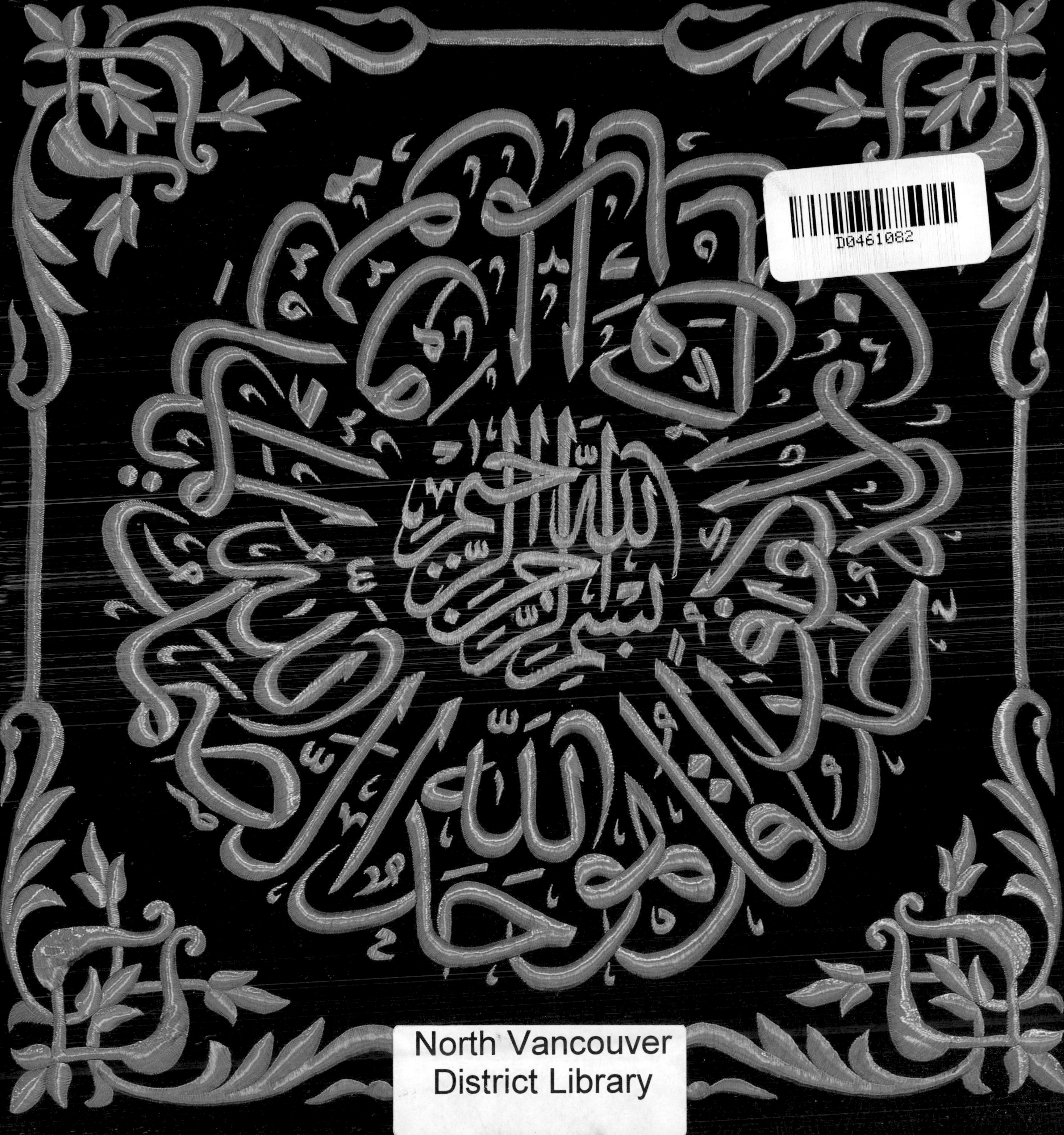
بسم الله الرحمن الرحيم

Pilgrims at Jabal Uḥud north of Medina before dawn. It was here that on 23 March 625 (AH 3) the Islamic army led by the Blessed Prophet suffered a crushing defeat at the hand of the Meccan army in a major battle of the early history of Islam during which the Prophet himself was injured.

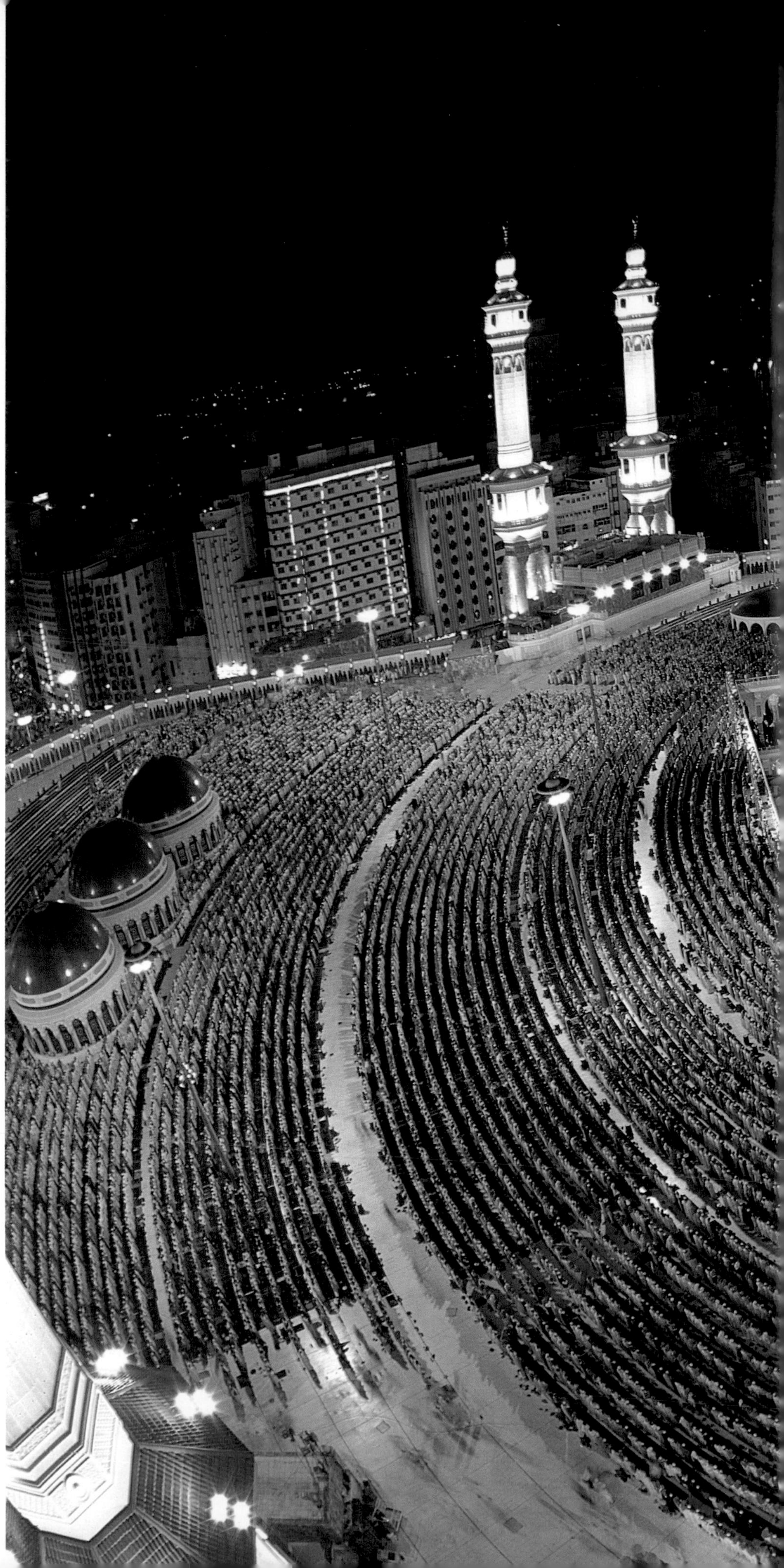

The *Ḥaram* in Mecca during the holy month of fasting. The 27th of Ramaḍān, is one of the holiest nights of the Islamic calendar, the night when the Noble Qurʾān began to be revealed to the Prophet.

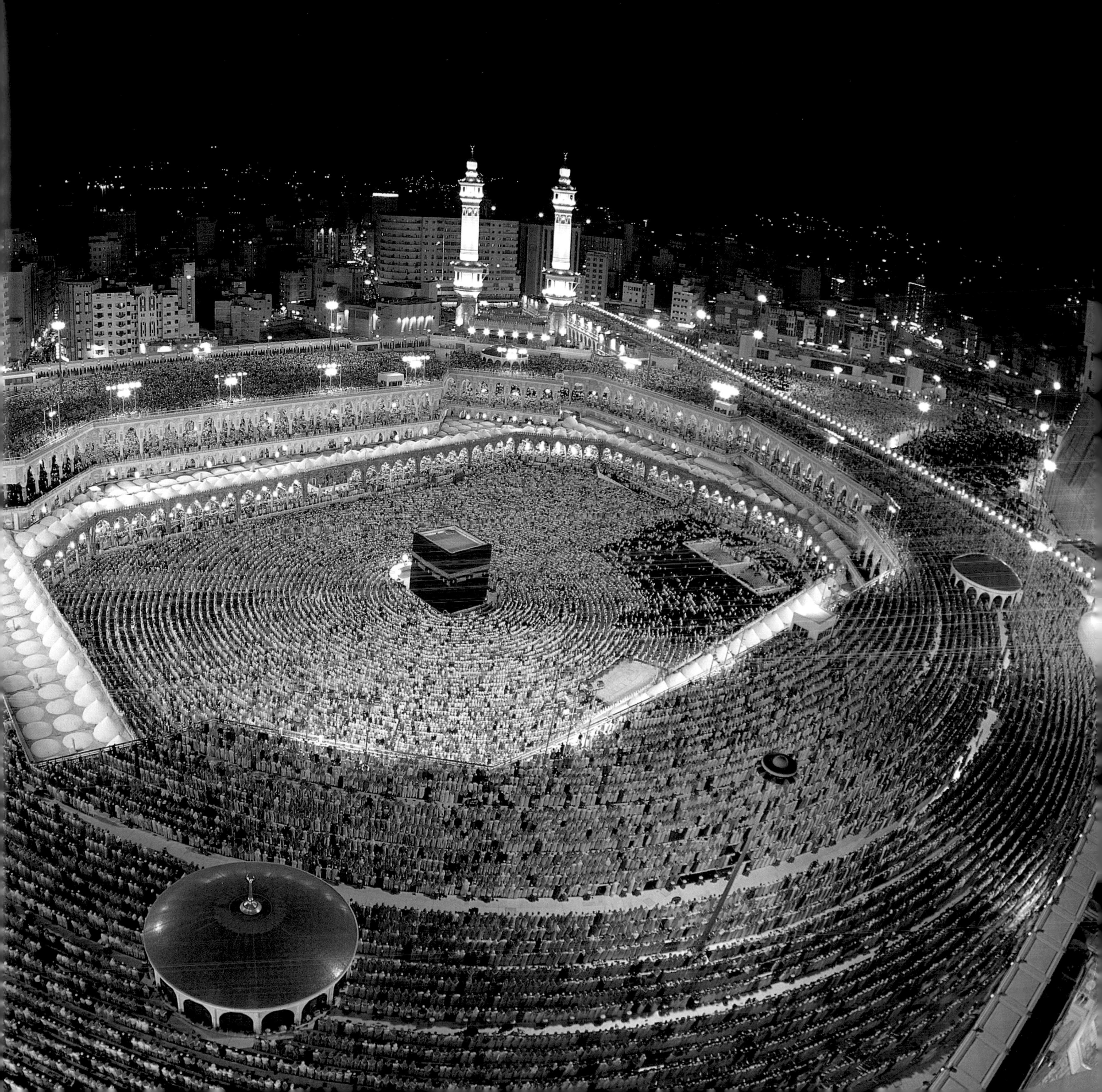

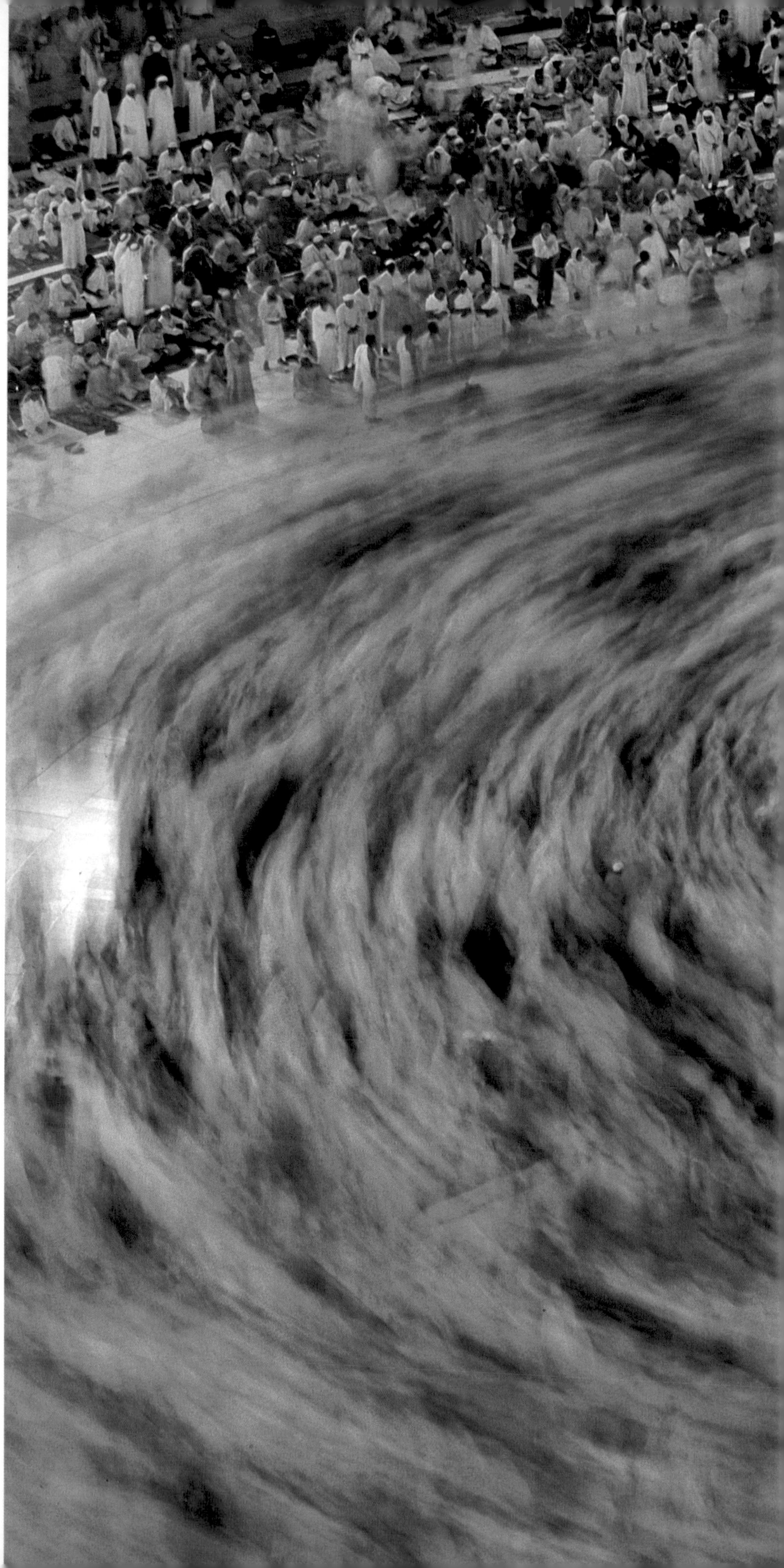

*Ṭawāf* or circumambulation around the *Ka*ʿ*bah*. *Ṭawāf* is a required part of *ḥajj* and must be performed seven times counter-clockwise starting at the south-eastern corner of the *Ka*ʿ*bah* where the Black Stone, symbol of the original covenant between God and man, is embedded.

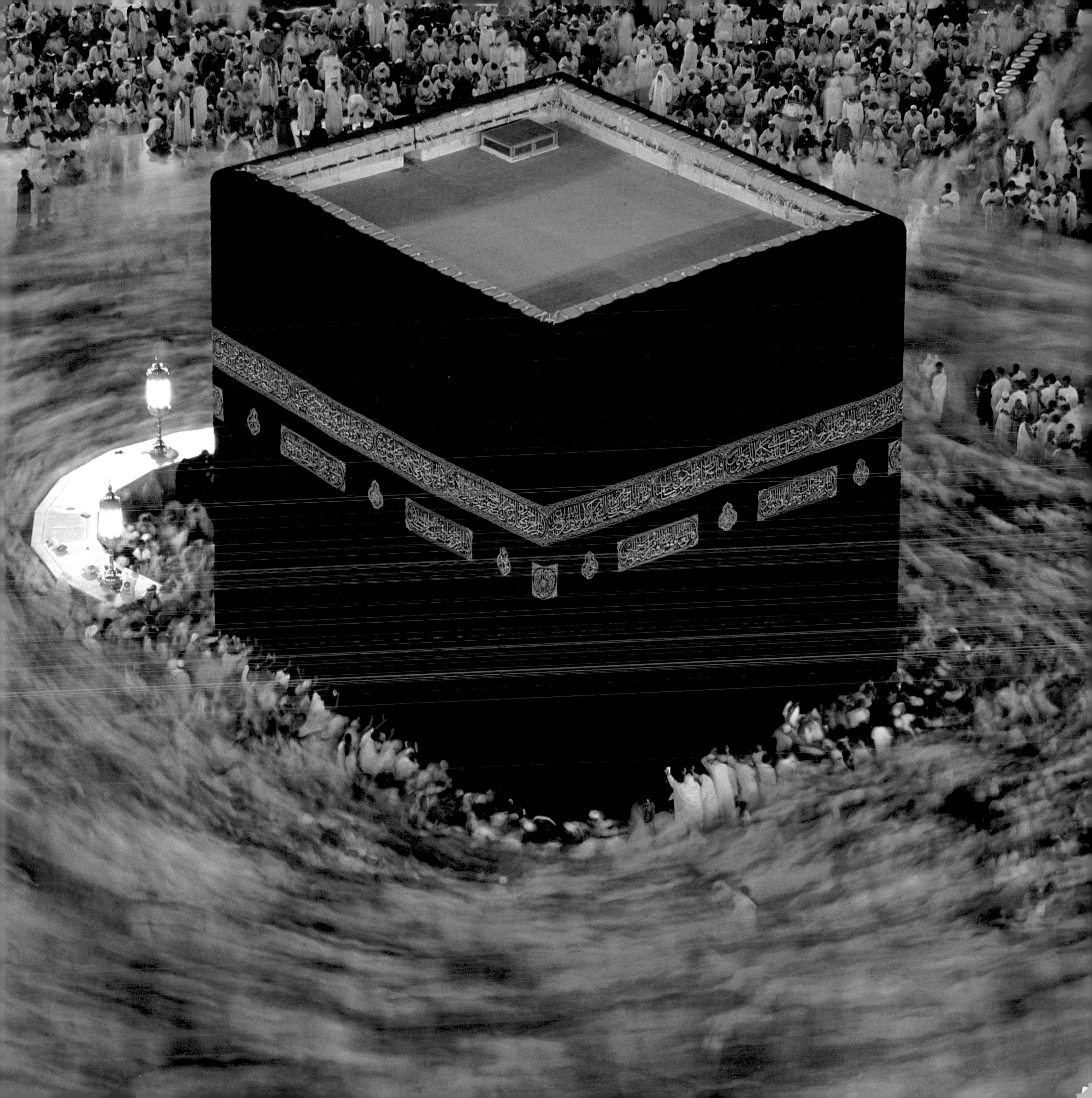

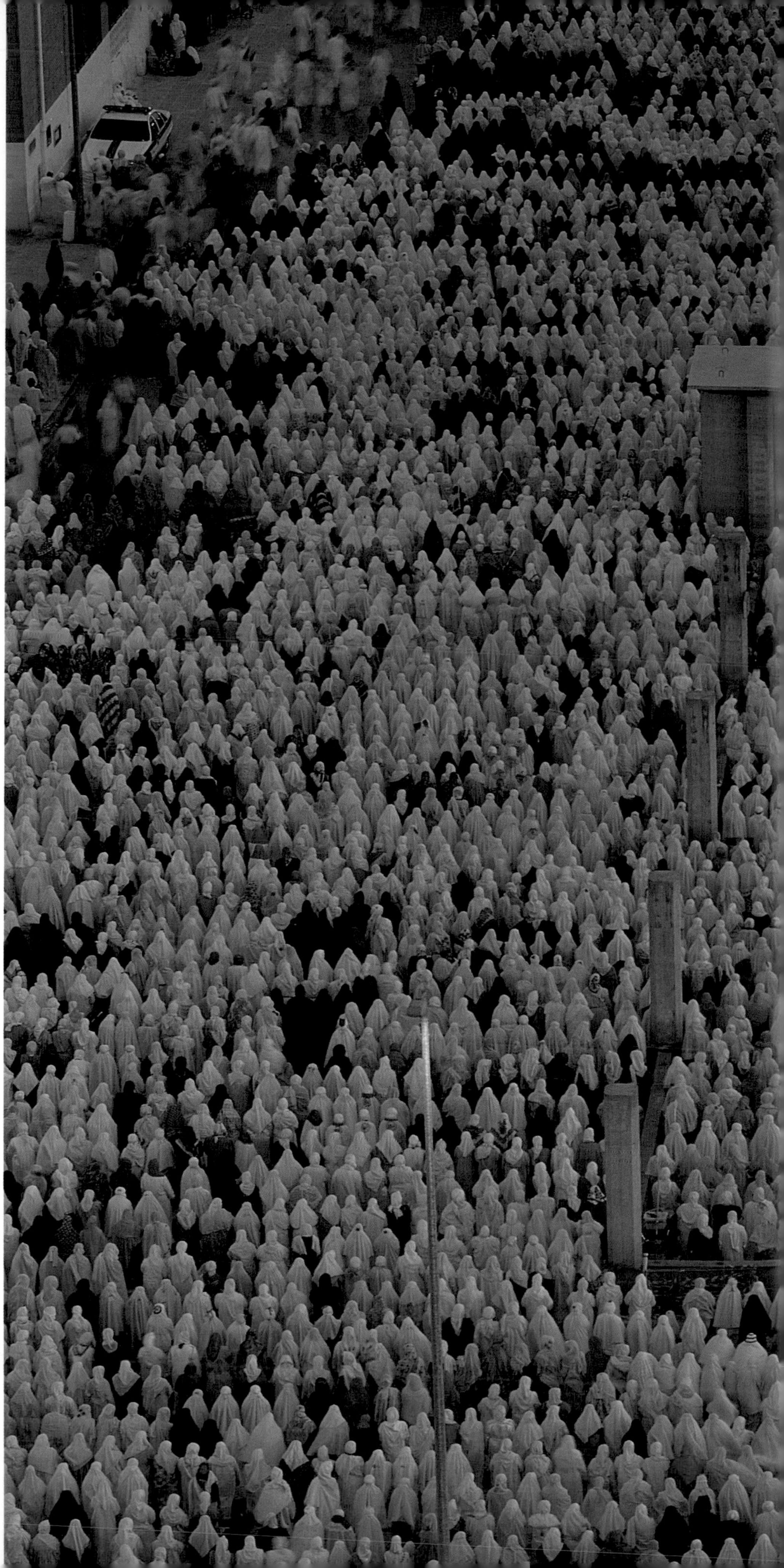

The sunset (*maghrib*) prayers at the Prophet's Mosque in Medina during the week before the annual season of *ḥajj* when a very large number of pilgrims assemble in Medina. The picture shows female pilgrims in an adjacent garden of the Mosque.

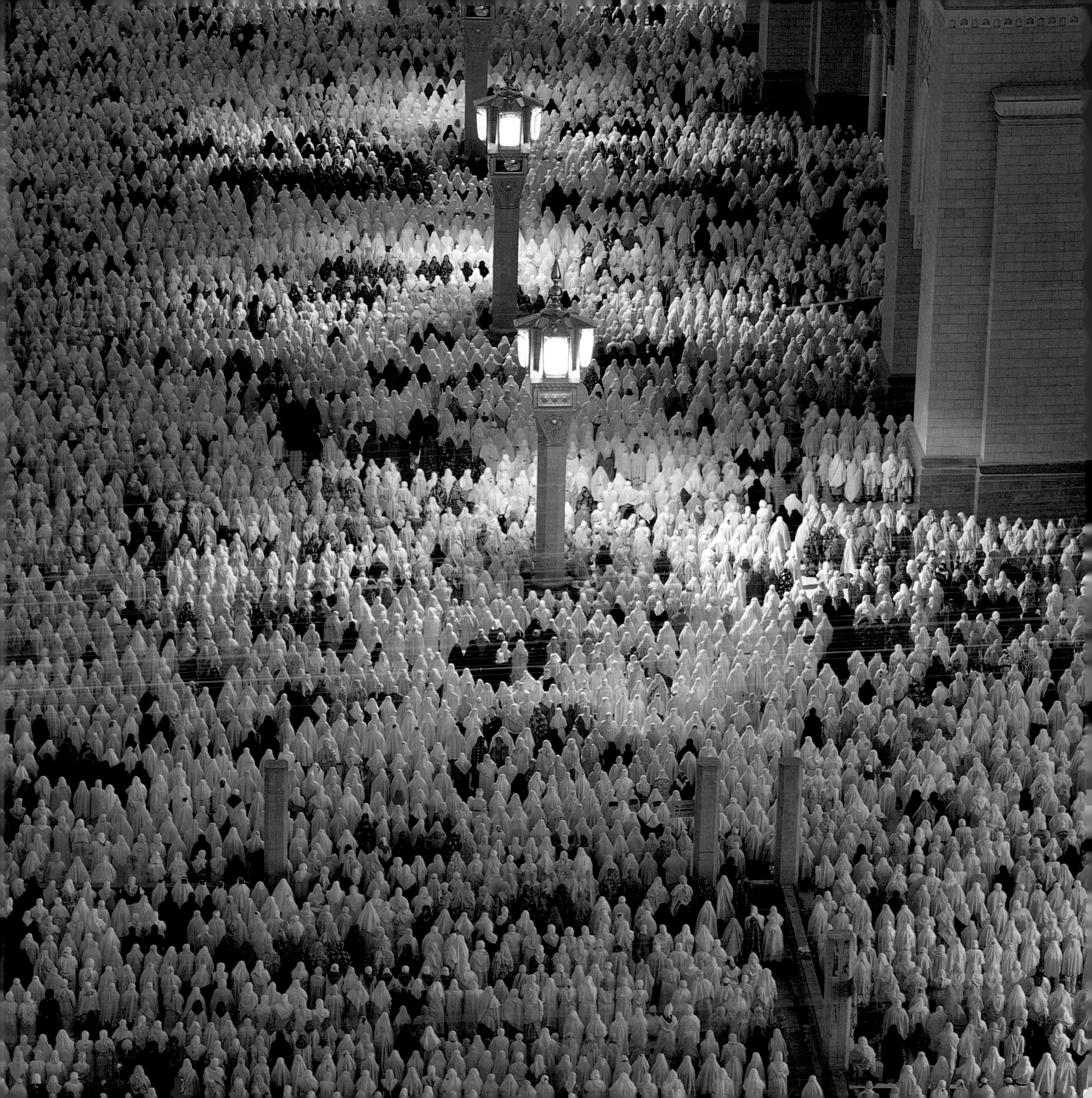

# Mecca
THE BLESSED
# Medina
THE RADIANT

## The Holiest Cities of Islam

*Photographs by Ali Kazuyoshi Nomachi*
*Essay by Seyyed Hossein Nasr*

*Aperture*

First published in 1997 in the United States of America and in Great Britain by Aperture Foundation, Inc.  A book project realized with the support of Thaara International, Jeddah, Saudi Arabia.



Library of Congress Catalog Card Number: 97-73709
Hardcover ISBN: 0-89381-752-X

Jacket design by Peter Bradford

The Staff at Aperture for *Mecca the Blessed, Medina the Radiant* is:
Michael E. Hoffman, Executive Director
Lois Brown, Editor
Elizabeth Franzen, Managing Editor

The publisher wishes to thank Gray Henry, Fyodor Gouverneur, and Adnan Bogary for their advice and guidance, and Patricia Salazar for her expert editing of the text. Also thanks for permission to reproduce the picture on page 29 by C Snouck Hurgronje from Makkah A Hundred Years Ago, Immel Publishing 1986.

Printed and bound in Hong Kong

Aperture Foundation publishes a periodical, books, and portfolios of fine photography to communicate with serious photographers and creative people everywhere. A complete catalog is available upon request. Address: 20 East 23rd Street, New York, New York 10010. Phone: (212) 598-4205. Fax: (212) 598-4015.

Aperture Foundation books are distributed internationally through:

**Canada:** General Publishing, 30 Lesmill Road, Don Mills, Ontario, M3B 2T6. Fax: (416) 445-5991. **United Kingdom:** Robert Hale, Ltd., Clerkenwell House, 45-47 Clerkenwell Green, London EC1R OHT. Fax: 171-490-4958. **Continental Europe:** Nilsson & Lamm, BV, Pampuslaan 212-214, P.O. Box 195, 1382 JS Weesp, Netherlands. Fax: 31-294-415054.

To subscribe to the periodical *Aperture* in the U.S.A. write Aperture, P.O. Box 3000, Denville, NJ 07834. Tel: 1-800-783-4903. One year: $40.00.
For international magazine subscription orders for the periodical *Aperture*, contact Aperture International Subscription Service, P.O. Box 14, Harold Hill, Romford, RM3 8EQ, England. Fax: 1-708-372-046. One year: £30.00. Price subject to change.

First edition
10 9 8 7 6 5 4 3 2 1

ACKNOWLEDGMENTS

This collection of photographs is the result of a publishing endeavour by Al Seyyed Mostafa Al Mehdar, Representative Director of Tharaa International of Jeddah, Saudi Arabia.

Of the many holy lands in the world, Mecca and Medina, the holiest places of Islam, are the most difficult to photograph.

Many photographers before me attempted to get permission to photograph in Mecca and Medina but were rejected. Without the generous understanding of the following persons, the success of this project would have been impossible:

H.R.H. Prince Majed Bin Abdul Aziz Al Saud,
*Governor of Mecca Region;*
H.R.H. Prince Abdul Majeed Bin Abdul Aziz Al Saud,
*Governor of Medina Region;*
H.R.H. Prince Saud Bin Abdul Muhsen,
*Deputy Governor of Mecca Region;*
H.E Mr. Ali Al Shair,
*Former Information Minister of Kingdom of Saudi Arabia;*
Dr. Rabya Dahallan,
*Second Deputy Governor of Mecca Region;*
Engineer Abdul Aziz Al Hossein,
*Mayor of Medina.*

And, above all, I am grateful to my friend Al Seyyed Mostafa Al Mehdar who moved many people with his enthusiasm and resolute persuasion to realize this project.

If this book contributes in any way to the understanding of Islam, my reward, as a photographer, will be infinite.

In addition, I would like to thank the staff of Aperture for bringing intelligence and energy to this project.

Ali Kazuyoshi Nomachi

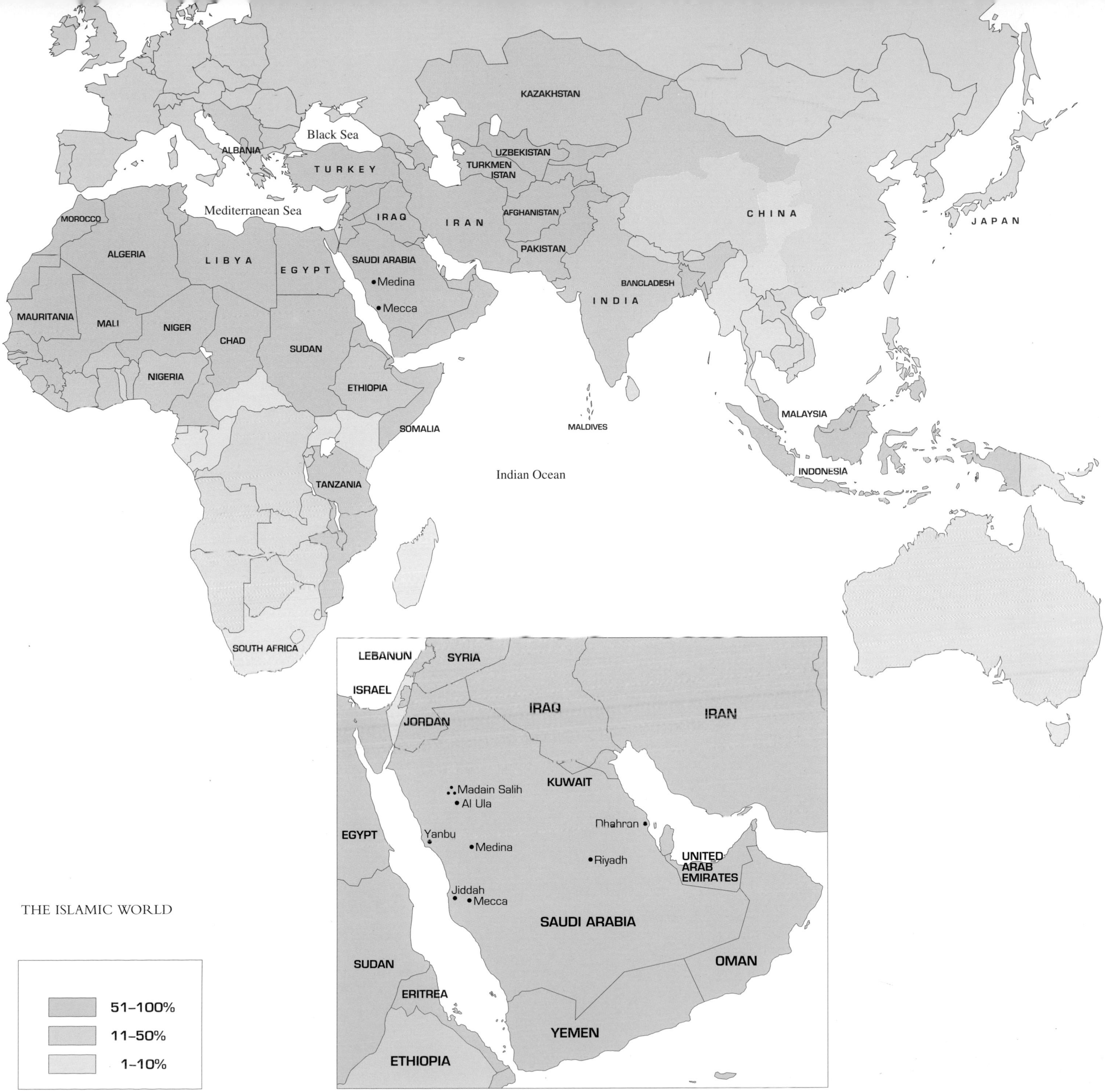


THE ISLAMIC WORLD

# CONTENTS

بِسْمِ اللّٰهِ الرَّحْمٰنِ الرَّحِيمِ

# In the Name of God—The Infinitely Good, the All-Merciful

## The Blessed and Radiant
## Cities of Islam—Mecca and Medina

by Seyyed Hossein Nasr

*"And this is a Book which We have sent down full of blessings and confirming what [was revealed] before it: that thou mayest warn the Mother of Cities [Umm al-qurā—Mecca] and its surroundings. Those who believe in the hereafter believe herein and they are constant in their prayers."* (Qur'ān VI:92. Yusuf Ali translation modified.)

"Medina is best for them if they only knew. No one leaves it through dislike of it without God putting in it someone better than he in place of him, and no one will remain there in spite of its hardship and distress without my being an intercessor on his behalf on the day of resurrection." (Saying of the Prophet of Islam, *ḥadīth*, transmitted by Muslim in the *Mishkāt al-maṣābīh* of Tabrīzī, trans. James Robeson, Lahore, Muhammad Ashraf, 1981 pp. 586-7.)

## The Two Holy Cities

Two events, which in fact are two aspects of the same reality, cast the cities of Mecca *(Makkah)* and Medina *(Madinah)* in a short period upon the pages of world history. These events were the birth in AD 570, the maturity and prophethood of Muḥammad ibn 'Abd Allāh—peace and blessings be upon him—and the descent of the Qur'ānic revelation upon him during a 23-year period from 610 until his death in 632. These events of cosmic proportions established Islam, the last plenary religion of humanity, upon the earth thereby transforming not only the history of Arabia, or of the Mediterranean basin and the Persian and Byzantine Empires, but also of lands as far away as France and the Philippines and in fact ultimately the whole of the globe. The revelation of the Noble Qur'ān, the verbatim Word of God for Muslims, began in Mecca where the Blessed Prophet was born and continued in Medina where he died. The very landscape of these two cities still reverberates with the grace *(barakah)* of the revelation and echoes the presence of that most perfect human being who was chosen by God to receive His last message and thereby to bring to completion the cycle of prophecy which had begun with Adam himself.

Mecca the Blessed *(al-Makkat al-mukarramah)* and Medina the Radiant *(al-Madīnat al-munawwarah)*, as they are known to Muslims, became intertwined by the very events of the Islamic revelation. Mecca, the city where the primordial Temple and House of God, the *Ka'bah*, is situated was where the Prophet was born and raised while Medina became his city by virtue of his migration there in AD 622, which marks the beginning of the Islamic calendar. The very name Medina, which in Arabic means simply "city", is in fact the abbreviation of *Madīnat al-nabī*, "the City of the Prophet," which replaced the older name of Yathrib, after the Blessed Prophet migrated to that city where he established the first Islamic community and the first mosque.

The testimony whereby a person embraces Islam is simply *la ilāha illa'Llāh*, "there is no divinity but Allah", and *Muḥammadun rasūl Allāh*, "Muḥammad is the messenger of God", "Allāh" being simply the Arabic word for God considered in His absolute Oneness beyond all hypostatic differentiations. These two formulas are inseparable in Islamic

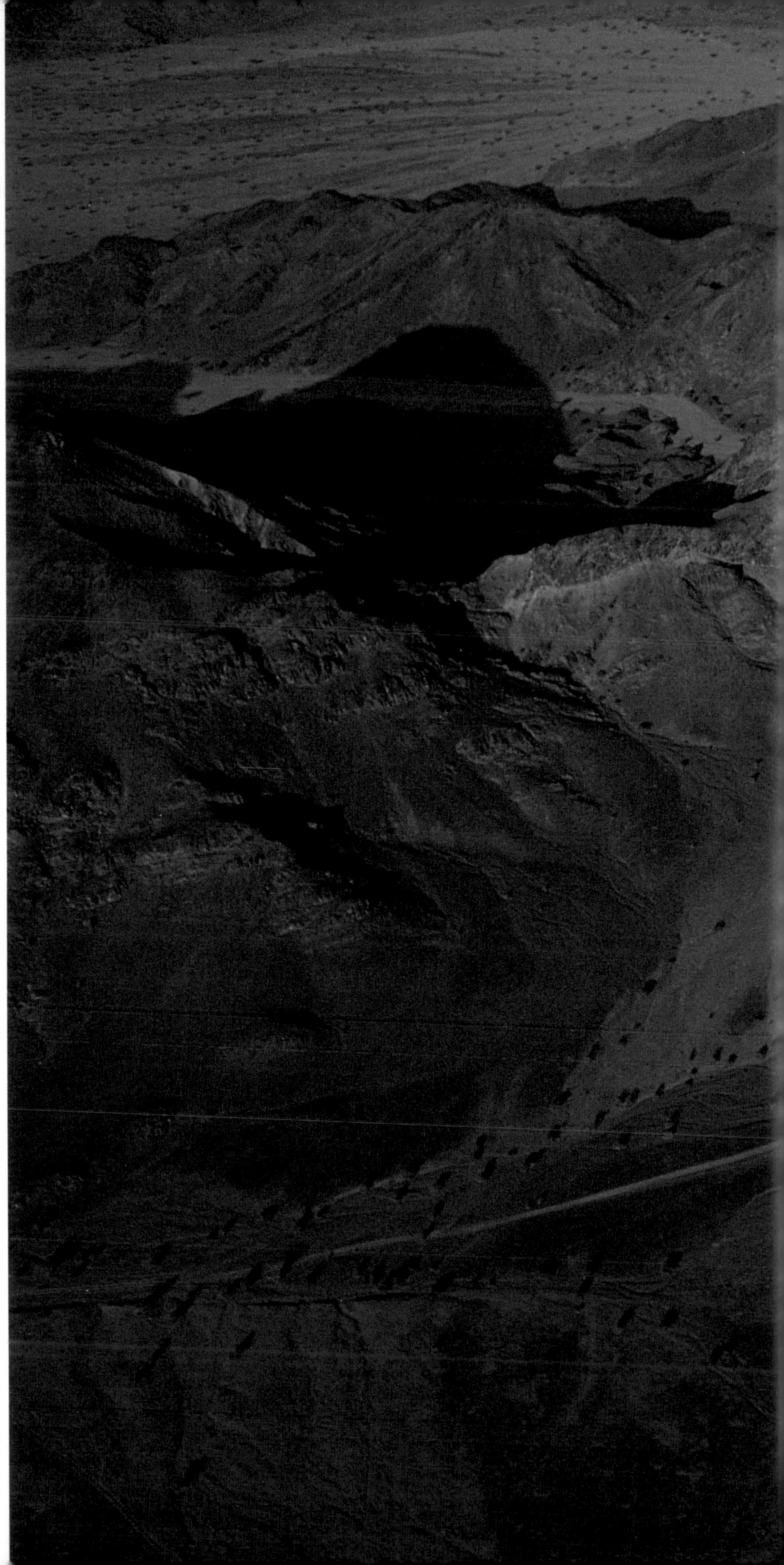

The wilderness stretching to the north of Medina forms a striking contrast to the desert area lying at the center and east of the Arabian peninsula. The Hijaz region in which both Mecca and Medina are located has mountains extending both north and south, some retaining volcanic activity.

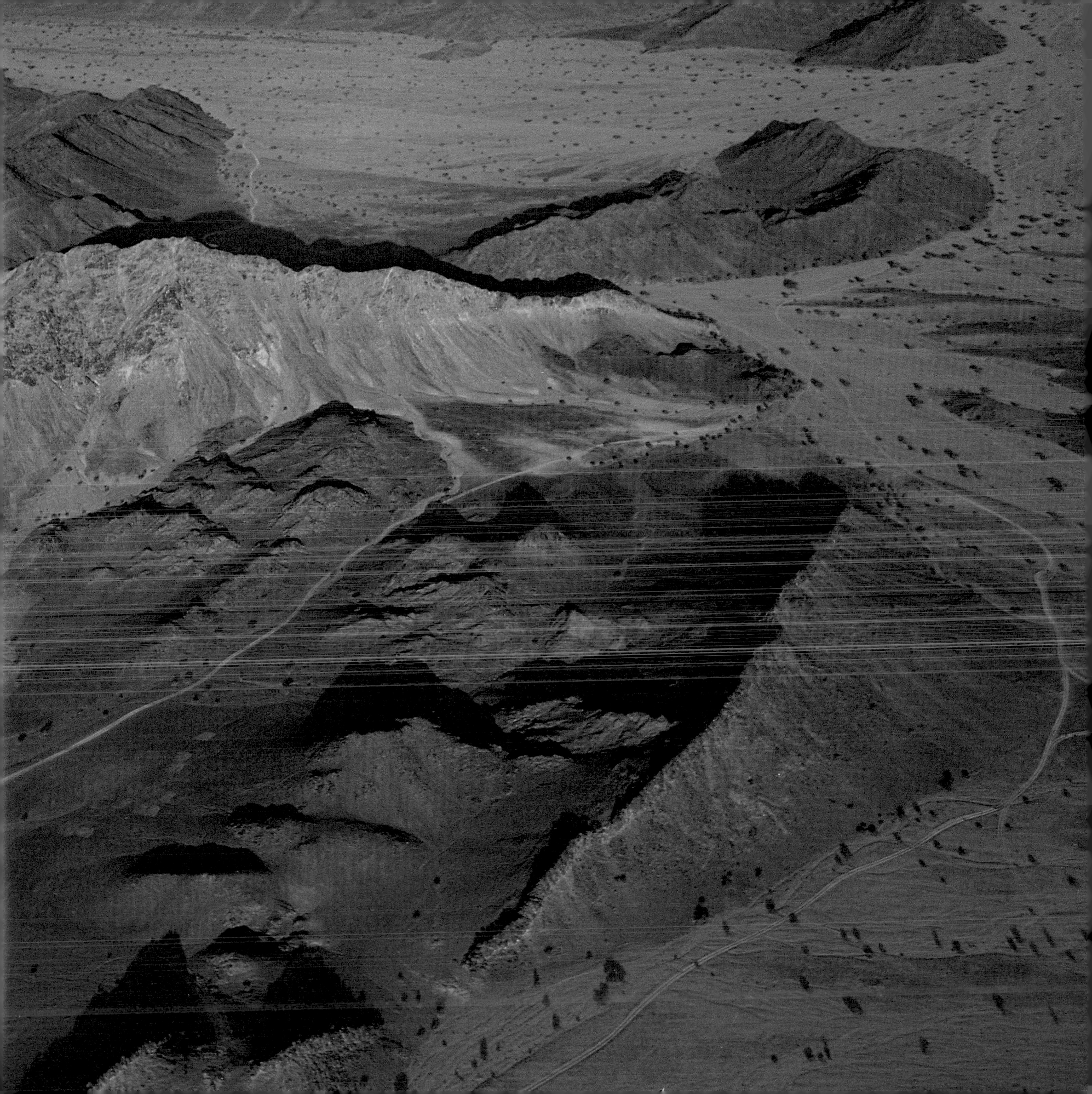

life and are seen by Muslims as being inwardly united. One may say that such is also the case of Mecca and Medina, the two holy centers of Islam, whose significance is inseparable in the religious life and thought of Muslims. Mecca is primarily the city of God by virtue of the *Kaʿbah* and may be said to correspond to *la ilāha illa'Llāh* while Medina, where the Mosque of the Prophet and his tomb are to be found, is of course primarily the city of the Prophet and corresponds to *Muḥammadun rasūl Allāh*. And in the same way that five times a day the call to prayer, *(al-adhān)*, heard from minaret and roof-tops as well as in streets and houses throughout the Islamic world, announces the two testimonies of faith together, the *barakah* and significance of those holy cities remain organically united. At the same time their influence, and the second by virtue of the first, has over the centuries dominated not only the heartland of Islam in Arabia, but all Islamic lands near and far, and love for them is cherished in the hearts of men and women of all different races and climes where there has been a positive response to the call to unity *(al-tawḥīd)* of the Islamic message.

## Arabia

The peninsula of Arabia is located at the crossroad of three continents, Asia, Africa and Europe, its northern regions neighboring the Mediterranean world, its eastern realms Persia, and its southern shores Africa, with which it has always enjoyed close links in trade, migration of ideas and also people, as it has with its other neighbors. The southern region of the peninsula, home to ports through which goods were brought from the Indian Ocean, has always been more green than the north and was the home of many ancient civilizations. Its people, who considered themselves as descendants of Qaḥṭān became known for the wonderful plants and perfumes which they cultivated. The frankincense and myrrh of southern Arabia were so well known in the Roman Empire that the Romans called this region *Arabia Odorifera*. It is sufficient to think of the Queen of Sheba and her world to recall the great regard that peoples of antiquity held for the high civilizations of southern Arabia.

As for the northern part of the peninsula, it was adjacent to the great Semitic civilizations of Mesopotamia the influence of whose art is to be seen in the artifacts found in the north. Later, there were also close contacts with the Persian and Byzantine Empires. In the centuries between the rise of Christianity and the advent of Islam, there were in fact local kingdoms in the north such as the Nabataean and the Ghassanid which exercised influence upon certain aspects of the cultures of Arabia, the latter having been Christian.

The heartland of Arabia consisting of Hijaz and Najd continued, however, to be dominated mostly by Arab nomads who had remained on the margin of the major historical developments to their north and, not greatly influenced by either Judaism or Christianity despite the presence of members of both communities in the cities of Arabia. As far as Hijaz, the sacred land in which Mecca and Medina are located, is concerned, it is the name of the western region of the Arabian peninsula consisting of a fairly narrow tract of land about 875 miles long east of the Red Sea with the Tropic of Cancer running through its center. The land is called Hijaz, meaning barrier, because its backbone, the Sarat Mountains, running parallel to the Red Sea, separates the flat coastal area called Tihamah from the highlands of Najd. The Sarat Mountains consist of volcanic peaks and natural depressions creating a stark and rugged environment dominated by intense sunlight and with little rain. And it is in one of the natural depressions of this mountain range that is to be found the sacred city of Mecca, the hub of the earth and its center for the descendants of Ismāʿīl (the biblical Ishmael).

Arabia is dominated by deserts that before modern times could not be crossed except with the help of camels which, therefore, became indispensable to the life of its people. The population centers have always been situated around wells and springs in the desert which have created the oases for which certain desert areas are well known. The majority of the population of Arabia consisted of nomads although cities such as Mecca existed in Arabia even before the rise of Islam. It is, however, only during the present century that the vast majority of the nomads of Arabia have become sedentarized and attempts made to make use of the vast underground water sources of the peninsula to create agriculture for the settled nomads. Throughout history, however, the Arabs, the descendants of Ishmael (Ismāʿīl), were mostly nomads of Semitic stock. Something essential of the spiritual dimension of Semitic nomadism was in fact adopted by Islam and has therefore become a basic aspect of the spiritual universe of all Muslims.

## Early Sacred History

From the Islamic point of view, Mecca, the *Kaʿbah* and the environs of the holy city are associated with the very origin of humanity and Islam's sacred history which, being based on the chain of prophecy, begins with Adam himself. The spiritual anthropology of Islam stated in the Qur'ān begins with the creation of Adam and Eve in Paradise, their subsequent fall, which is not, however, associated with original sin in the Christian sense, and their search for each other on earth. Traditional sources mention that Adam descended in the island of Sarandib, or

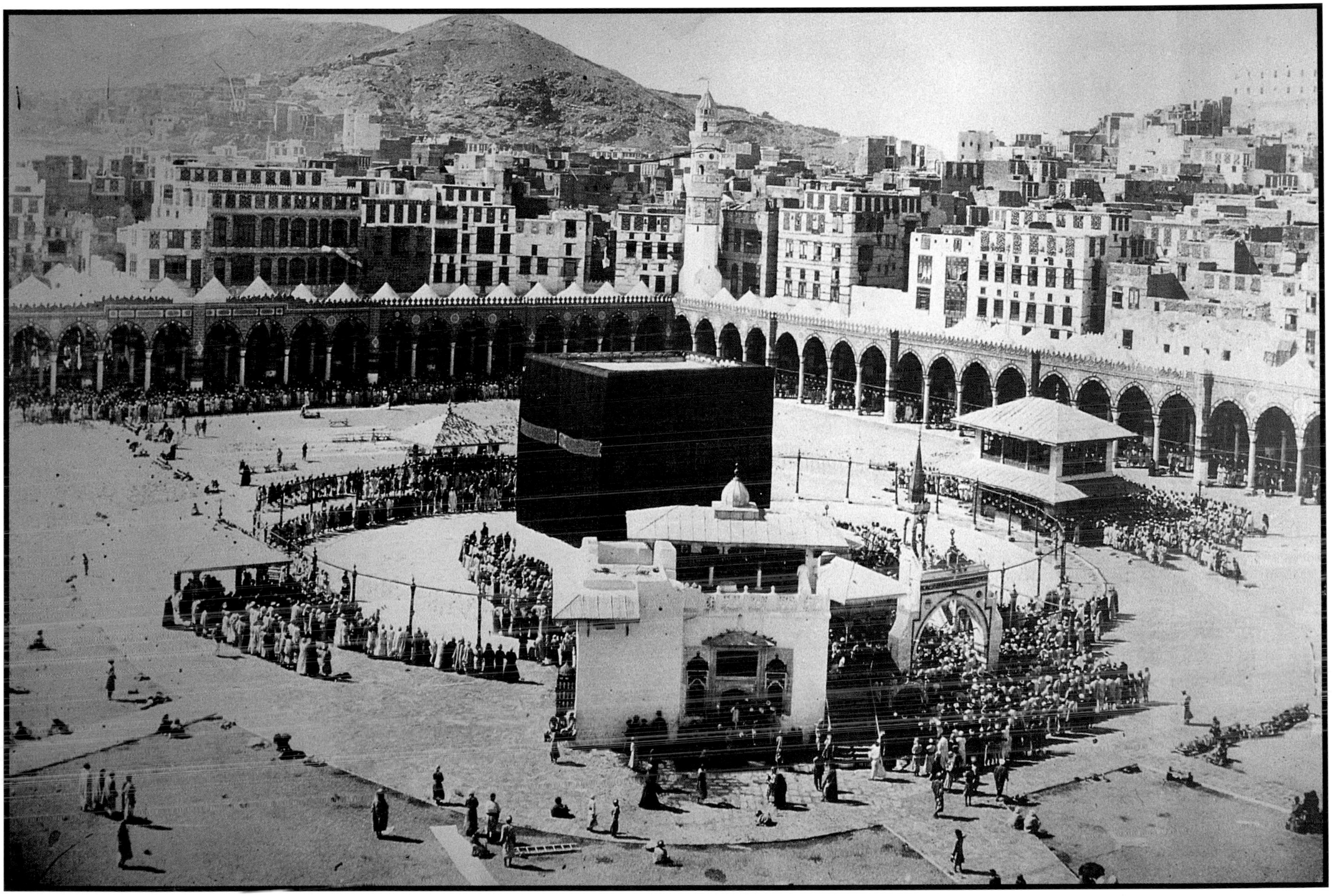

A picture of the *Ḥaram* or Grand Mosque of Mecca a hundred years ago. In this photograph the sacred spring Zamzam is located in a peak-roofed building adjacent to the *Kaʿbah*. Today, the buildings in the near proximity of the *Kaʿbah* have been demolished and the access to the spring of Zamzam moved underground.

present day Sri Lanka, and Eve in Arabia. Adam then set out to find Eve and finally encountered her at the plain of ʿArafāt, so central to the rite of the annual pilgrimage to this day. Here the two halves of primordial man, in the sense of *anthropos* and not only the male, became united again and therefore it is here that one must search for the origin of the human family. It was also in this area in Mecca, then called Becca (Bakkah, or narrow valley), that Adam built the first temple, the *Kaʿbah*, as the earthly reflection of the Divine Throne and the prototype of all temples. Adam is said to have died and been buried in Mecca and Eve in Jeddah by the sea which still bears her name, *jiddah*, meaning maternal ancestor in Arabic. The area of Mecca with the *Kaʿbah* at its heart is therefore associated with primordiality, essential to Islam which considers itself as the reassertion of primordial monotheism and addresses what is primordial in the human soul, hence its also being called *dīn al-ḥanīf* (the primordial religion) and *dīn al-fiṭrah* (the religion of one's primordial nature).

Nor are the main later stages of Islamic sacred history separated from the area of Mecca. According to tradition, when the flood occurred, the body of Adam, which had been interred in Mecca, began to float on the water while the ark of Noah circumambulated around it and the *Kaʿbah* seven times before setting out north where it landed after the flood. A thousand years later the great patriarch of monotheism, Abraham, or Ibrāhīm, came to Mecca with his Egyptian wife Hagar (Hājar) and their child Ishmael (Ismāʿīl). It was he who discovered the mount left after the flood underneath which lay God's first temple built by Adam. And it was there that Abraham set out to rebuild the *Kaʿbah* which in its present form owes its origin to him.

Leaving his wife and child with some water and dates, Abraham left Mecca on God's command. Hagar suckled her son and they drank the remaining water. Soon, however, both faced great thirst and the child began to cry. Hagar began to run between two mounds named Ṣafā and Marwah looking for water, repeating the journey seven times until an angel appeared to her, striking the ground with his wing, with the result that the spring of Zamzam, which Muslims consider as a "tributary" of the water of Paradise, gushed forth. Henceforth Mecca was to be blessed with a source of water which has continued to this day. It was because of the Zamzam that the Jurhum tribe from northern Yemen came to settle in Mecca where they adopted Ishmael (Ismāʿīl), taught him Arabic and made him one of their own.

Muslim historians also believe that it was at Mount Thabir situated north of the Mecca valley that Abraham, upon returning to Mecca, took Ishmael (Ismāʿīl) to be sacrificed for God. In the Islamic version of the binding of the son of Abraham, the son himself was perfectly resigned to the Will of God as was the father. *So when they both surrendered [to Allāh] and he had flung him upon his forehead We called out to him: 'O Abraham! Thou hast already fulfilled the vision.' Lo! Thus do We reward the good. . . . Then We ransomed him with a tremendous sacrifice. And we left for him among the later folk (the salvation): 'Peace be upon Abraham!'* (Qur'ān xxxvii:103-9) This great episode of sacred history, shared in different versions by Jews, Christians and Muslims alike, is thus again associated by the Muslim mind with the area of Mecca.

It was after this event and the departure and return of Abraham to Mecca that the most lasting mark of the Patriarch in Mecca was created. Upon his return Abraham discovered that his wife Hagar had died. Then he called upon his son, Ishmael (Ismāʿīl), who is called "the father of the Arabs" and was the ancestor of the Prophet of Islam, to help him in the construction of the House of God, *bayt al-ʿatīq* or the Ancient House as the Arabs called it. The Divine Peace *(al-sakīnah)* descended in the form of a wind which brought a cloud in the shape of a dragon that revealed to them the site of the old temple. Abraham and Ishmael (Ismāʿīl) dug the ground until they discovered with awe the ancient temple built by Adam. A stone came to light on which there was the following inscription: "I am the God of Becca. I have created compassion and love as my two appellations. Whoever attains these virtues shall meet Me. And whoever removes himself from these virtues, is removed from Me." Already Allāh, whose Name is inseparable from the qualities of compassion and mercy in Islam and who was to reveal *Bismi'Llāh al-Raḥmān al-Raḥīm* (In the Name of God—the Infinitely Good, the All-Merciful) as the formula of consecration in the Noble Qur'ān, had spoken. And He had spoken at the place which was to become inseparable from the celebration of His Names of *Raḥmān* and *Raḥīm* from the time of the advent of Islam.

Abraham or Ibrāhīm, known in Islam also as *Khalīl Allāh* or Friend of God, built the *Kaʿbah* as a sign of his perfect faith in his Friend. Thus does the Qur'ān address him *"Associate naught with Me and purify My house for those who make the round (thereof) and those who stand and those who bow and make prostration. And proclaim unto mankind the Pilgrimage."* (Qur'ān xxii:26-7)

He made the first pilgrimage with his son Ishmael (Ismāʿīl), and in the presence of the archangel Gabriel, performed all the elements which constitute the rite of *ḥajj* today. Under Divine Command he established a rite which was revived by the Prophet of Islam and which is inseparable from the reality of Mecca and its meaning for Muslims the world over to this day. Abraham was to leave Mecca to die in Palestine in al-Khalīl, but he left an important part of himself and his heritage in Mecca. And so Abraham raised his hands in prayer and said

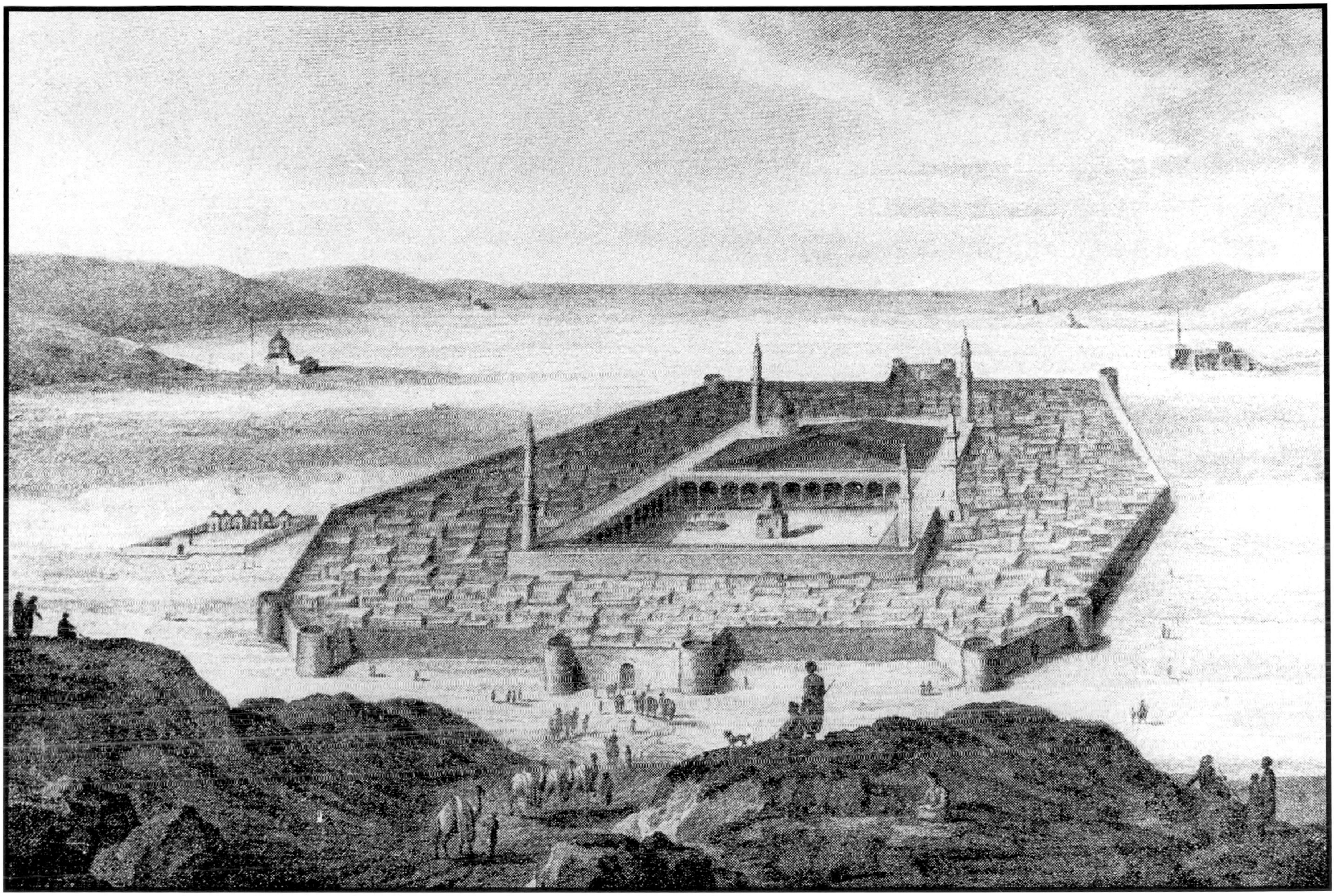

Map of the center of Medina dated 1790 when the city was surrounded by ramparts with the Mosque of the Prophet at its heart. The ramparts seen here were completed in 948/1541, having a total length of 2,300 meters with four gates.

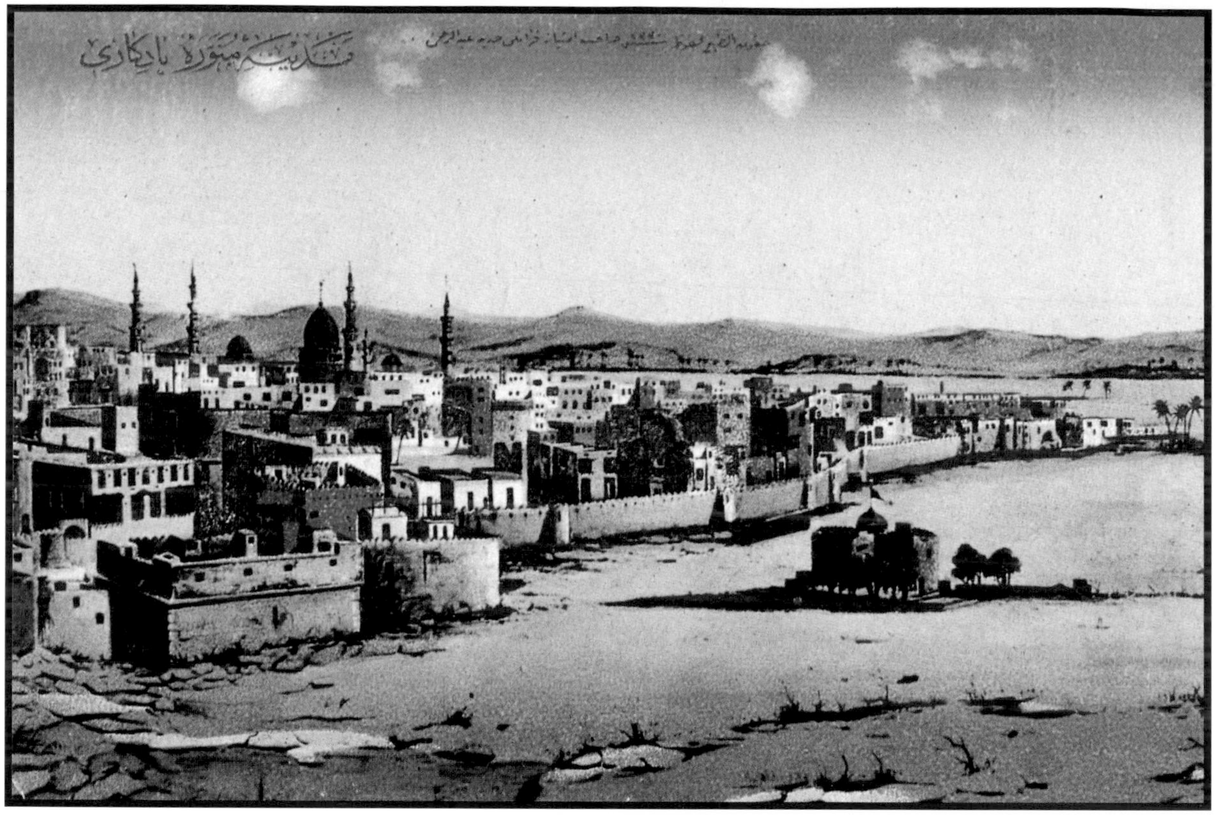

A postcard of Medina (date unknown) shows that the city had grown in comparison with the map on the previous page.

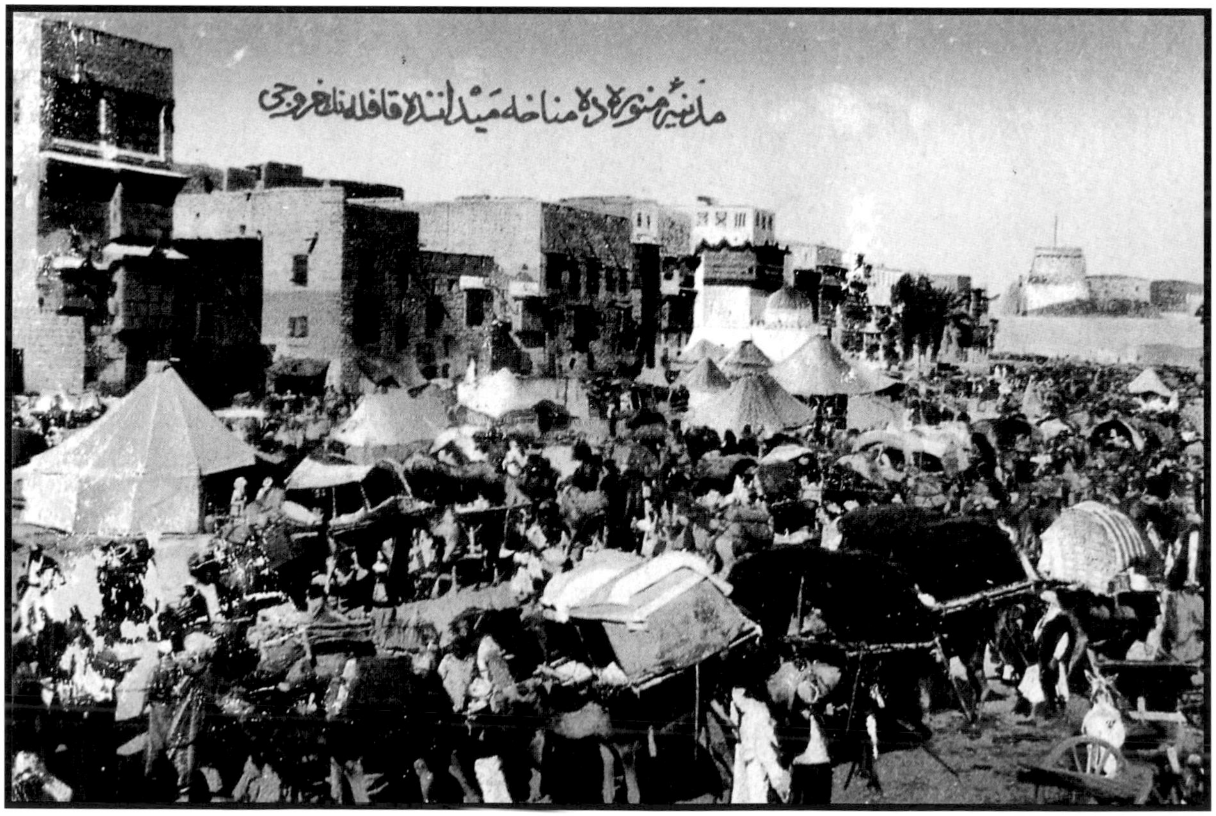

Caravans of pilgrims with palanquins on camels go through Medina.

according to the Noble Qur'ān, *"Our Lord, I have settled a part of my offspring in an infertile vale near Thy Sacred House, our Lord! That they may establish proper worship."* (Qur'ān xiv:37) Henceforth Mecca became inseparable from Abrahamic monotheism and despite the rise of Arabian paganism in later centuries in that city, it was finally here that the religion of the One was re-established in its final form with the advent of Islam. Mecca's sacred history links it therefore inalienably to the message and heritage of Abraham, whose progeny continued to live there. Eventually they gained power over the city and finally, as a result of their indulgence in idolatry, lost that power because of the revelation of the message of the One to one of their own, namely, Muḥammad—may blessings and peace be upon him—who destroyed the idols and renewed fully the monotheism of his ancestor Abraham.

## *The Proto-history of Arabia and the Holy Cities of Mecca and Medina*

Already in an inscription of the Assyrian King Salmanazar II dating from 854 BC there is reference to the "Arabs" probably meaning "desert dwellers". The Arabs were Semites who with the help of camels were able to navigate the Arabian peninsula around 1000 BC while creating settlements such as Aram and Eberin in the north of the Peninsula. Divided into tribes, they guarded jealously their genealogy and tribal customs and until the advent of Islam their allegiance was first and foremost to their tribe while inter-tribal skirmishes and warfare characterized their lives. Some of these tribes remained in a particular region while others such as the ʿAmālīq, mentioned in the Bible as the Amalekites, were to be found throughout the Arabian peninsula.

It was a branch of this tribe known as the ʿAbil that founded the city of Yathrib, later to be known as Medina. Blessed by much underground water, the plain of Yathrib, lying between the ranges of the Sarat Mountains, became the site of a prosperous community. But its people disobeyed God and so were punished by natural calamities such as pestilence and also the Prophet Moses sent an army to punish them. Centuries later, Jews, probably fleeing from Nebuchadnezzar, migrated to Yathrib and formed the community whose descendants the Prophet of Islam was to meet upon his migration to that city.

According to Arab custom going back to the earliest known historical period, it was forbidden to fight in the vicinity of the *Kaʿbah*. Another branch of the ʿAmālīq taking advantage of the fact that the descendants of Ishmael (Ismāʿīl) who were the custodians of the *Kaʿbah* would not engage them in battle there, attacked them and drove them out. The descendants of Ismāʿīl took refuge in the gorges around Mecca as nomads, some wandering to other parts of Arabia and others remaining close to the House of God erected by their ancestors Abraham and Ishmael (Ismāʿīl). Gradually Mecca grew in stature as the chief sanctuary of Arabia and tribes would come from every corner of the peninsula to pray in and around the *Kaʿbah*, which had by now become defiled, from the Islamic point of view, with idols of various tribes, the original significance of the structure as the House of the One God, eclipsed and forgotten by the majority save the few who, however, remained attached to Abrahamic monotheism and whom Islam calls the *ḥunafā'* or "primordialists". It was also as a result of the presence of these idols that Jews ceased to visit the *Kaʿbah*. The structure of the *Kaʿbah* remained, however, unchanged and it was rebuilt exactly as it was before by the ʿAmālīq after a flood inundated and destroyed it. What changed over the centuries was that floods brought sedimentation from adjacent hills which raised the ground around the *Kaʿbah* to such an extent that the original mound upon which Abraham had built the *Kaʿbah* was no longer visible.

It was the victory of the Jurhum tribe from the Yemen over the ʿAmālīq and their conquest of Mecca that accentuated polytheism in the Sacred City. But they were in turn defeated by the Khuzāʿah, an Arab tribe of Ismāʿīlite descent, which had migrated to the Yemen and then returned north. The ʿAmālīq did not leave Mecca, however, without seeking to ravage it, including among their actions the burial of the spring of Zamzam. In entering Mecca the Khuzāʿah continued to protect the city as a center of pilgrimage for the Arab tribes and themselves brought the famous idol Ḥubal which they placed within the *Kaʿbah* and which they made the chief idol of Mecca.

## *The Rise of the Quraysh, the Hāshimites and the Birth of the Prophet*

Around the fourth or fifth Christian century another Ismāʿīlite tribe, the Quraysh, one of whose members was to be chosen as the final prophet of God, began to gain ascendance in Mecca. One of their members Quṣayy married the daughter of the chief of the Khuzāʿah tribe and later became the ruler of Mecca and custodian of the *Kaʿbah*. He ruled over both the Quraysh who lived near the sanctuary and those who lived farther away. He was a capable ruler and it is said that it was he who built the city of Mecca in the form of concentric circles around the *Kaʿbah* with the inhabitants of each circle being determined by their social rank, with those of higher rank living closer to the

"Ancient House". This original plan of the city lasted well into the historical period and its traces could in fact be found until the advent of the urban development of recent decades.

The grandson of Quṣayy was named Hāshim, after whom the clan of the Prophet, the Hāshimite, is named. Hāshim was also a competent ruler and succeeded in making Mecca prosperous by expanding trade routes through the city. He married Salmā, one of the most influential women of Yathrib of the tribe of Khazraj, and from this union was born Shaybah. Brought up originally by his mother in Yathrib, he was taken to Mecca upon the death of his father by his uncle Muṭṭalib. Since he was riding behind his uncle in entering the city, he was called in error ʿAbd al-Muṭṭalib (the slave of Muṭṭalib), a name with which he came to be identified. This remarkable figure of great spiritual stature and statesmanship finally became the ruler of Mecca.

Once, while sleeping by the area adjacent to the *Kaʿbah* known as Ḥijr Ismāʿīl, he dreamt that he should dig for the spring of Zamzam buried long before by the ʿAmālīqs. The dream occurred twice and so ʿAbd al-Muṭṭalib began to circumambulate the *Kaʿbah.* After completing this ancient ritual, he saw a number of birds strutting to a place a hundred yards away from the *Kaʿbah.* And so he began to dig in that spot to which he was led by the sign from Heaven. Soon the long-lost spring of Zamzam gushed forth as if foretelling of the re-assertion of primordial monotheism and the re-consecration of the *Kaʿbah* to the One in the near future. The tribe of Hāshim was given the right of supervision over the water of the Zamzam, a privilege whose significance can hardly be over-emphasized.

ʿAbd al-Muṭṭalib had vowed that if he were to have ten sons, he would sacrifice one of them to God to whom he, as a *ḥanīf,* always prayed, never bowing before the idols of Mecca. After the drawing of lots, ʿAbd Allāh, his most beloved son, was chosen for sacrifice but his mother, Fāṭimah, from the powerful Makhzūm tribe, was opposed to this act. After much consultation and prayer, ʿAbd al-Muṭṭalib accepted to sacrifice a hundred camels instead. The future father of the Prophet of Islam was thereby saved and ʿAbd Allāh who, because of his physical beauty was called the Joseph of his time, was married in 569 according to his father's choice to Āminah, a descendant of the brother of Quṣayy.

There lived at that time a *ḥanīf* in Mecca by the name of Waraqah who had become a Christian. A holy man in touch with other Christians of the region, he declared that the coming of a new prophet was imminent. The rabbis had also believed in this news but they considered the new prophet to be a descendant of Isaac while Waraqah thought that he could be an Arab. Before the marriage ceremony, as ʿAbd Allāh and his father ʿAbd al-Muttalib were walking toward the place where the ceremony was to take place, the beautiful and pious sister of Waraqah, Qutaylah, was standing at the door of her house. She saw ʿAbd Allāh and became startled by the light in his face which she knew to be the light of prophecy. She offered herself in marriage to him for the hundred camels that were sacrificed by his father in his place, but ʿAbd Allāh could not disobey his father and therefore refused the offer. After the consummation of the marriage, the next day when ʿAbd Allāh saw Qutaylah again she showed no interest in him and when he asked the cause, she said that the light in his face had disappeared. That light was to manifest itself in the being of the child who was conceived the night before. But ʿAbd Allāh did not live long enough to see his son Muḥammad, who was born in the Year of the Elephant, that is 570, as an orphan.

That year was indeed a momentous one for Mecca, Arabia and ultimately most of the world. The Christian ruler of Abyssinia, Abrahah, had conquered the Yemen and built a cathedral in Sanʿā' with the hope that this monument would replace Mecca as the center of religious activity in Arabia, but the cathedral was defiled by a member of the Kinānah tribe who managed to escape to safety. Abrahah thus decided to take revenge upon Mecca by razing the *Kaʿbah* to the ground. He assembled a vast army with an elephant leading in front. Approaching Mecca he asked for the leader of the Quraysh to come out to meet him, saying that he had nothing against the people of the city but wanted only to destroy the *Kaʿbah.* ʿAbd al-Muṭṭalib came out to meet him and to the great surprise of the latter did not ask for the *Kaʿbah* to be saved but only for his two hundred camels, taken by the Abrahah's soldiers, to be given back. When Abrahah asked why this was his only demand, ʿAbd al-Muṭṭalib said that he was responsible only for his camels and that the Lord of the *Kaʿbah* would take care of his own House. ʿAbd al-Muṭṭalib then returned to the *Kaʿbah,* asking God for help and then left with all the Meccans to the adjacent hills.

Abrahah then decided to march upon Mecca, but near the city the elephant in front of the army refused to move and simply sat on the ground. No amount of beating could change its will. Suddenly the sky turned black and a cloud of birds appeared which pelted the army killing most of the soldiers, the rest fleeing back to the Yemen. Hence the year, so famous in Islamic sources, became known as the Year of the Elephant. As a result, Mecca, which was soon to enter into the full light of history, was saved and the Quraysh gained greater respect among the other tribes as the people of God because their prayers were answered.

The momentous nature of this year was not only, however, in the miraculous saving of the *Kaʿbah,* but most of all in the birth of the

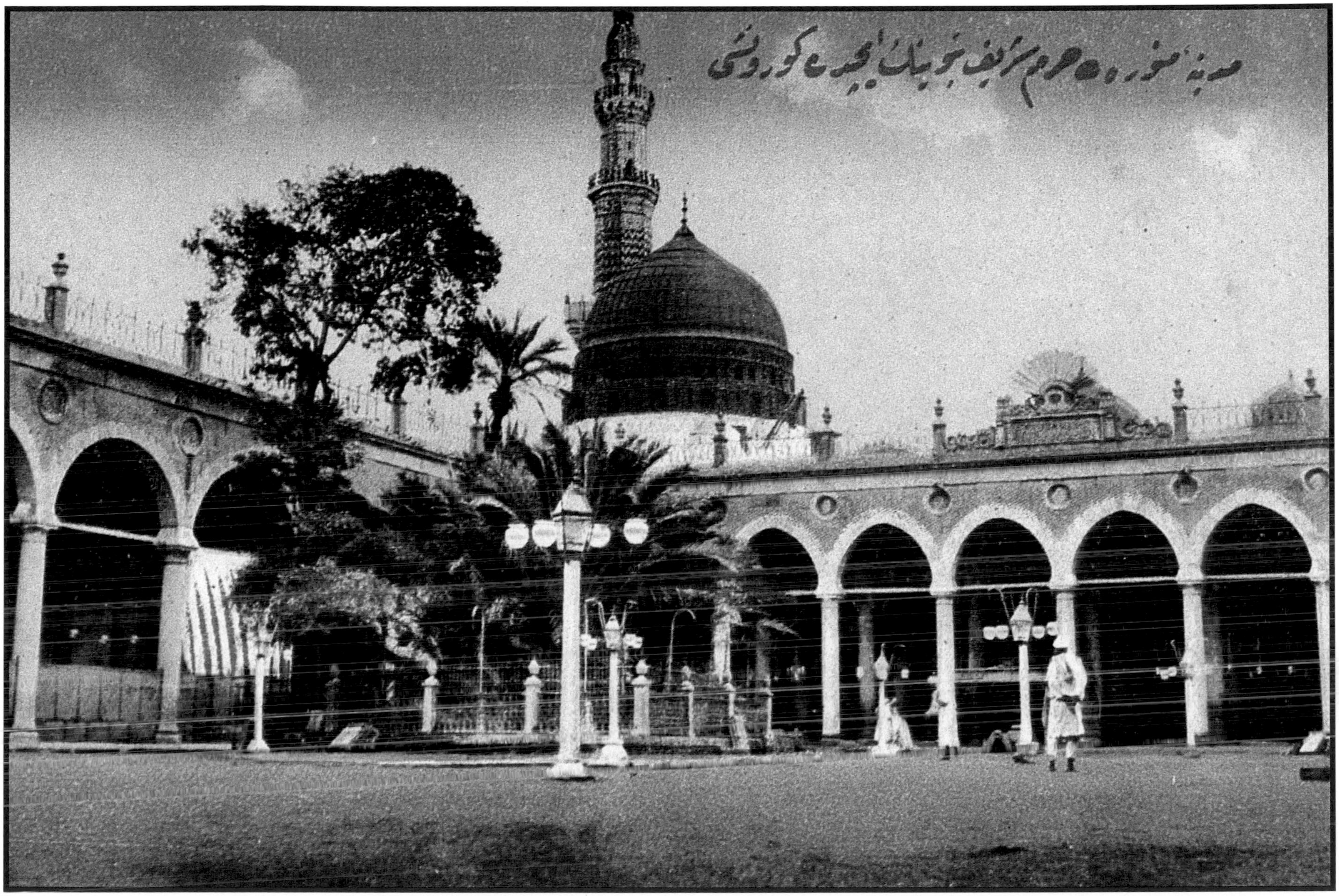

The Mosque of the Prophet with its green dome built in 678/1279. The color green is associated with the Blessed Prophet and his family and the green dome has become since the last century, along with the *Kaʿbah*, a global symbol of Islam.

person who, forty years later, would be visited by the archangel Gabriel in Mecca and who would rid the *Kaʿbah* of all the dross of forgetfulness of the One which, over the centuries, had covered its original face. Muḥammad ibn ʿAbd Allāh—upon whom be blessings and peace—was born to Āminah in Mecca and was given this name by God's command. His grandfather ʿAbd al-Muṭṭalib took the new-born child immediately to the *Kaʿbah* where he offered prayers to God. Thus the life and later message of the Prophet became intertwined with the *Kaʿbah* from the earliest moments of his earthly life and a link was established which, according to Islam, will last until the Day of Judgement.

## *The Life of the Prophet in Mecca and Medina*

The life of the Prophet of Islam was spent nearly completely in the two holy cities of Mecca and Medina where his *barakah* is ubiquitous for pious Muslims to this day. It was in Mecca that he was nurtured and raised, while spending some time in the care of the nomadic tribes in the areas around the city as was the tradition of the time. It was in Mecca that he gained fame as a just and trustworthy person and was bestowed with the title of al-Amīn, the Trusted One, even before being chosen as prophet. It was in this city that he married Khadījah and where his children were born. In fact the foundations of his house were visible in Mecca until the recent expansions of the Great Mosque. It was from here that he led the caravans of Khadījah, his wealthy and faithful wife, to Syria and back. It was in the hills around this city that he took refuge to be alone with God and it was on the top of one of these hills, al-Ḥirā', which stands just outside today's Mecca, that in the year 610 he was visited by the archangel Gabriel and the first verses of the Noble Qur'ān were revealed to him.

The advent of the revelation of course transformed the life of the Prophet completely, placing upon his shoulders the responsibility of establishing God's religion based upon the doctrine of Divine Unity *(al-tawḥīd)* amidst a society given to idolatry and in a tribe which derived its power from idol worship. Although his message was accepted immediately by his beloved wife Khadījah, trusted friend Abū Bakr, and intimate cousin and future son-in-law, ʿAlī, it was in the middle of his own city of Mecca that the Prophet was to encounter the most severe challenges, opposition, humiliation and threats, and experience the bitterness of being the object of enmity of so many of the members of his own Quraysh tribe. But also it was here that he persevered and succeeded in creating the nucleus of the first Islamic society.

It was also from the blessed city of Mecca that God chose to have him ascend during the Nocturnal Journey *(al-miʿrāj)* with the help of the archangel Gabriel, from Mecca to Jerusalem and from Jerusalem to the Divine Throne. Jerusalem was the first direction of prayer for Muslims *(al-qiblah al-ūlā)* and then, while the Prophet was in Mecca, God ordered that city to become the *qiblah*. The *miʿrāj* reconfirmed for all later generations of Muslims the spiritual connection between Jerusalem and Mecca, the first and second *qiblahs* and the center of monotheism as a whole and Islamic monotheism respectively; two cities whose spiritual reality will, according to Islamic eschatological teachings, become reunited at the end of time, while being deeply interconnected here and now.

The Prophet was to leave a Mecca in deep enmity against him, where even his life was now threatened, for the hospitality of the city which was to take his name and become known as the City of the Prophet, *madīnat al-nabī*. He was to return to his city of birth several years later to perform the pilgrimage in peace and finally to enter Mecca in triumph in the moment which marked the crowning achievement of his earthly life. He was to order ʿAlī and Bilāl to rid the *Kaʿbah* of the idols of the Age of Ignorance *(al-jāhiliyyah)* and to re-establish it as the primordial temple dedicated to the One God. His final departure from Mecca left that city as the unquestionable center of the new religious universe created by the Qur'ānic revelation. At once the site of the *Kaʿbah*, the birthplace of the Prophet, the place of the first revelation of the Qur'ān and the *qiblah* of all Muslims, Mecca thus became and remains the holiest of Islamic cities.

It was, however, the city of Yathrib to the north that opened its arms to the Prophet at a moment when his life and that of the nascent Islamic community were threatened by the intractable enmity of the Quraysh in Mecca. The Prophet thus set out with his trusted companion Abū Bakr for what was to become Medina, having sent his followers, known as *al-muhājirūn*, literally "the immigrants," in small groups before him to that city with a few to follow afterwards. It was at the outskirts of Medina at the site of the present Qubā' Mosque where he performed his prayers. It was to the present site of his mosque that his camel was to take him—by its own will so as to avoid contention between different groups that wanted to offer him hospitality at their homes.

Medina was integrated by the Prophet into the first fully-fledged Islamic society to become henceforth the model for all later Islamic societies. The Prophet had a Constitution prepared for the city which is the earliest Islamic political document. Here he established norms which were to become models for later Islamic practice and promulgated laws which became foundational to Islamic Law or *al-Sharīʿah*.

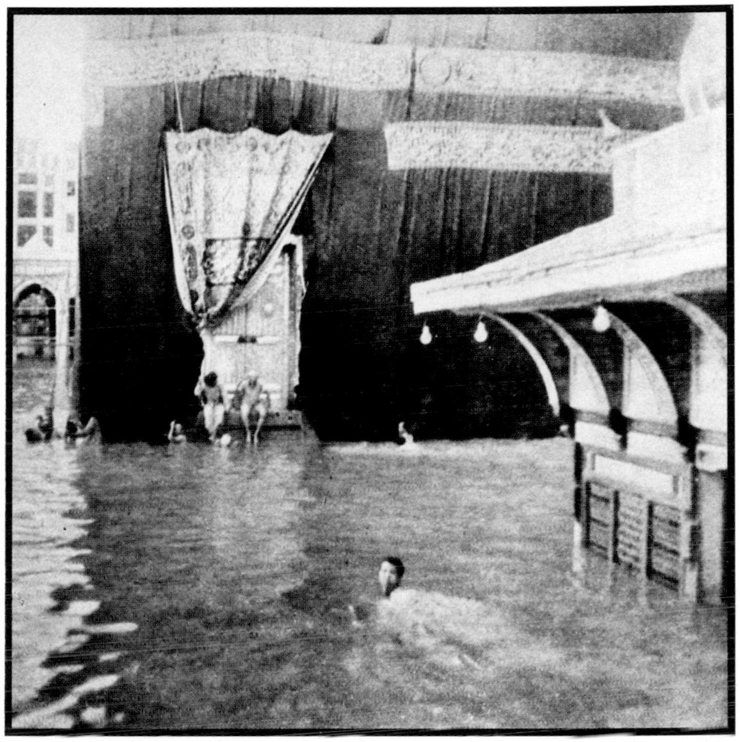

A rare photograph of the *Kaʿbah* taken in 1941 when an unusual deluge in an ordinarily very dry region covered the entire area around the *Kaʿbah* which stands on lower ground than most of the other mosques in the ravine of Mecca.

While the revelation continued in Medina, the community became transformed from a small number of scattered adherents to a fully organized society, the heart of a vast religious universe which was in the process of formation. But the challenge of Meccan forces against Islam continued and Medina and its environs were witness to crucial battles which decided the fate of the new community. The first great battle *(al-ghazz)* was al-Badr, in which a vastly outnumbered Muslim army overcame the Meccan army, with the help of angels, according to traditional sources, at a site just outside of Medina. The battle of Uḥud, in which the Muslims were defeated and the Prophet injured without the Meccans pursuing their victory, likewise took place close to the present limits of the city, while the site of the battle of Khaybar, in which ʿAlī showed exemplary valor, is not far away. Medina was even besieged once and saved only by the wise decision of Salmān al-Fārsī, the first Persian to embrace Islam, to dig a ditch around the city, hence the name of the battle as *al-Khandaq* or the Ditch.

It was in and around Medina that both successes and failures took place militarily as well as socially and politically, but while the failures were short-lived and overcome by never-ending hope and reliance of the Prophet upon God, the successes increased and the strength of the Islamic community augmented from day to day until gradually all of Arabia became united under the banner of Islam during the lifetime of the Prophet with Medina serving as the socio-political capital and center of this newly-integrated world. The man who rode with his close friend Abū Bakr from Mecca to the city of Yathrib became within a decade in that city which had now become Medina, the prophet-king of the whole of Arabia and the founder of a new religious civilization and society whose boundaries were to stretch in less than a century from China to France. And it was to this city, in which God had bequeathed upon him the mastery and dominion of a whole world, that he returned from his city of birth, Mecca, to spend the last few months of his life. Furthermore, it was there in Medina that he died in 10/632 to be buried in his own apartment next to the mosque which he had ordered to be built, the *masjid al-nabī* or Mosque of the Prophet, that is the prototype of all later mosques. Medina therefore became the second sacred city of Islam, reflecting to this day, and despite the loss in recent years of much of its traditional architecture and palm groves, (some planted by ʿAlī and other companions of the Prophet), crucial stages in the life of the Prophet, his family and companions. One can still sense the perfume of his presence in that beautiful oasis city, *al-Madinah*, which Muslims cherish the world over.

## *Mecca and Medina in Later Islamic History*

Through all the later vicissitudes of Islamic history, Mecca and Medina have continued as the spiritual and religious centers of the Islamic world, but the political heart of the Islamic world was to leave Arabia a little more than two decades after the death of the Prophet. Abū Bakr, ʿUmar and ʿUthmān, the first three caliphs, ruled the ever-expanding Islamic world from Medina, where they enlarged the Mosque of the Prophet as well as the limits of the city itself. But the fourth caliph, ʿAlī, facing the rebellion of the garrison in Syria moved to Kufa in Iraq to prepare an army to put down this revolt. His coming to Kufa, which henceforth became the capital until ʿAlī's assassination, moved the political center of Islam out of Arabia forever. For after ʿAlī, the Umayyads who gained political power did not return to Mecca or Medina but made Damascus their capital while their successors, the Abbasids, built Baghdad as their capital. Both dynasties, however, influenced the architecture of the two holy cities. During the early Umayyad period the people of both Mecca and Medina resisted strongly Umayyad directives. The grandson of Abū Bakr, ʿAbd Allāh, led a revolt in Mecca against the Umayyads as a result of which the *Kaʿbah* became seriously damaged and was rebuilt with the help of architects and craftsmen using Yemeni building techniques. But the city was attacked again by the Umayyad general al-Ḥajjāj and all of ʿAbd Allāh's work on the *Kaʿbah* was destroyed and the monument reconstructed. Likewise in Medina many of the houses of the *ahl al-bayt* or household of the Prophet, including the house of Fāṭimah, were destroyed by the Umayyads. Some believe in fact that the Umayyads built the monumental mosques of Jerusalem and Damascus so that Muslims would pay less attention to Mecca and Medina but such was not to be the case.

Although raids and skirmishes continued from time to time, the most famous being that of the Carmathians in the fourth/tenth century during which they stole the Black Stone of the *Kaʿbah* for twenty-one years, Mecca and Medina continued to be revered as the spiritual centers of the Islamic world. They even resisted the more worldly art that the Umayyads had developed farther north and had sought to impose upon the two holy cities. During the Abbasid as well as Mamluk and Ottoman periods great attention continued to be paid to the two cities and many fine monuments were created some of which survive to this day for it was the greatest honor and responsibility to be custodian and protector of the two holy cities. Since 1926 after the demise of the Ottoman Empire and the defeat of the Hāshimites of Mecca by the Saudis, Hijaz has been a part of Saudi Arabia. Under the new situation

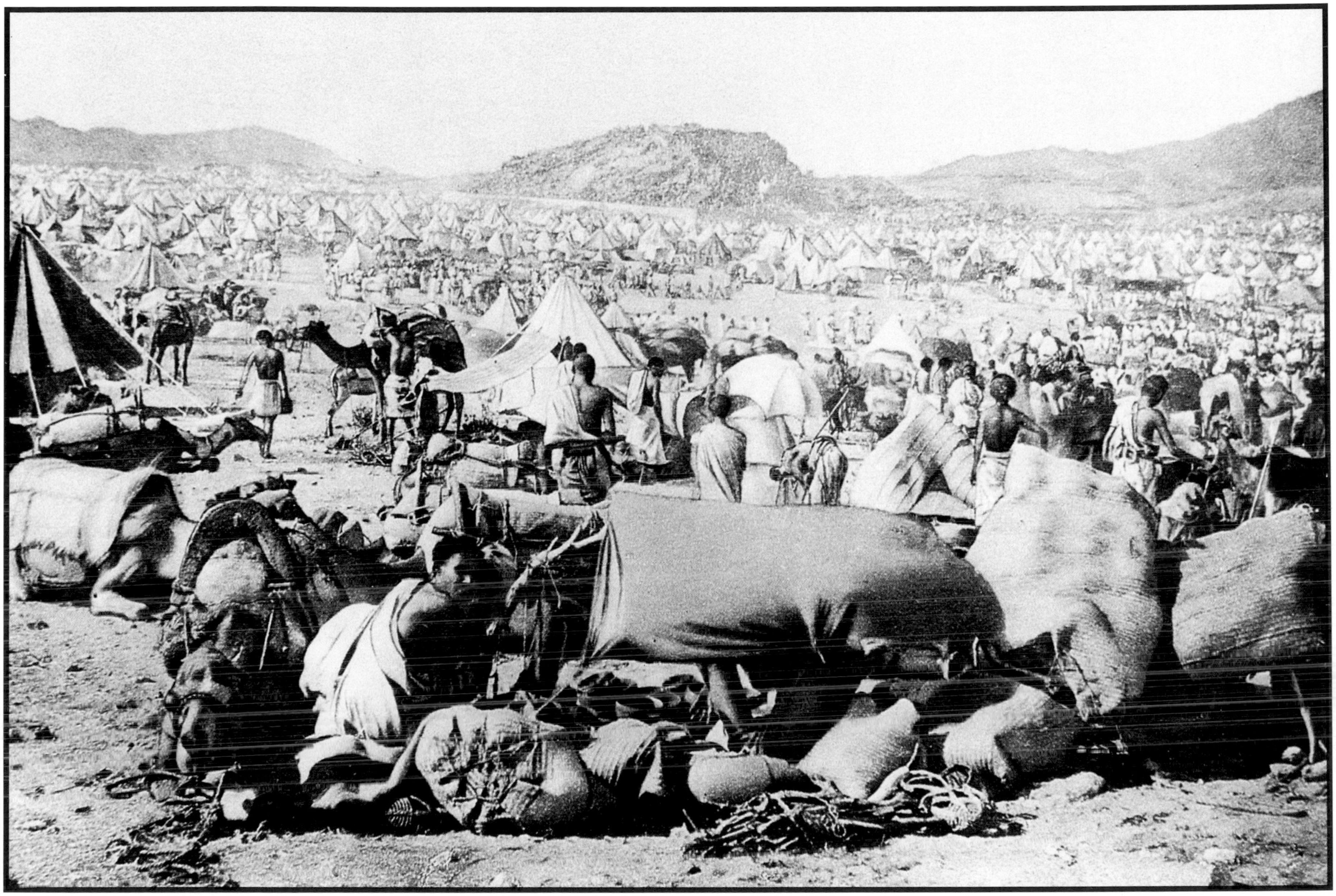

A scene of ʿArafāt photographed during the *ḥajj* in 1885. The photo, taken by the Dutch orientalist Snouck Hurgronje whose Muslim name was ʿAbd al-Ghaffār, shows a number of pilgrims around the Mount of Mercy (Jabal al-Raḥmān) shown at the center.

the custodianship of the two holy cities continued to be seen as the greatest honor by the Saudis to the extent that the King of Saudi Arabia is not referred to as "His Majesty" but as "Custodian of the Two Holy Mosques".

During all the centuries of Islamic history Mecca and Medina remained outside the major turmoils in the heartland of the Islamic world farther north. The tremors of the Crusades and the Mongol invasion hardly reached them while they continued to be visited by streams of pilgrims from the east to the west of the Islamic world, many of whom in fact took refuge in the calm and peace of these cities from either turmoil in their place of birth, or the din of the life of the world, as we see in the case of Bahā' al-Dīn Walad, the father of Jalāl al-Dīn Rūmī who, fleeing the Mongol invasion in Khurasan, came with his young son to Mecca before settling in Anatolia; or Imam al-Ghazālī who spent years in seclusion in the holy cities. Many of those Islamic scholars, who are called Makkī or Madanī, hailed in fact from other regions of the Islamic world but settled in the two holy cities. These cities remained over the centuries as the heart of Islamic civilization whose more evident and well known centers as far as political, intellectual and artistic life are concerned, lay north, east and west of the sacred land of Hijaz, the birthplace of Islam. Hijaz itself continues to this day to be the religious center of the Islamic world as a result of the ever-living presence and continuing significance of Mecca and Medina.

## *The Kaᶜbah*

This House of God and primordial temple dedicated to the One, which is the object of the *ḥajj* and the focal point for the daily prayers or the *qiblah* of all Muslims, stands at the heart of Mecca as testimony to the nature of Islam as the pure monotheism which revived the monotheism of Abraham and ultimately the primordial message of unity revealed to Adam, at once the father of humanity and first prophet. The *Kaᶜbah* is the concrete symbol of the origin of Islam, and in Muslim eyes, of all religion. To come to the *Kaᶜbah* is to return to one's origin. But it is also the supreme center of Islam by virtue of which all Muslims turn to it in their daily canonical prayers. Like all veritable traditional civilizations, Islam is dominated by the two realities of Origin and Center and these two fundamental dimensions of Islamic life are present in the *Kaᶜbah*. Throughout his or her life on earth a Muslim, whether living by one of the volcanic peaks of Java or in the desert of Mauritania, is aware of the *Kaᶜbah* as the point on earth which links him or her to the origin of himself or herself, of his or her religion, Islam, and ultimately of humanity as such. The Muslim is also aware that all points of space on earth are linked by an invisible line to a unique center which is the *Kaᶜbah* towards which one directs one's face five times a day in prayer. The Muslim therefore has a relation to the *Kaᶜbah* which is at once static and dynamic, static for there is a constant link between every point of the space of the Islamic cosmos and the *Kaᶜbah* and dynamic because it is toward the *Kaᶜbah* that one journeys during the pilgrimage. In a sense the daily prayers *(al-ṣalāh)* represent that static relation and the *ḥajj* the dynamic one. Together they confirm the overwhelming and majestic presence of the *Kaᶜbah* as at once Origin and Center in the Islamic religious universe, not because of the *Kaᶜbah* in its earthly reality but because of what it signifies as the House of God, for in reality it is God alone who is the Origin and Center of a Muslim's life.

The *Kaᶜbah* is considered by Muslims to be a reflection here below of the celestial temple surrounding God's Throne *(al-ᶜarsh)* except that by inverse analogy, here below, one can speak of surrounding the Throne while in the principial domain it is the Throne that surrounds all things as the Qur'ān asserts. The archaic nature of the *Kaᶜbah* points to its primordial character. Being a cube (hence the name *Kaᶜbah* which means cube in Arabic) or almost a cube, it is 12 meters long, 10 meters broad and 16 meters high, possessing therefore dimensions which are in harmonic relation with each other according to the Pythagorean meaning of harmony. As a cube, the *Kaᶜbah* also symbolizes the stability and immutability that characterize Islam itself, a religion based on harmony, stability and immutability in its basic reality, hence the truth that Islam can be renewed but not reformed. It is of interest to note that the Holy of Holies in Jerusalem in which the Ark of the Covenant was kept was also in the form of a cube. And like the ark, the *Kaᶜbah* is considered to reflect the Presence of God. It is like a living body; hence its being dressed in the black cloth *(al-kiswah)*, with golden Qur'ānic verses. This dressing of the Sacred House of God, an old Semitic tradition not found in the Graeco-Roman world, is renewed every year and the old *kiswah* is cut up and distributed so as to allow the *barakah* of the *Kaᶜbah* to emanate among those to whom pieces of the cloth are given. From the earliest centuries of Islamic history the kiswah was made in Egypt and carried with great care to Mecca but now it is made near the holy city itself.

The *Kaᶜbah* is a structure with cosmic and even metacosmic significance. It lies on the axis which unites Heaven and Earth in the Islamic cosmos. It is situated at the hub of the world at the point of intersection between the *axis mundi* and the earth. Its properties reflect cosmic harmony. Its four corners point to the four cardinal directions which represent the four pillars *(al-arkān)* of the traditional cosmos. As for the Black Stone *(al-ḥajar al-aswad)* at its corner, it is a meteorite, therefore from beyond the earthly ambience. Abraham (Ibrāhīm) and Ishmael (Ismāʿīl) are said to have brought it from the hill of Abū Qubays nearby Mecca where it had been preserved since coming to earth. According to the Prophet, the stone had descended from Heaven whiter than milk but turned black as the result of the sins of the children of Adam although something of its original luminosity survives. The stone also symbolizes the original covenant made, according to the Qur'an, between God and Adam and all his progeny, through which all members of humanity accepted on that "pre-eternal moment" *(al-azal)*, when the covenant was made, the Lordship of God.

The communal prayer around the *Kaʿbah* is the most tangible sign of perfect submission to God's Will as the circumambulation around it marks the return of man to his original Edenic perfection. By emptying the *Kaʿbah* of the idols, the Prophet not only re-consecrated the Primordial Temple as the House of the One God but also taught all Muslims that in order to be truly Muslim they must empty the heart, which is the microcosmic counterpart of the *Kaʿbah*, of all idols, of all that is other than God, making the heart worthy of receiving the Divine Presence.

The *Kaʿbah* is a form, yet the symbol of the Formless. It is proto-architecture, yet the source of all Islamic architecture. The black color of the *kiswah* is the symbol of that darkness which is none other than the intensity of light, the color beyond all colors which contains all colors, all forms. The golden letters of the Noble Qur'ān embellishing it are the evident manifestation of the Divine Essence from which the Word originates in the golden color of the sun, itself symbol of the Divine Intellect. The black and gold reveal the relation between the Word in the manifested world *(al-shahādah)* and the Unmanifested to which the Qur'ān refers so often as the Invisible *(al-ghayb)*. To stand before the *Kaʿbah* is to behold the miracle of manifestation in relation to its invisible Source in revelation as well as in creation which is also God's primordial revelation. That is why the *Kaʿbah* is at once the House of God, the center of the Islamic cosmic ambience and outward symbol of the heart of God's slave, man, the heart which when purified reveals its true nature, according to the famous saying *(ḥadīth)* of the Blessed Prophet, as the Throne of the Compassionate (*al-Raḥmān*, which is a Name of the Divine Essence).

## *Pilgrimage and* the *Pilgrimage* (al-ḥajj)

Life itself is not only a journey but in reality a pilgrimage whether man is aware of it or not, for at the end of the journey of life stands the gate of death and encounter with the Sacred, in the same way that the journey of the pilgrim leads him to the sacred precinct which is the very goal and purpose of the journey. Islam has taken this essential truth and made it an integral element of the religious life by making the pilgrimage to Mecca obligatory. But pilgrimage to more local sites is also part and parcel of the life of traditional Muslims. Whether it be Mulay Idrīs in Morocco, Ra's al-Ḥusayn in Cairo, the Dome of the Rock in Jerusalem, numerous sites in Iraq and Iran such as Najaf, Karbala', Samarrah, and Kazimayn, Mashhad and Qom, all revered especially by Shiʿites, or the mausoleums of Dādājī Ganjbaksh in Lahore and Muʿīn al-Dīn Chistī in Ajmer in India, all these sites, to which pilgrimage is made by millions of the faithful annually, are reflections of the holy cities of Mecca and Medina. The grace *(barakah)* of these sacred precincts thus flows to the other regions of the Islamic world like blood which, issuing from the heart, reaches all the limbs of the body. It is not accidental that all these sites are associated with events in the life of the Prophet and his household or are mausoleums of those who were either biological or spiritual children of the founder of Islam.

These forms of pilgrimage are, however, but echoes to loci of sacred presence, of the supreme pilgrimage which is the *ḥajj*, one of the obligatory pillars of Islam. The *ḥajj* recapitulates the whole spiritual journey of man on earth. As the rite instituted by Abraham in commemoration of the One God of pure monotheism and revived by the Prophet, every part of it goes back to Prophetic example and his wonts *(sunnah)*. The performance of the *ḥajj*, which countless Muslim men and women have undertaken over the centuries, coming in heat and cold from near and far, on foot or on camels, in boats or on horses, from high mountain valleys or distant islands, is itself a *jihād* or exertion in the path of God. It implies sacrifice and hardship leading sometimes, even in the present age of so-called modern convenience, to death which Muslims espouse with open arms for they are then promised the death of a martyr and entry into Paradise if their intentions have been pure.

It is enough to understand the real significance of each of the elements of the *ḥajj*, to grasp the transforming power of this unique rite which unites Muslims from all over the world once a year before the majestic presence of the House of God. In approaching the holy precinct *(al-ḥaram)*, whose boundaries were delineated by the Prophet, the pilgrim must perform the complete ritual ablution *(al-ghusl)* to wash away the impurities of worldly existence. Each pilgrim must then put on the *iḥrām*, two pieces of seamless white cloth, so as to be in a consecrated state. Henceforth the pilgrim must abstain from all evil thoughts and the cares of the world and also from gratification of sexual passions.

The men and women who are to perform the *ḥajj* in this state must die to the world and the white color of the *iḥrām* does not only signify purity but also spiritual death. That is why most pilgrims put their *iḥrāms* away at the end of the pilgrimage to be used for their shroud which in Islam is also always white. The *iḥrām* also signifies primordial man's "nakedness" in standing before God, as all Muslims will do on the Day of Judgement.

Upon entering Mecca the pilgrims must make the circumambulation *(al-ṭawāf)* around the *Kaʿbah* seven times and try to kiss the *ḥajar al-aswad* at its corner. The movement of the circumambulation is counter clockwise for in performing this rite man reverses the process of the fall and all the imperfections which he has accrued within himself as a result of the consequences of the downward flow of time. The circumambulations re-integrate the men and women who actualize the meaning of the rite within themselves into the Edenic state, in that condition in which all the children of Adam bore testimony to God's Oneness. The kissing of the Black Stone is in a sense the renewal of the pre-eternal covenant *(al-mīthāq)* with God. Furthermore, in relation to that Edenic perfection outward distinctions are irrelevant; hence the performance of the *ḥajj* in a dress which is the same for all, whether king or beggar, for in the sight of God, *the noblest of you . . . is the best in conduct,* (Qur'ān xlix:13) and outward social and class distinctions play no role. In making the *ṭawāf* amidst a vast sea of humanity, black, white and yellow, Arab and non-Arab, dark haired and blond, without awareness of a person's wealth or position in society, one gains a glimpse of the reality that the only basic distinction of human beings before God is their inner purity and spiritual character, while in the realm of creation there are diversities of race, age, gender, language and culture which are themselves willed by God. The *ṭawāf* reveals a unity in diversity which is overwhelming and at the very antipode of a quantitative egalitarianism which mistakes uniformity for unity.

The *saʿy* or rapid walk between Ṣafā and Marwah, celebrating the rapid movement of Hagar and her son Ishmael (Ismāʿīl) in quest of water, which appeared miraculously in the form of the sacred spring of Zamzam, represents our quest in this world for the life-bestowing bounties of God and His Mercy which fulfills our quest. The spring of Zamzam itself is an earthly "tributary" flowing from the springs of Paradise. Its water heals body and soul and is brought back by pilgrims and distributed throughout the Islamic world as a blessing. It is one of the most precious gifts that a pilgrim can bring back to his family and friends.

The events outside of Mecca are intimately related to sacred history and eschatological realities. The great plain of ʿArafāt where all the pilgrims assemble in a vast congregation and where the deepest prayers are offered for the forgiveness of one's sins as well as the welfare of others, symbolizes the plain of *Maḥshar* or Resurrection when everyone will stand before God on the Day of Judgement denuded of all accessories and paraphernalia with one's only possession being one's actions in this world and the effect they have had upon the soul. In the middle of ʿArafāt stands Jabal al-Raḥmah or the Mount of Mercy where the last verses of the Noble Qur'ān were revealed and where one of the famous farewell addresses of the Blessed Prophet was delivered. It is here that the alchemy of union between various aspects of human nature takes place and men and women regain their primordial wholeness for it was in the plain of ʿArafāt that Adam and Eve are said to have found each other again after their fall on earth from Paradise. All of us, whether male or female, contain the two poles of the human reality symbolized by Adam and Eve within ourselves. But these two poles, representing our active and passive natures and tendencies, are now in discord. The alchemical wedding, whose fruit is gold or the perfection of the soul, is none other than the harmonious wedding between the Adam and Eve of our soul, a wedding which can become actualized, for those aware of the profound significance of the rites of the *ḥajj*, at the great plain of ʿArafāt where in sacred history such a union took place on the objective plane at the dawn of our earthly existence.

It is at Mina, where the Prophet delivered his last eloquent words during his final pilgrimage, that pilgrims cast stones against pillars representing Satan *(al-Shayṭān)*. This rite is, however, not only an external act but also an external support for the inner battle with the demon within, a battle that must be carried out incessantly until final victory. Muslims usually begin ritual actions, including recitation of the Qur'ān, by taking refuge in God from the accursed Satan which in the Arabic formula, *al-Shayṭān al-rajīm*, means literally Satan against whom the stone is cast. The ritual at Mina actualizes, in a scene which is unforgettable for those who participate in it, a reality of human life of which we must be always aware no matter what our religious and spiritual accomplishments, that reality being the need for the constant battle against the forces of evil and dispersion within the soul. This unforgettable experience remains a powerful weapon in the journey of life, one which those pilgrims who make the rites with pure intention and devotion will never forget.

Finally, there is the sacrifice of an animal in emulation of the sacrifice of Abraham, the flesh of the sacrificed animals being given to the poor. Like Judaism, Islam obliges its followers to slaughter ritually those animals which are permitted by religious Law to eat, sacrificing them

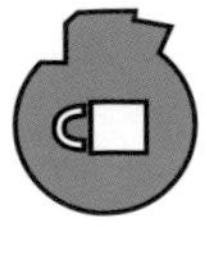

Extension by
the Quraysh
AD 604

Extension by
ʿUmar ibn al-Khaṭṭāb
in 17 AH (AD 638)

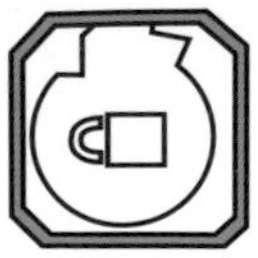

Extension by
ʿUthmān ibn ʿAffān
in 26 AH (AD 646)

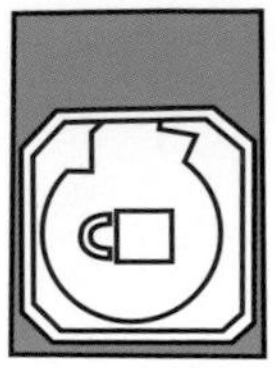

Extension by
ʿAbd Allāh ibn al-Zubayr
in 65 AH (AD 684)

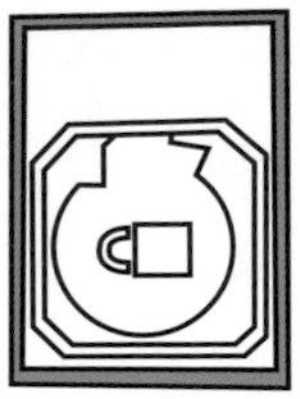

Extension by
al-Walīd al-Malik
in 91 AH (AD 709)

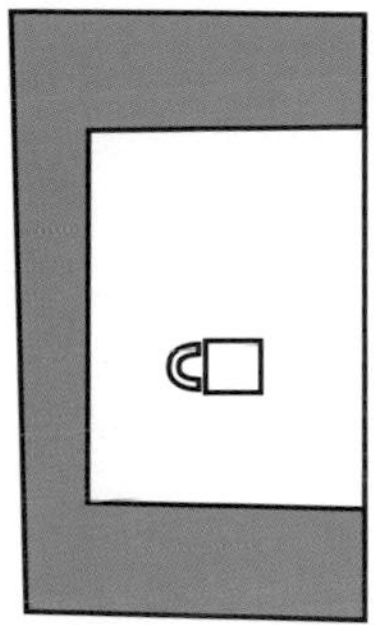

Extension by
Abū Jaʿfar al-Manṣūr
in 137 AH (AD 754)

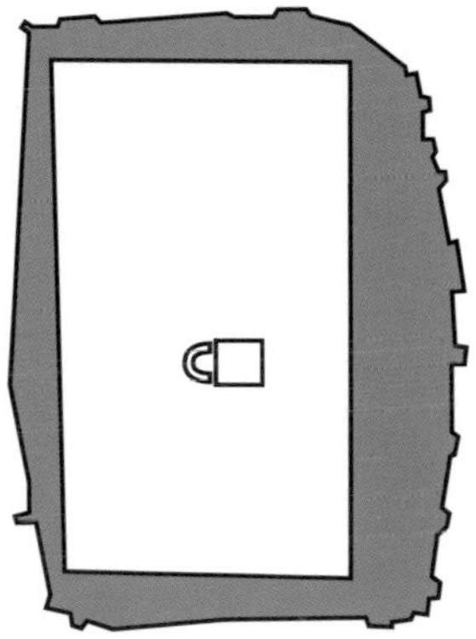

Extension by
al-Mahdī al-ʿAbbāsī
in 161-164 AH (AD 777-780)

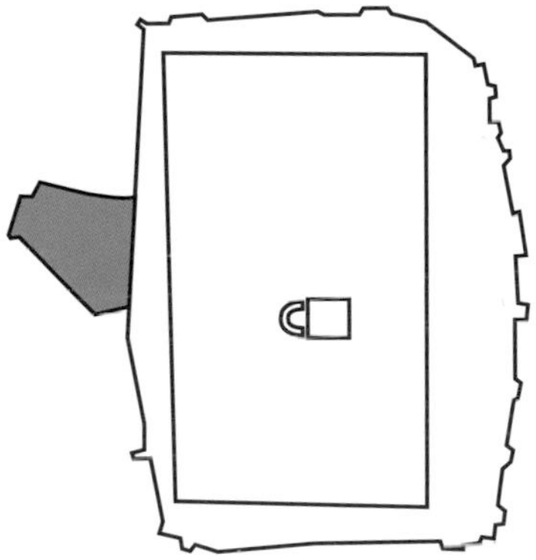

Extension by
al-Muʿtaḍid al-ʿAbbāsī
in 284 AH (AD 897)

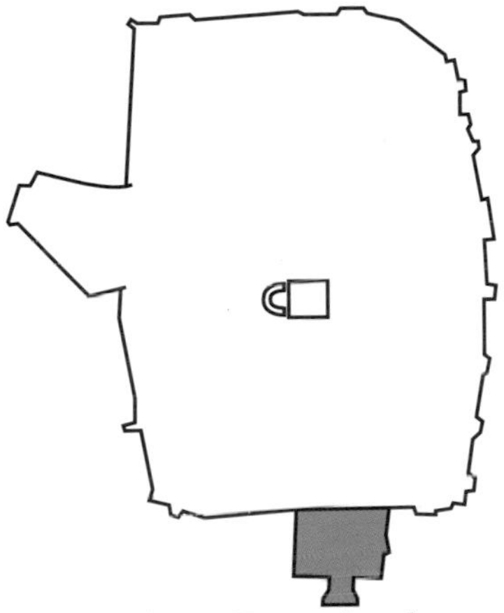

Extension by
al-Muqtadir al-ʿAbbāsī
in 306 AH (AD 918)

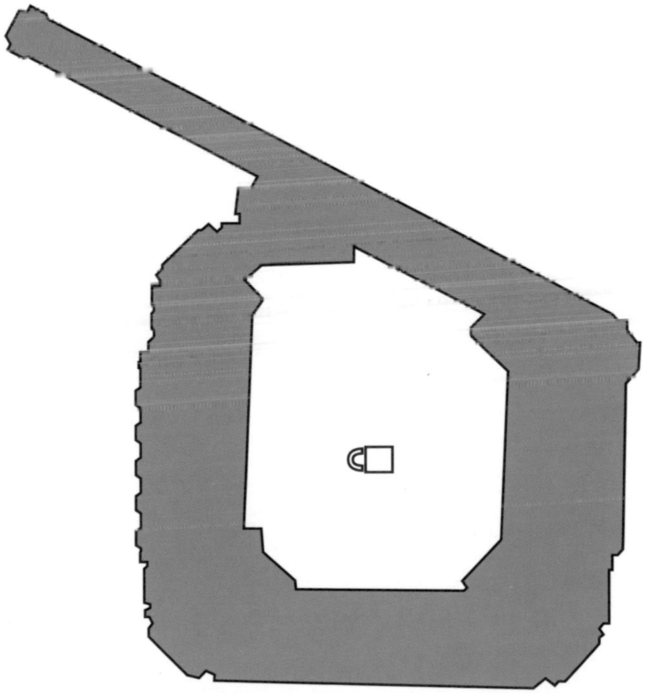

Extension by King Abdul Aziz Al-Saud
in 1375-1396 AH (AD 1955-1976)

# Expansion chart of the Holy Mosque of Mecca

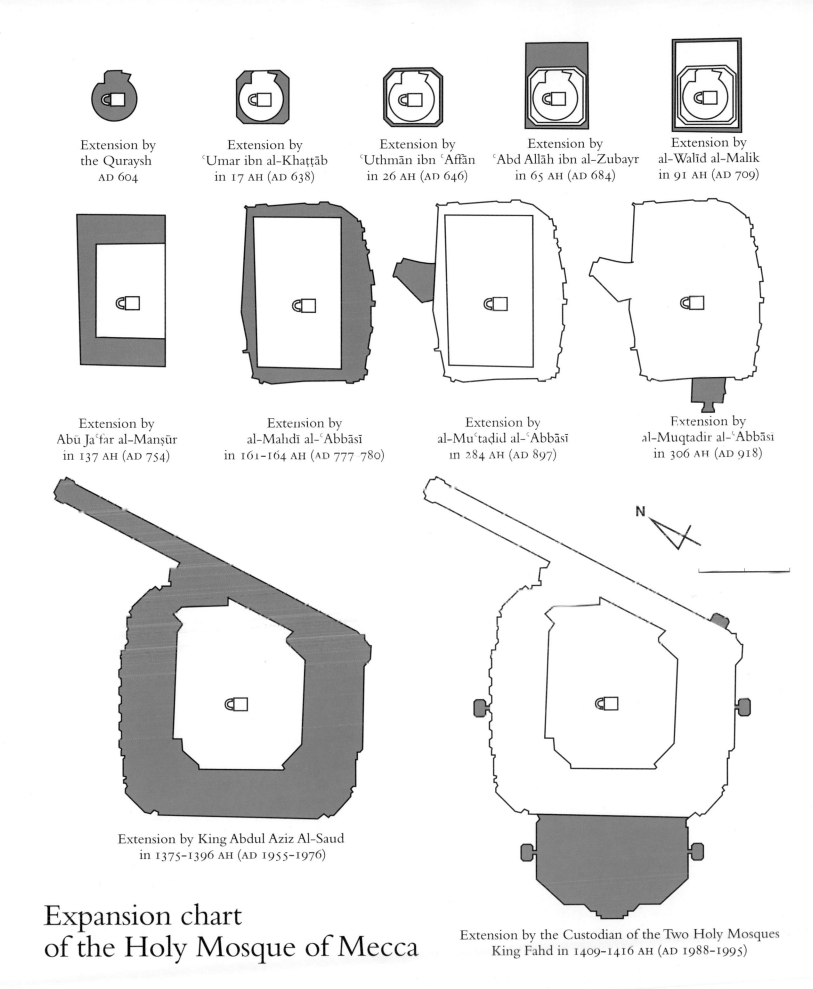

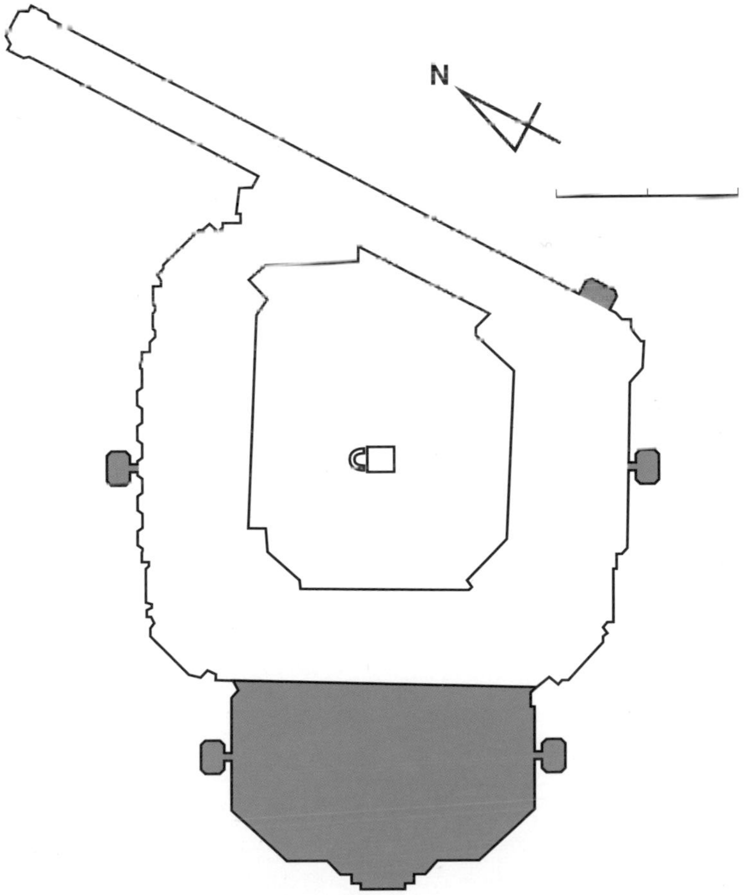


Extension by the Custodian of the Two Holy Mosques
King Fahd in 1409-1416 AH (AD 1988-1995)

before God. The sacrifice at the end of the *ḥajj*, not only reasserts the significance of this Islamic practice, but also symbolizes the sacrifice of the soul before God, for the greatest sacrifice that we can make before God is that of our carnal and passionate soul. It was to this battle, to overcome the lower soul, that the Blessed Prophet referred as *al-jihād al-akbar* or greater exertion upon the path of God, in comparison to ordinary *jihād*, to defend Islam and its borders to which he referred, upon returning from the battle of Badr that determined the future of the newly-born religious community, as the lesser *jihād* or *al-jihād al-aṣghar*.

The rite of sacrifice is so significant that the great celebration at the end of the *ḥajj* is called the Feast of Sacrifice (*ʿīd al-aḍḥā* or *ʿīd-i qurbān* in Persian). But it must be remembered that the root of the word *aḍḥā* possesses another meaning which is that of clarity and lucidity and is related by certain Muslim writers to the Day of Resurrection. This meaning of the term is also mysteriously present at the end of the *ḥajj* for the pilgrim has now been washed of his or her sins and begins life anew, resurrected as a potentially perfect servant of God. The final farewell visit to the *Kaʿbah* is to seal the remembrance of the Center and the new life it has given to the pilgrim who is now called a *ḥājjī* (male) or *ḥājjiyah* (female). That is why when the pilgrim returns home, everyone comes to visit him or her to gain something of the *barakah* of the Center and the purity of the pilgrim born into a new life which must now be an exemplar of righteousness, piety and virtue.

## *The Holy Cities Today*

Modern methods of transportation have increased the number of pilgrims greatly during the past few decades. Some two million people now make the annual pilgrimage, coming from all over the traditional areas of the Islamic world as well as from Western Europe, North and South America and Australia where the presence of Islamic communities is more recent. One can now see pilgrims from Los Angeles, Caracas and London as well as Dakar, Baku, Samarqand and Jakarta—not to speak of the central areas of the Islamic world. This vast increase in the number of pilgrims has caused the Great Mosque at Mecca and the Mosque of the Prophet to be expanded immensely but at the cost of the destruction of many quarters around the two sacred areas, quarters which contained historic houses and were scenes of many of the events of the sacred history of Islam.

What is remarkable is that despite the ravages of modernism, the rite instituted by the Patriarch Abraham and re-established by the Prophet of Islam continues as a unique event in today's world. Every year during the lunar Islamic month of *Dhu'l-ḥijjah* pilgrims come to Mecca and also visit Medina. The image described in traditional sources of Mecca as a womb which once a year grows immensely and is then emptied still holds but one must add that the Great Mosque is now never empty. Now, throughout the whole year outside of the season for the annual *ḥajj* many Muslims make the pilgrimage to the two holy cities to perform the lesser pilgrimage which is called *al-ʿumrah*, and even in the middle of the night throughout the year thousands can be seen circumambulating around the *Kaʿbah* in a constantly moving circle of humanity crying *labbayka allāhumma labbayk* (at Thy service, O Lord, at Thy service). To behold such a site with its constancy day and night, season after season, is to see the earthly reflection of the heavens rotating around the solar star and according to the Qur'ān praising God constantly.

The *ḥajj* remains, as in the days of old, also the occasion for the purchase and exchange of gifts and of ideas, some historians of science having called the *ḥajj* of the earlier centuries the first international conference on the sciences. The *ḥajj* continues to be, moreover, a powerful means for various parts of the Islamic community *(al-ummah)* to know each other and therefore instrumental in the integration of the community. But despite all the outward changes related to communication, facilities and the like, the *ḥajj* remains first and foremost what it has always been, a return to our Center and Origin, a death and rebirth, a spiritual rejuvenation and a renewal of our pre-eternal covenant with God. It remains a powerful way, along with other Islamic rites, of realizing the Unity of God *(al-tawḥīd)* and in the light of that unity, the interrelation of all of His creation. That is why Mecca and its twin city Medina flourish as the heart and sacred Center of the Islamic universe and will continue to do so as long as there are men and women who accept the truth of *Lā ilāha illa'Llāh* and *Muḥammadun rasūl Allāh*, whose hearts palpitate with the rhythms of the psalmody of the Noble Qur'ān and whose minds and souls remain nourished by the message of the Noble Book first revealed in Mecca to a man who was born in that city and who died in Medina, the man with whom the cycle of prophecy for present humanity came to a close.

*wa'l-ḥamdu li'Llāh waḥdahu*
All praise belongs to God in His Oneness

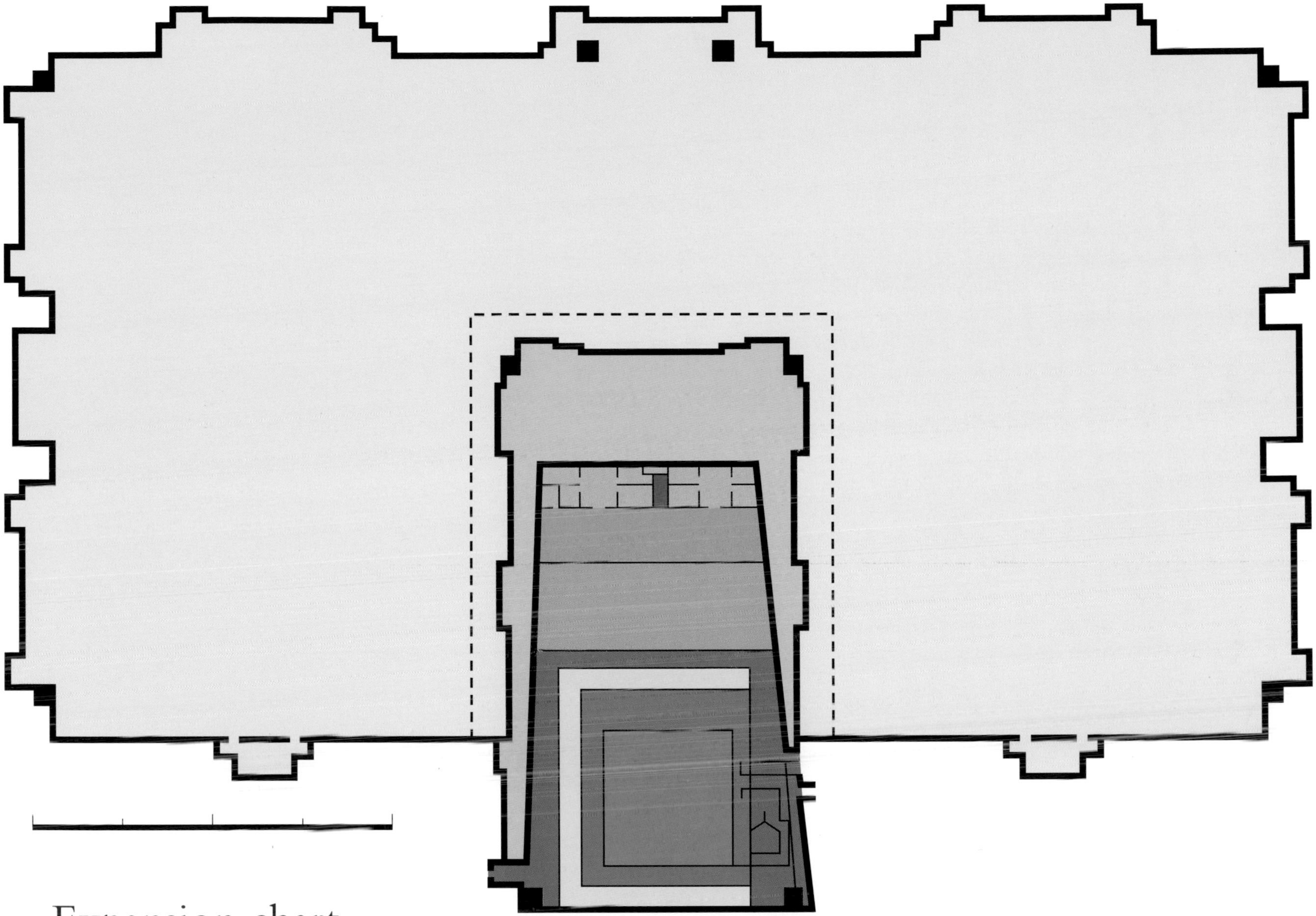

# Expansion chart of the Prophet's Mosque of Medina

LEGEND

- Construction by Prophet Muḥammad
- Extension by Prophet Muḥammad after Conquest of Khaybar in 7 AH (AD 628)
- Extension by ʿUmar ibn al-Khaṭṭāb in 17 AH (AD 638)
- Extension by ʿUthmān ibn ʿAffān in 29-30 AH (AD 649-650)
- Extension by al-Walīd al-Umawī in 88-91 AH (AD 706-709)
- Extension by al-Mahdī al-ʿAbbāsī in 161-165 AH (AD 777-781)
- Extension by Sultan Ashraf Qutabai in 888 AH (AD 1483)
- Extension by Sultan ʿAbd al-Majīd al-ʿUthmānī in 1265-1277 AH (AD 1848-1860)
- Extension by King Abdul Aziz al-Saud in 1372 AH (AD 1952)
- Extension by the Custodian of the Two Holy Mosques King Fahd in 1406-1416 AH (AD 1985-1995)

# *Mecca*

Here is the heart of the Islamic world, and even the Islamic cosmos by virtue of containing at its center the Kaʿbah, the point where the world axis of the Islamic universe connecting Heaven and earth touches our human world. This is the city upon whose soil Abraham and Ismāʿīl/Ishmael walked, in one of whose precincts the most perfect creature of God, Muḥammad ibn ʻAbd Allāh—may God's blessings and peace be upon him—was born, in whose vicinity God revealed the first verses of the Noble Qur'ān. It was here that the earliest Islamic community was born and where the Prophet experienced his greatest trials and triumphs. Its streets were traversed by the great companions such as Abū Bakr, ʿUmar and ʿUthmān, while ʿAlī was born in the *Kaʿbah* at the heart of the city. The house of the Prophet where Fāṭimah was born stood in Mecca until only recently. Are there other cities which have produced so many figures who transformed world history? And then there are all those great Islamic scholars, scientists, theologians, philosophers and Sufi saints who have visited Mecca over the ages. Their spirit seems to hover over the city as does the spirit of all the great men of action who came as humble pilgrims to its doors.

Mecca is the city of God reflecting His absoluteness. To be there is to be at the center. To stand before the *Kaʿbah* is to realize the journey's end. There is nowhere else to go here on earth for here is the goal of all terrestrial wayfaring. From Mindanao to Mauritania Muslims keep the love of Mecca, this mother of cities, in their heart and yearn to come to its welcoming embrace, to stand before God's House in a city which was honored to be the birthplace and site of most of the life of God's friend, *ḥabīb Allāh*, the Prophet whose supreme triumph in life was to return to Mecca toward the end of his earthly journey victorious in being able to re-establish the religion of the One, *al-tawḥīd*, in a land which had long ago been witness to the cry of the father of monotheism, Abraham, to the One God. Mecca was never to forget the religion of Divine Unity again and remains to this day and in fact will remain to the end of time the spiritual center of the religion of Islam whose very *raison d'être* is to bear witness to the One who ultimately is the sole Reality that abides for "all things perish save the Face of God."

Seyyed Hossein Nasr

A number of pilgrims gain the special opportunity of standing before the door of the *Kaʿbah* in prayer. Every year during the *ḥajj* season this golden door is opened by the governor of Mecca and washed with perfume. To enter the *Kaʿbah* is a very rare honor and privilege bestowed upon a few dignitaries each year.

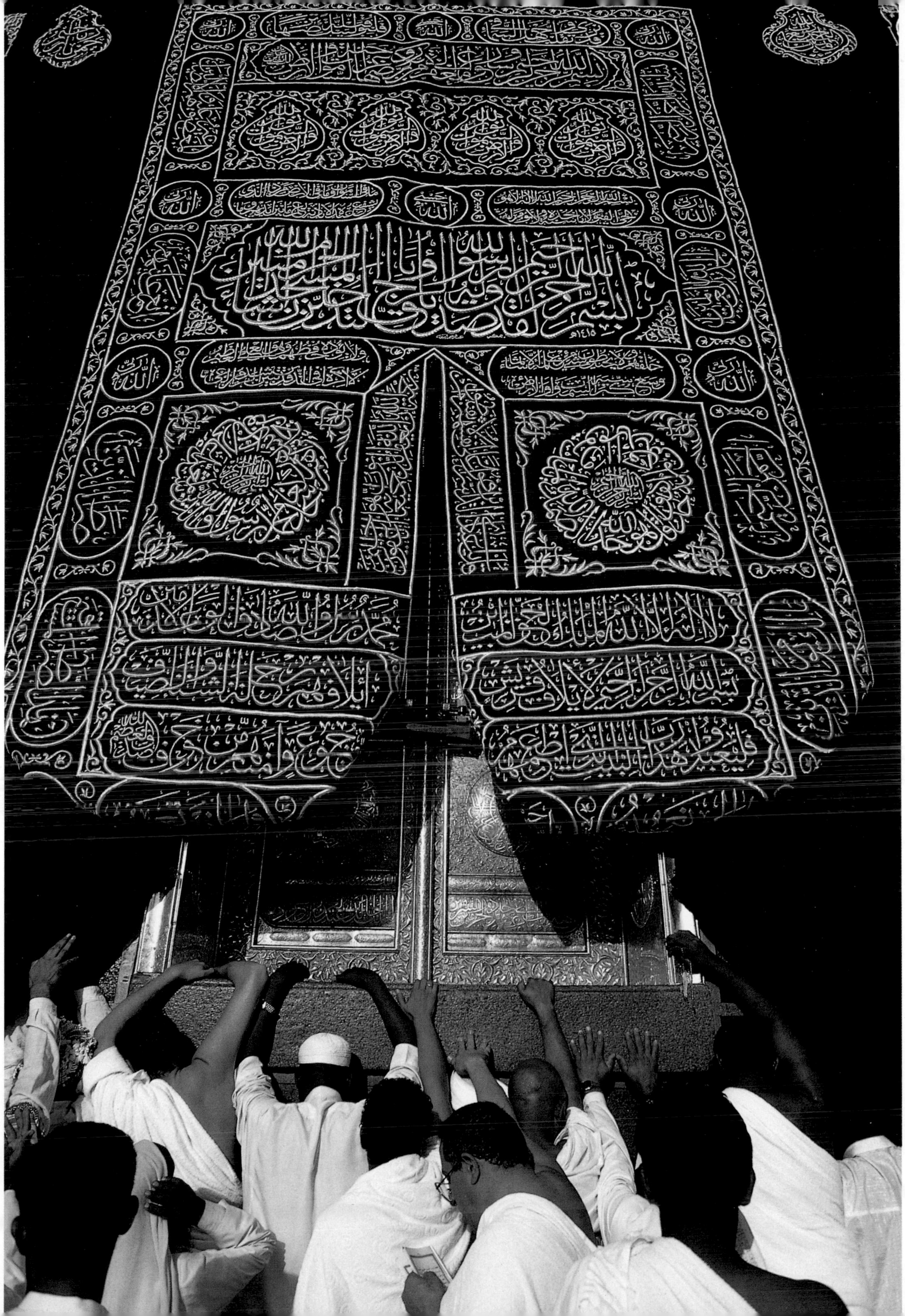

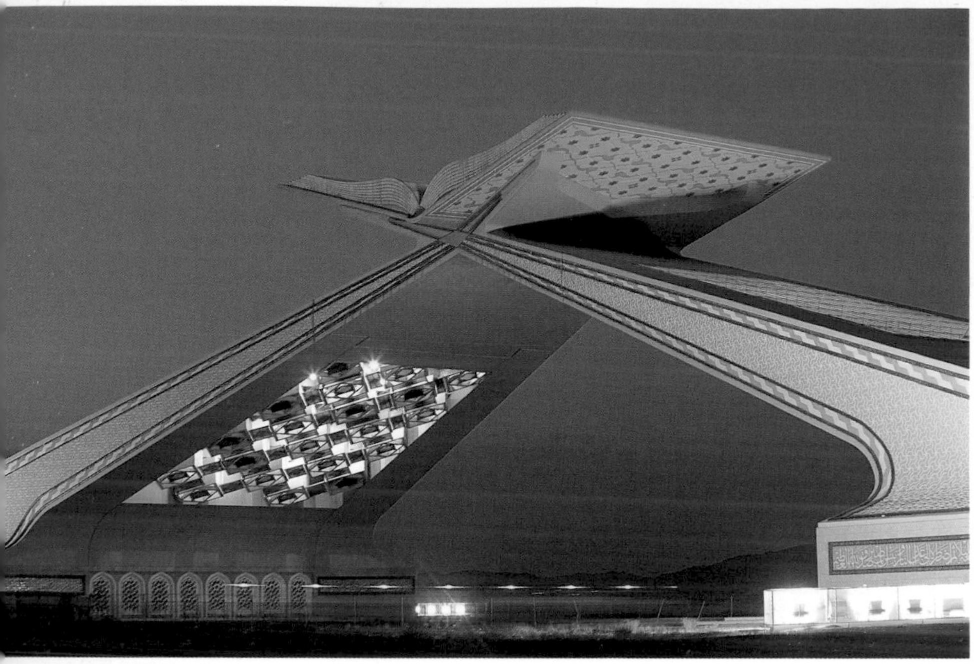

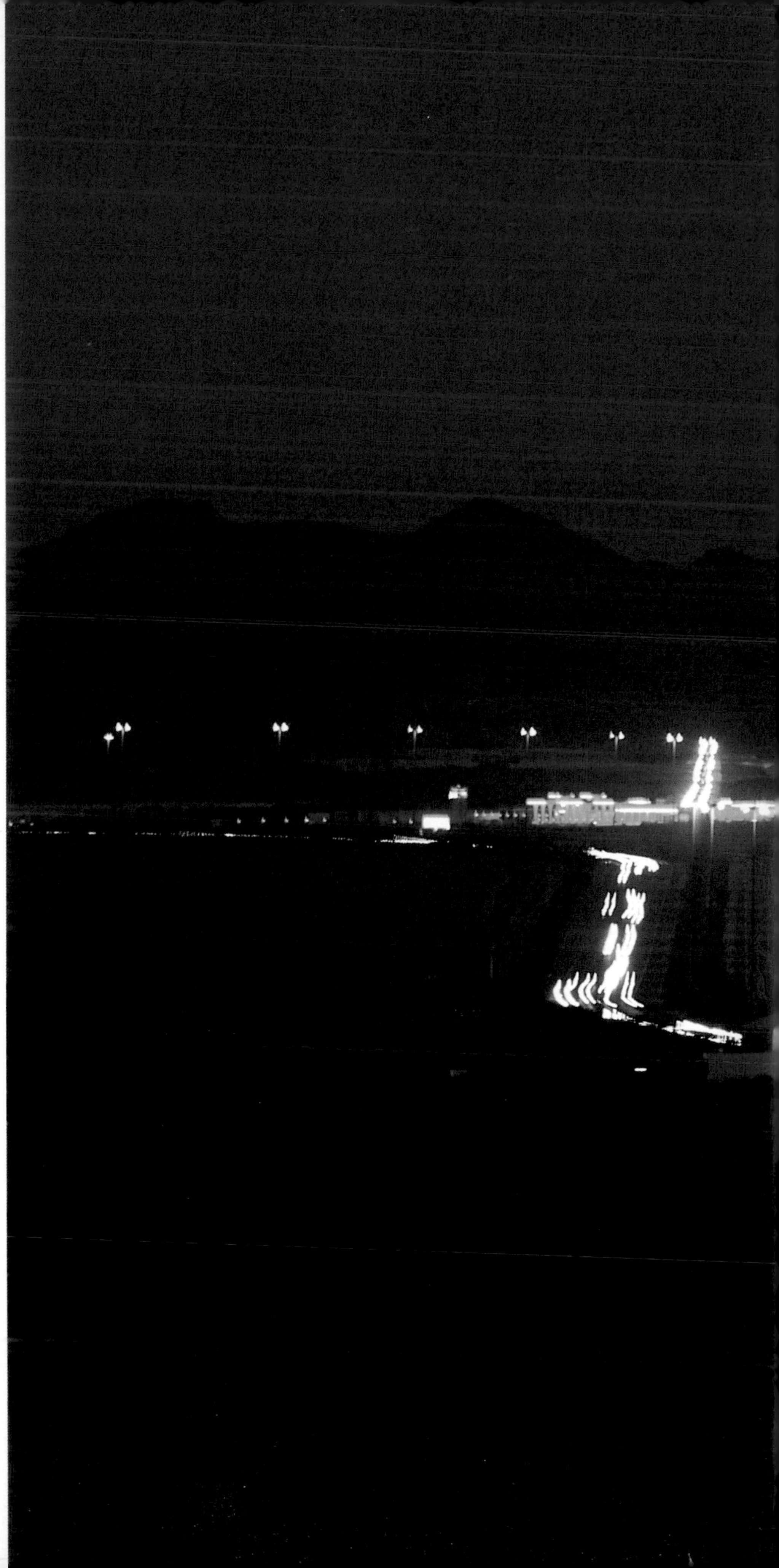

This new gateway designed as a Qur'ān holder stands over the main highway connecting Jeddah to Mecca. There is a check-point on the Jeddah side of this gate marking the boundaries of the sacred precinct beyond which non-Muslims are not permitted to travel.

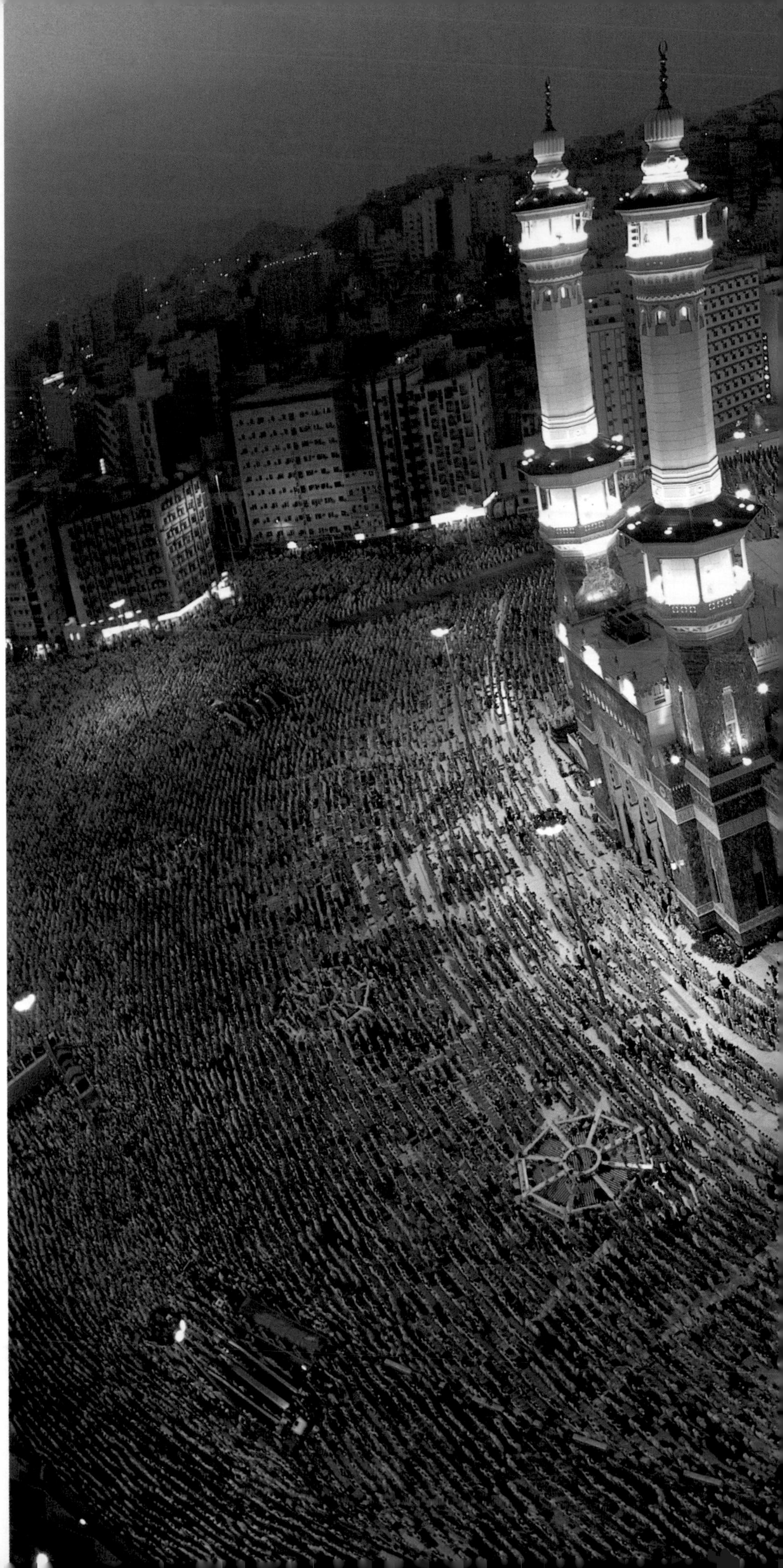

*(also following pages)*
The prayer of sunset (*maghrib*) performed at the Grand Mosque in Mecca shortly before the annual *ḥajj* when some two million pilgrims gather in that city. The steep and craggy rock mountain beyond the *Kaʿbah* is Mount Hirāʾ. At top of it is located the cave in which the Blessed Prophet received the first Qurʾānic revelation.

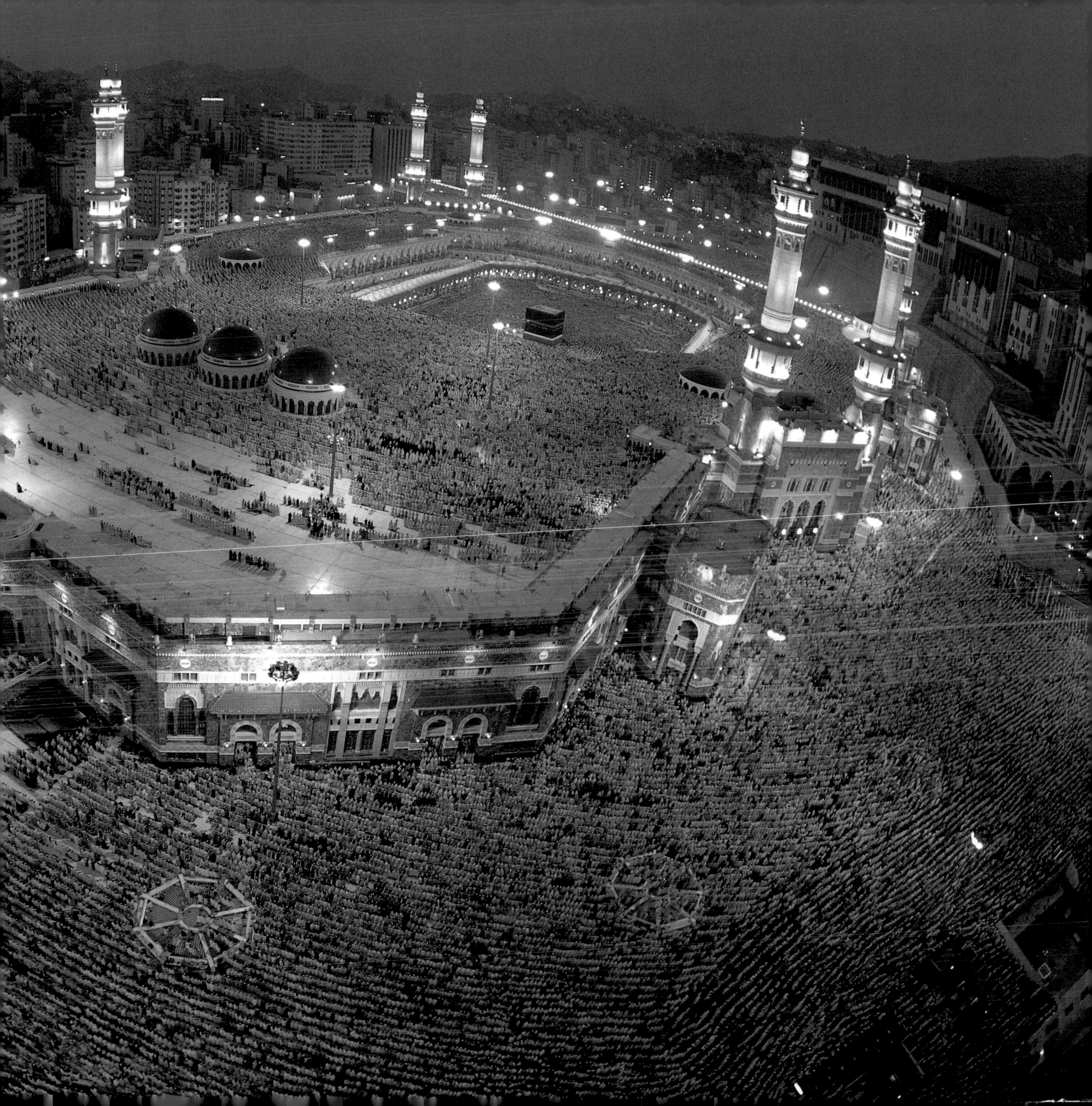

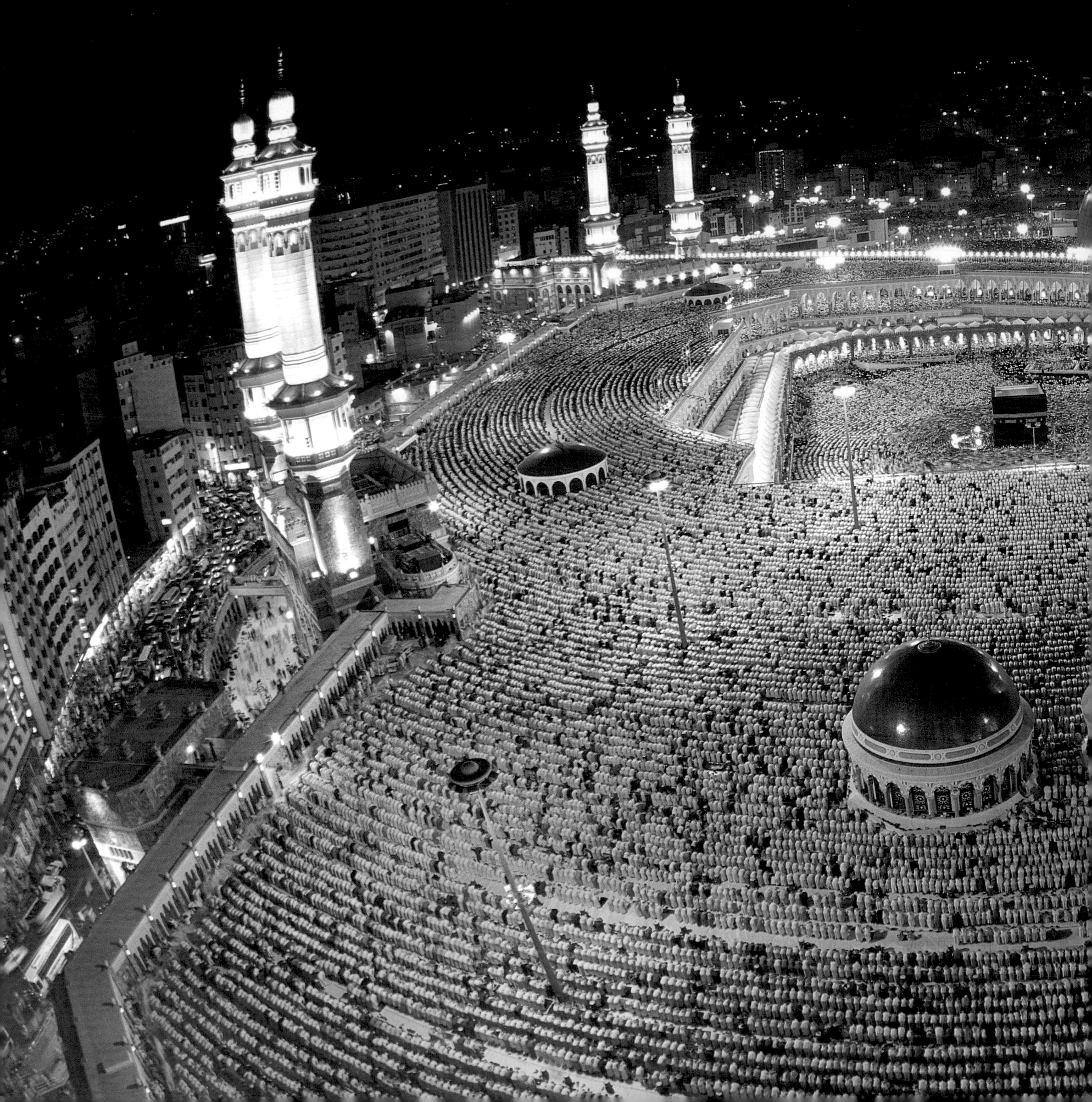

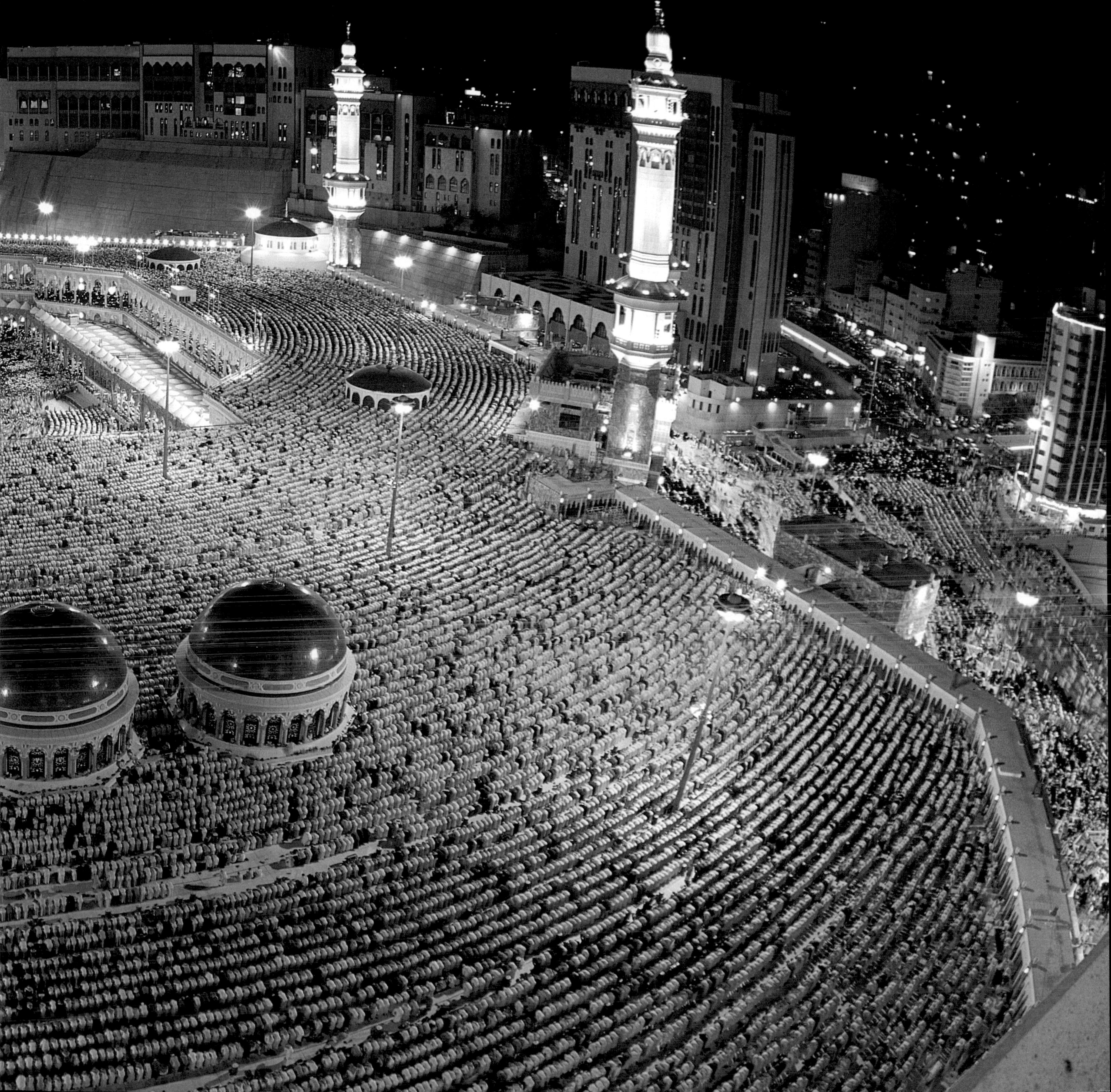

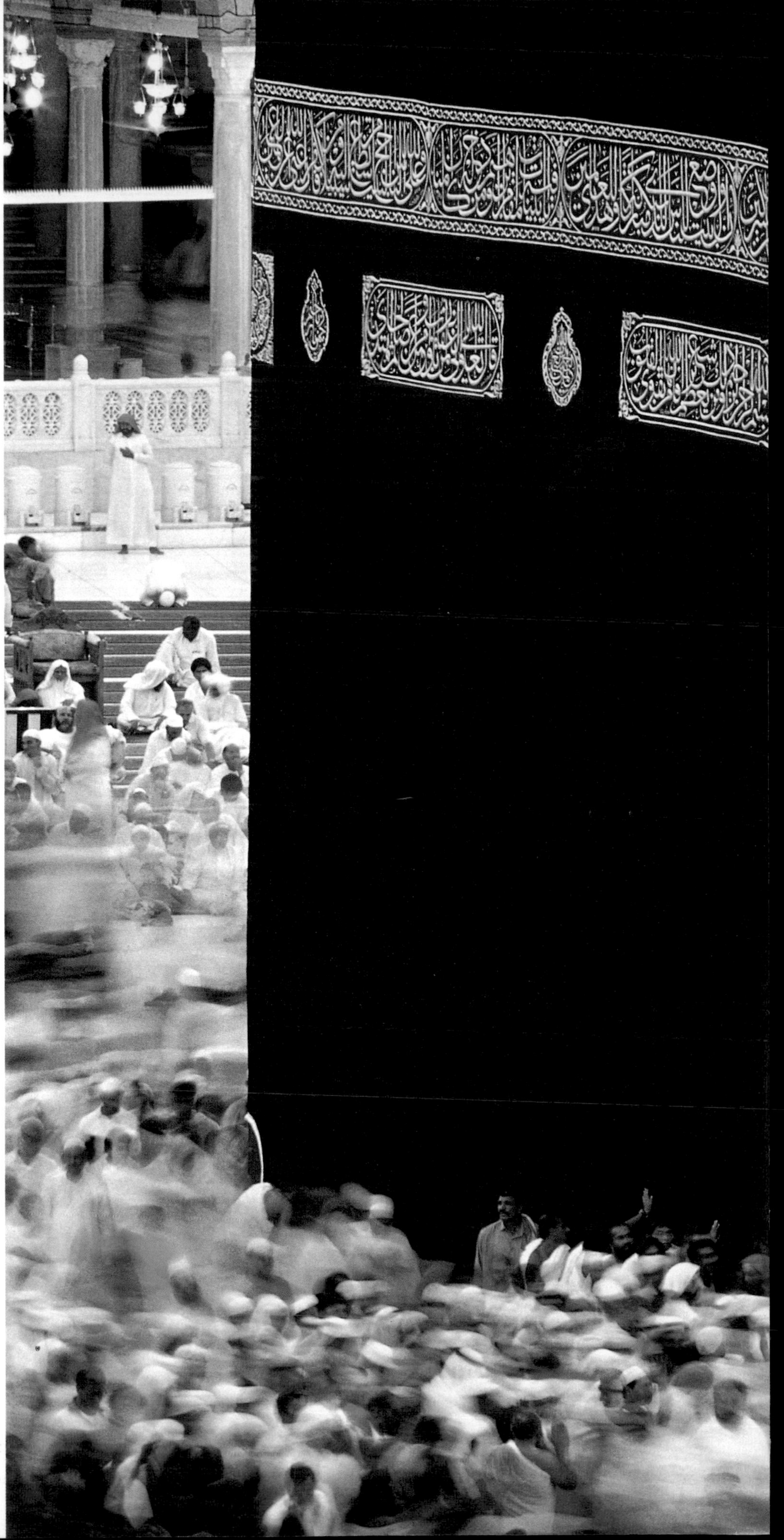

The building of the *Ka'bah* covered by a black cloth adorned by golden verses from the Noble Qur'ān and called the *Kiswah*.

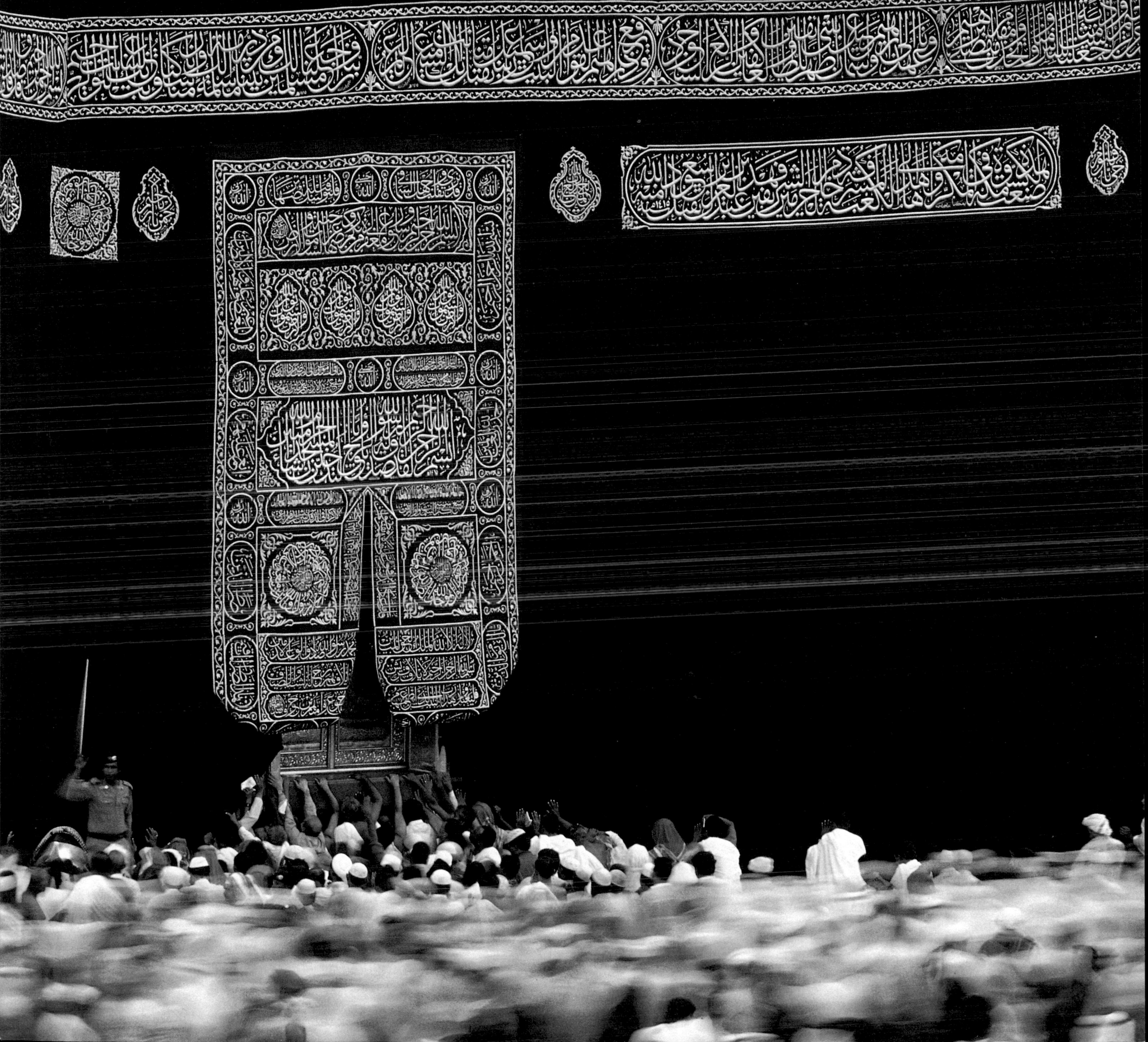

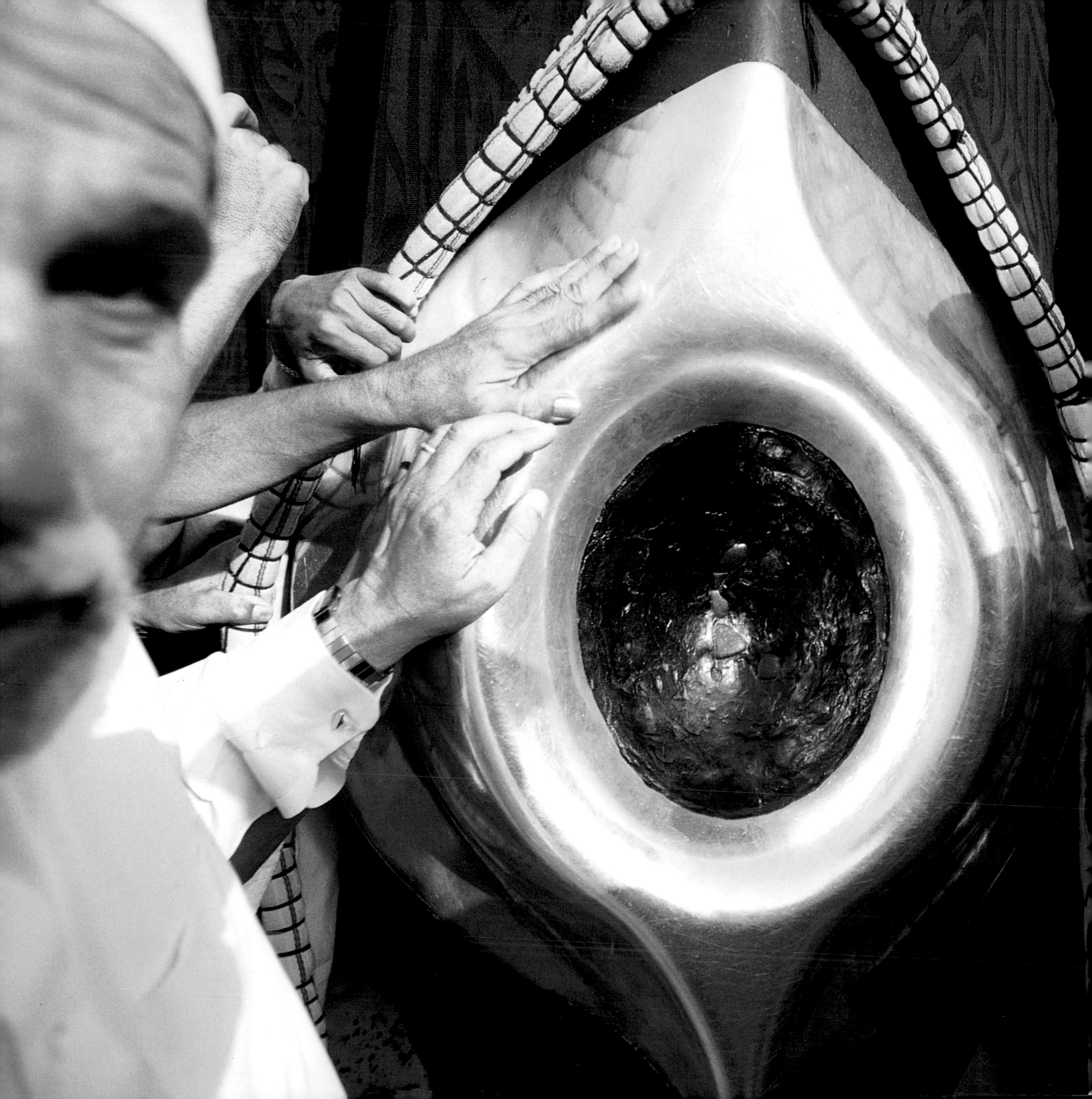

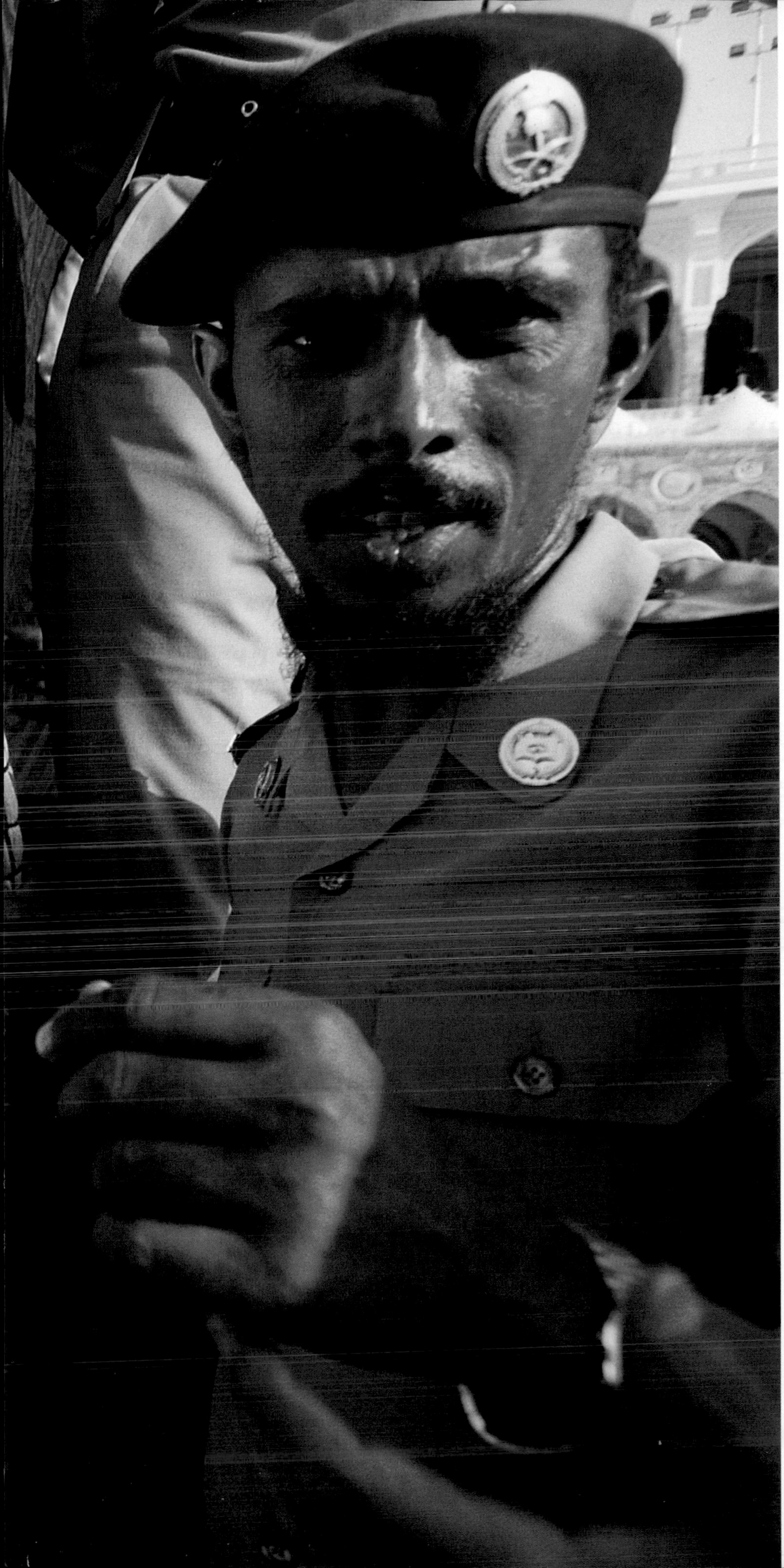

The Black Stone (*hajar al-aswad*) considered by Muslims to have descended from Heaven as the symbol of the covenant made between God and Adam and his progeny.

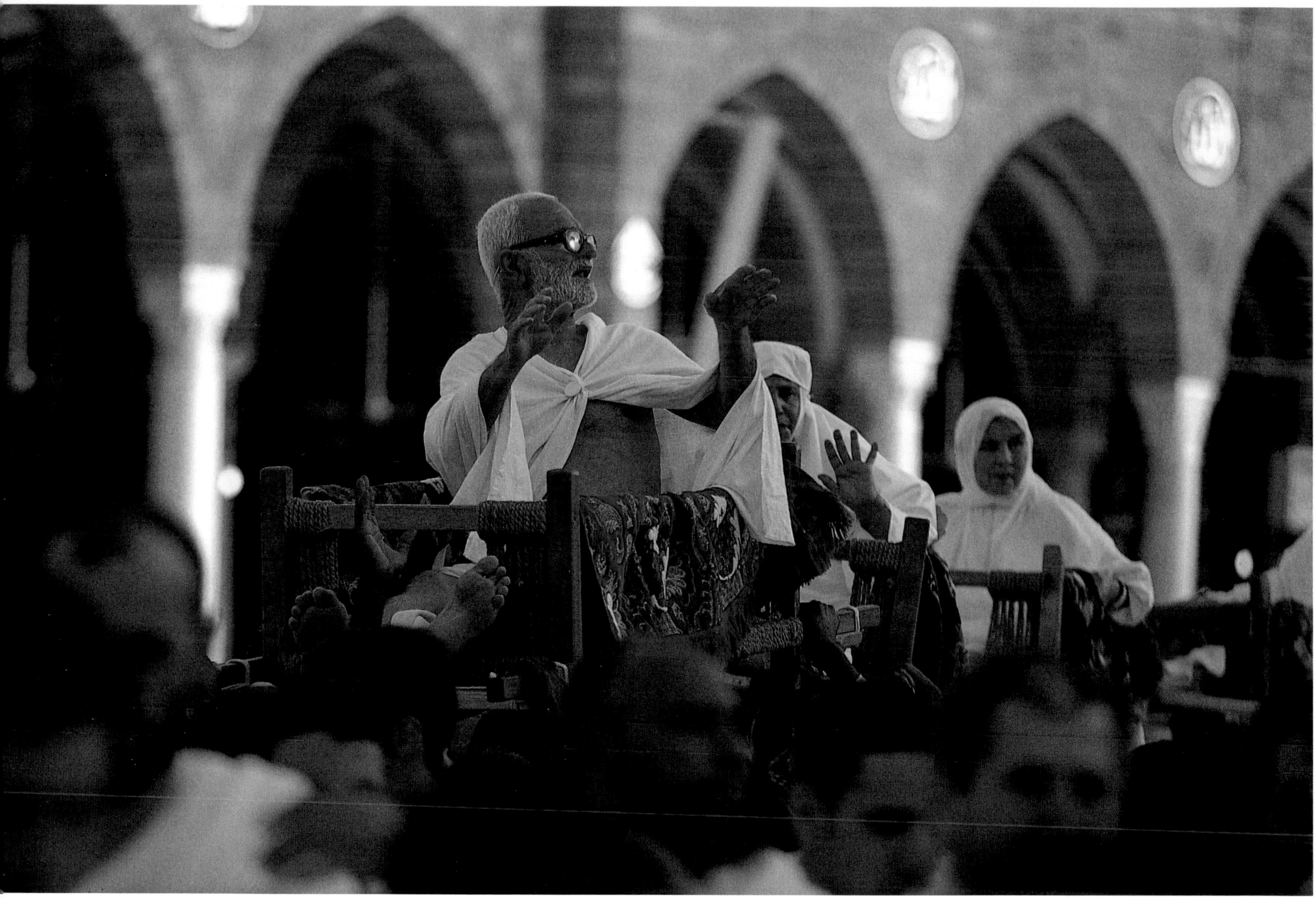

Some elderly people who have trouble walking, make the *Ṭawāf* on a palanquin carried by two men. When they come to the corner of the Black Stone, they hold up their hands in order to receive the *barakah* from the stone.

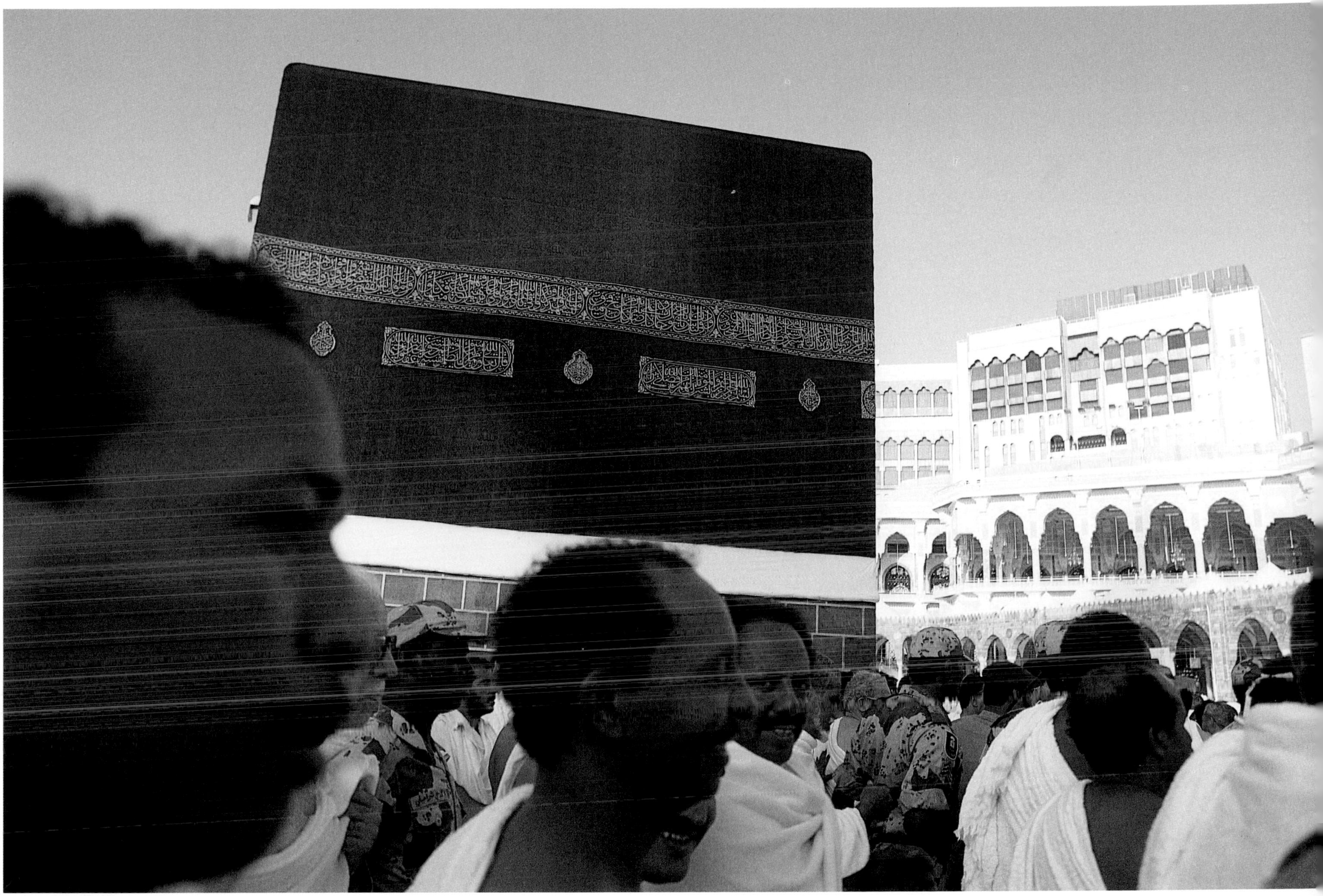

Pilgrims making *Ṭawāf*. The black cloth covering the *Kaᶜbah* is called *Kiswah*. The pilgrims chant the *talbiyah* during the *Ṭawāf*.

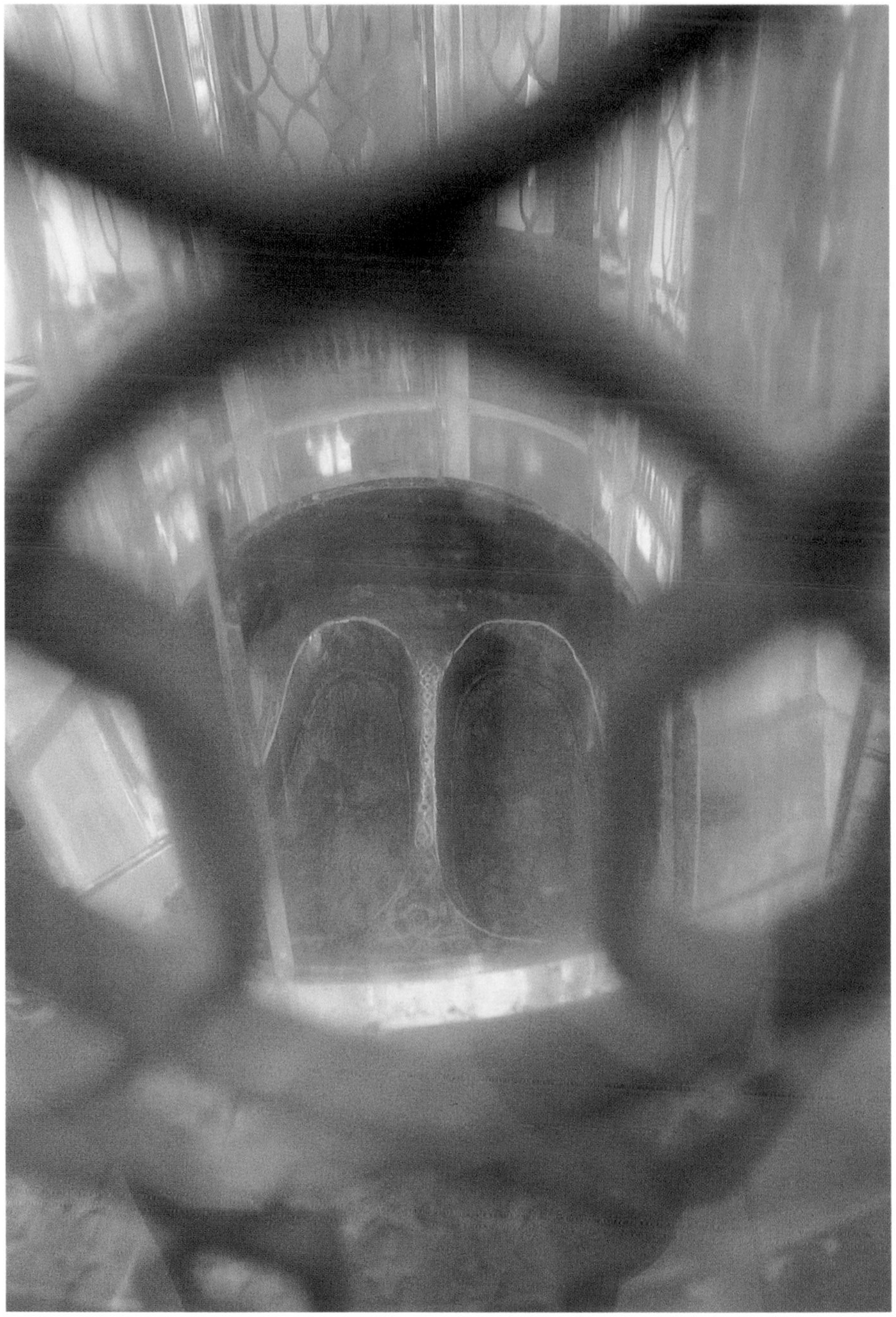

Footprints at the place where Abraham (Ibrāhīm) stood called Maqam Ibrāhīm. The footprints are protected in a glass case to east side of the *Kaʿbah*.

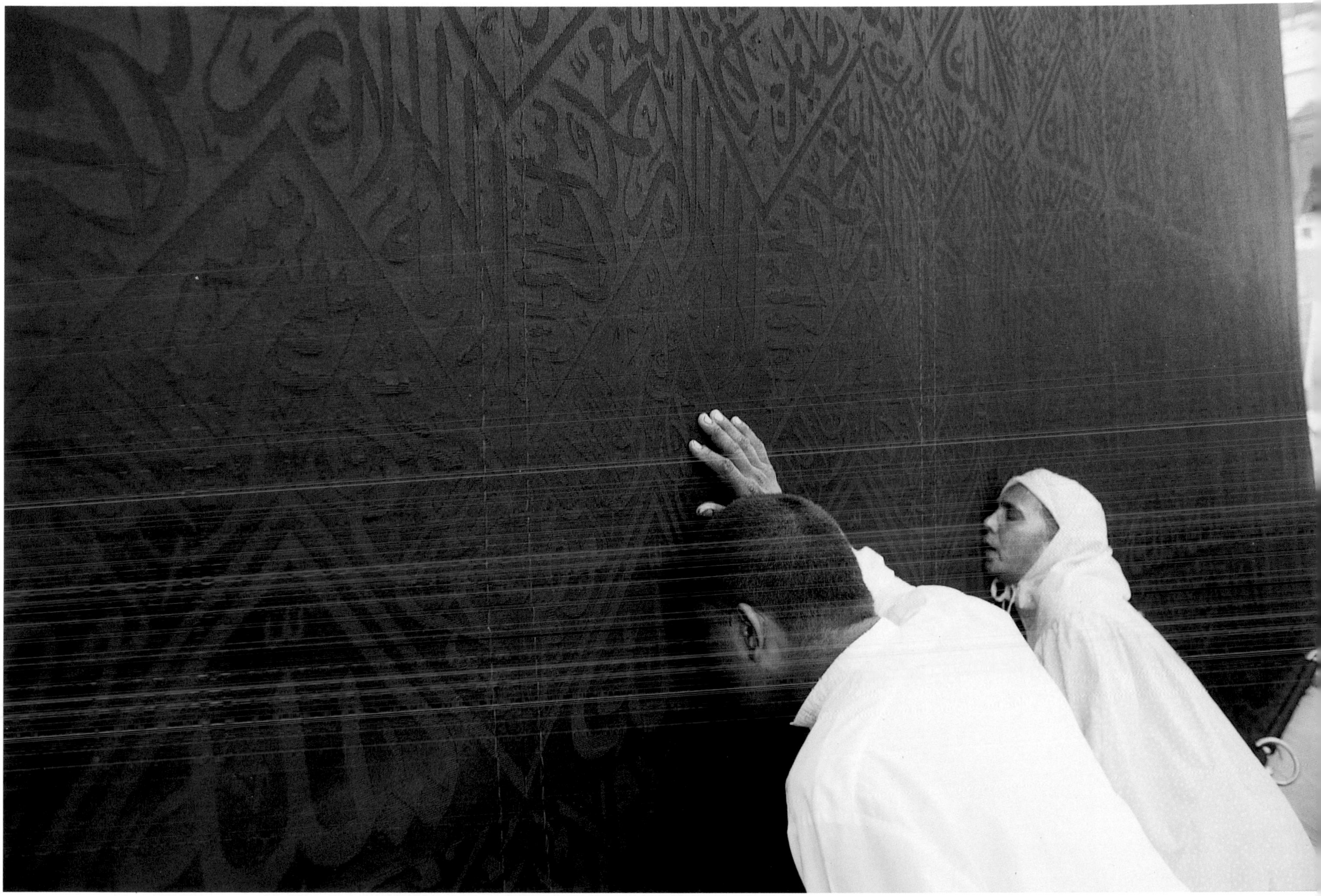

A Pakistani pilgrim couple holding on to the *Kiswah* while praying. The *Kiswah* is made of black silk cloth and is changed for a new one once every year on the ninth day of the month of pilgrimage when all the pilgrims gather outside leaving the *Ka<sup>c</sup>bah* empty.

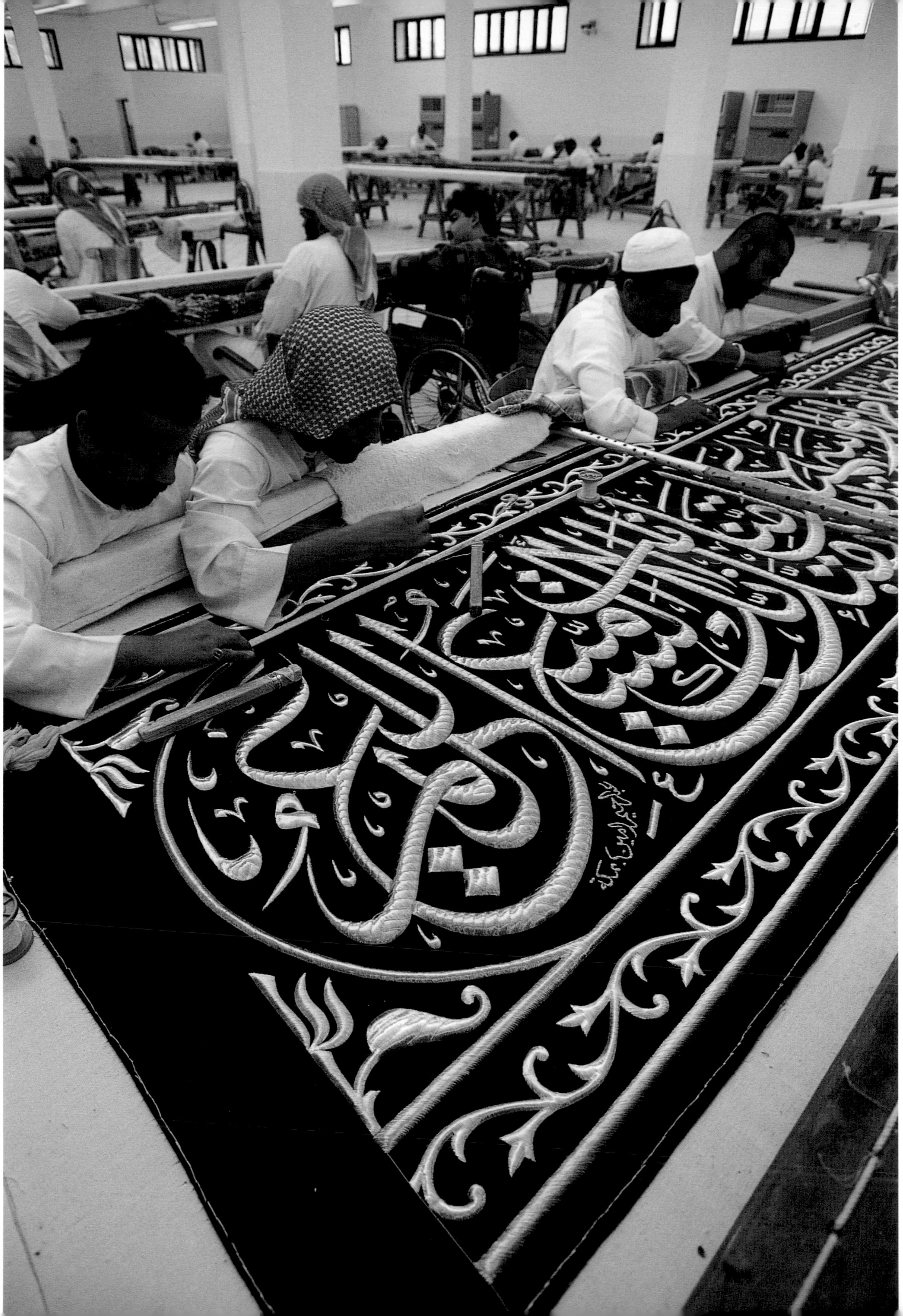

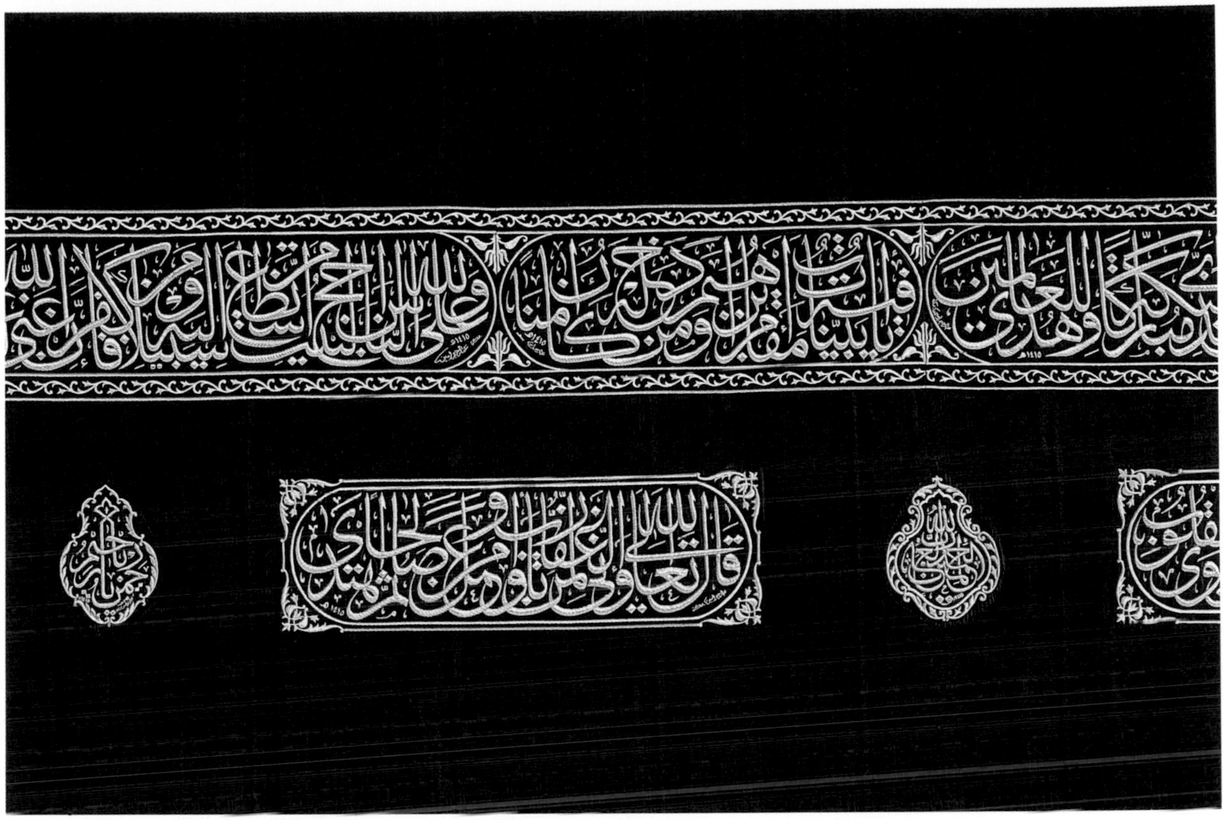

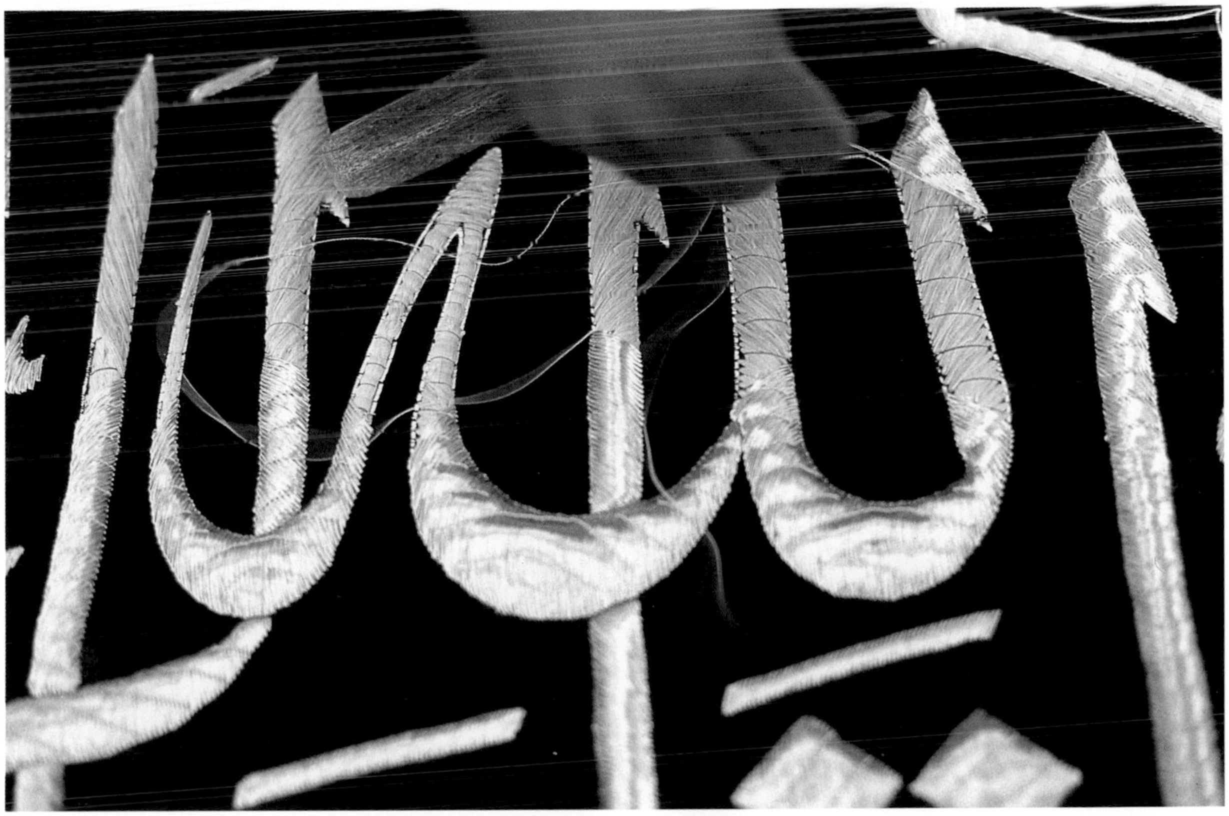

*(Opposite)*
Embroidering the *Kiswah* by hand using gold threads at a factory in Mecca. Until recently the *Kiswah* was made in Egypt and presented to the *Kaʿbah* but it is made in Saudi Arabia today. Each year the old *Kiswah* is cut into small pieces and donated as precious gifts to certain individuals and organizations.

*(Top)*
A band decorating the south side of the structure of the *Kaʿbah*. It was a tradition among Semitic people even before the advent of Islam to dress a sacred temple with cloth, a practice followed in Islam.

*(Bottom)*
The Divine Name "Allāh," the Supreme Name of God in Islam, adorns the center of this part of the band of the *Kiswah*.

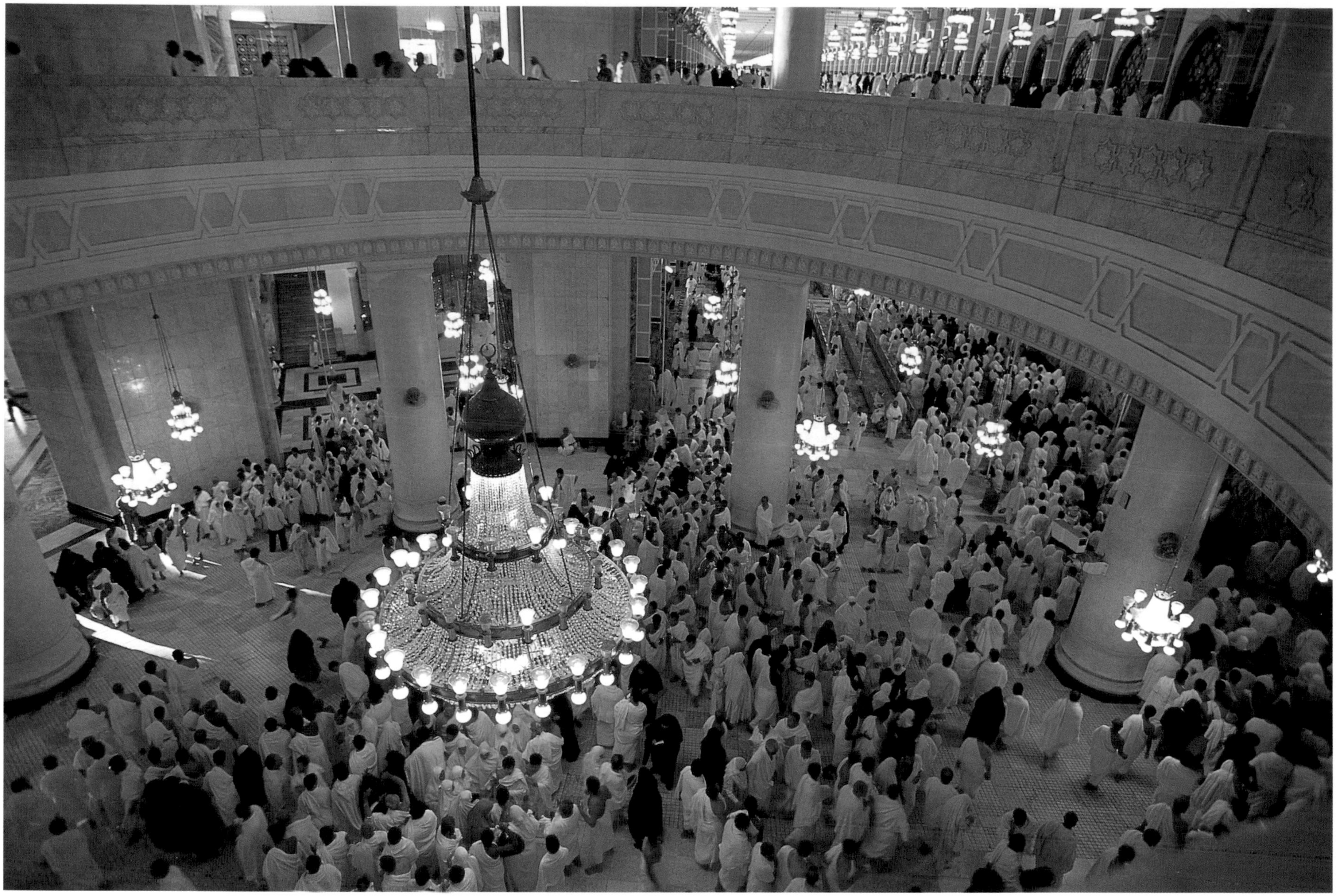

*(Above)*
Ṣafā and Marwah are two stations in the vicinity of the *Ka*ʿ*bah* between which pilgrims must walk quickly almost at the pace of a run, or what is called *sa*ʿ*y*. This is part of the ritual of the *ḥajj* seen here photographed from the side of Ṣafā.

*(Opposite)*
Upon completion of the ritual of *sa*ʿ*y* pilgrims pray toward the *Ka*ʿ*bah* from the hill of Ṣafā. The rapid walk of *sa*ʿ*y* recapitulates symbolically the running to and fro of Hagar (Hājar), the wife of the Prophet Abraham (Ibrāhīm), in search of water for her son Ishmael (Ismāʿīl). Her search ended when the spring of Zamzam gushed forth miraculously.

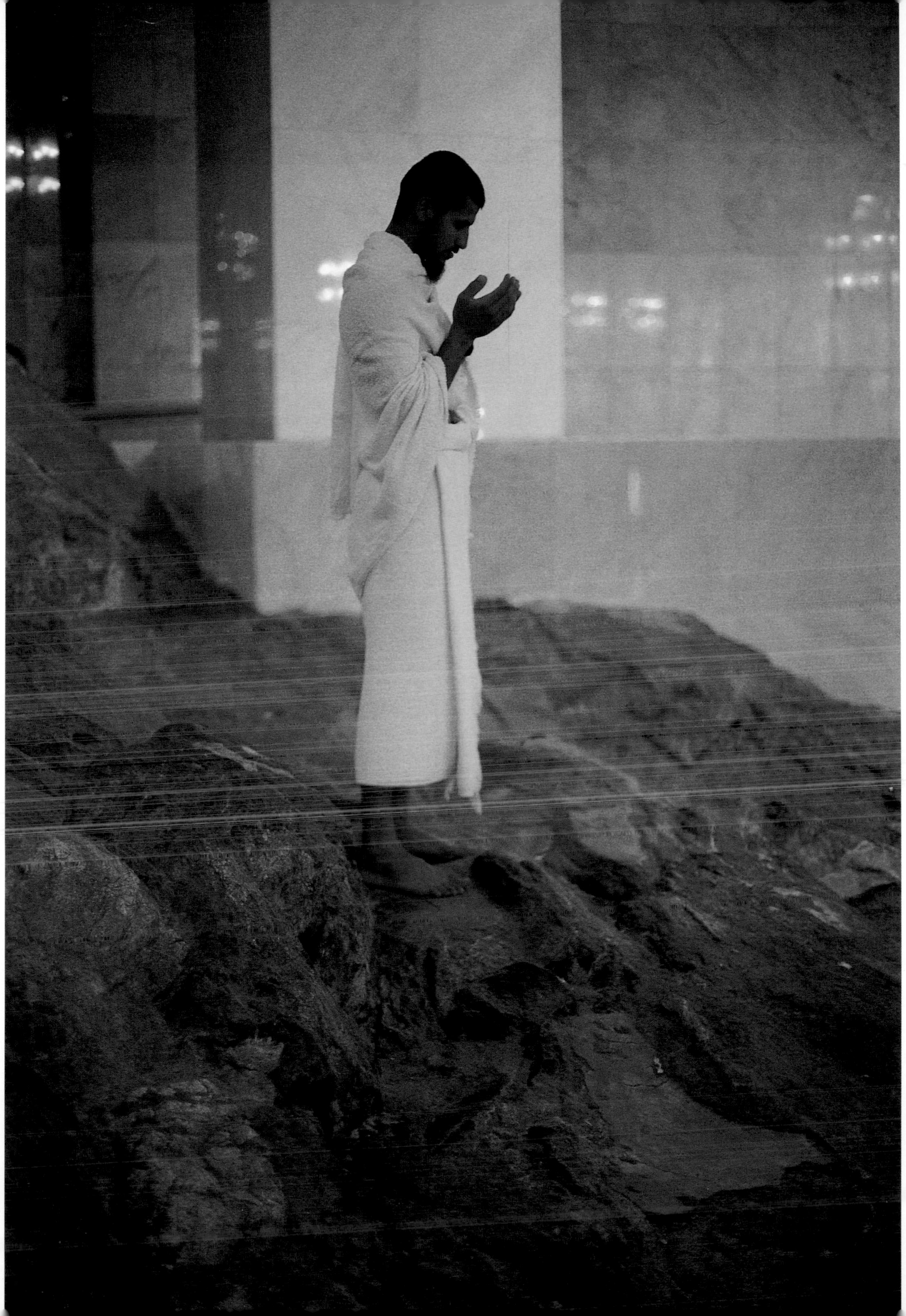

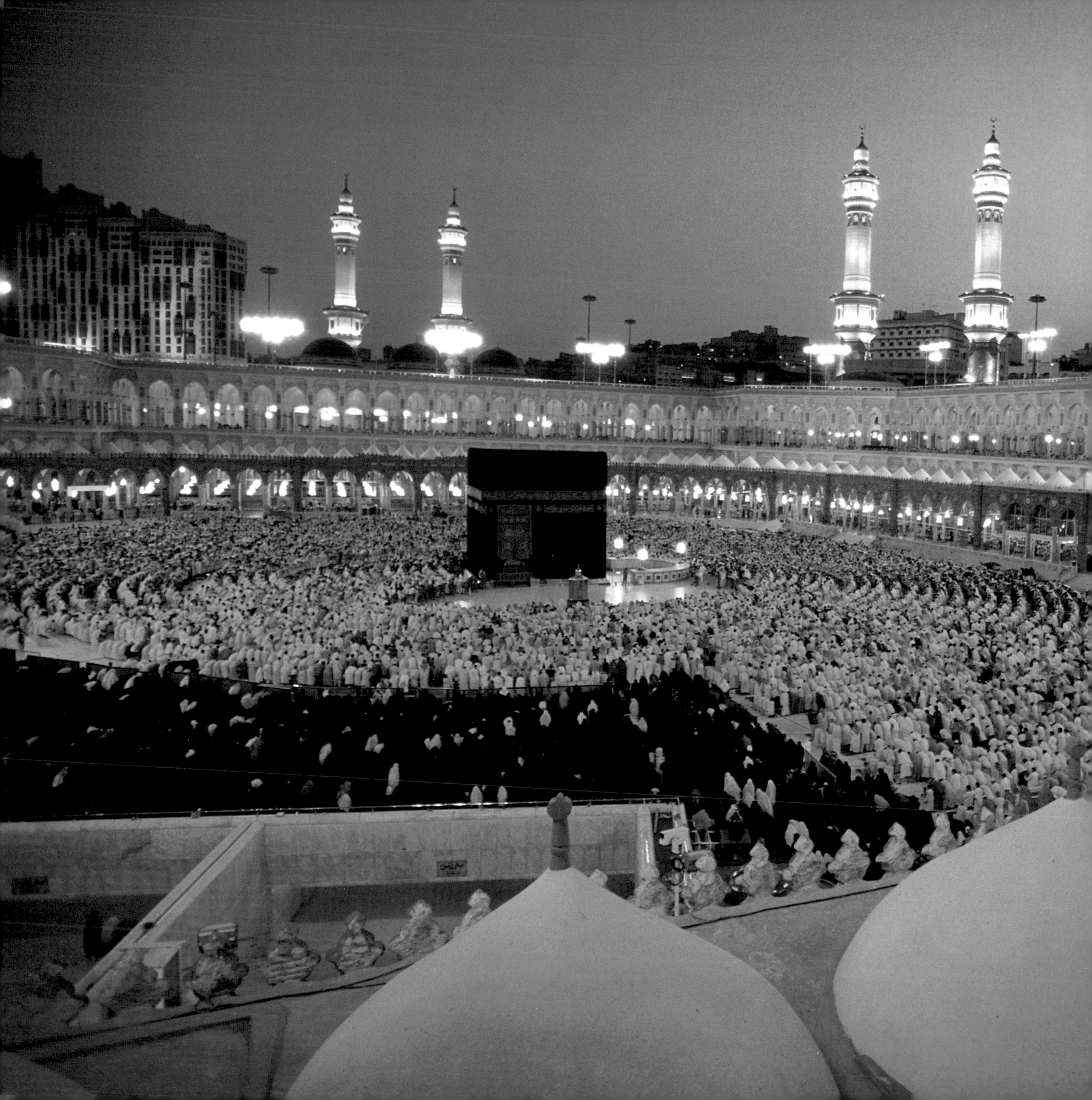

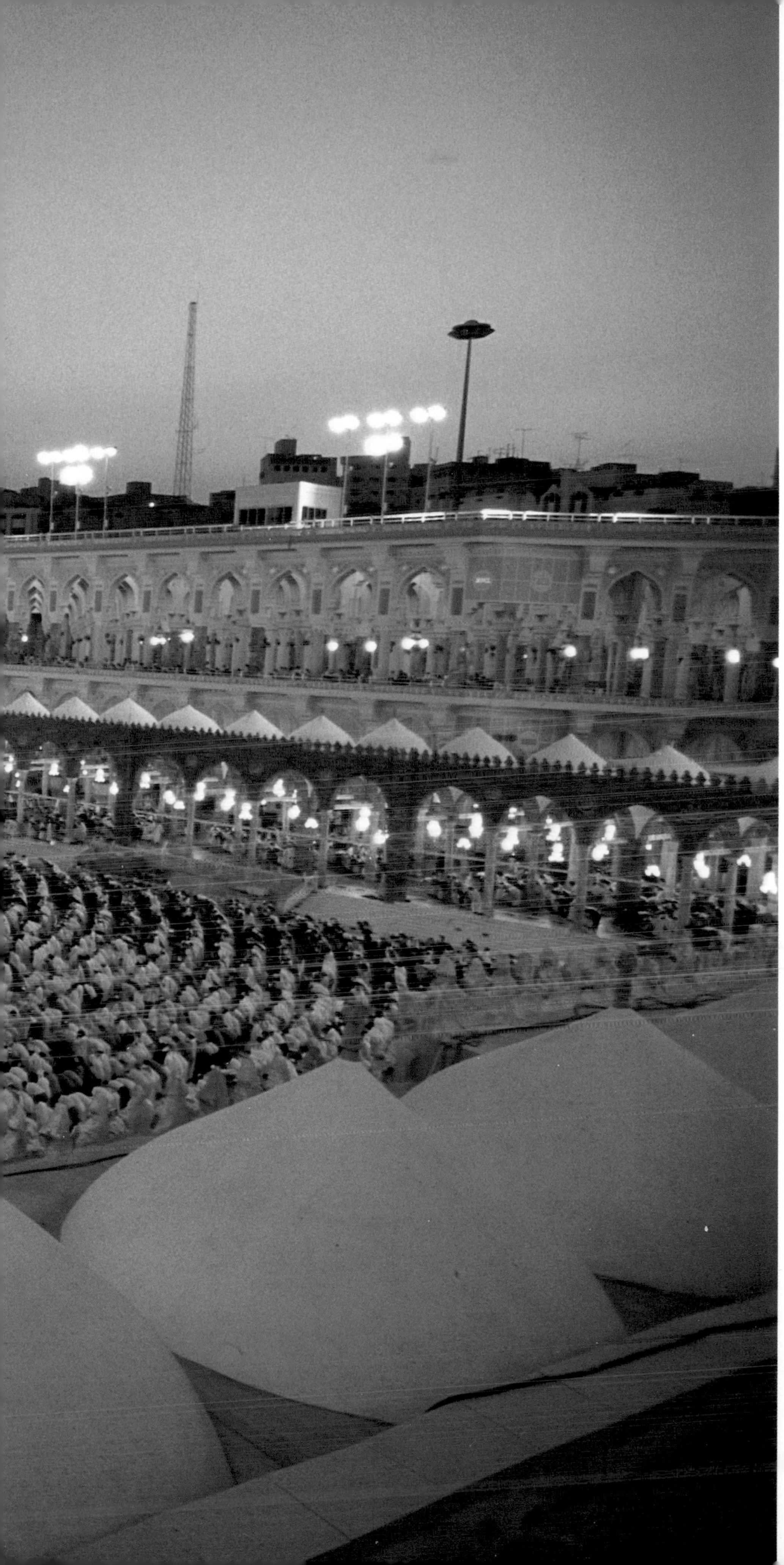

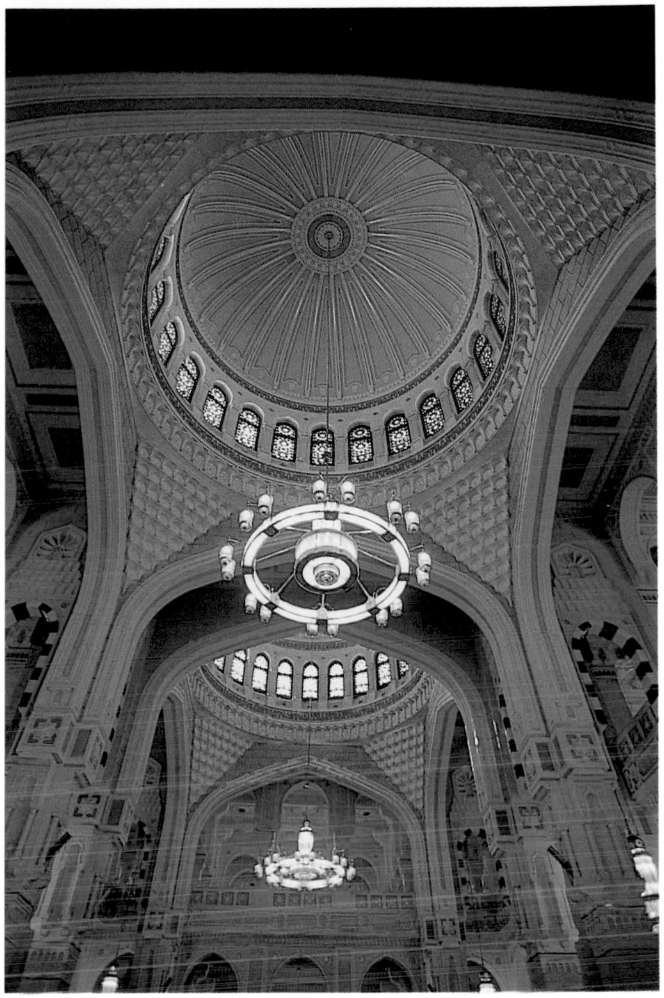

*(Above)*
The open domed roof was part of the extension of the Grand Mosque carried out under the Saudi King Fahd from 1988 to 1995.

*(Opposite)*
The *maghrib* prayers at the Grand Mosque in Mecca. Those wearing black are women. The Grand Mosque today consists of four stories including the basement and the roof with access to the spring of Zamzam being located underground.

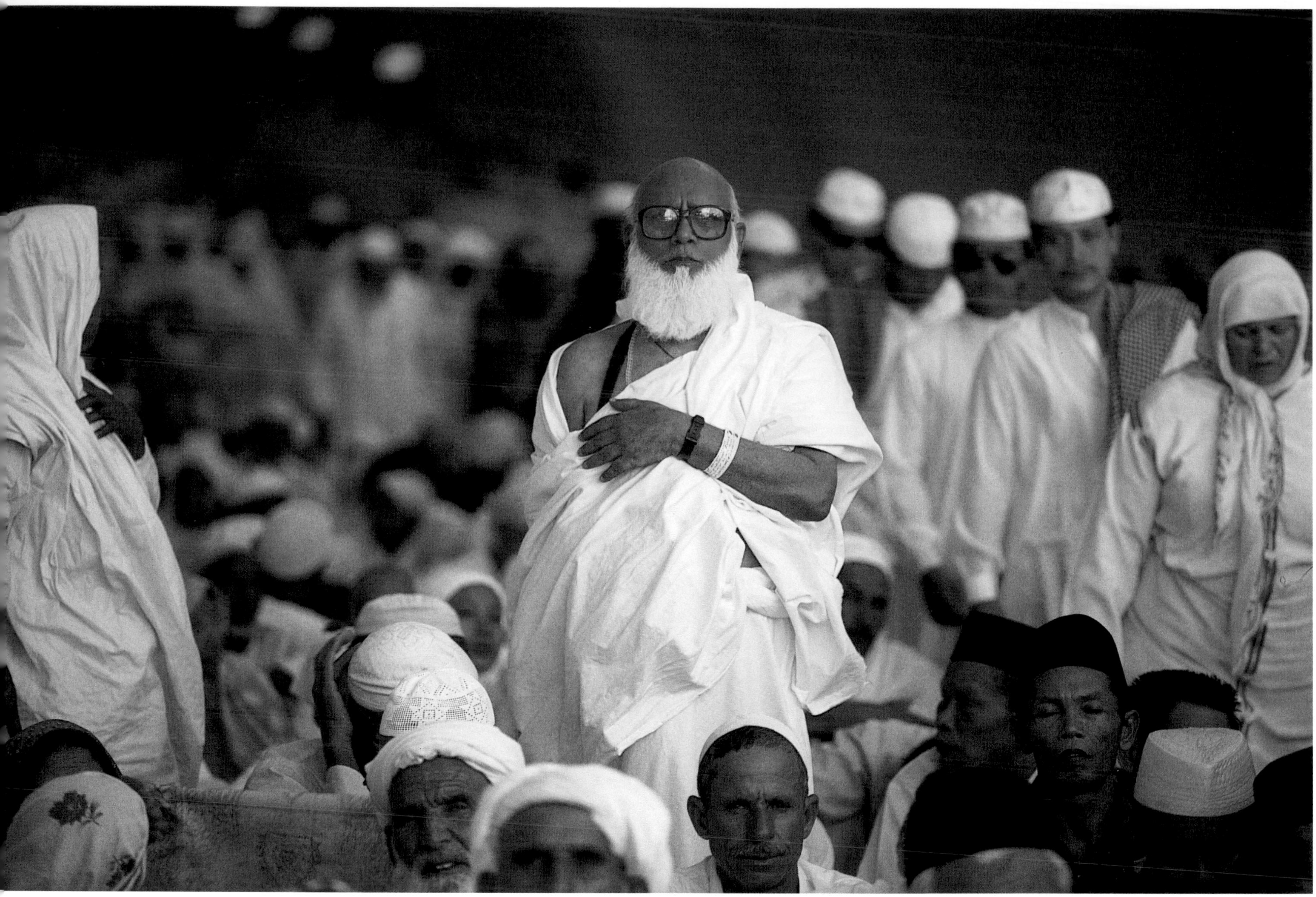

Pilgrims standing in a tunnel connected to the Grand Mosque before the performance of the Friday congregational prayers during the period nearing the annual pilgrimage.

Those who come first occupy the shade while later comers have to stand and sit during the rites in the sun where the temperature often reaches 50 °c.

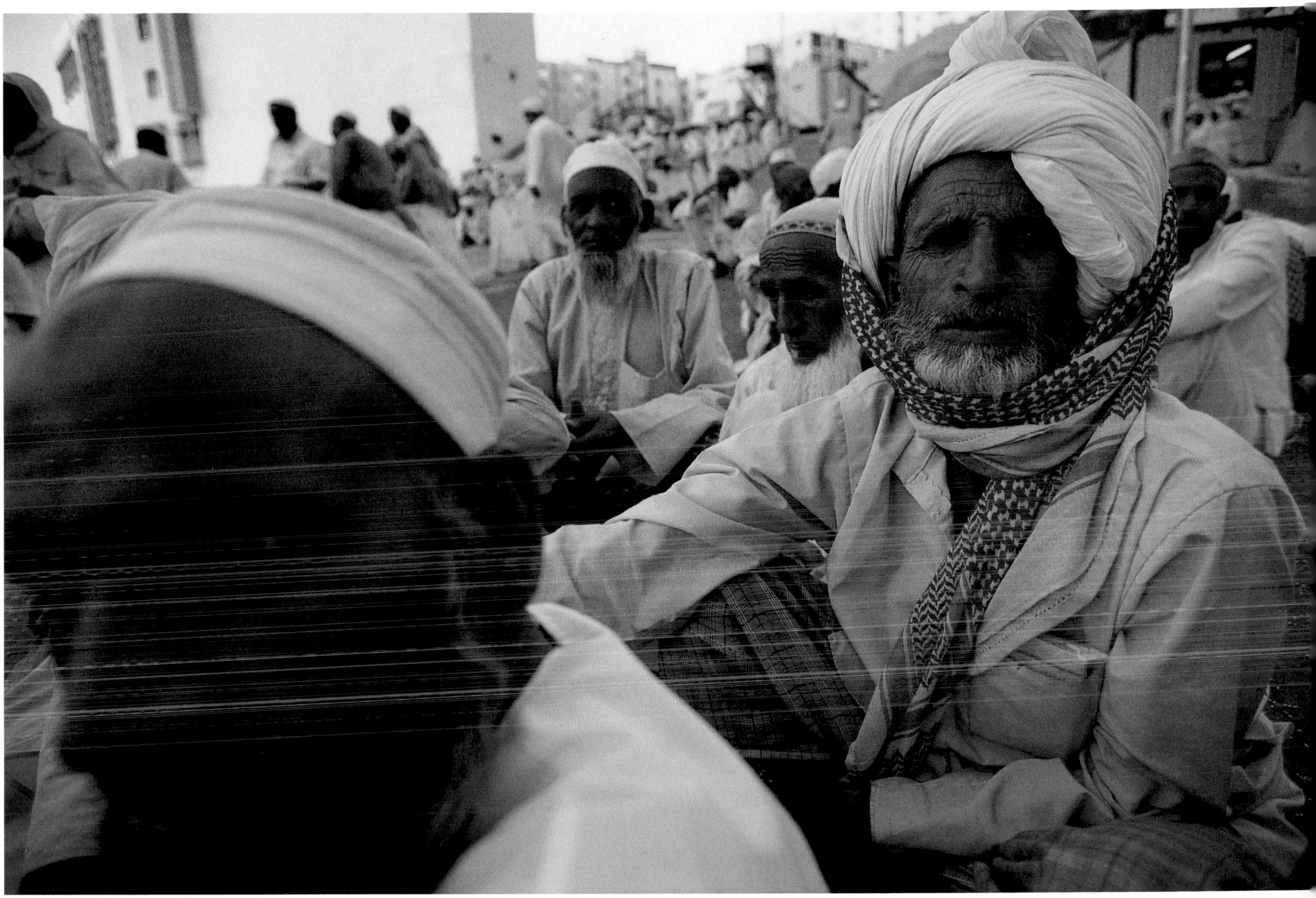

A group of Indian pilgrims waiting for the *maghrib* prayers at the Grand Mosque. The area around the *Ka*ʿ*bah* as well as around the Mosque of the Blessed Prophet in Medina are called *Ḥaram* which means sacred precinct within which all dispute and confrontation is prohibited.

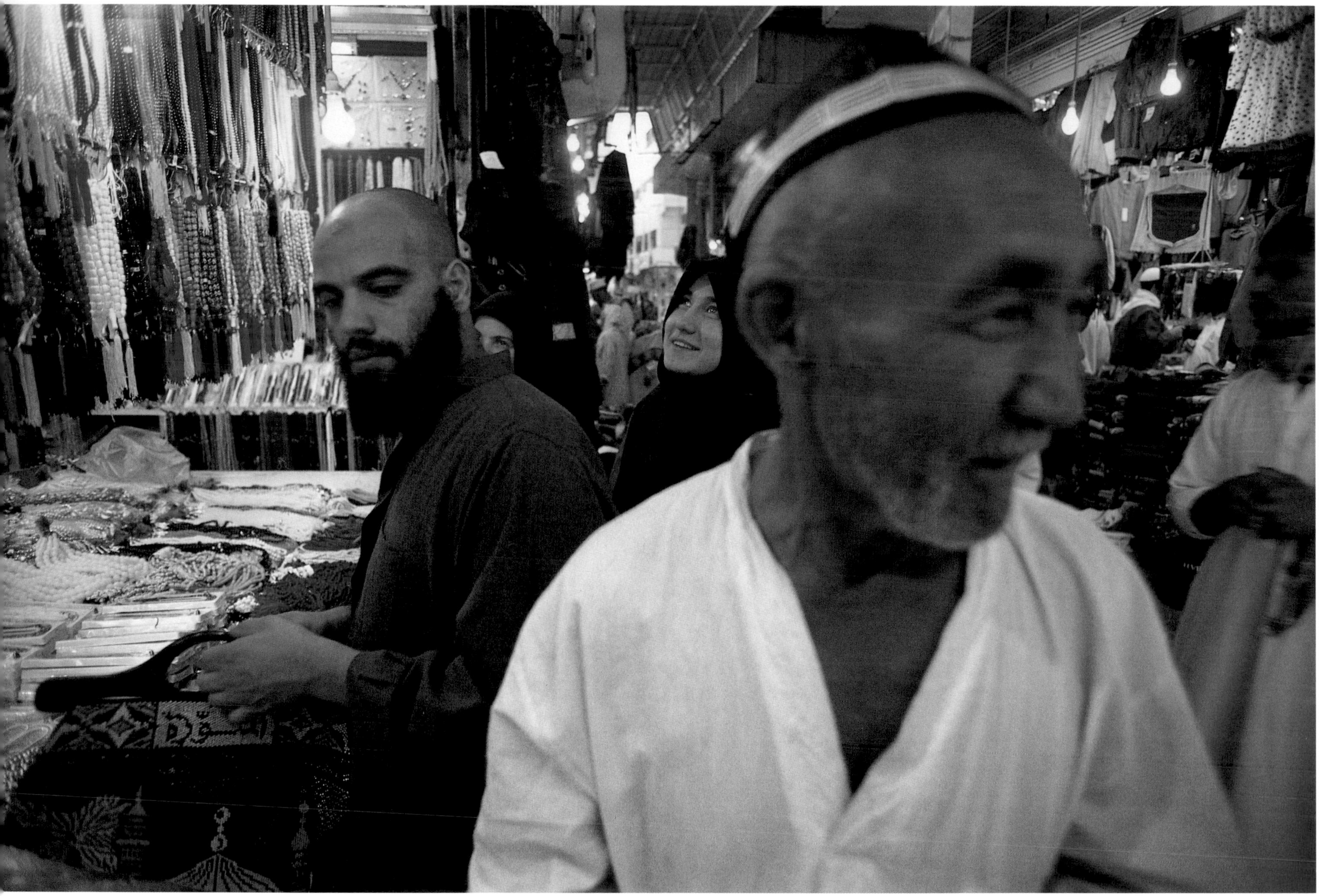

*(Above)*
The most popular merchandise sold in the shops around the *Ḥaram* is the rosary (*subḥah*). The Islamic rosary has 99 beads corresponding to the ninety-nine "Beautiful Names of God" (*al-asmā' al-ḥusnā*).

*(Opposite)*
Although most of the older buildings of Mecca and Medina were destroyed as a result of the "urban development" of the past few years, some of the older buildings remain. Here is one with the wooden lattice windows (*mashrabiyyah*) which has the effect of cooling the air inside the building.

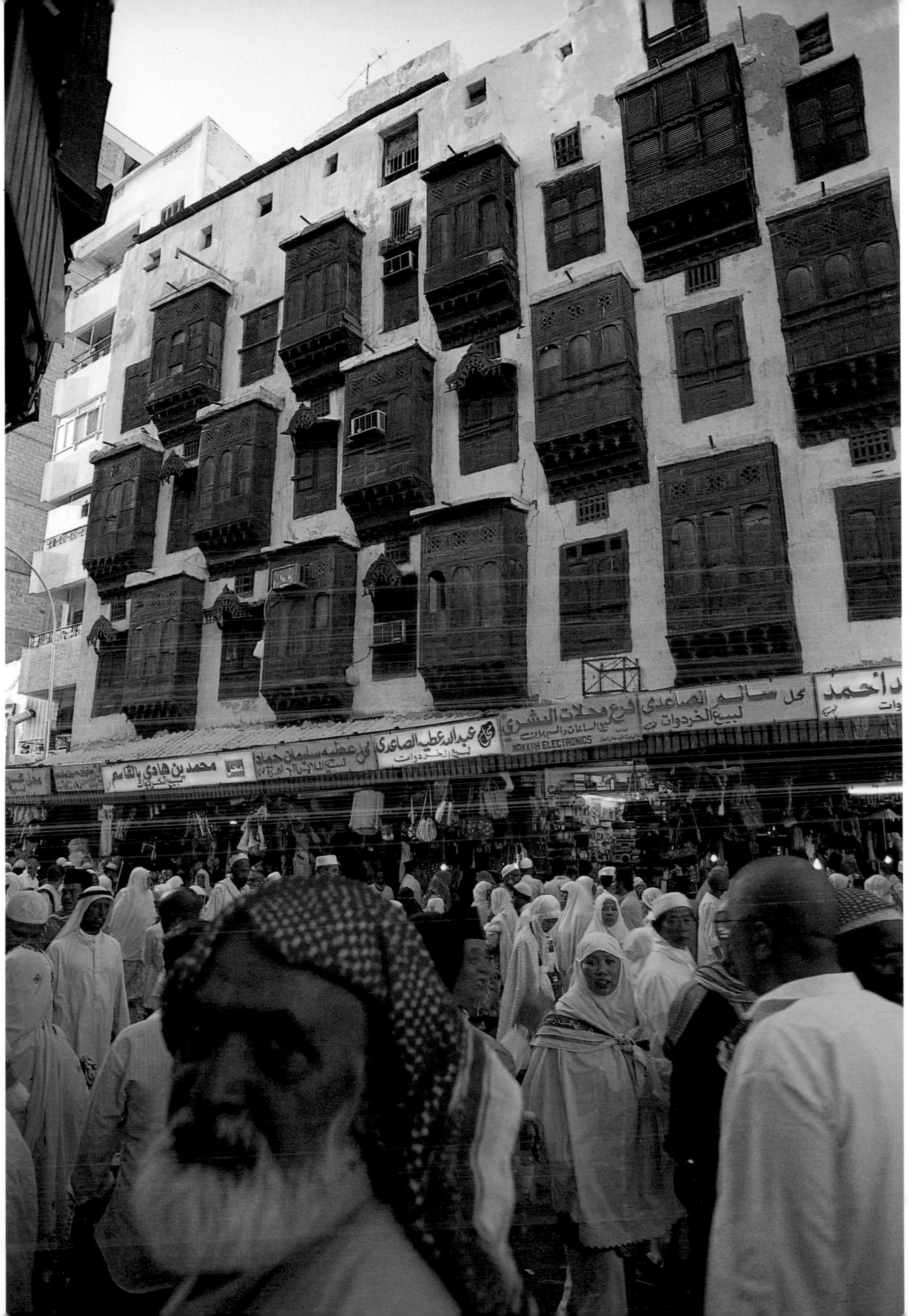

محل سالم الصاعدي
لبيع الخردوات
فرع محلات البشري
MAKKAH ELECTRONICS
عبدالله عطيه الصاعدي
لبيع الخردوات
محل عطيه سليمان حماد
محل
محمد بن هادي بالقاسم

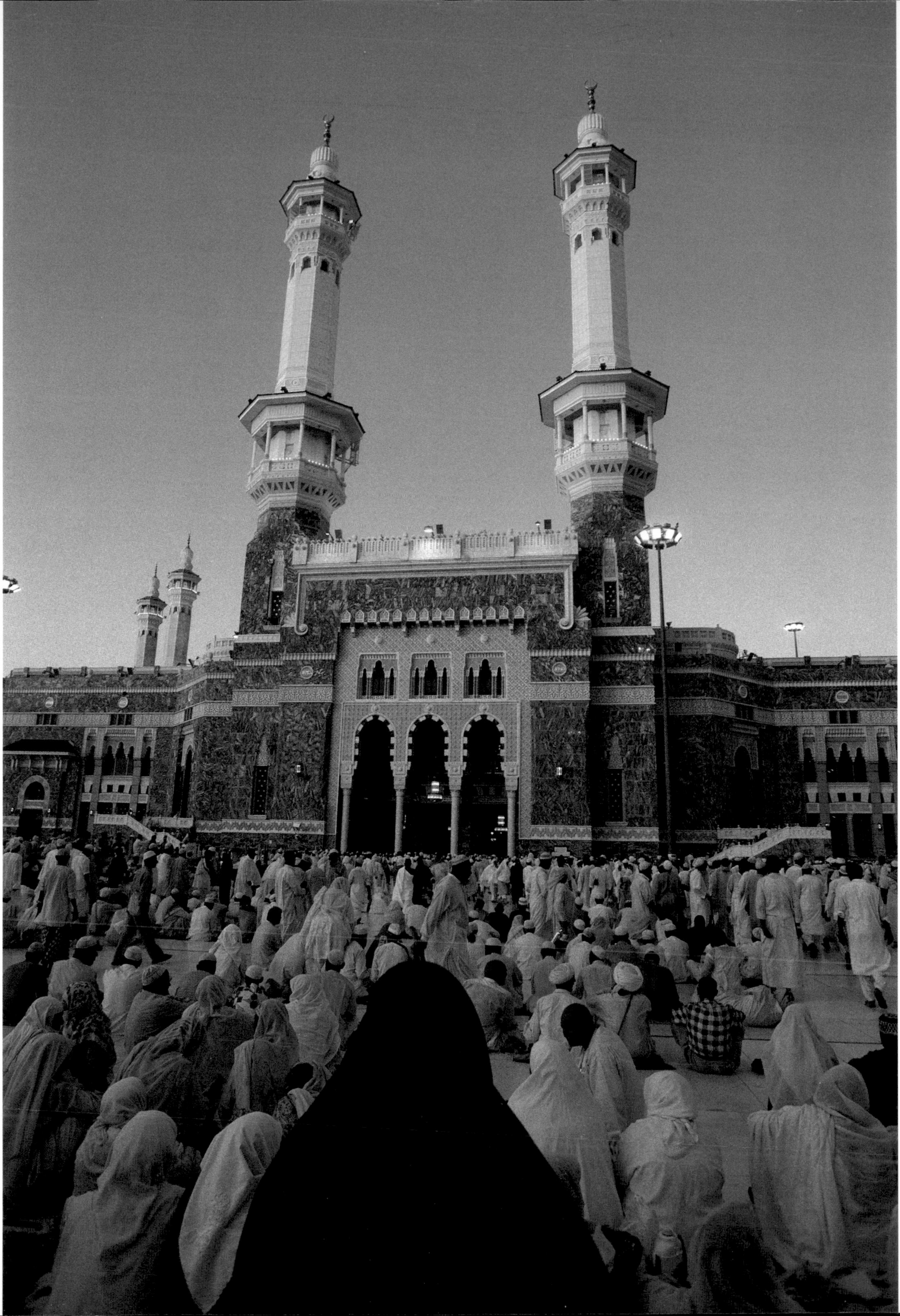

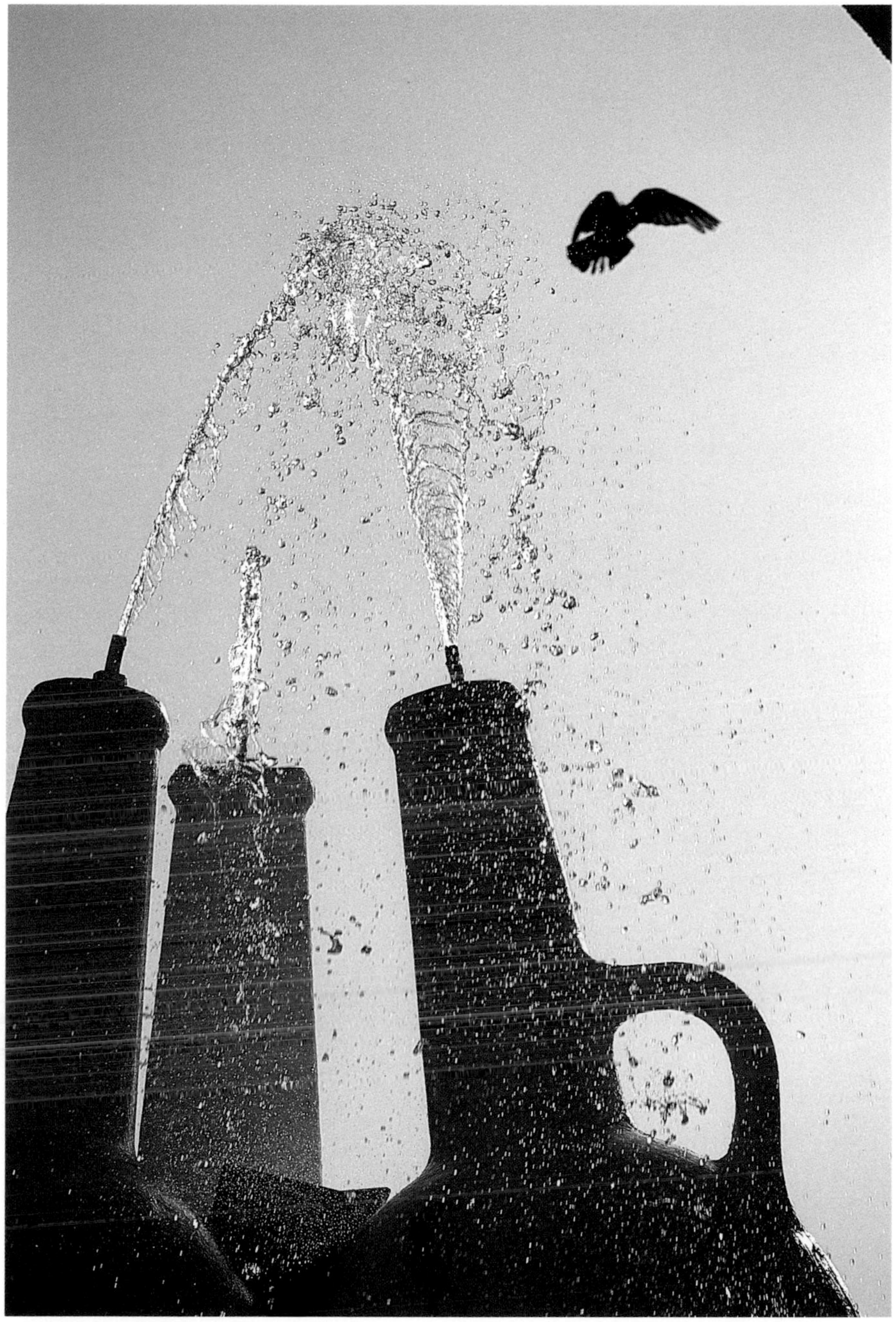

*(Opposite)*
People are gathering for the *maghrib* prayers around the Grand Mosque. The minarets which rise 93 meters are lit up at dusk.

*(Above)*
A fountain at the entrance of Mecca district. In the Noble Qur'ān water symbolizes Divine Mercy and in traditional Islamic cities water fountains are to be found nearly everywhere.

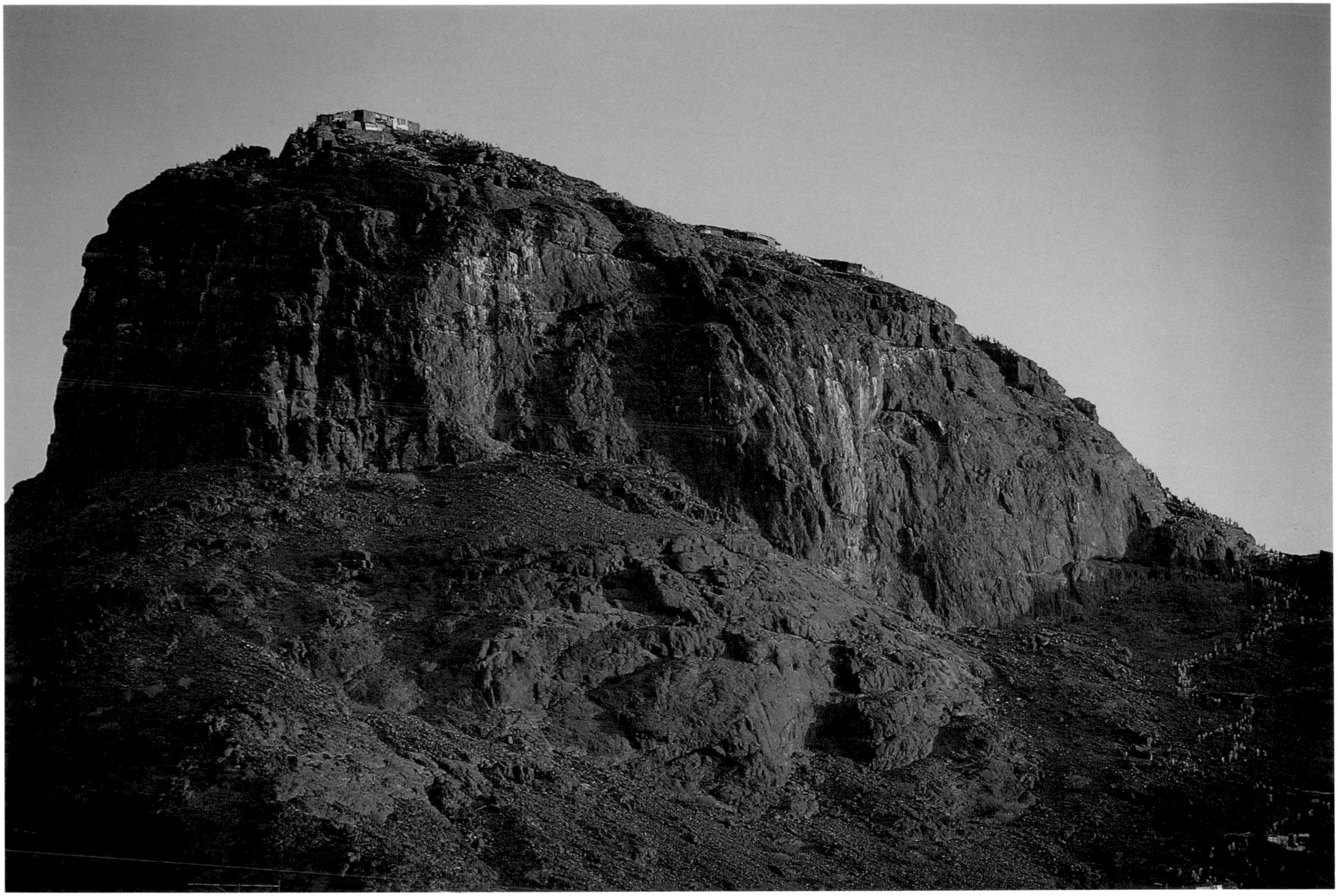

*(Above)*
A distant view of Mount Ḥirā' where the Blessed Prophet received the first revelation. The photograph reveals many pilgrims climbing up the mountain despite signs saying "Do not climb," "Do not remove stones," etc.

*(Opposite)*
Underneath a rock painted white there is the small cave to which the Prophet would often come for meditation even before being chosen as prophet and where he heard the first verses of the Qur'ānic revelation. This site remains extremely holy in the eyes of nearly all Muslims.

*(Following page)*
Pilgrims leaving Mina for ʿArafāt in the gray of the morning of the ninth day of Dhu'l-ḥijjah (the twelfth month of the Islamic calendar designated as the month for the annual *ḥajj*).

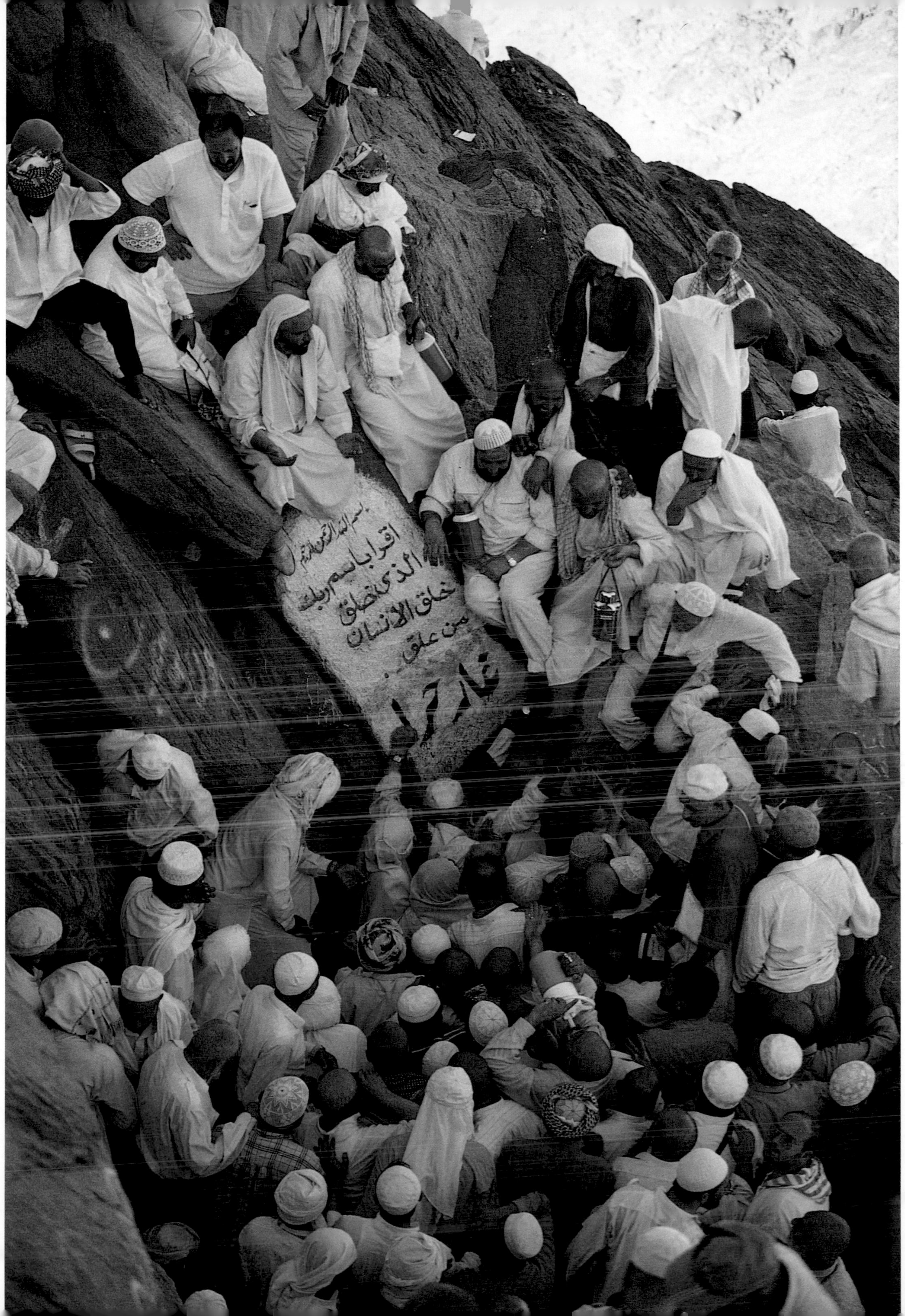
بسم الله الرحمن الرحيم
اقرا باسم ربك
الذى خلق
خلق الانسان
من علق

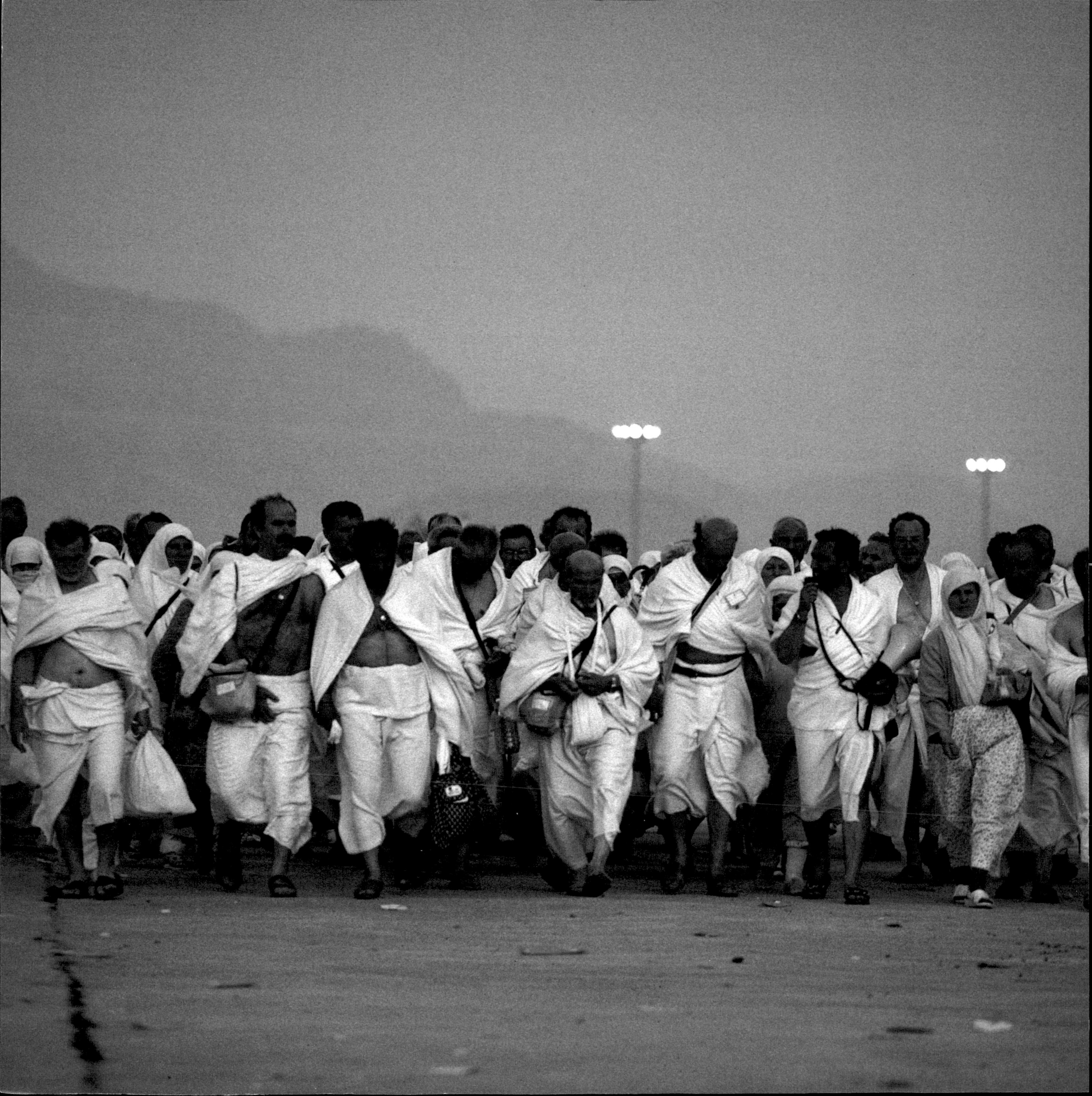

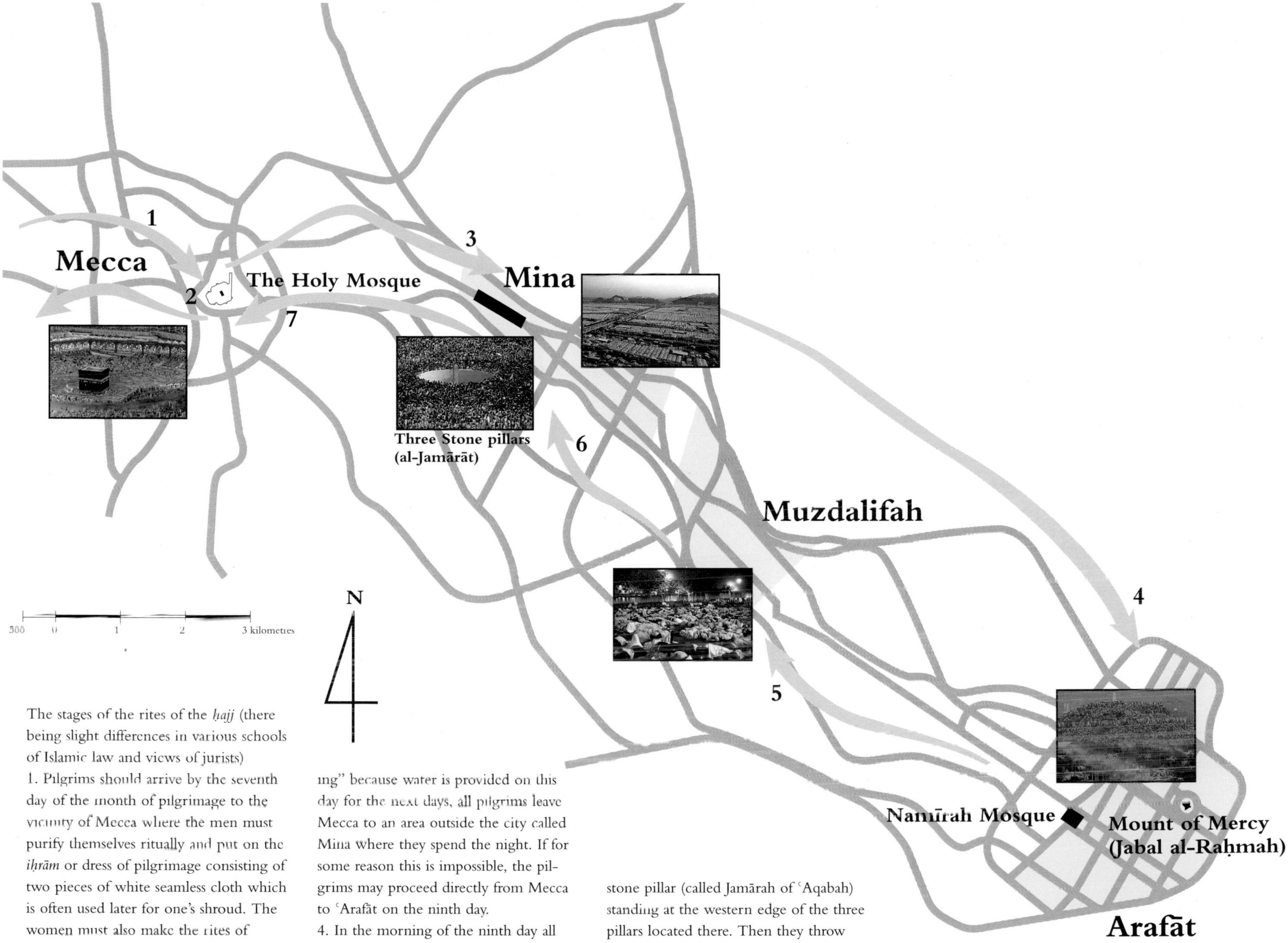


The stages of the rites of the *ḥajj* (there being slight differences in various schools of Islamic law and views of jurists)

1. Pilgrims should arrive by the seventh day of the month of pilgrimage to the vicinity of Mecca where the men must purify themselves ritually and put on the *iḥrām* or dress of pilgrimage consisting of two pieces of white seamless cloth which is often used later for one's shroud. The women must also make the rites of purification but do not have to put on the *iḥrām* as do men. What is expected of them is to wear clean and simple clothing which is modest according to Islamic norms of female dress.
2. Upon arrival at the Great Mosque, the pilgrims must perform seven *ṭawāfs* or circumambulations around the *Kaʿbah* and then perform the *saʿy* between Ṣafā and Marwah seven times. A special sermon is preached in the Great Mosque of Mecca.
3. In the morning of the eighth day, called *yawm al-tarwiyah* or "day of watering" because water is provided on this day for the next days, all pilgrims leave Mecca to an area outside the city called Mina where they spend the night. If for some reason this is impossible, the pilgrims may proceed directly from Mecca to ʿArafāt on the ninth day.
4. In the morning of the ninth day all pilgrims leave Mina for the plain of ʿArafāt. Here from noon to evening the Noble Qur'ān and prayers are recited (*wuqūf*) and people try to climb Jabal al-Raḥmān, the Mount of Mercy at the center of the plain of ʿArafāt.
5. With sundown as the signal, pilgrims leave ʿArafāt for Muzdalifah which lies midway to Mina and spend the night there. While there, they gather small pebbles (traditionally ten) to be used the next day at the rite of stone-throwing.
6. After midnight or at dawn pilgrims move to Mina and proceed to the largest stone pillar (called Jamārah of ʿAqabah) standing at the western edge of the three pillars located there. Then they throw the stones they gathered earlier at the pillar symbolizing the Devil. The rite is done with consciousness that in throwing the stones at the pillar one is also casting away the evil in one's heart and soul. After this rite an animal is usually sacrificed (hence the name of the celebration at the end of the pilgrimage as the *ʿīd* of Sacrifice). Men have some of their hair cut off and the *iḥrām* is taken off. Pilgrims stay there for two more days on the tenth and eleventh during which stones are thrown at the two smaller pillars also representing the Devil and then return to Mecca where the final circumambulation of parting (*ṭawāf al-ifāḍah*) is performed. Most jurists have given the view that the *ṭawāf* at the *Kaʿbah* should be done on the tenth.
7. All pilgrims leave Mina by the twelfth day and return to Mecca where those who had not completed the final *ṭawāf* do so. Then begins the great celebration of *ʿīd al-aḍḥā*, the Feast of Sacrifice, and the pilgrims gain the honorific titles of *ḥājjī* for men and *ḥājjiyah* for women.

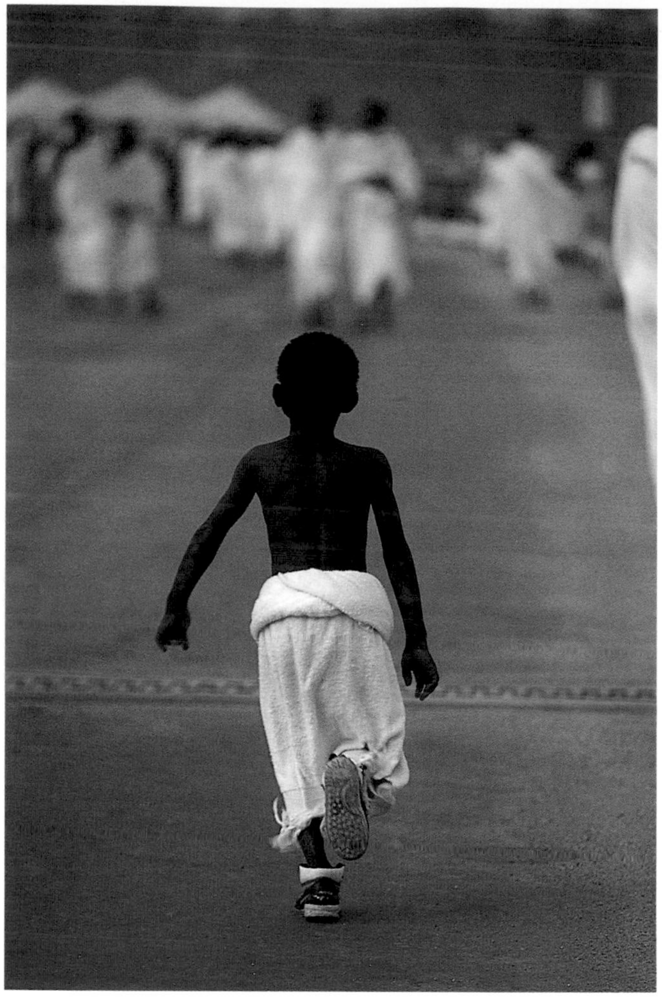

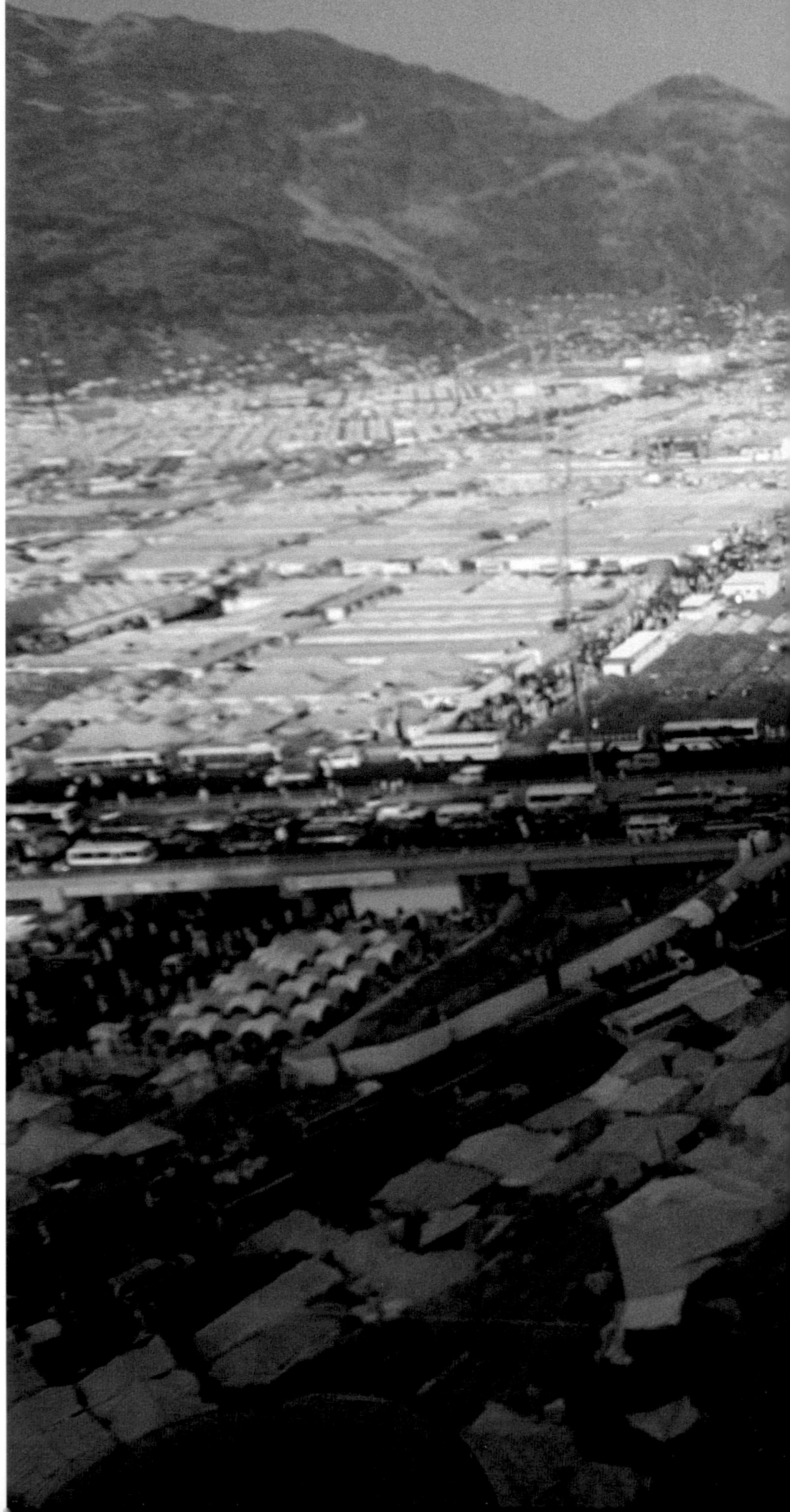

*(Above)*
A boy in *iḥrām*, the pilgrim's costume made of two pieces of white cotton cloth, following his parents during the *ḥajj*.

*(Opposite)*
Mina where some two million people throng during the *ḥajj*. Tents are allocated to pilgrims in groups according to their country of origin, the arrangements being made by a special agency, called the Mutawallā, which is in charge of all travel arrangements for the pilgrims.

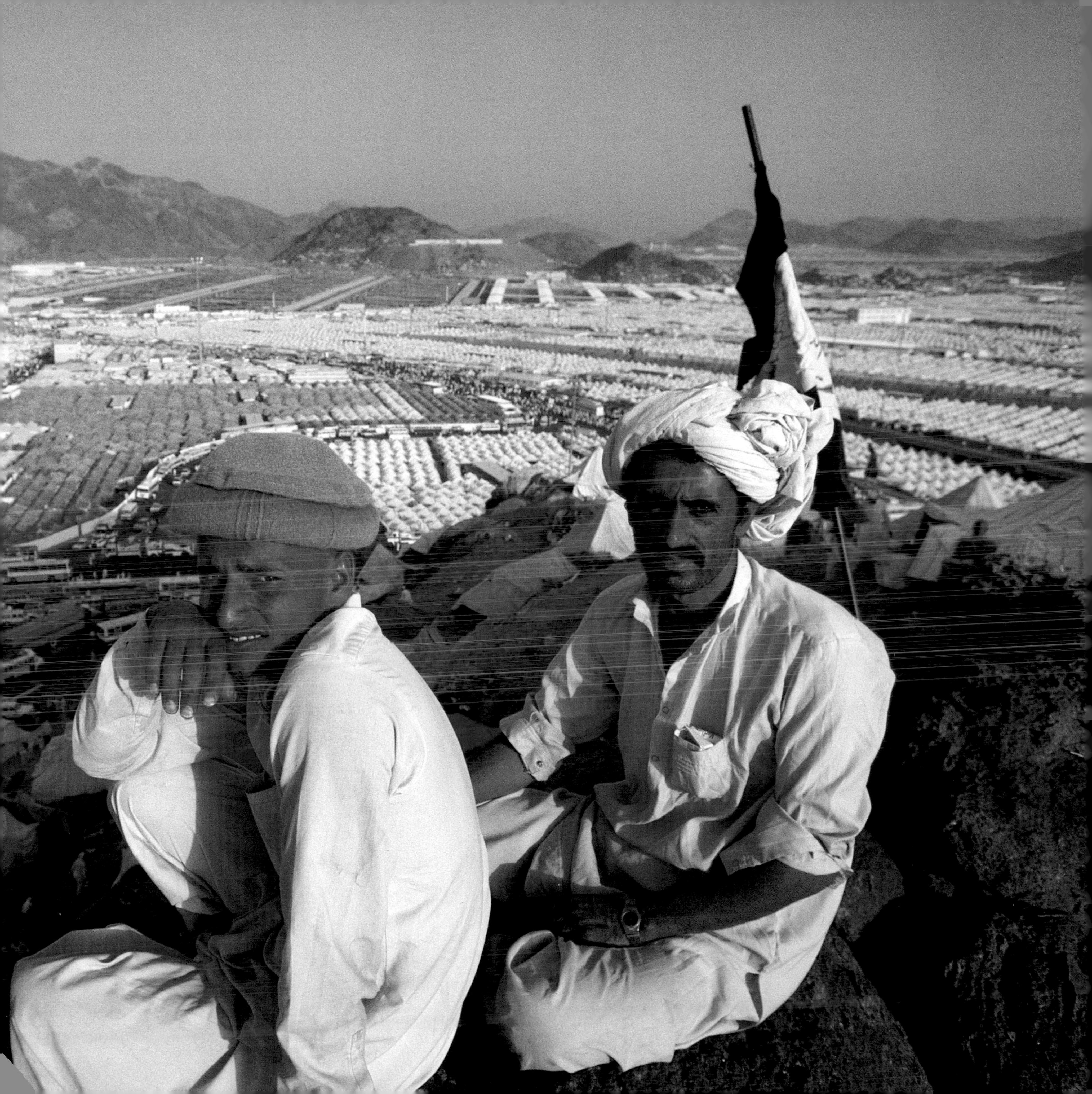

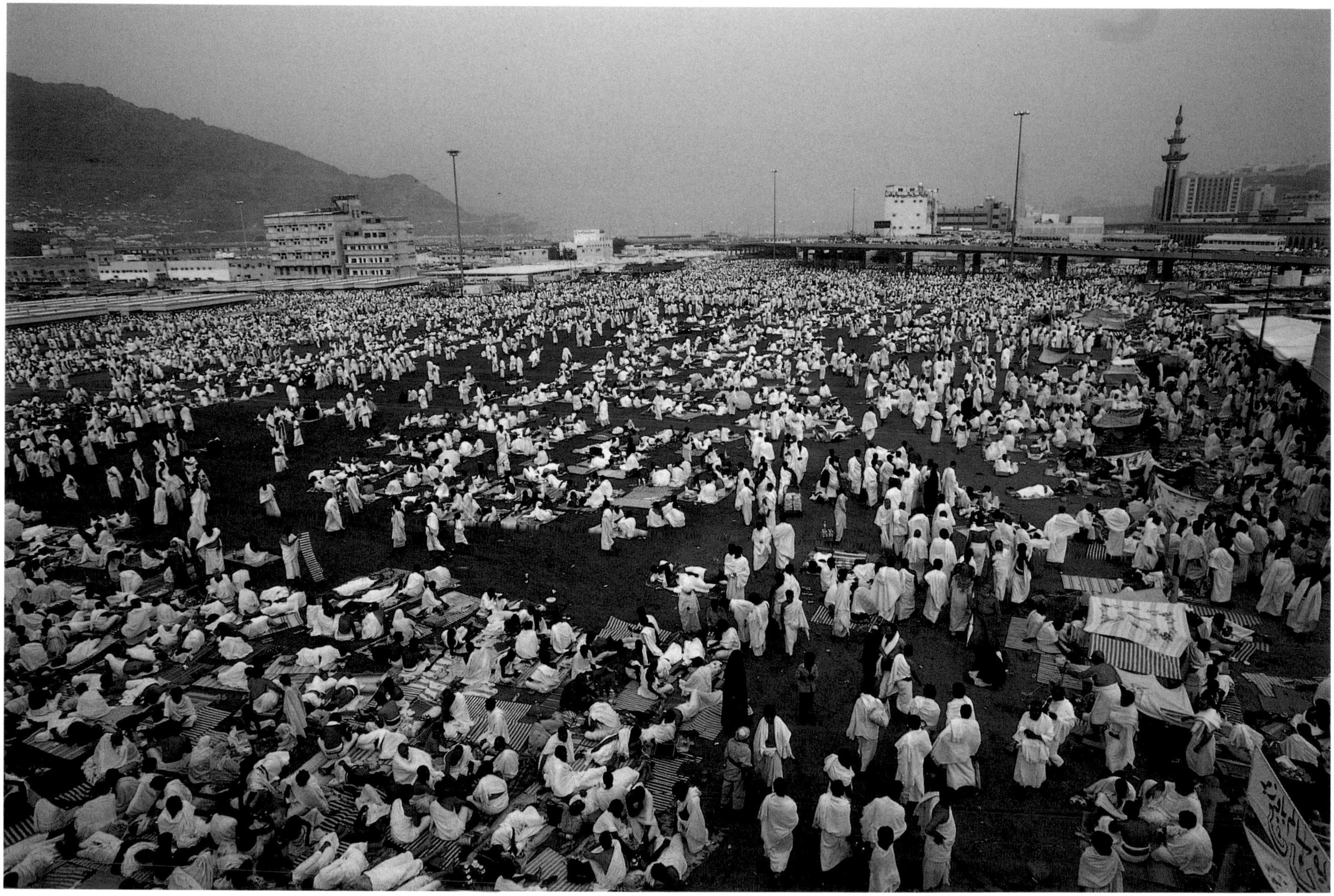

*(Above)*
Many pilgrims who cannot stay in the tents spend their nights on the street. A pilgrim becomes aware that he is part of the Muslim community through living alongside people of different races, languages and nationalities, yet wearing the same attire and praying together.

*(Opposite)*
An elderly couple who spent the night outdoors. Although uplifted by the feeling that their long-cherished desire is about to be fulfiled, pilgrims undergoing the mass migration to Mina and ʿArafāt, are jostled by the crowd and exposed to the blazing sun—a severe ordeal for some.

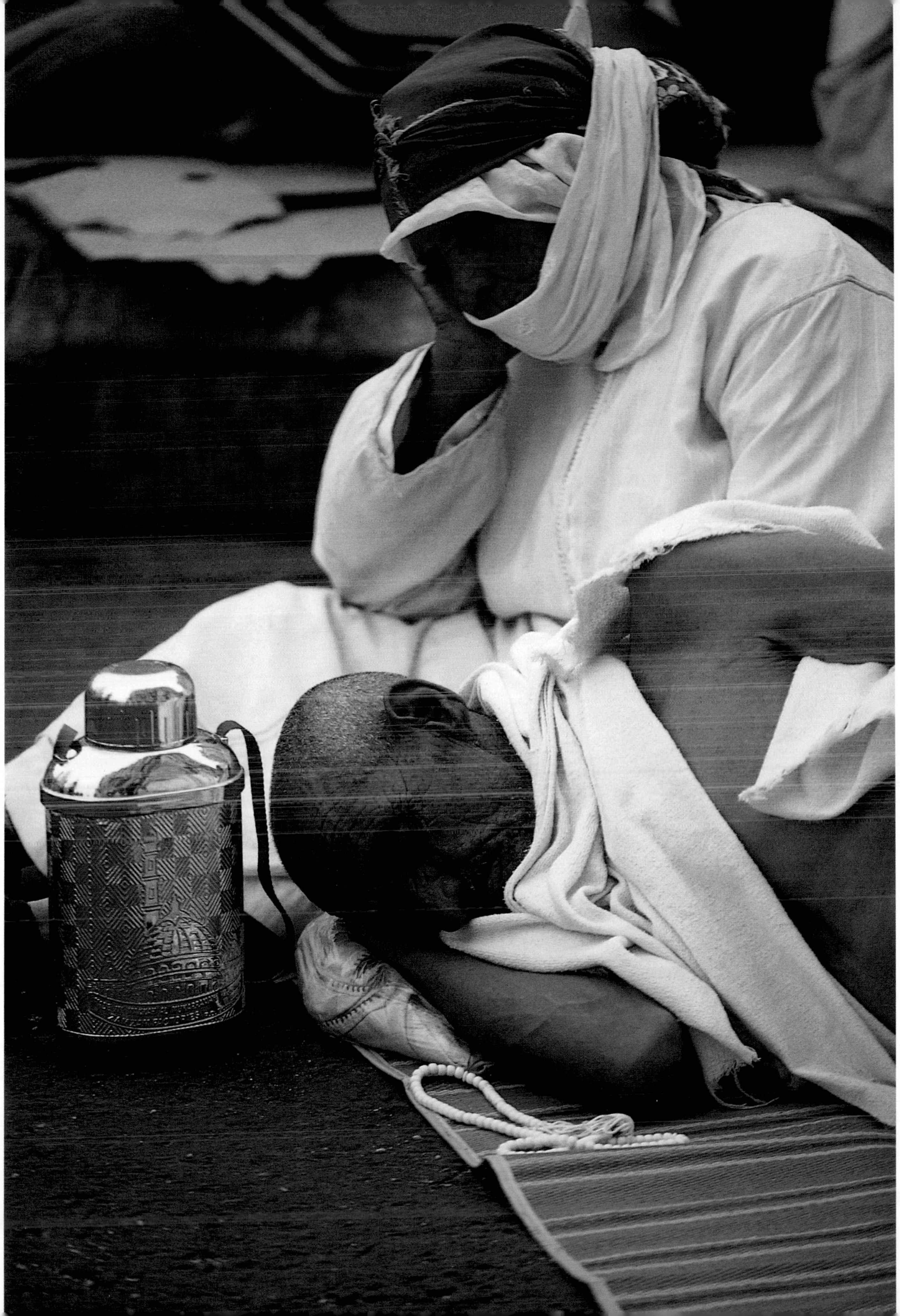

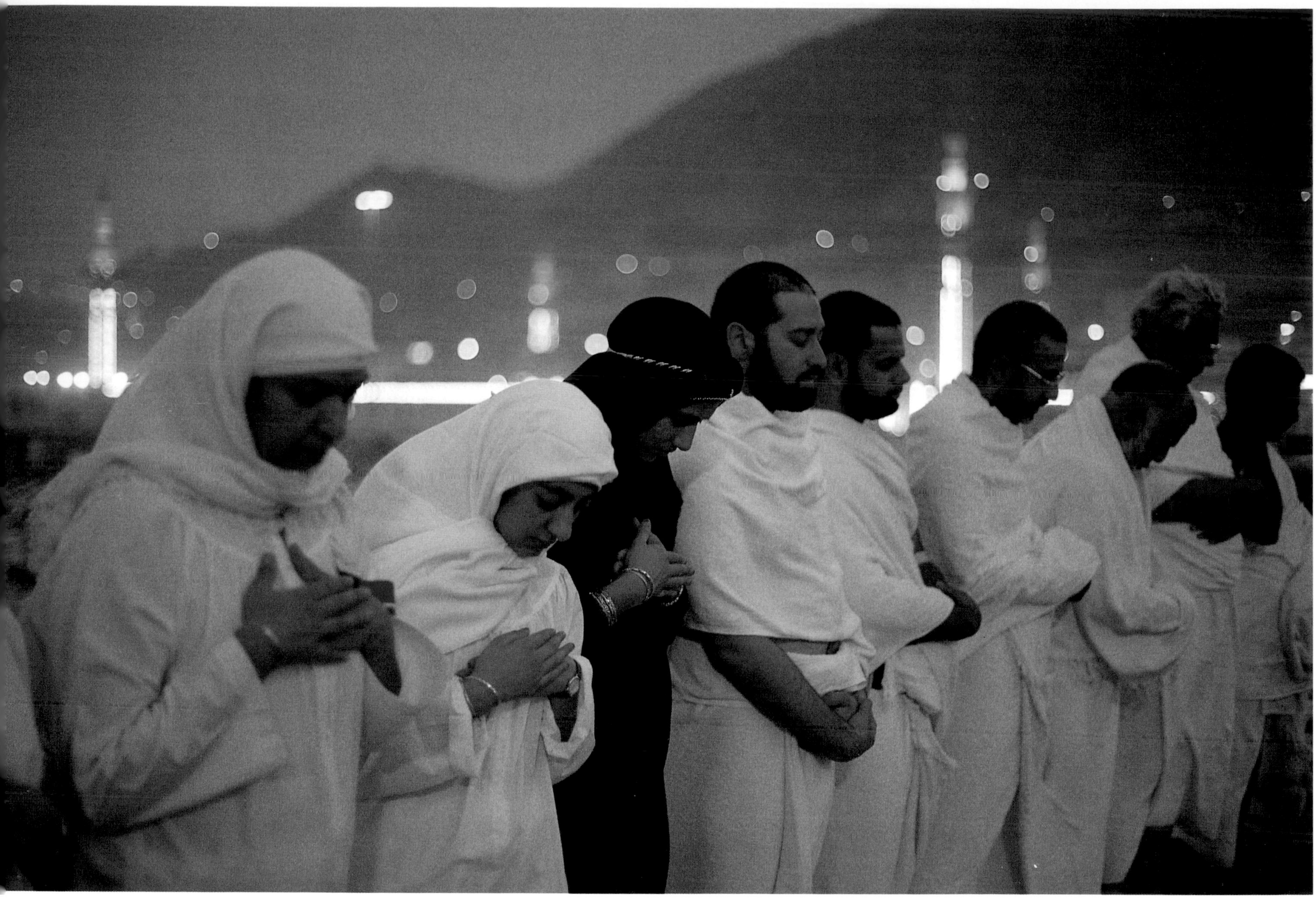

Pilgrims of Indian origin from South Africa performing the *maghrib* prayers at Mina. In contrast to what one observes in Arab countries, the women are standing not behind but adjacent to the men.

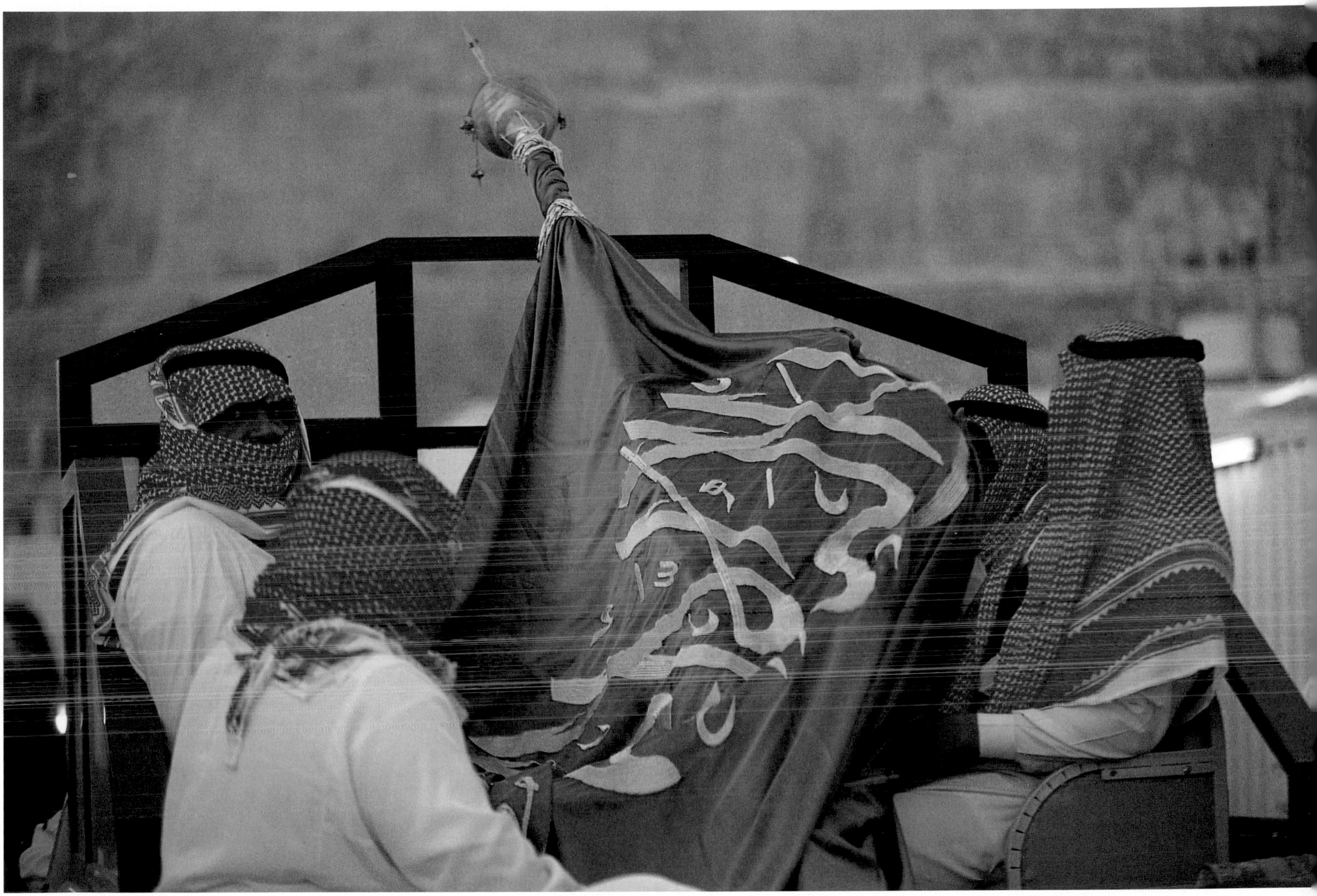

The national flag of Saudi Arabia, bearing the Islamic testimony of faith "There is no god but Allah and Muḥammad is His Messenger," flies from an escort car of the group of pilgrims who are guests of the Governor of Mecca.

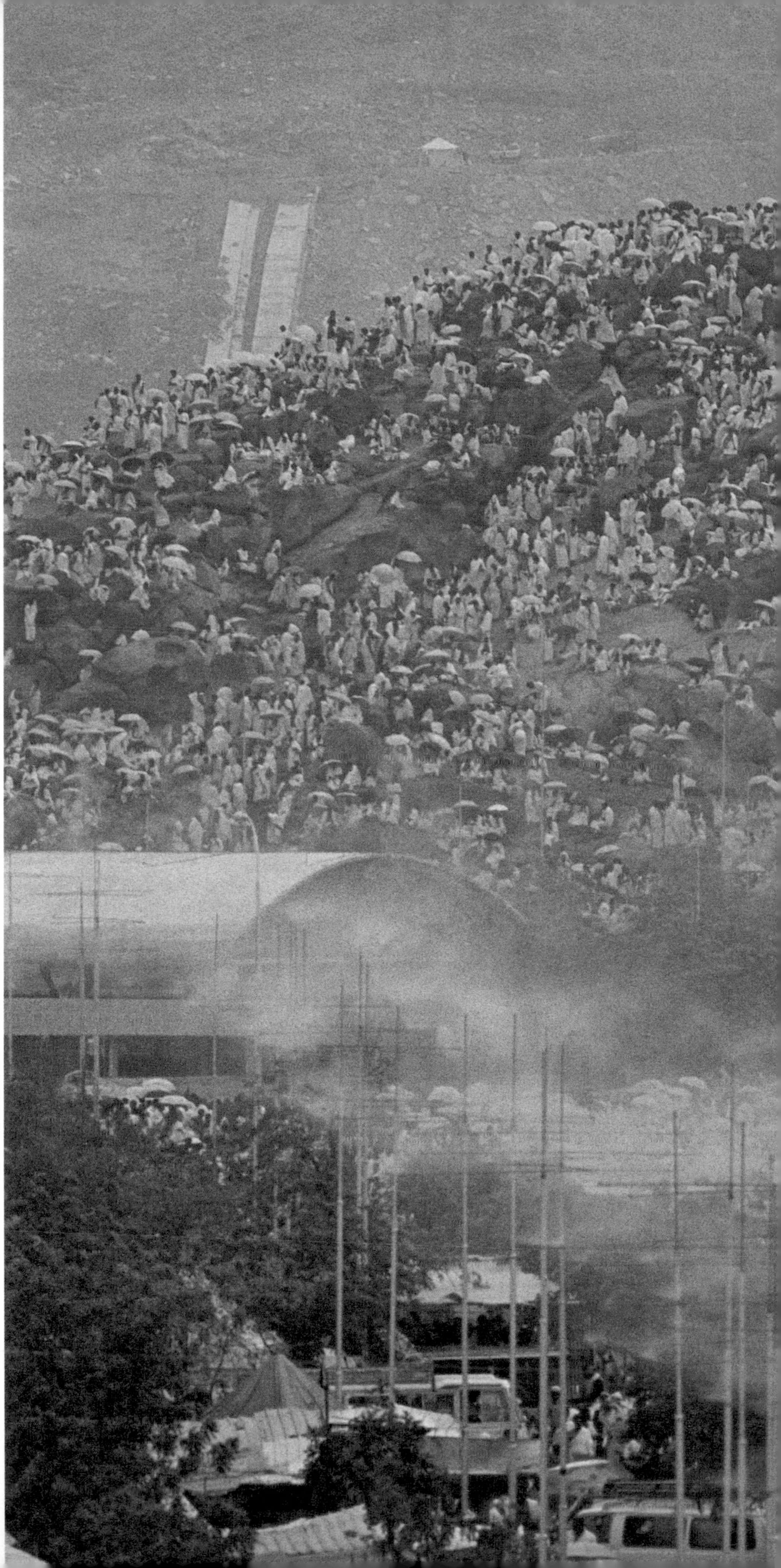

Pilgrims on the Mount of Mercy (Raḥmān) at ʿArafāt on the ninth day of the month of pilgrimage and the climax of the rites. Here they perform *wuqūf* which consists of the recitation of the Noble Qur'ān and intense prayer with all one's heart. Water-sprinklers function all day to subdue the excruciating heat.

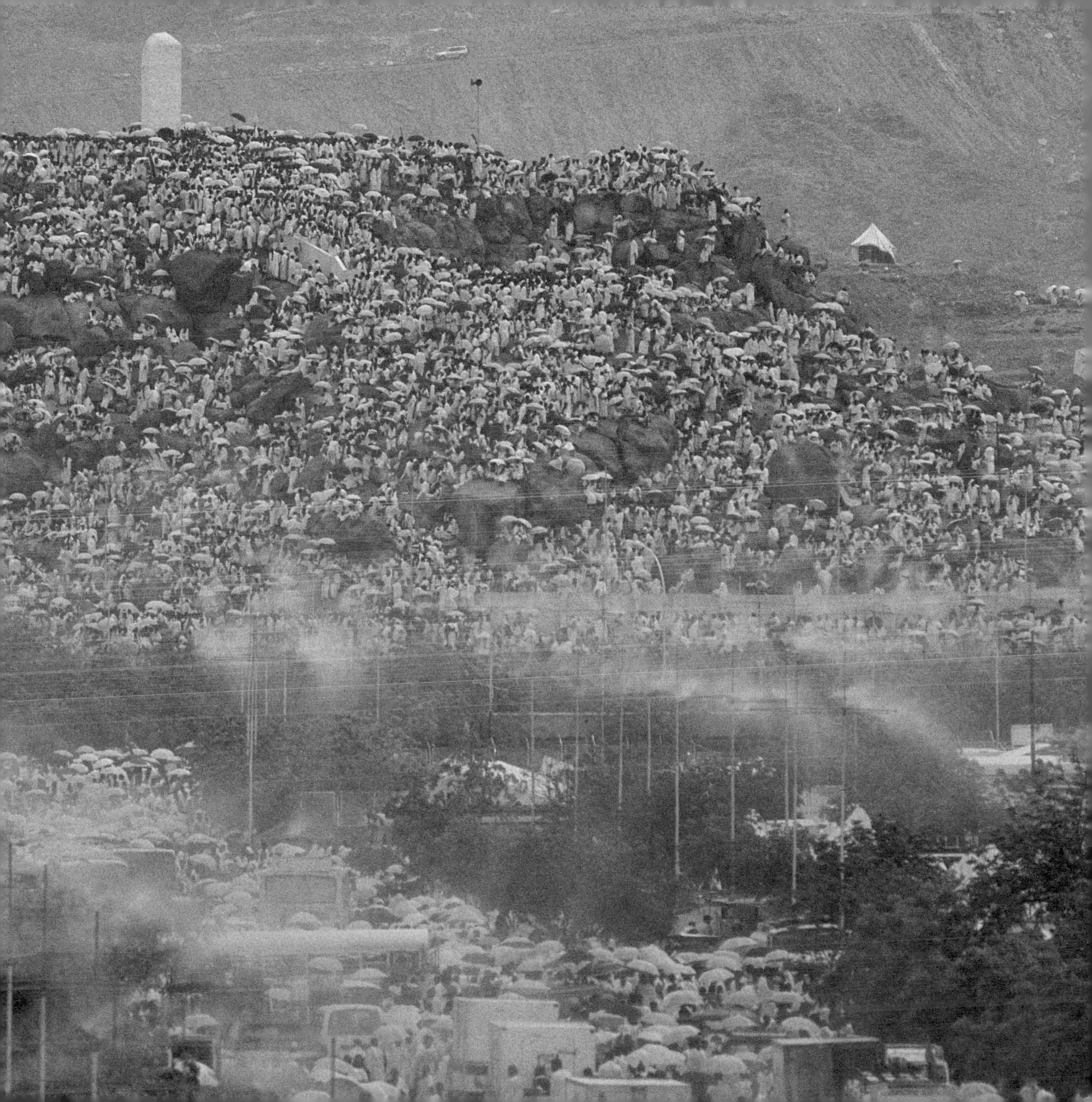

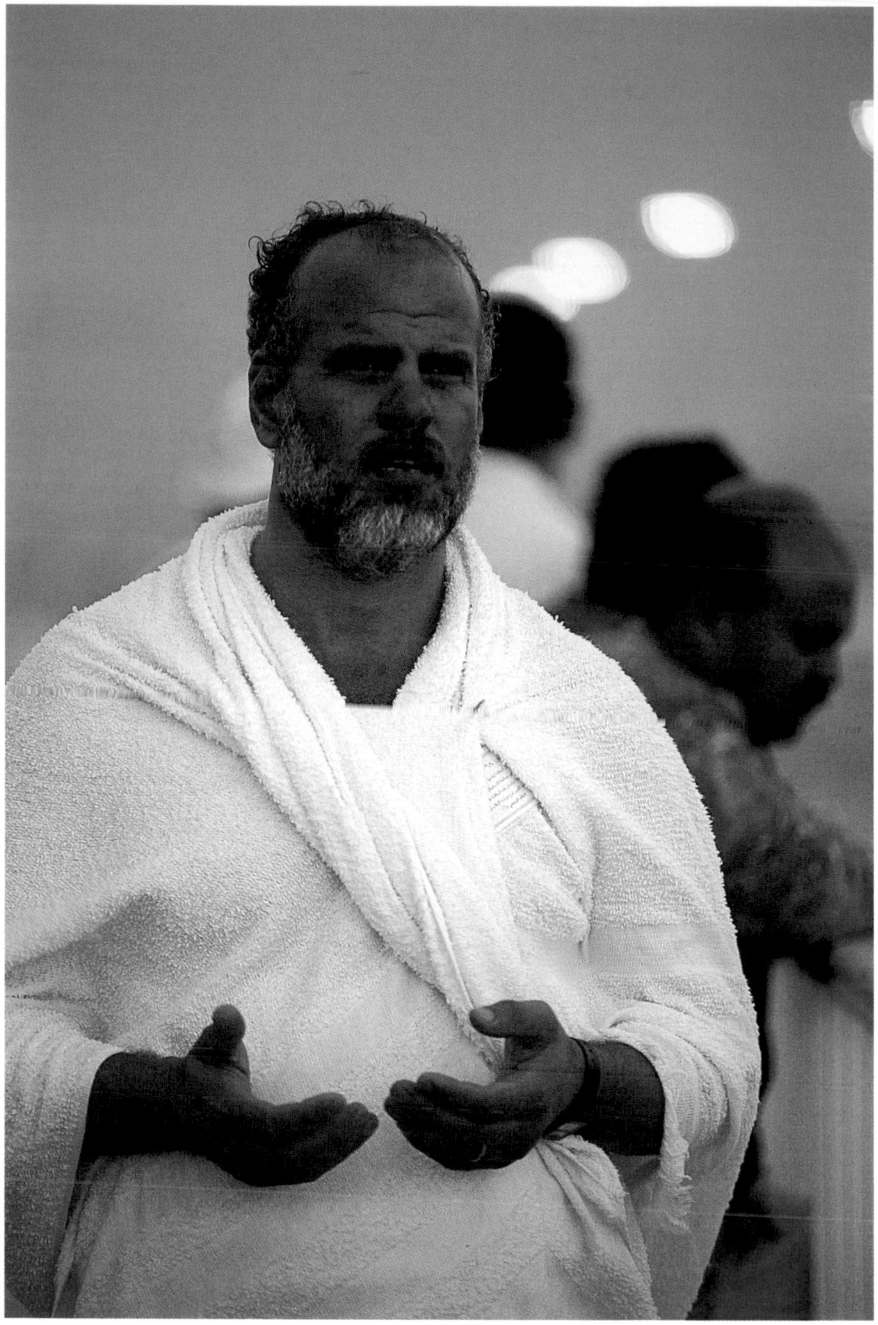

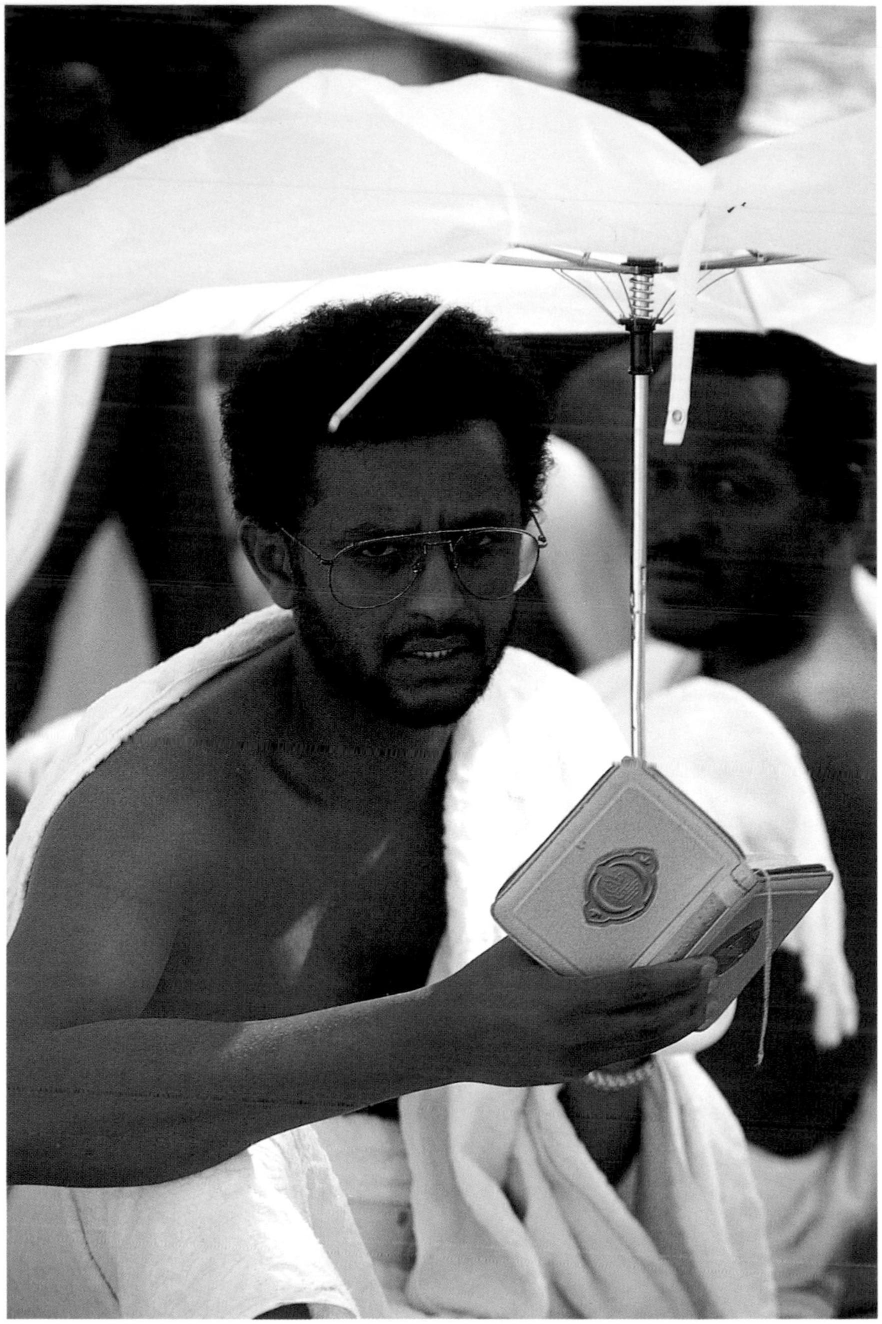

*(Above)*
Pilgrims performing *wuqūf* at ʿArafāt. During the rites of pilgrimage people recite continuously the *talbiyah* which is a prayer in praise of God starting with "*labbayka, allāhumma labbayk . . .*" (At Thy service, Oh Lord, at Thy service . . .).

*(Opposite)*
Pilgrims performing *wuqūf* at the Mount of Mercy. Nothing is allowed to be worn besides the *iḥrām*, but one is permitted to carry a parasol to ward off the sun.

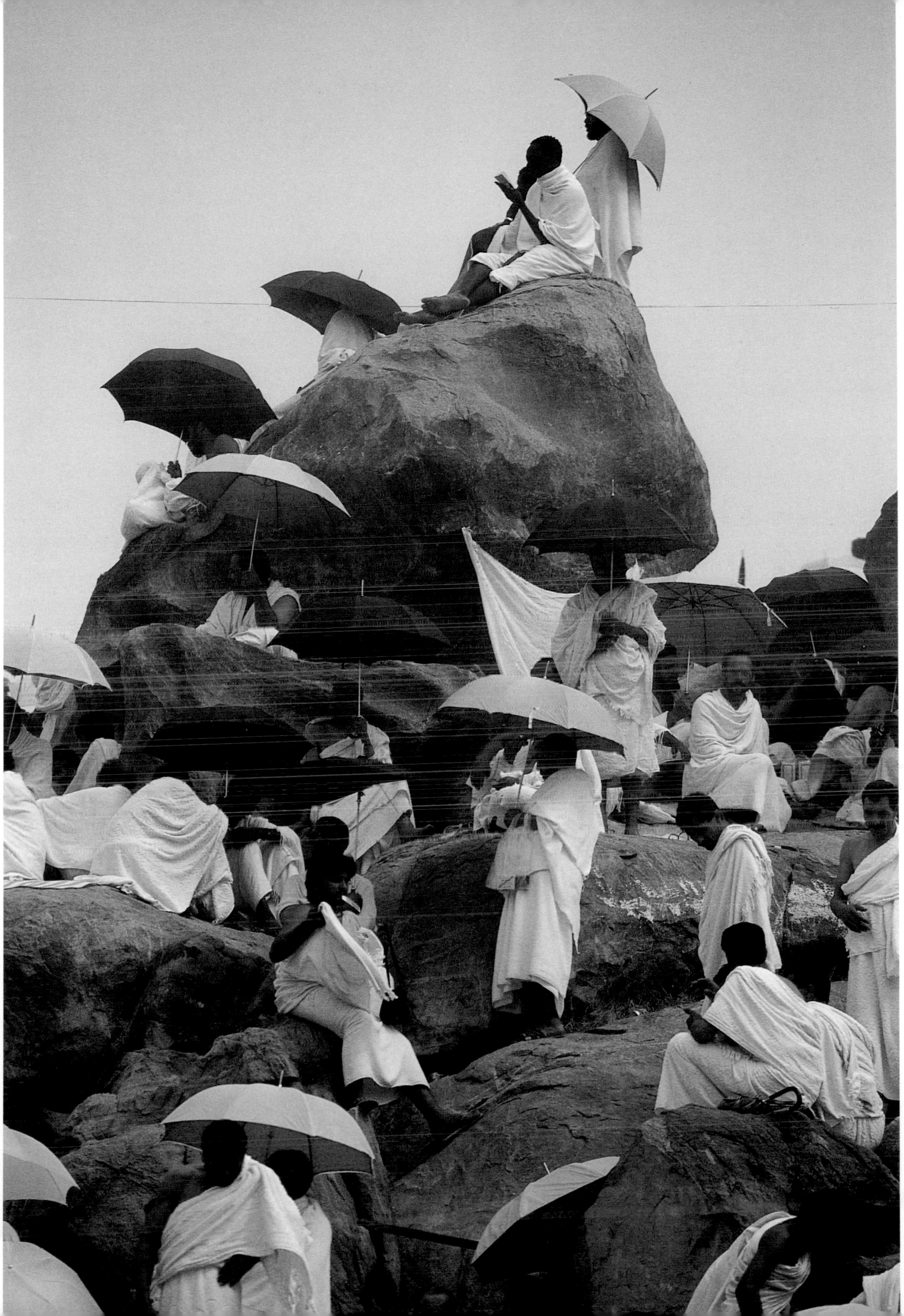

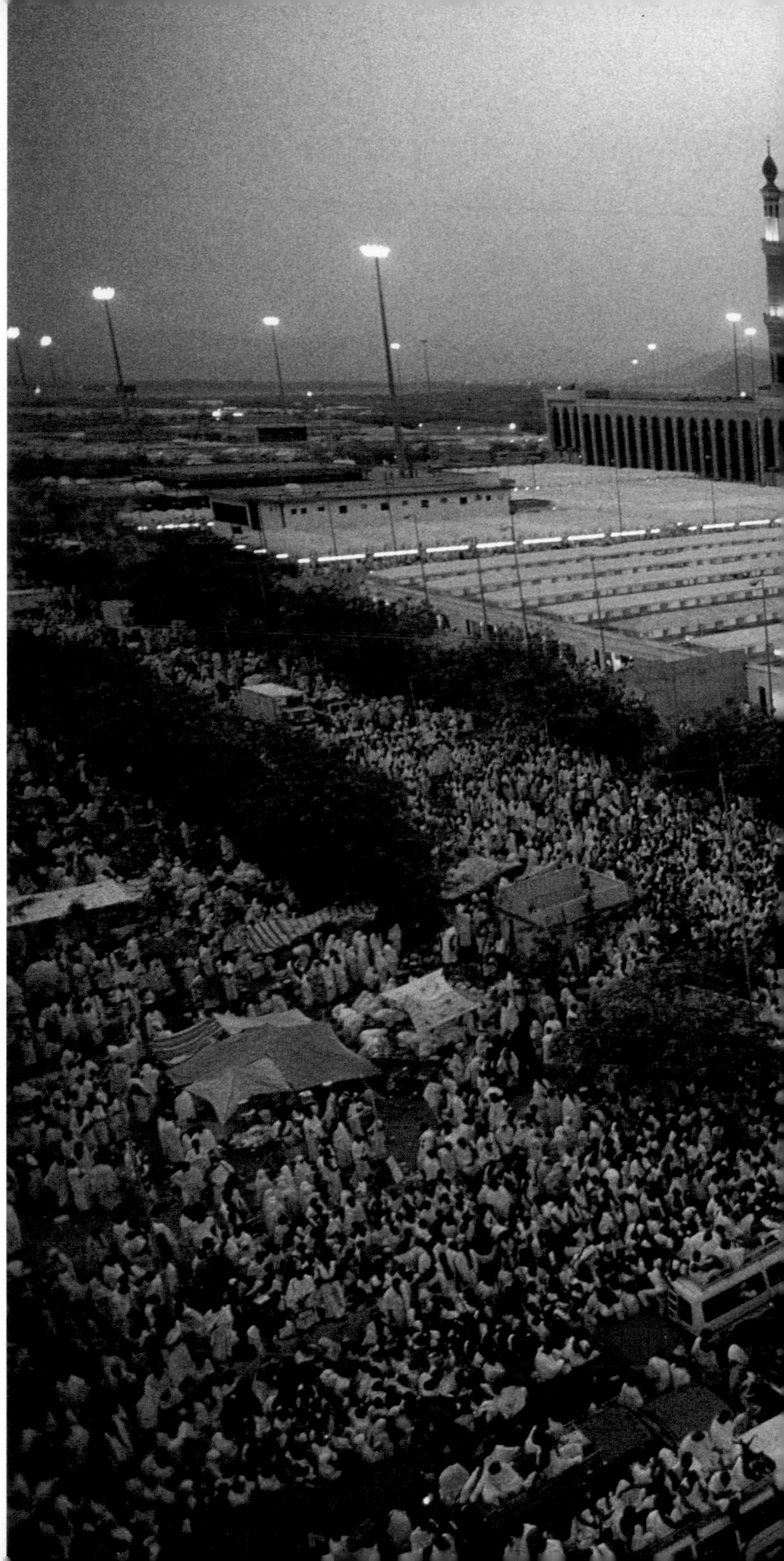

A vast crowd leaving ʿArafāt at the moment of sunset. At this time everyone, whether walking or in cars, prays audibly and the deep sound of the prayers reverberates throughout the vast plain of ʿArafāt. The building in front of the photo is the Namirah Mosque.

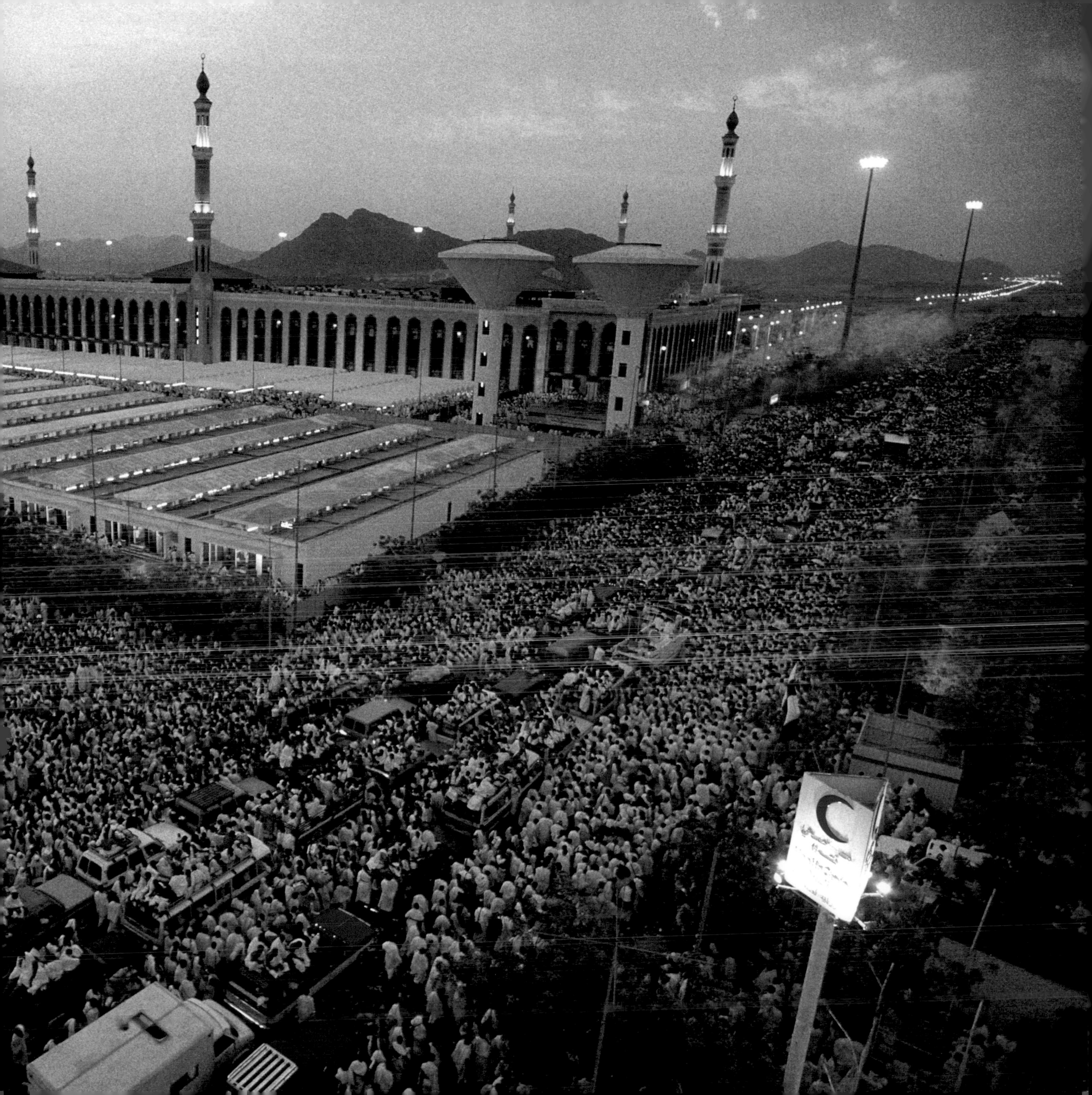

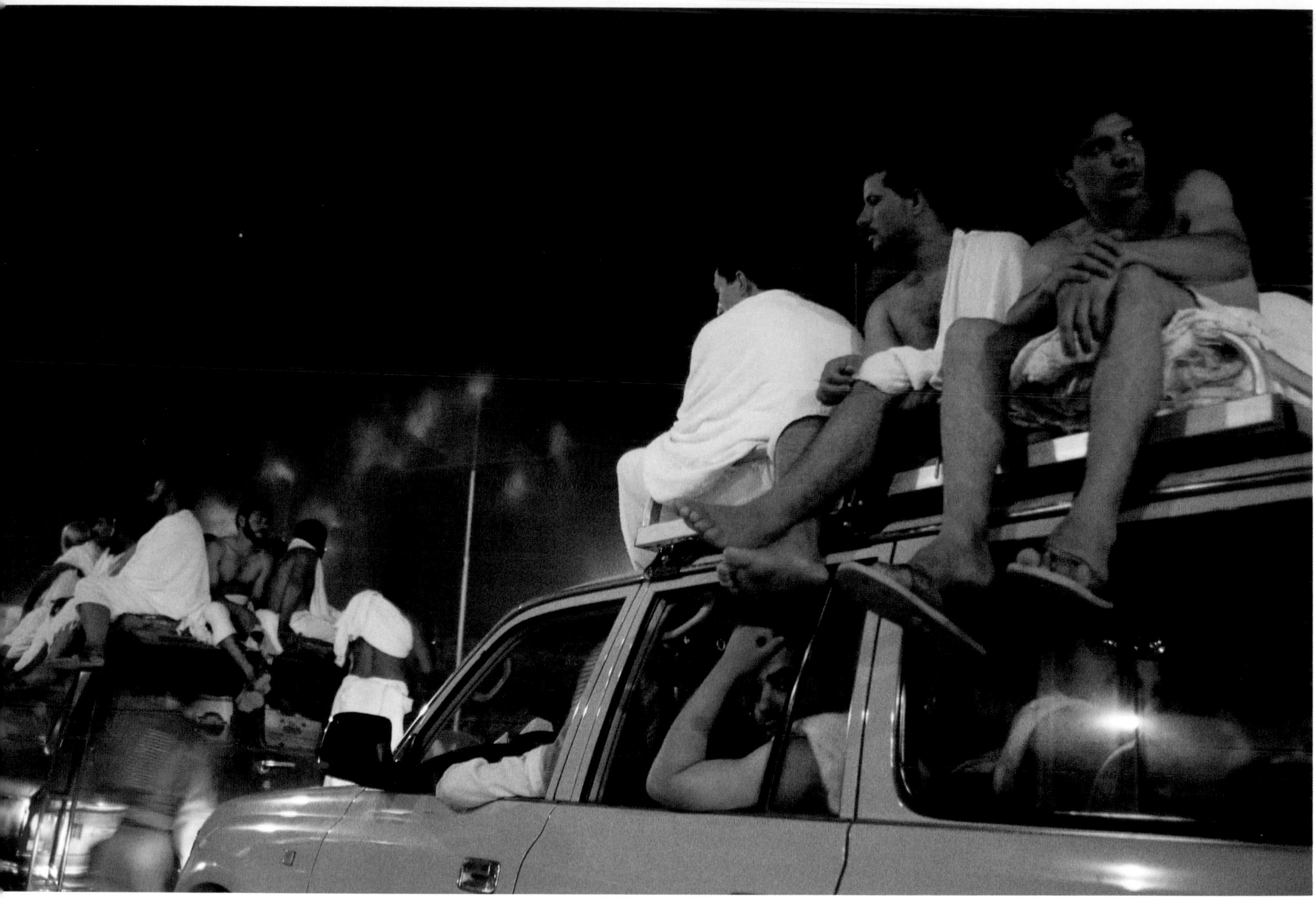

During the early evening hours of the ninth day people leave ʿArafāt for Muzdalifah. Because of the immense crowd all available large vehicles of Mecca are used for the occasion while small vehicles are banned from the pilgrimage area.

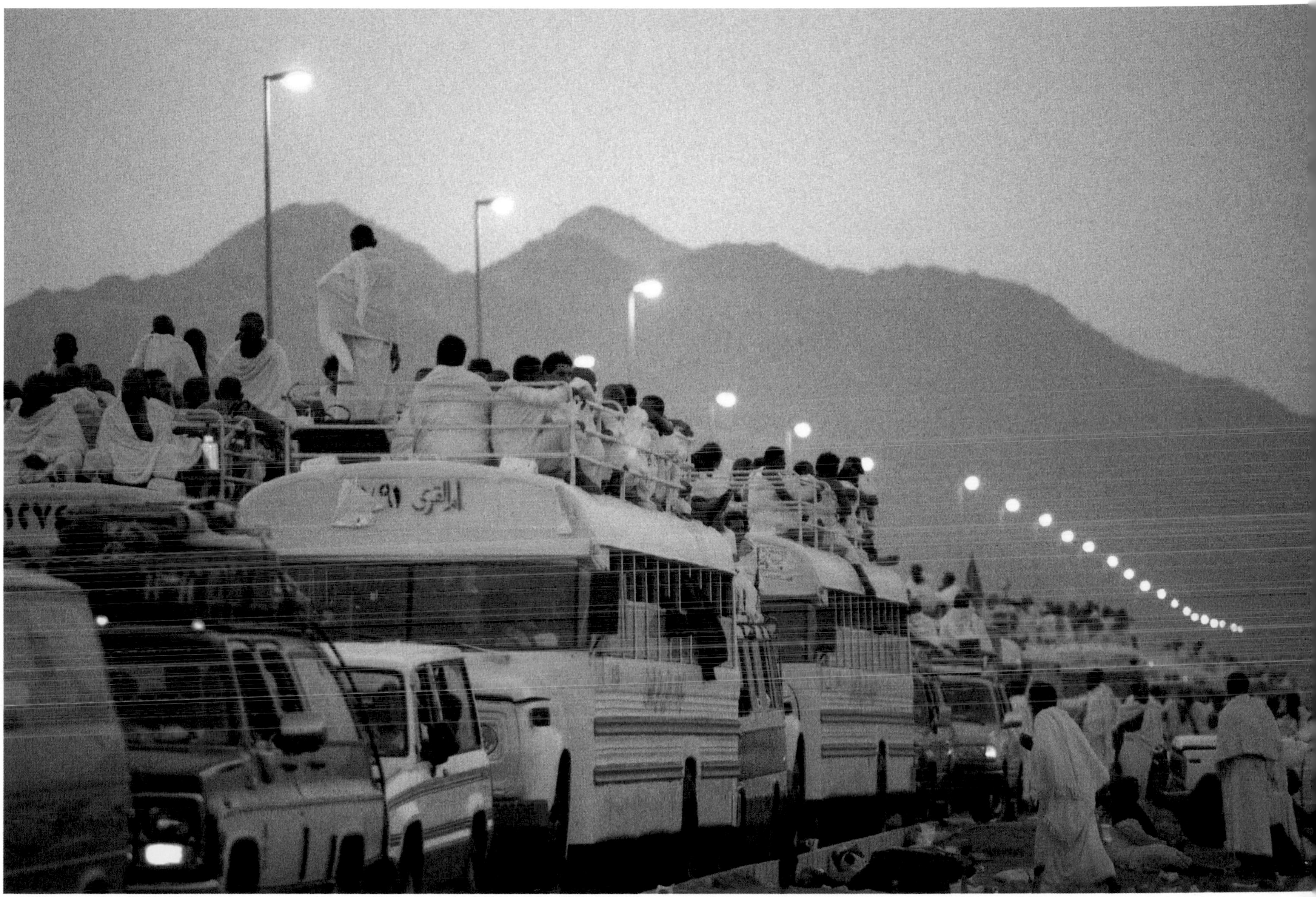

A pilgrim's bus remains stationary in congested traffic before Muzdalifah at dawn. The 5-kilometer journey starting from Mina is one long traffic jam because of the vast number of pedestrian pilgrims who block the way.

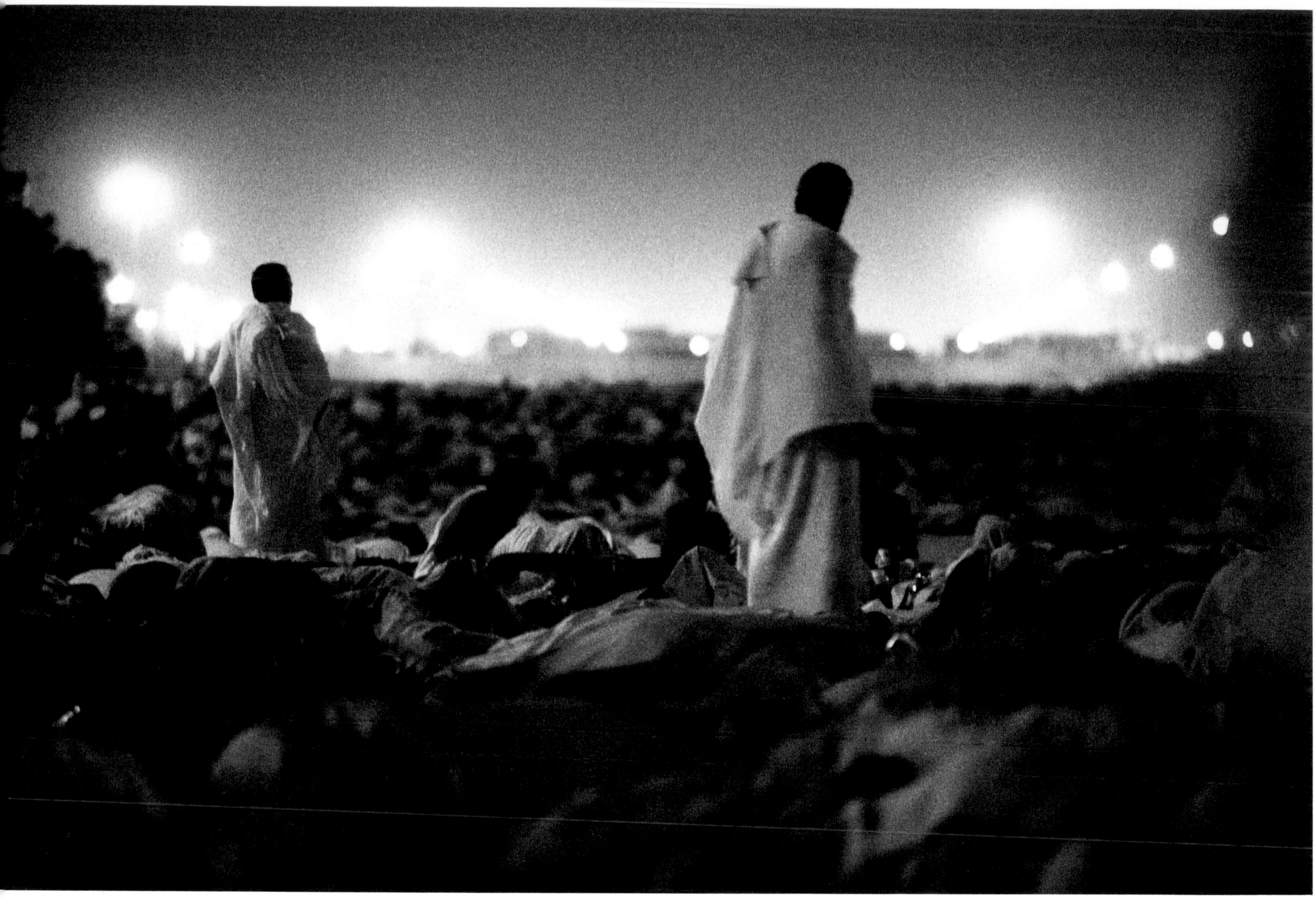

Pilgrims arriving from ʿArafāt to Muzdalifah must spend their time here after midnight. Therefore the wasteland of Muzdalifah becomes so crowded that there is hardly space to put one's foot. Here, most pilgrims gather the stones which they will cast later in Mina.

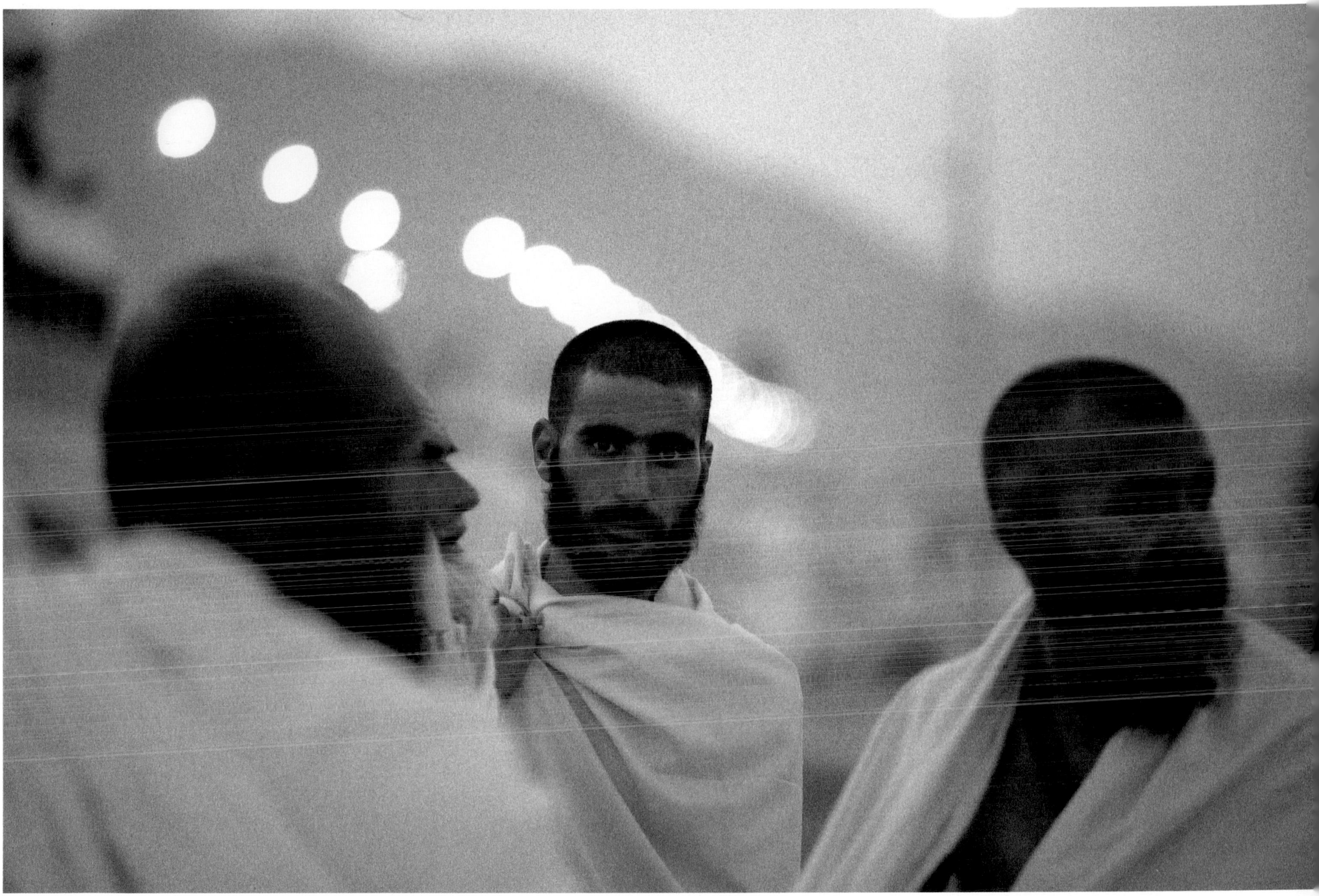

*(Above)*
After a brief rest in Muzdalifah, pilgrims set out for Mina many in a state of exhaustion from lack of food and sleep since the day before. Nevertheless, they continue to exclaim, "*labbayka, allāhumma labbayk*" (at Thy service, Oh Lord, at Thy service) thereby renewing their spiritual energy.

*(Following pages)*
On the tenth day, the pilgrims who have returned to Mina gather for the rite of the casting of stones at the pillars symbolizing the Devil. The area around the pillars is extremely crowded and dangerous for women, children, and the elderly, who may therefore ask one of the men accompanying them to perform the rite for them. On this day stone is cast only at the largest of the pillars.

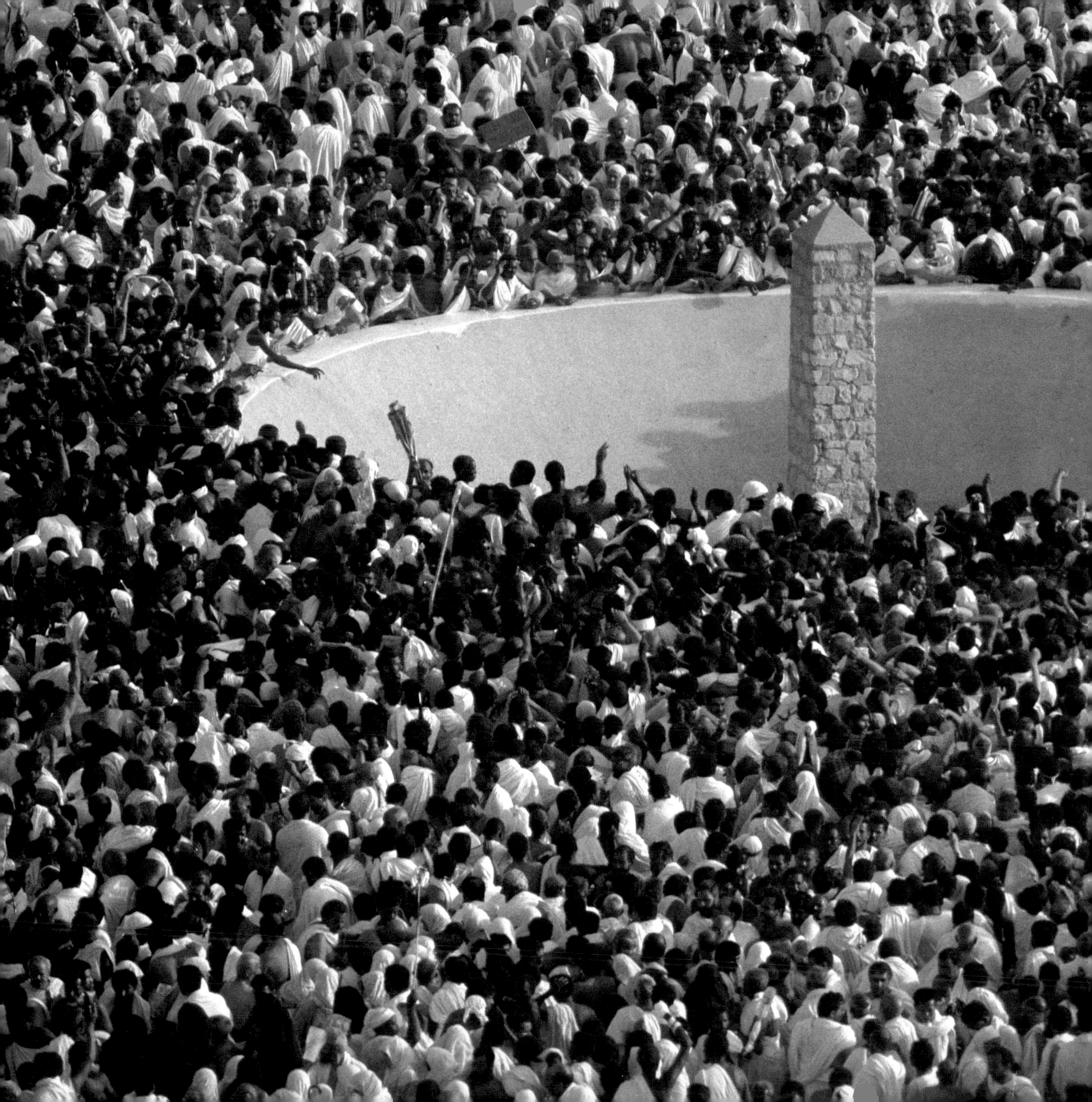

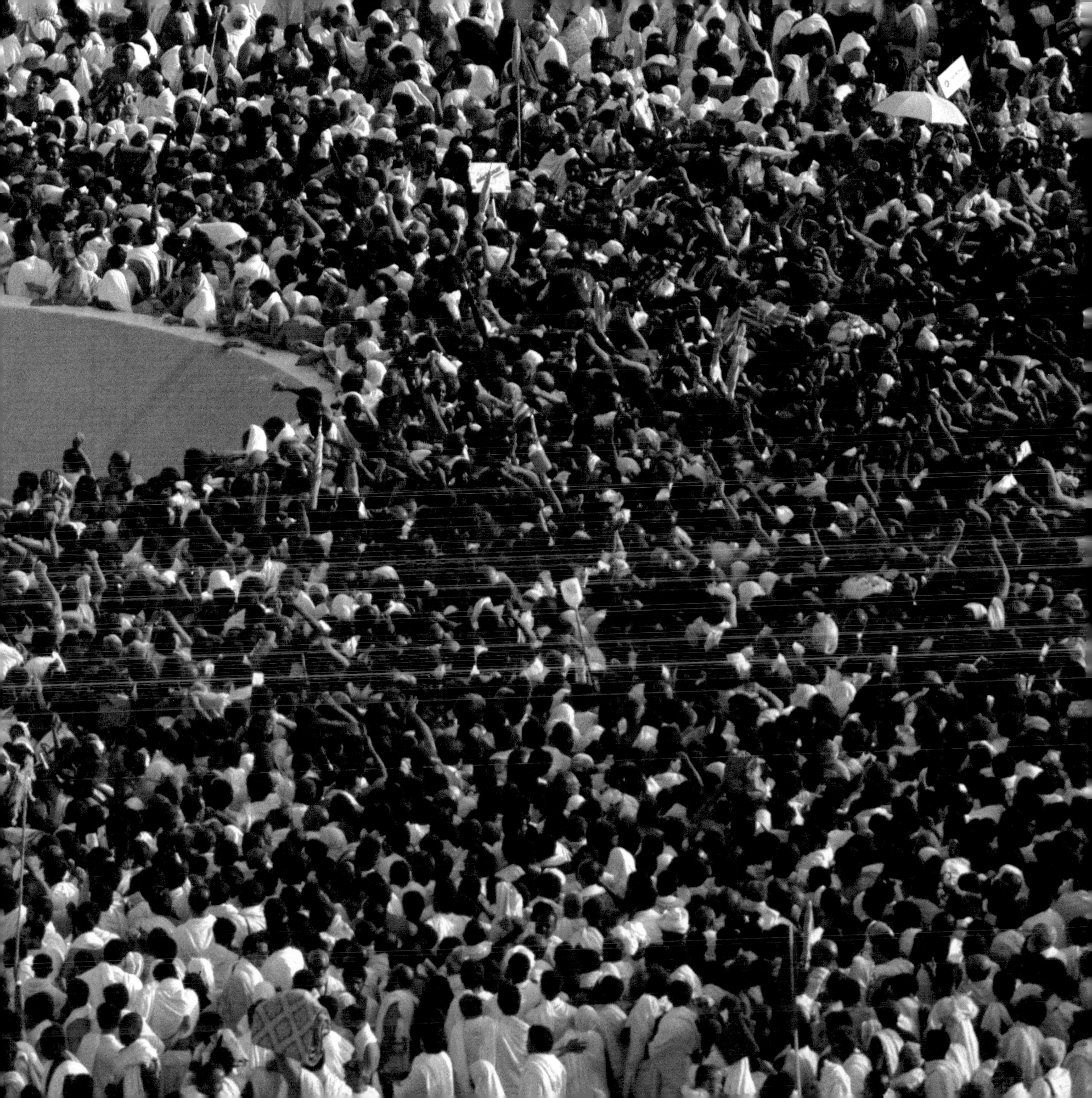

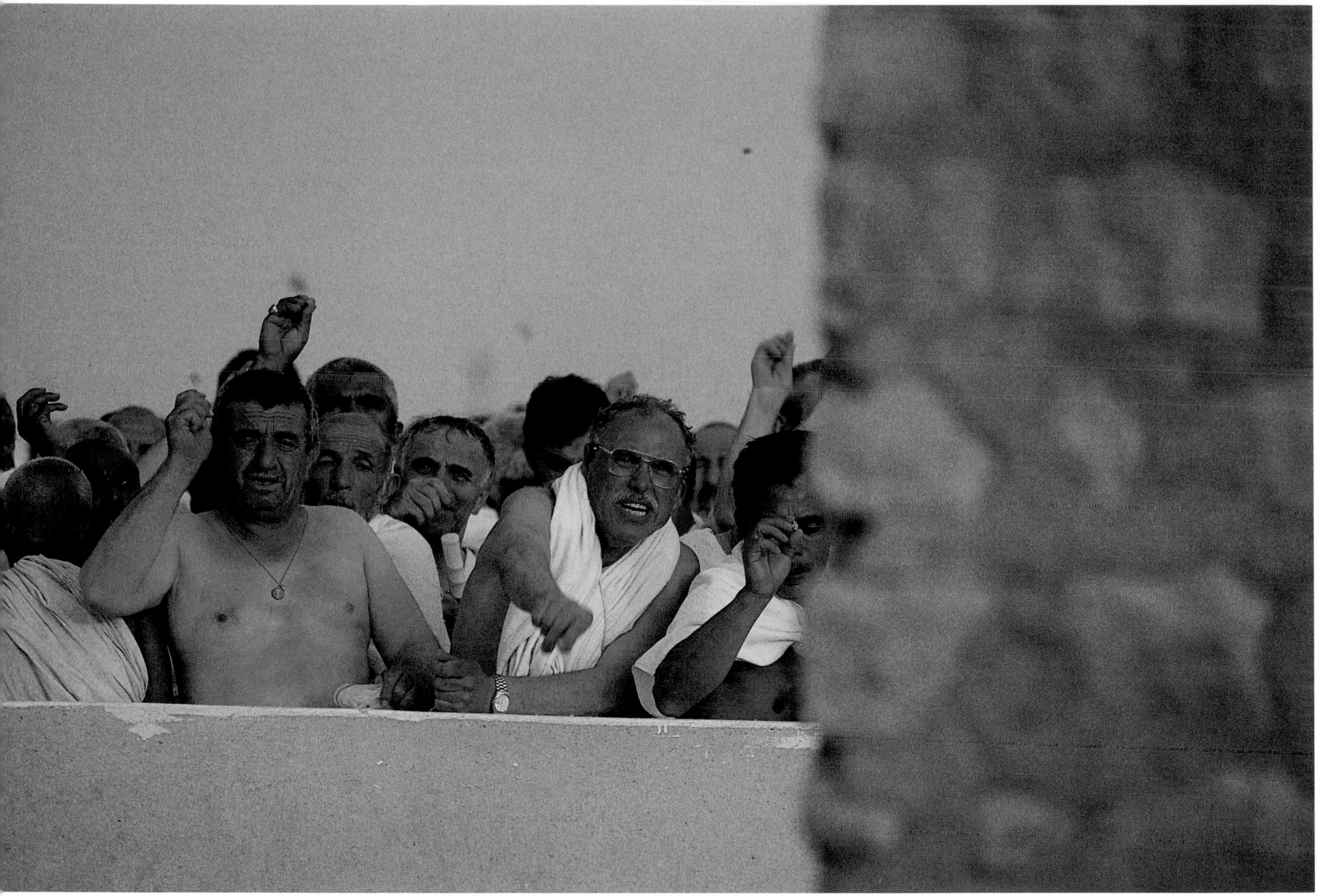

The rite of the casting of stones at the two smaller pillars, which like the larger one symbolize the forces of evil, takes place. The pillars are called *Jamārāt* in Arabic.

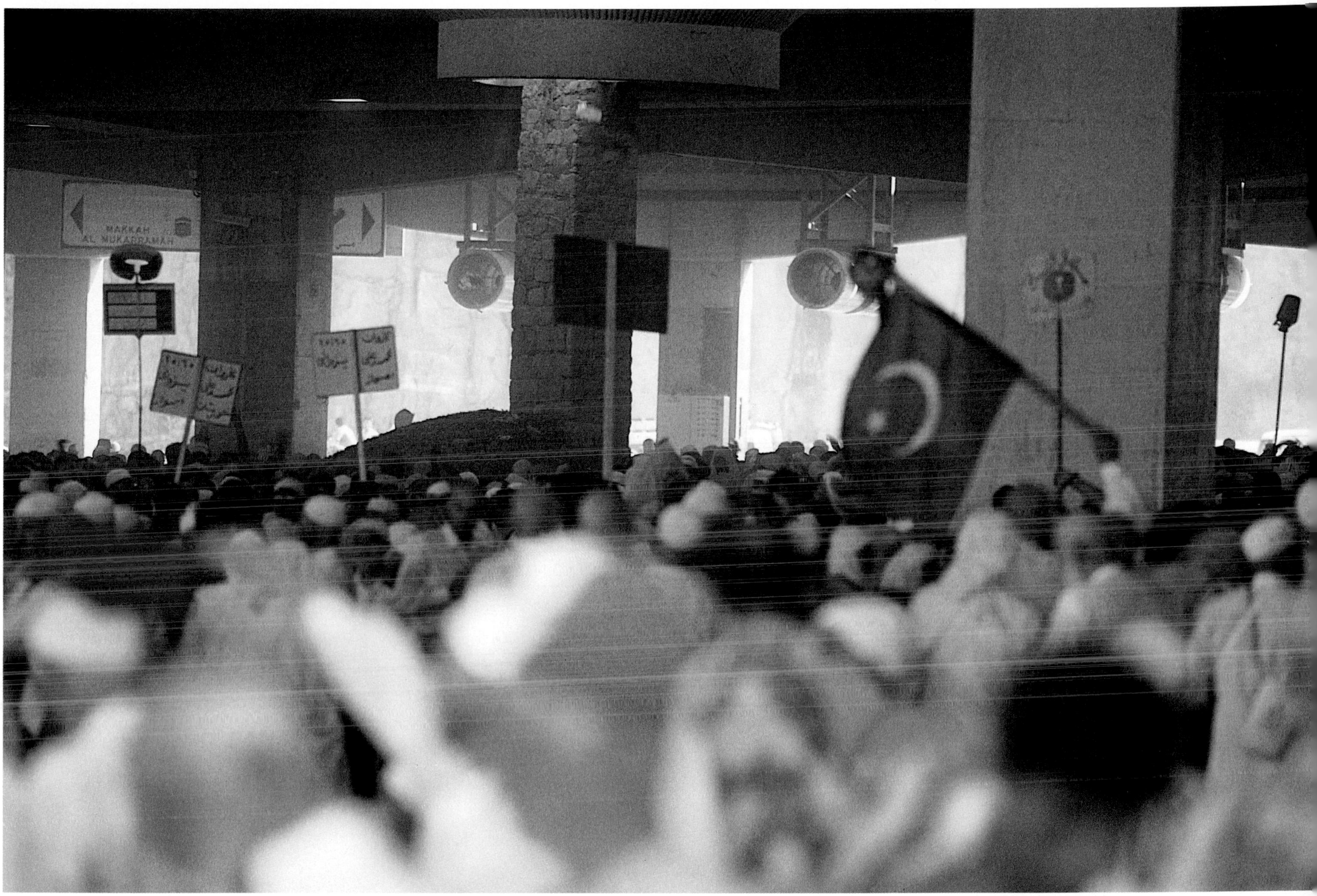


Pilgrims cast stones from the top of a large bridge nearby while some do so from the ground at the foot of the pillar.

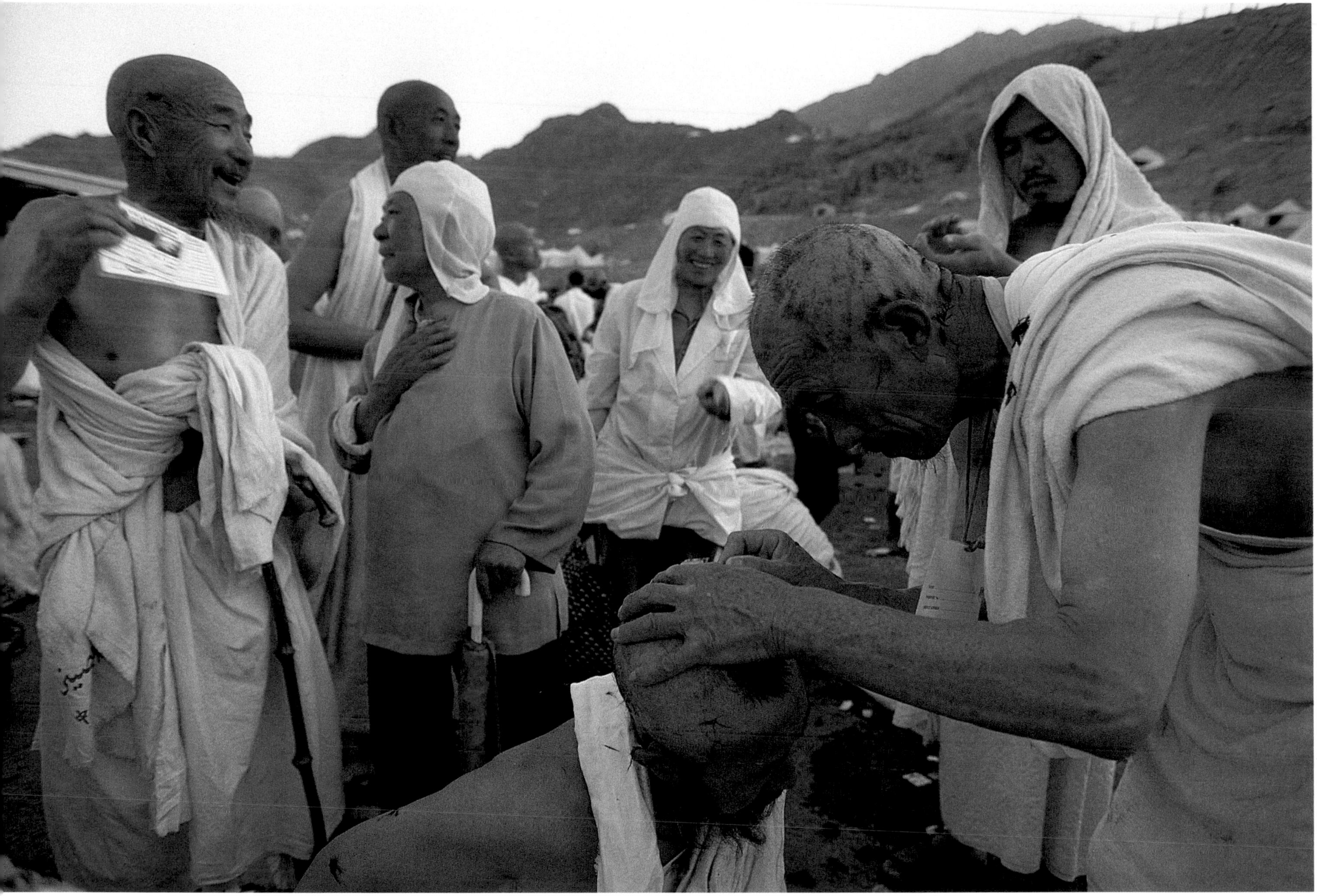

*(Above)*
It is traditional for people to cut off hair after the rite of the casting of stones. Women and some men cut only a lock or two of their hair while other men shave their heads completely as seen here.

*(Opposite)*
A pilgrim from Egypt after having shaved his head. After this ceremony pilgrims often look at each other and laugh at their sudden change of appearance.

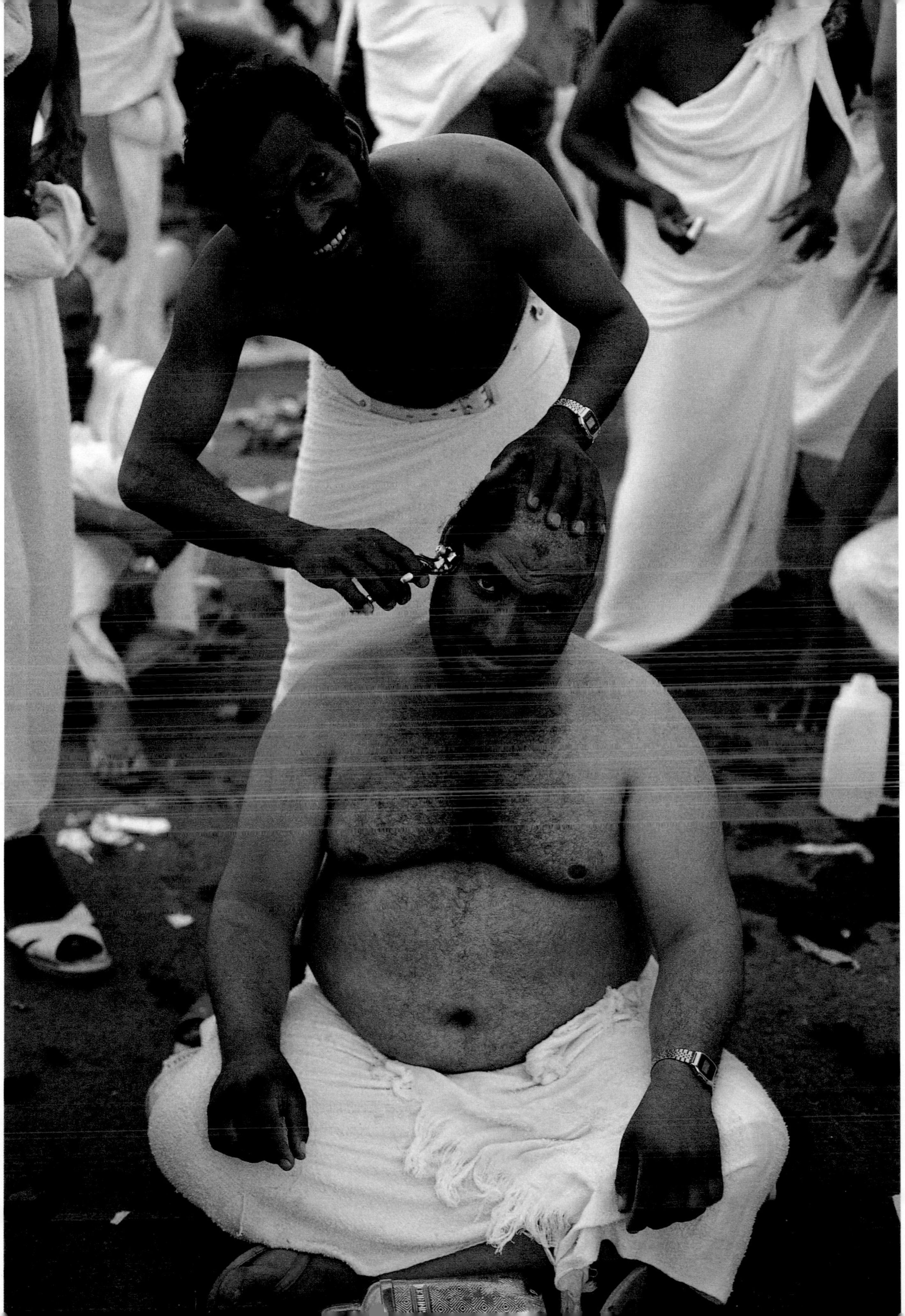

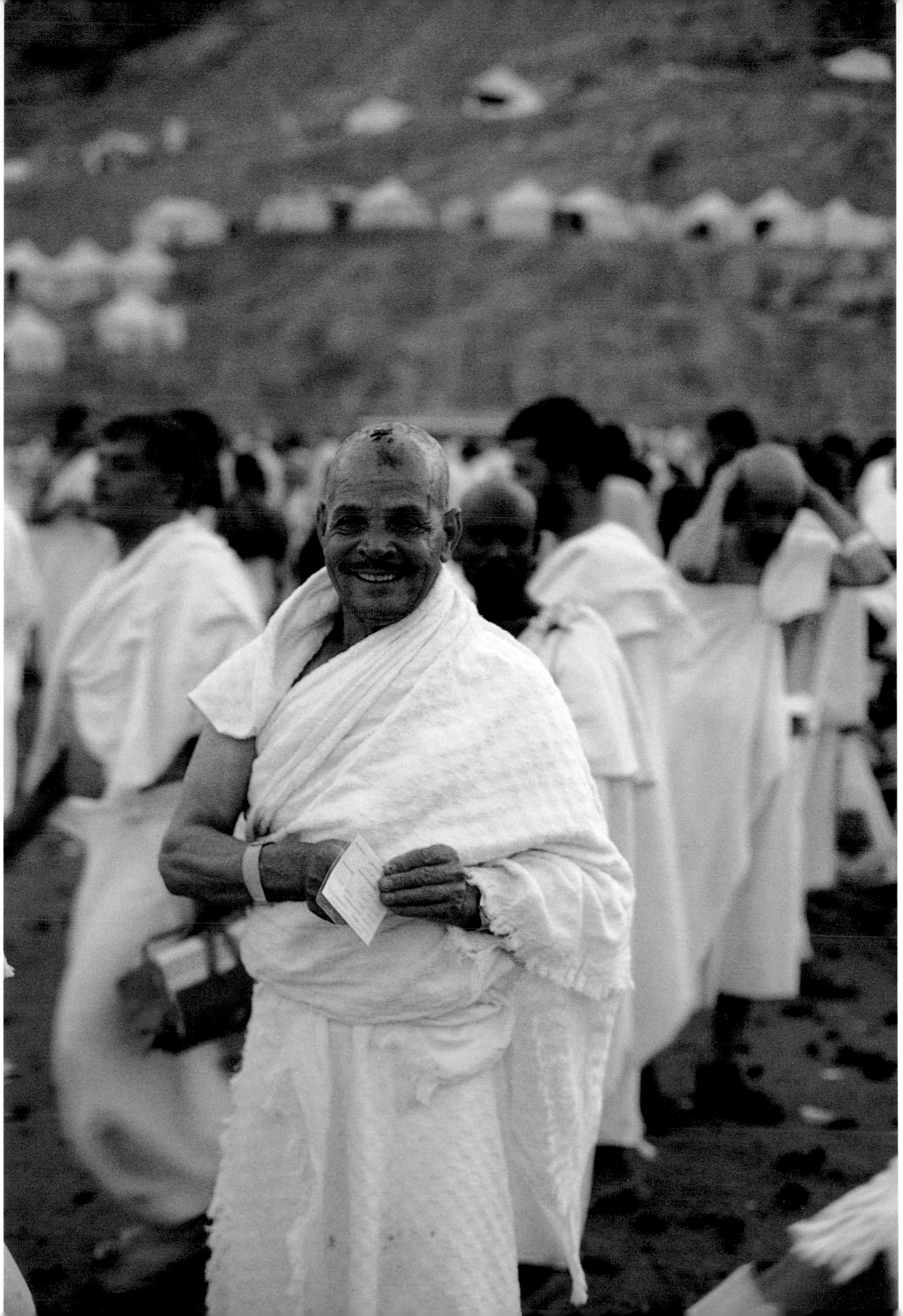

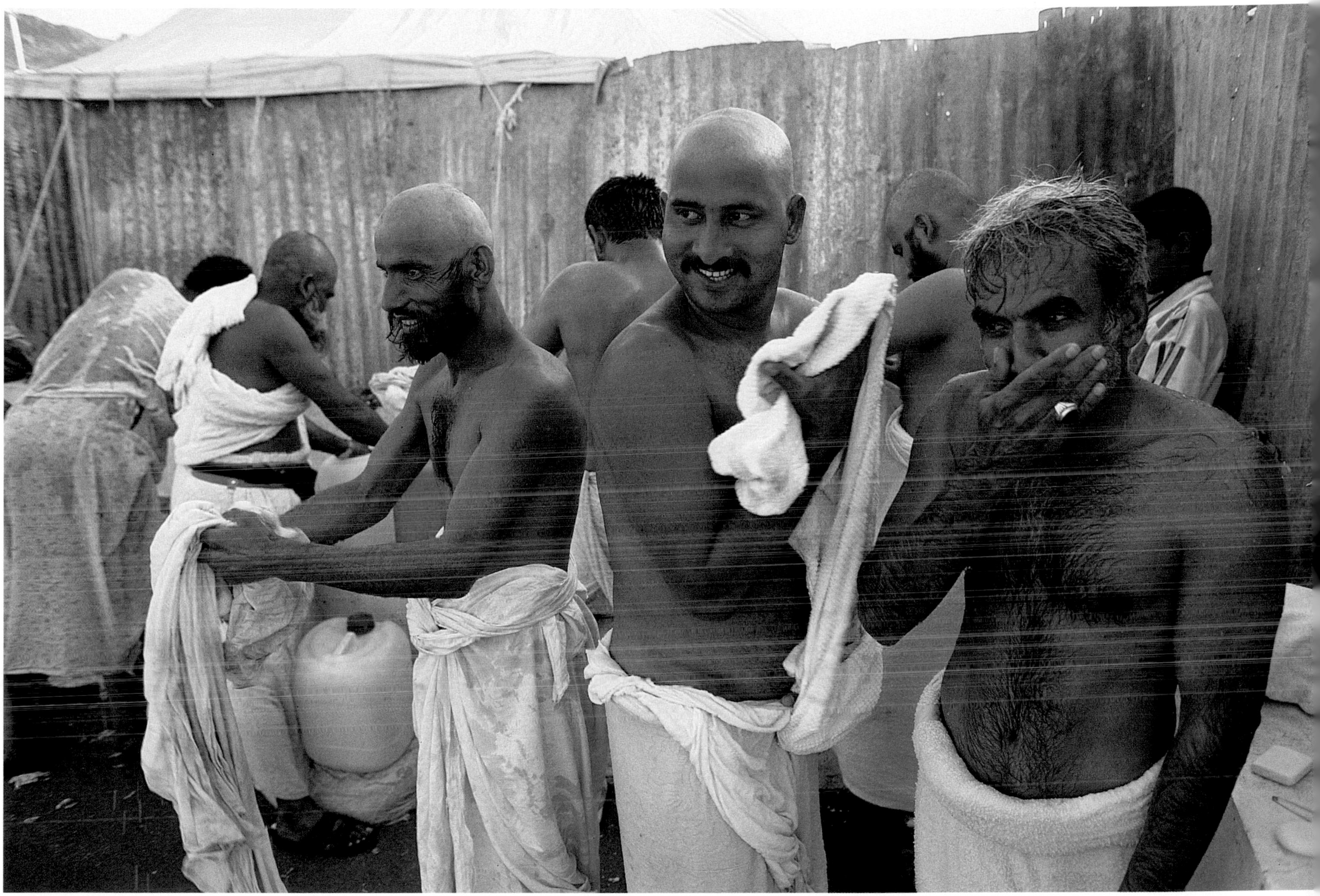

*(Opposite)*
A pilgrim with his head bleeding. This site is filled with an air of happiness in having completed successfully the pilgrimage which was the greatest wish of each pilgrim. After this event people take off their *iḥrām*, which is usually put away as their shroud, and return to their ordinary attire.

*(Above)*
Washroom and toilet facilities are provided along the way for the two million people who participated in the annual pilgrimage. Cold water and cold drinks are distributed free of charge by various Islamic charitable and philanthropic organizations.

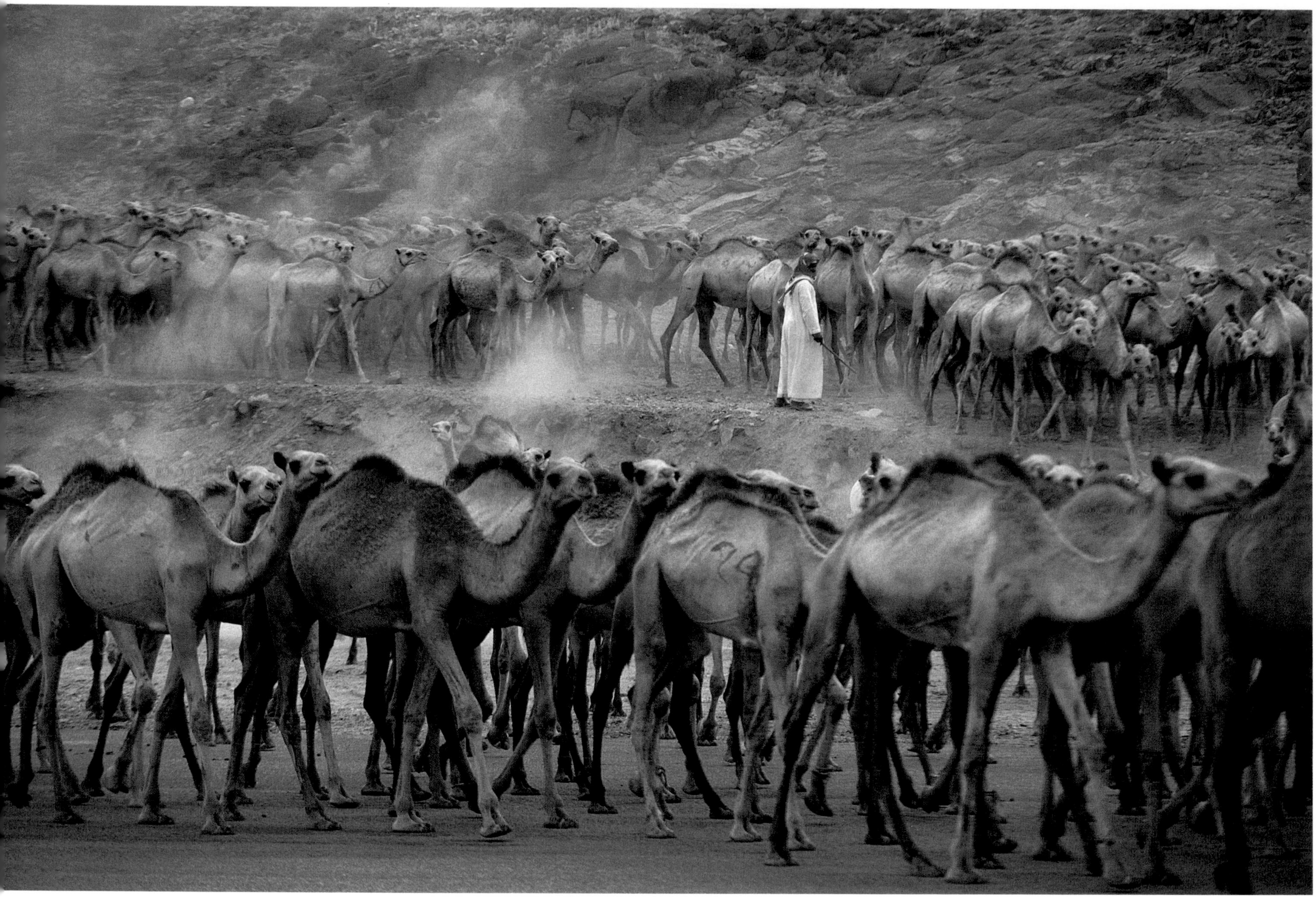

The end of the *ḥajj* is marked by the sacrifice of an animal in celebration of the sacrifice of the prophet Abraham (Ibrāhām). As one observes, a group of camels are being brought for sacrifice. The celebration at the end of the pilgrimage is called *ʿĪd al-aḍḥā* and it lasts four days during which those who had made the *ḥajj* before often also perform the sacrifice of an animal in their home town, the meat then being given to the poor.

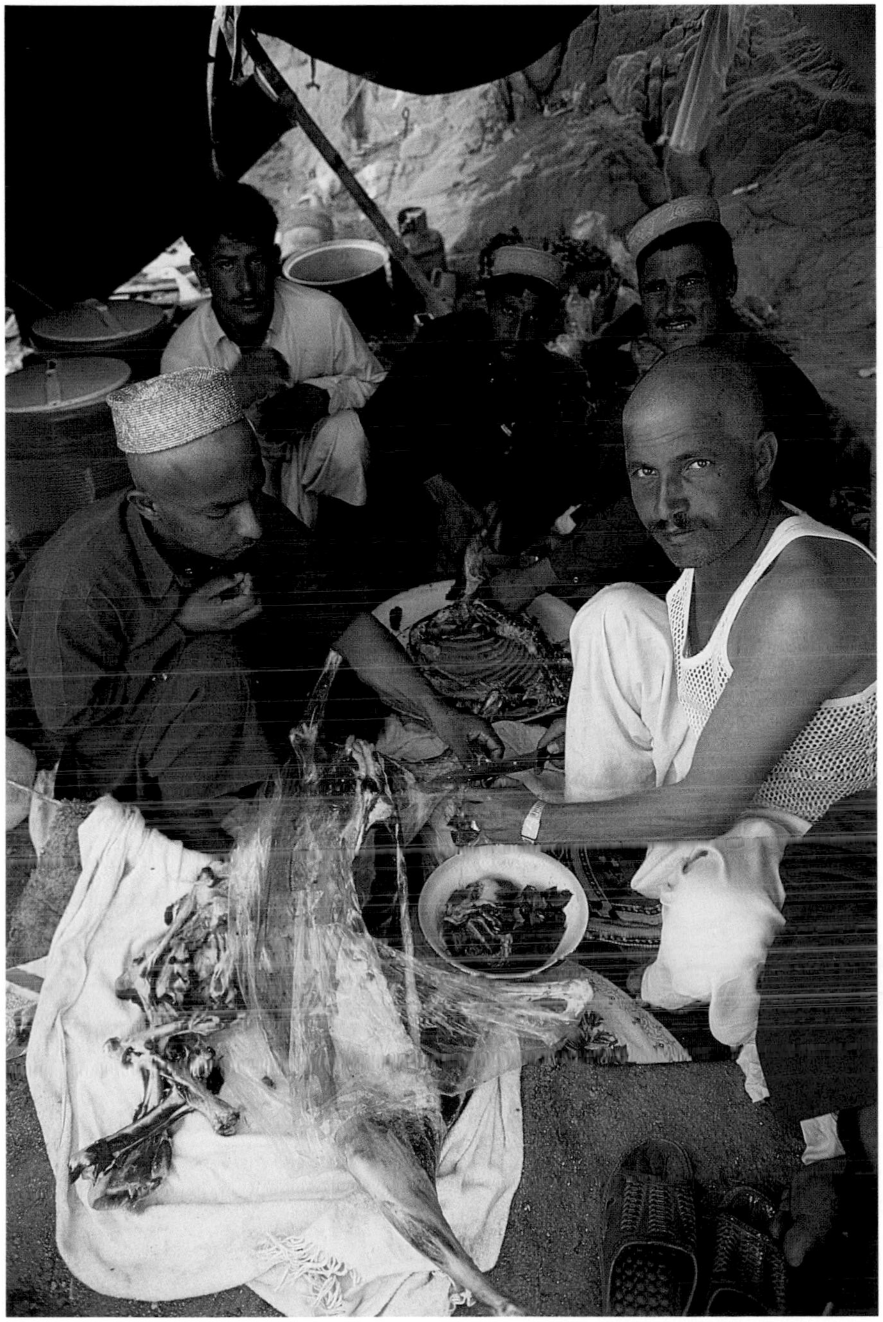

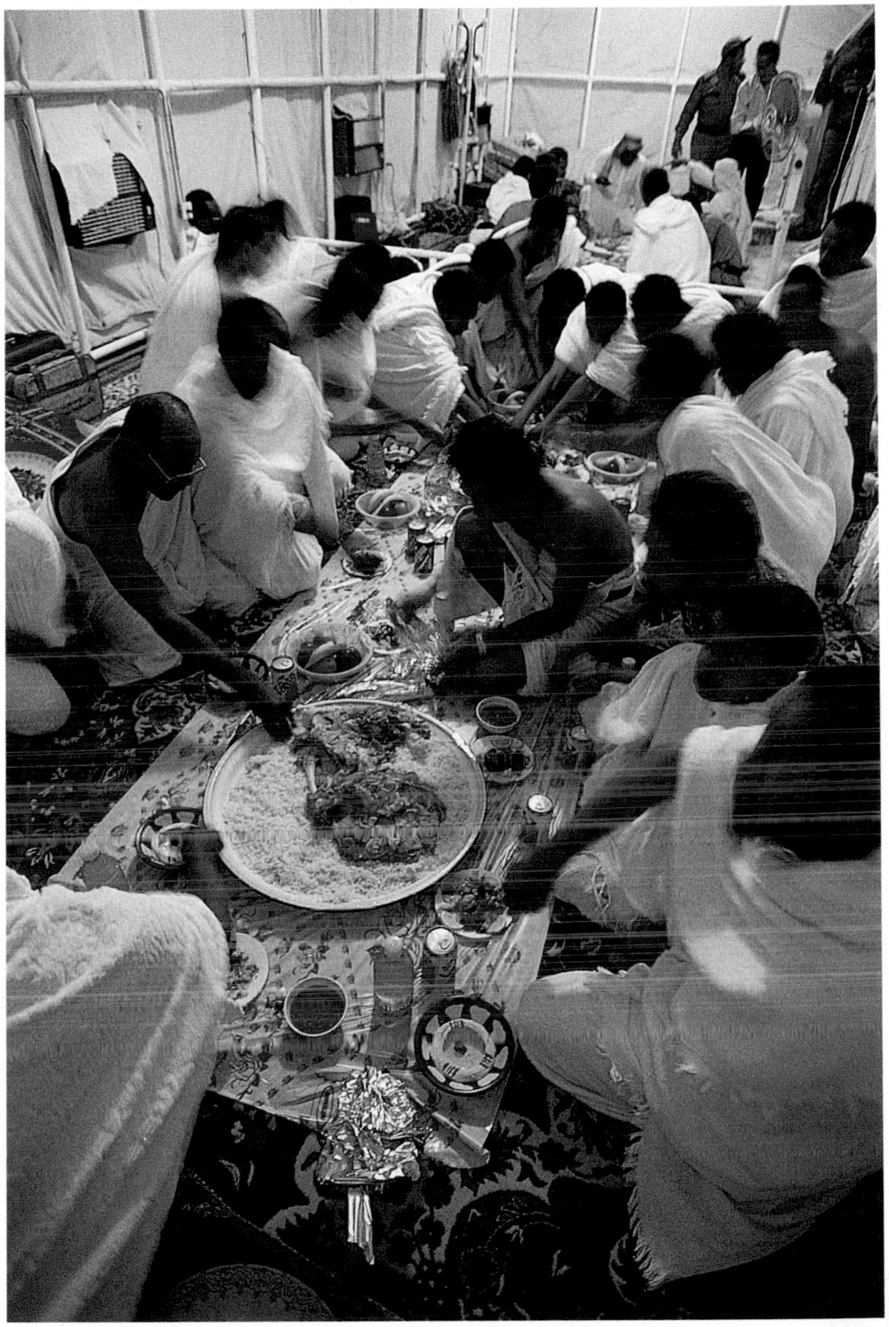

*(right)*
Pilgrims used to slaughter animals for the sacrifice themselves, but now it is mostly carried out in the slaughter-houses in Muzdalifah with the exception of a few pilgrims who do it themselves. The meat is distributed to the pilgrims. This photograph shows the evening meal on the eighth day of the month of pilgrimage.

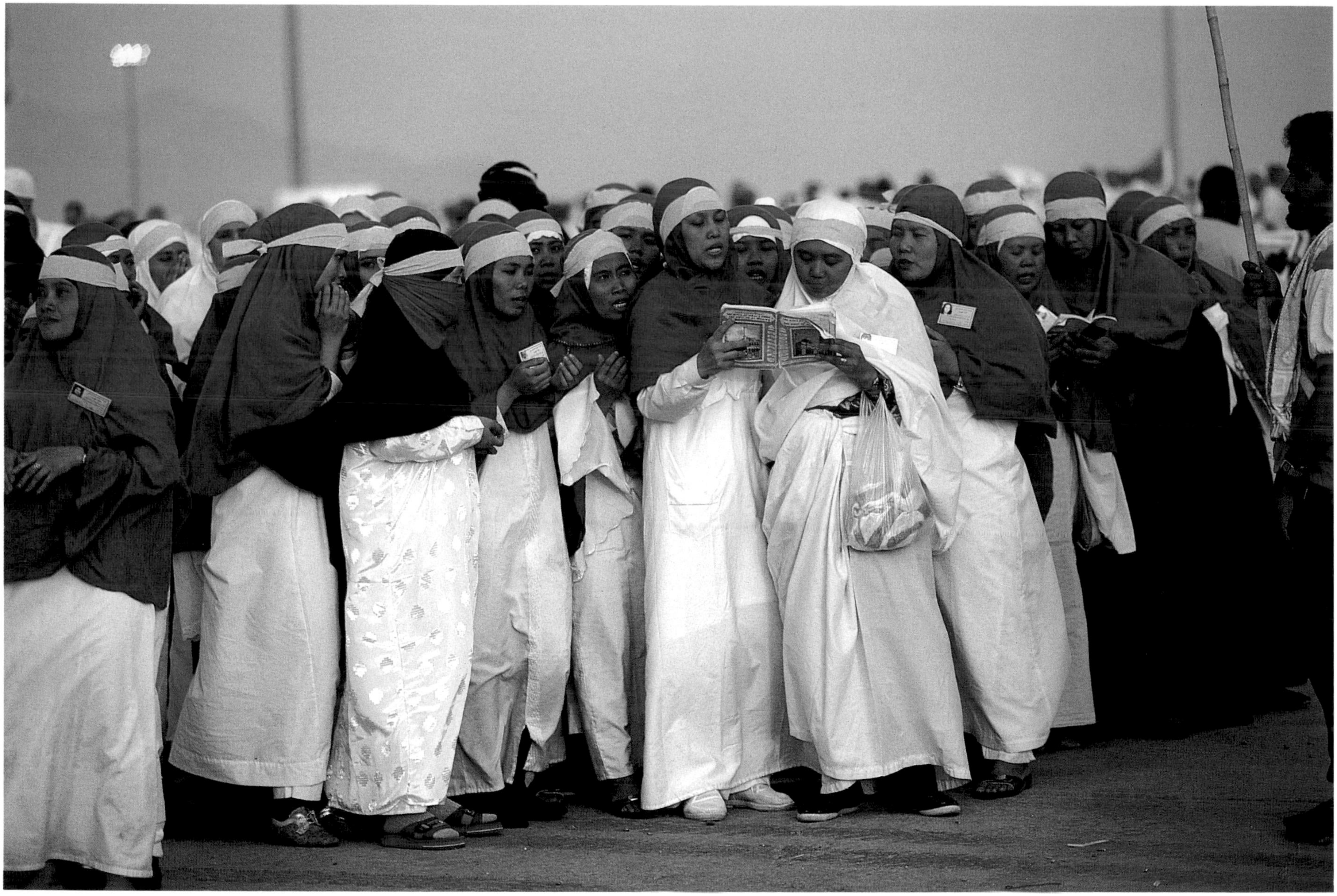

A group of pilgrims from Indonesia reciting prayers after the rite of casting of stones. All women, even those who hide their faces behind a veil in their own country, perform the pilgrimage with their faces revealed and only their hair covered.

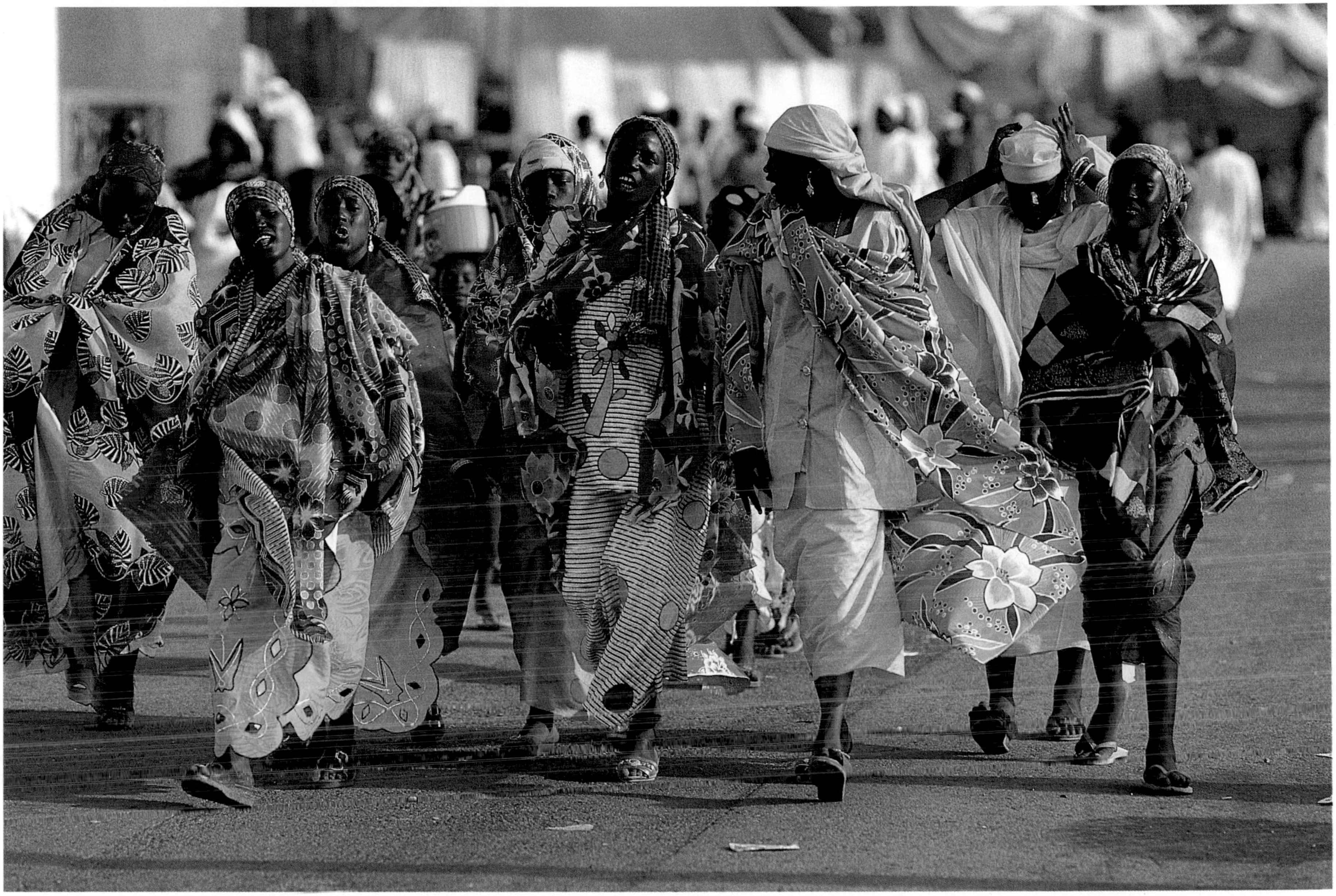

Men and women both wear their best clothing for the ʿĪd al-aḍḥā, the women usually dressing in black or white. But there is much diversity in traditional Islamic dress as the colorful habit of this group of African women reveals.

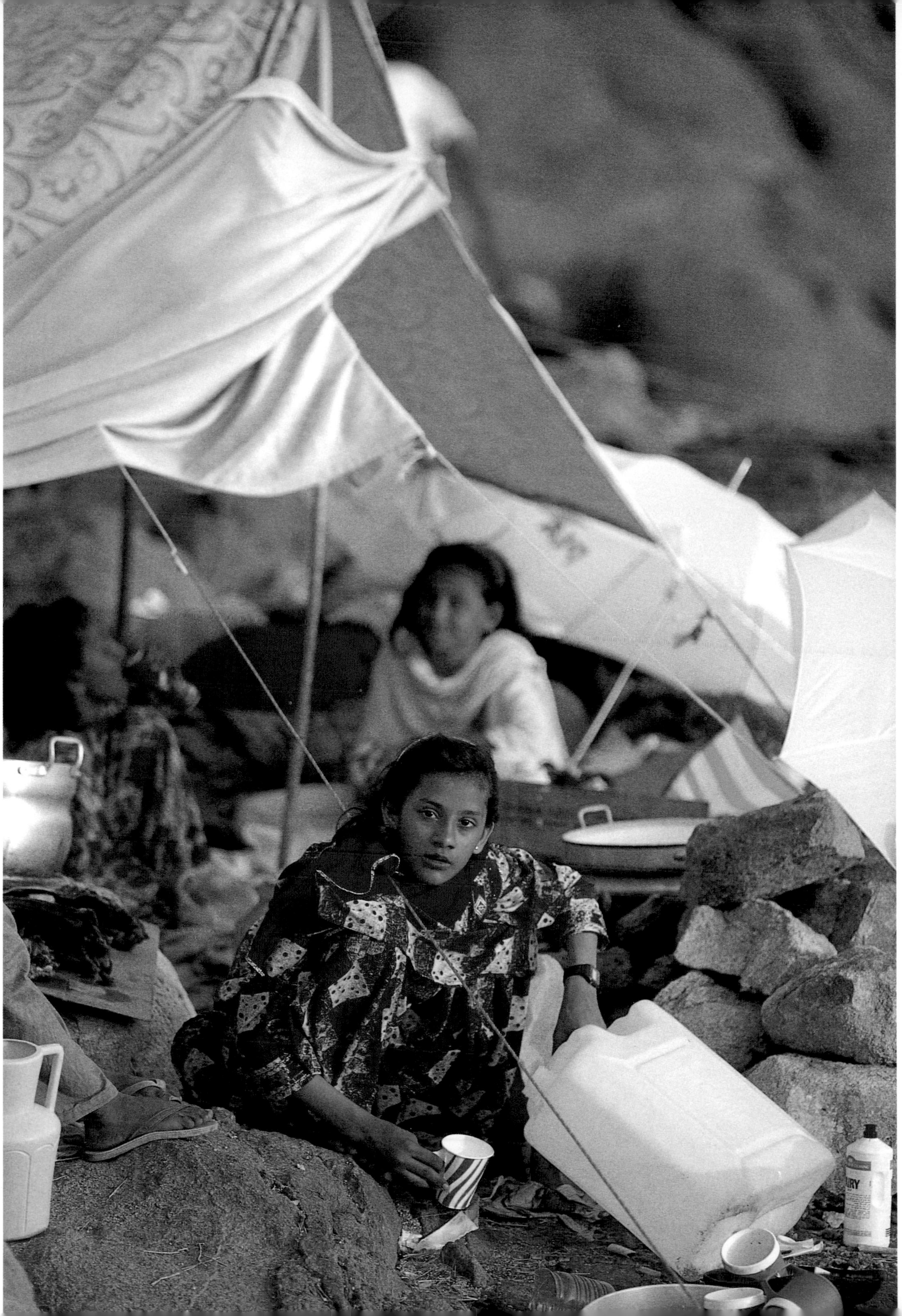

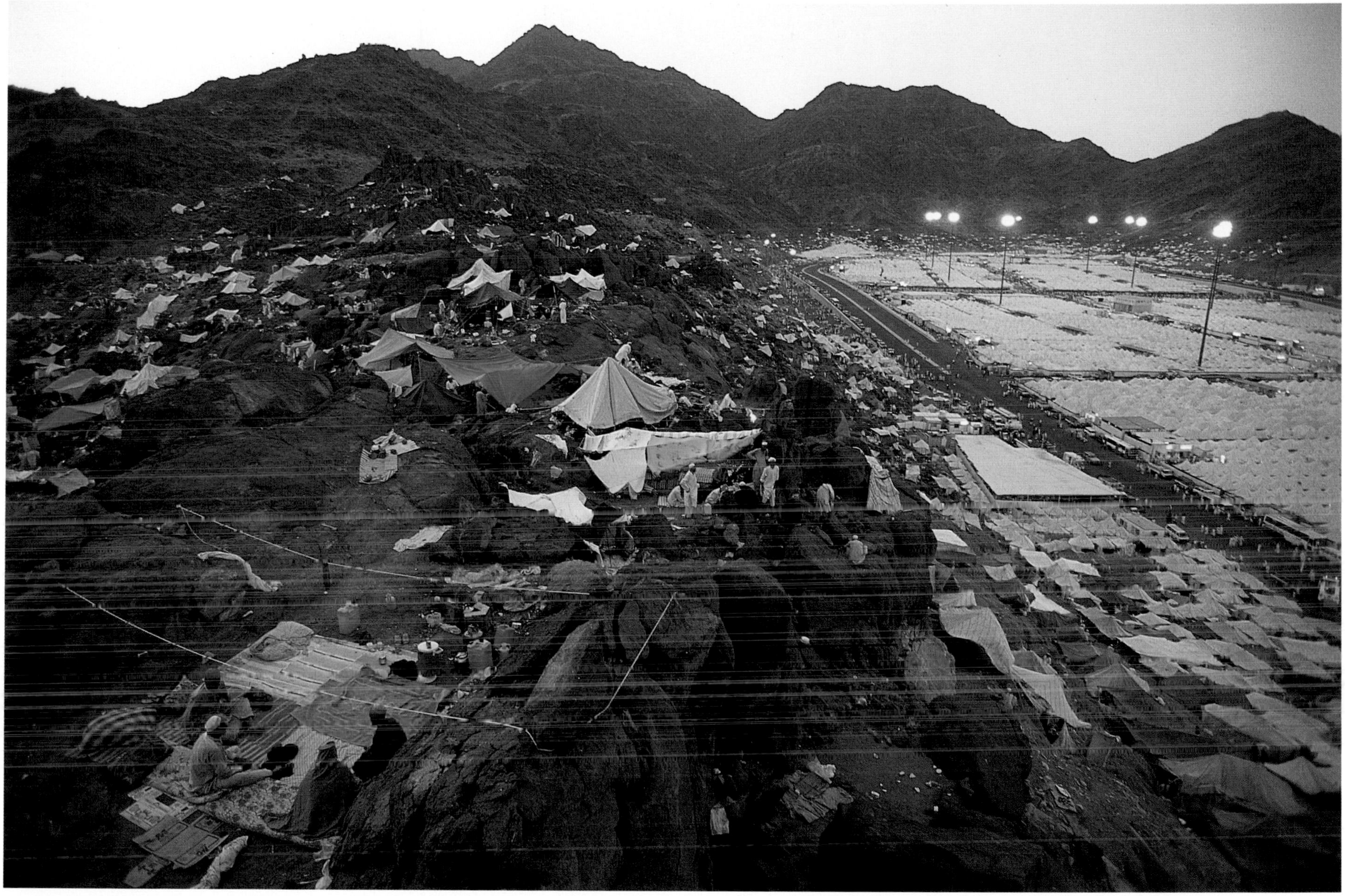

*(Opposite)*
Those who pitch tents on hilltops or surroundings are usually foreign workers in Saudi Arabia who often make the pilgrimage individually. There are some five million such workers and many among them perform the annual pilgrimage every year.

*(Above)*
According to government statistics, in 1996 some 1,080,000 pilgrims from outside of Saudi Arabia made the *ḥajj*. This figure was lower than other years because of the occurrence of contagious diseases in West Africa. With pilgrims from within Saudi Arabia the number of pilgrims for the year 1996 rose to over 1.6 million.

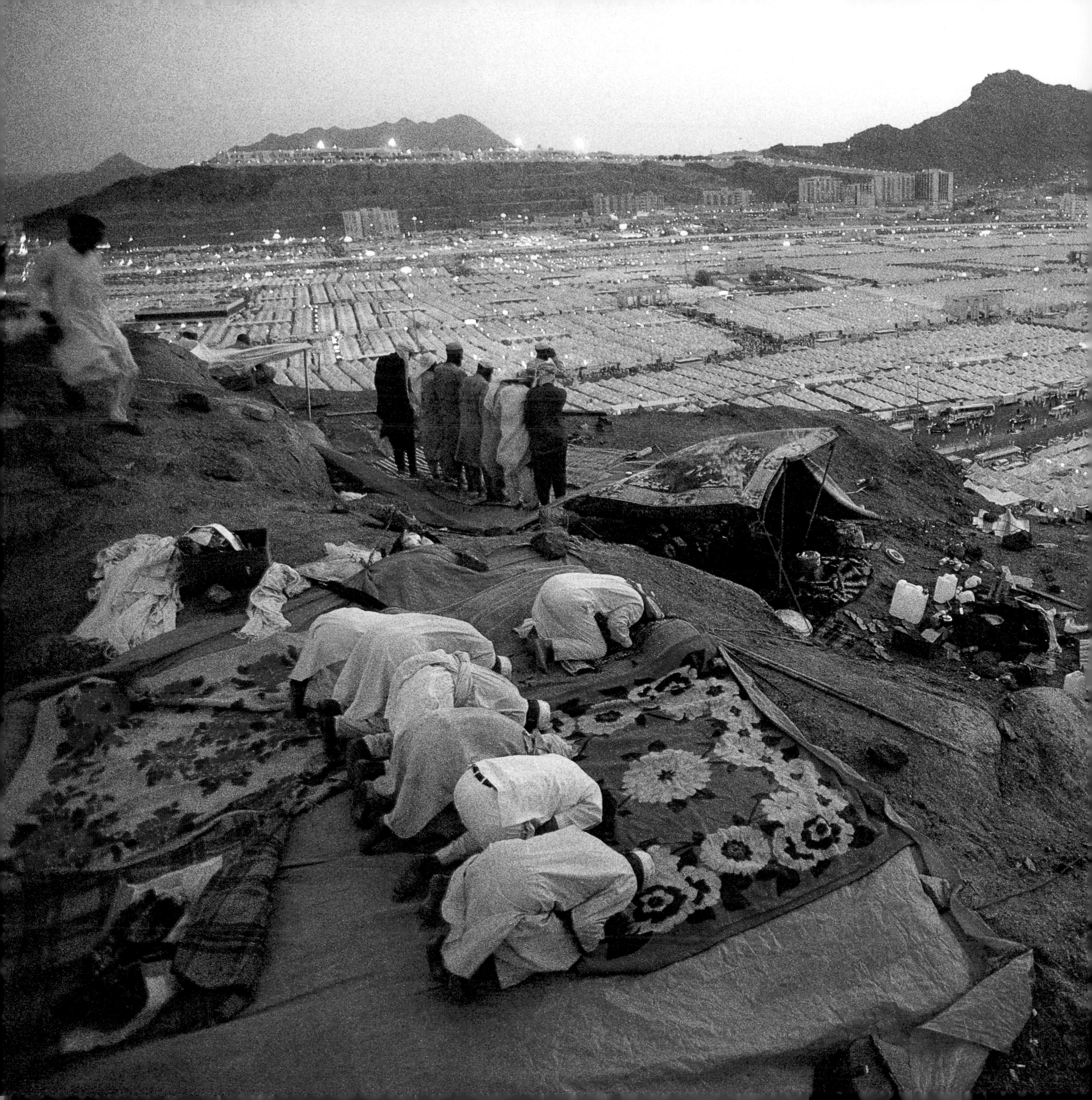

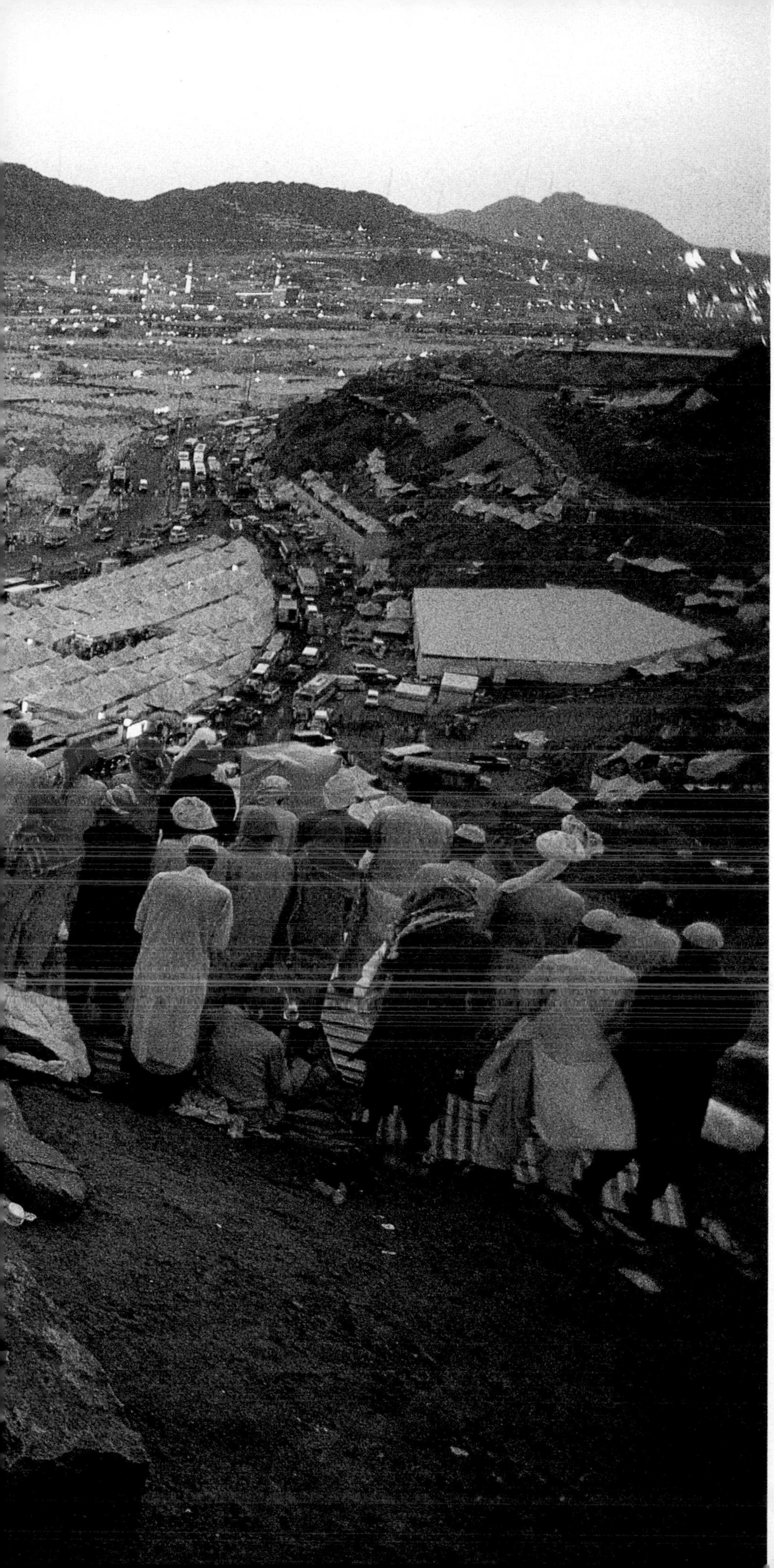

*(Opposite)*
Evening (*maghrib*) prayers at the camping area in Mina. Most pilgrims leave this area and return to Mecca on the twelfth day but they do spend at least one night at Mina. This and other steps in the *ḥajj* follow the precedent established by the wonts (*sunnah*) of the Blessed Prophet who made the pilgrimage in 10/632.

*(Following pages)*
After the completion of the rites at Mina pilgrims return to Mecca for the farewell *ṭawāf* or circumambulation (*ṭawāf al-widā'*). Those who cannot enter the holy precinct perform the *ṭawāf* on the second floor of the surrounding mosque, in the basement or even outside the immense complex of the Grand Mosque.

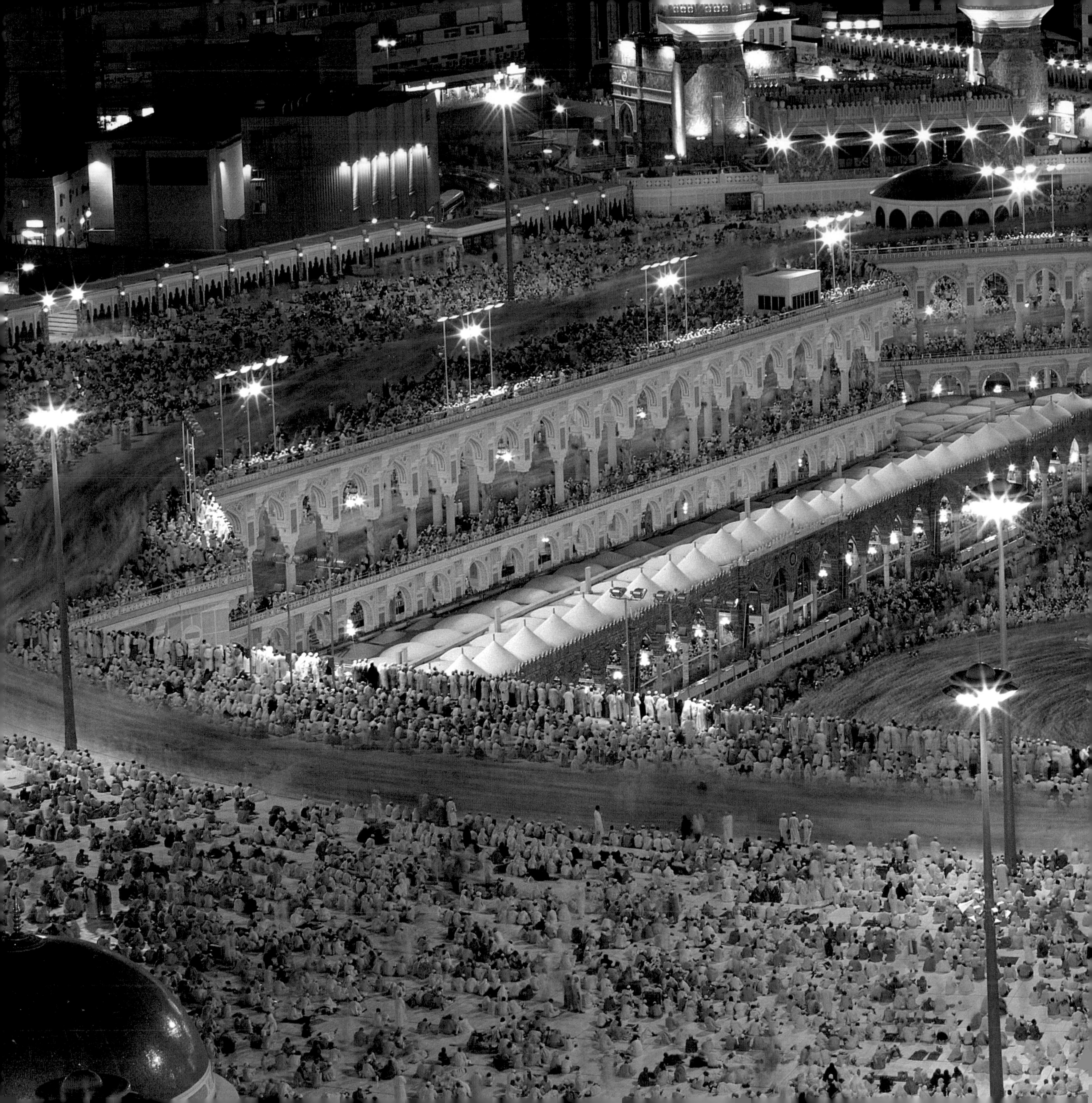

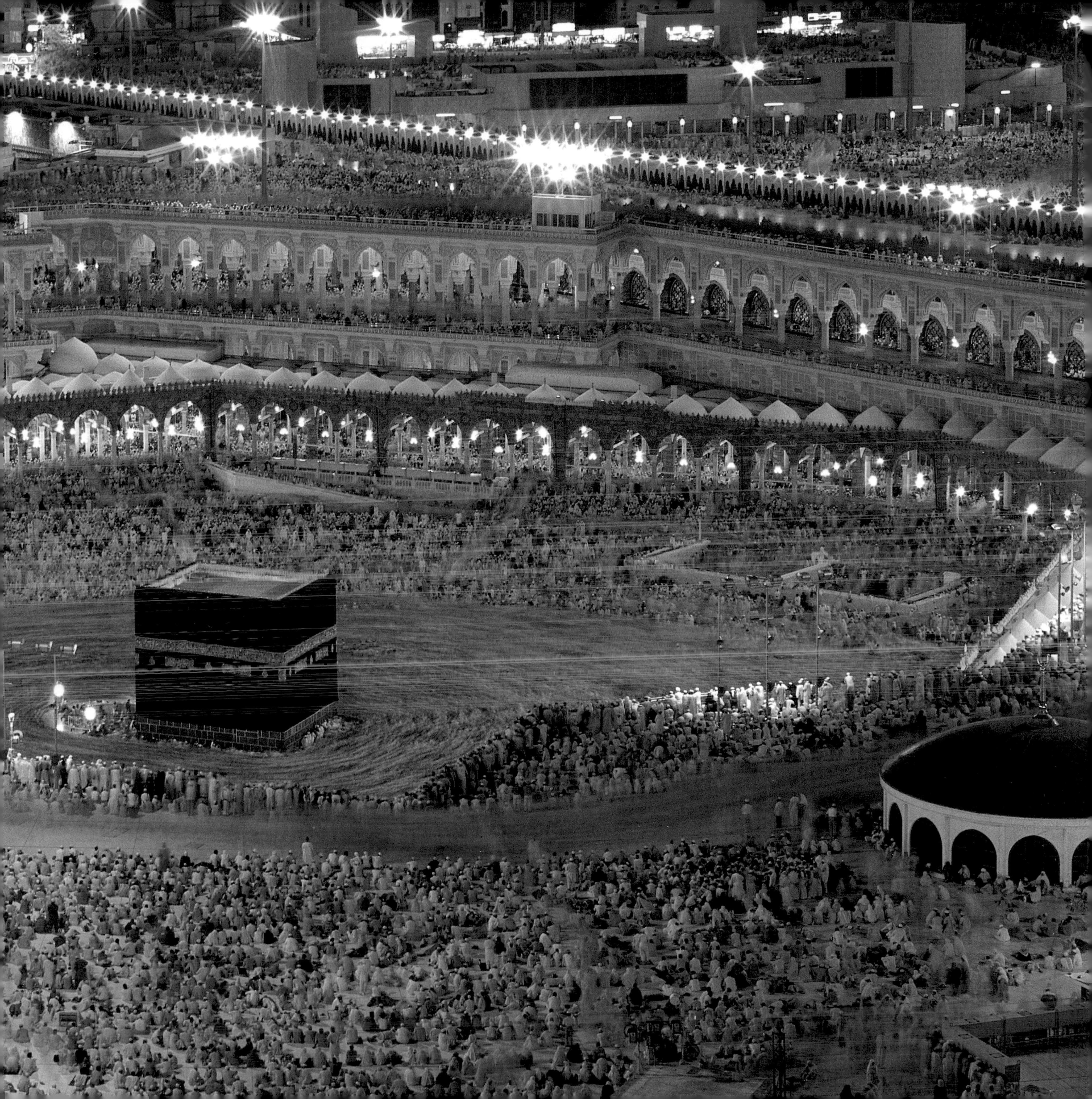

# *Medina*

It was in this miraculous oasis—gentle, hospitable and full of bounties, that the last years of the life of the Blessed Prophet were spent, where the first Islamic community was established, where the Prophet died and where many of his companions and closest members of his family are buried. The earth of Medina is blessed by the fact that it contains the body of God's last chosen prophet, a blessedness that one feels while walking on its hallowed ground. No wonder that in days of old many a pious man would dismount from his horse a long way outside of the city and would walk the rest of the way in order to be respectful of the land that contains in its bosom the earthly remains of such a precious being. Even a generation ago Medina was like a vast garden with majestic palm trees which surrounded the houses and markets of the city giving an impression of plenitude and bounty. One might in fact say that whereas Mecca represents the reality of the Divine as the Absolute, Medina reflects His reality as the Infinite. There is a feminine quality to the city in the sense that it is not harsh but gentle. Even its people display the trait of gentleness reflecting the character of the Prophet about whom the Noble Qur'ān has said, "O thou art of a tremendous character."

After all, this is the abode of the Prophet dominated by his mausoleum and mosque. His *barakah* is felt everywhere throughout the confines of the town. The heart yearns to visit Medina precisely because this is the city of the Prophet, its mosque the model of all mosques, its traditions the source of so many Islamic practices. To love God one must love His Prophet. To love Mecca also requires loving Medina. The two cities in fact form a single sacred reality for the vast majority of Muslims who live outside of their vicinity, a reality at once blessed and luminous. Yes, there is indeed something of the Muḥammadan Light, the light associated with the inner reality of the Blessed Prophet that still emanates in his city and bestows upon Medina a special *barakah*, a sweet presence which is associated with the being whom it welcomed to its fold, the being who is interred in its earth and who made Medina the capital of a vast new order.

Although that political order no longer exists as a unity, this first capital of the Islamic world continues to be loved by all Muslims near and far. Today as in days of old all the faithful pray for the opportunity to be able to experience the Muḥammadan *barakah* which is still so palpable within the confines of this "illuminated city", still the capital of the Blessed Prophet's dominion.

Seyyed Hossein Nasr

The tomb of the Blessed Prophet Muḥammad—may peace and blessings be upon him—in Medina. The green-colored dome and the *Kaʿbah* are the two most recognizable symbols of the religion of Islam.

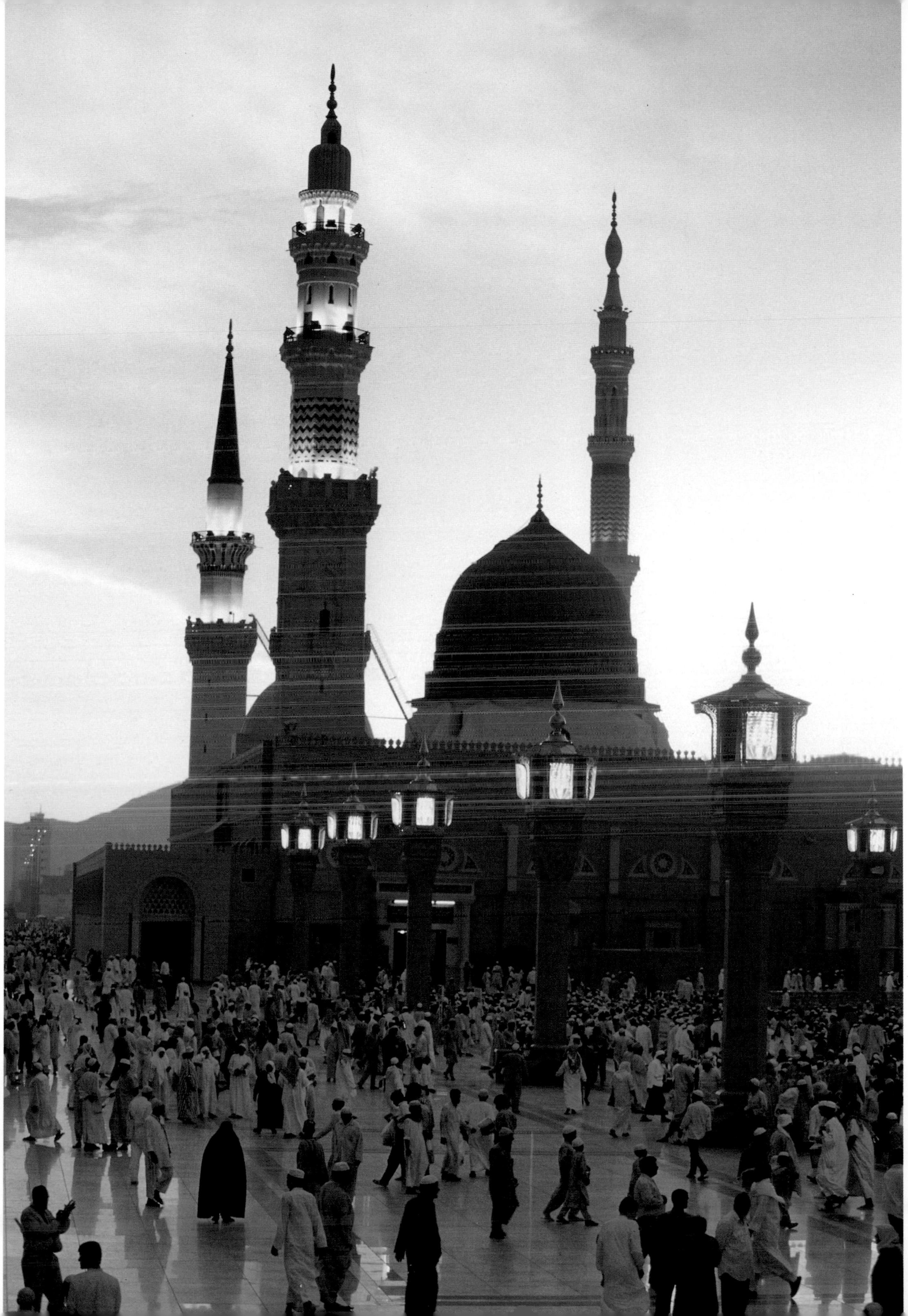

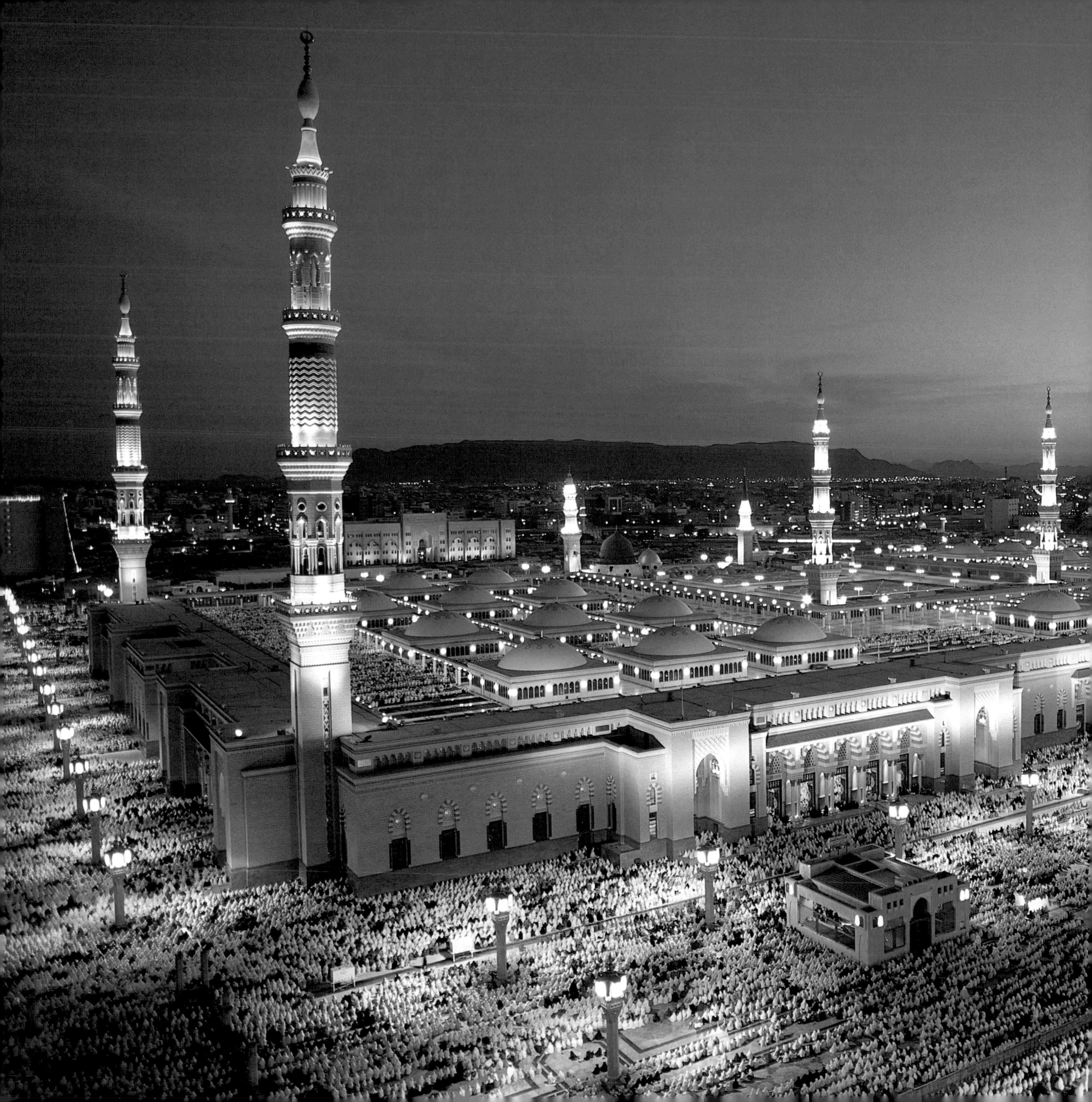

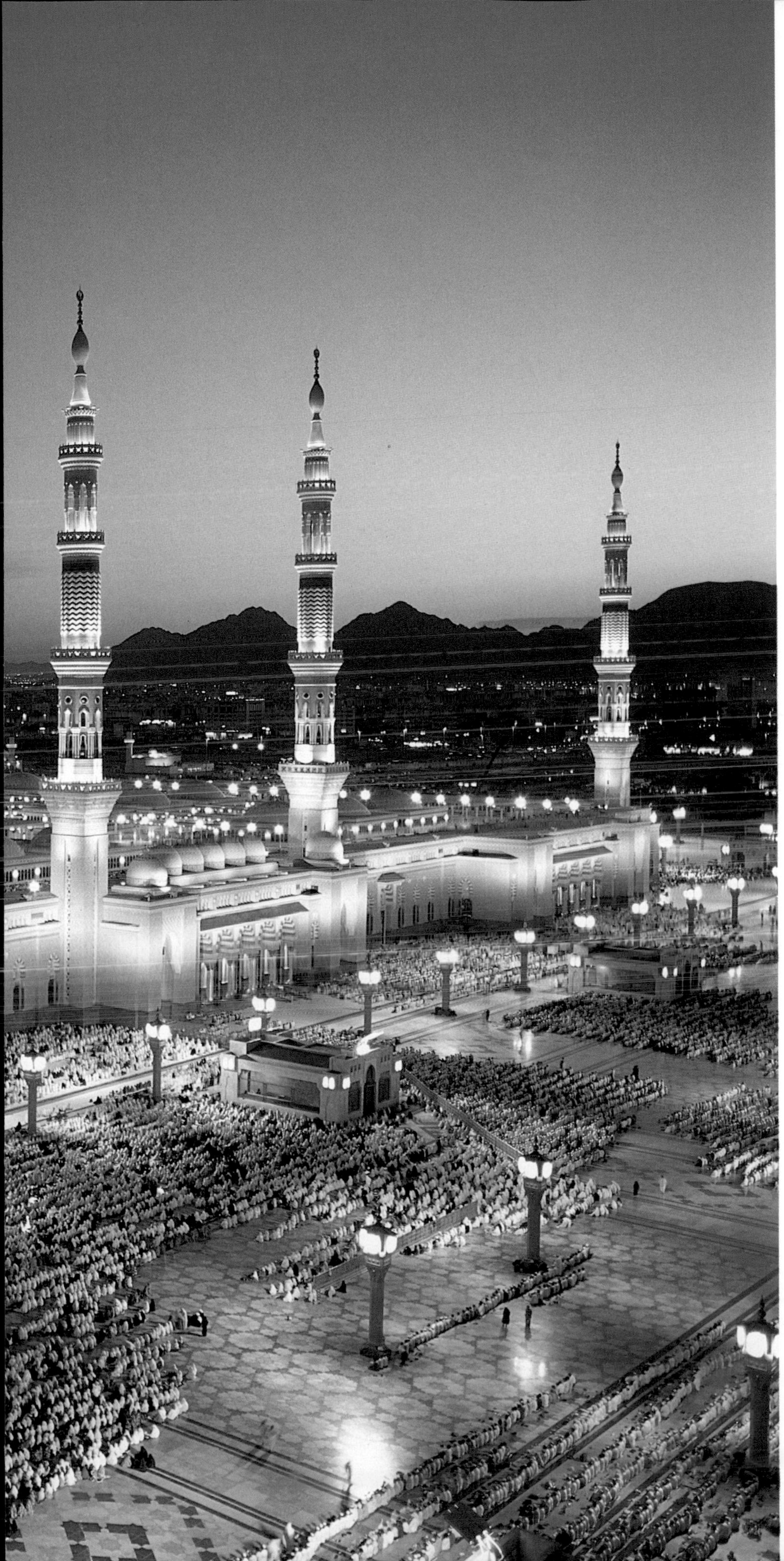

Evening prayer at the Mosque of the Prophet (*masjid al-nabī*). During the twenty days preceding and following the annual *ḥajj* nearly all the two million pilgrims visit Medina as well but they are not all there at the same time as is the case with Mecca.

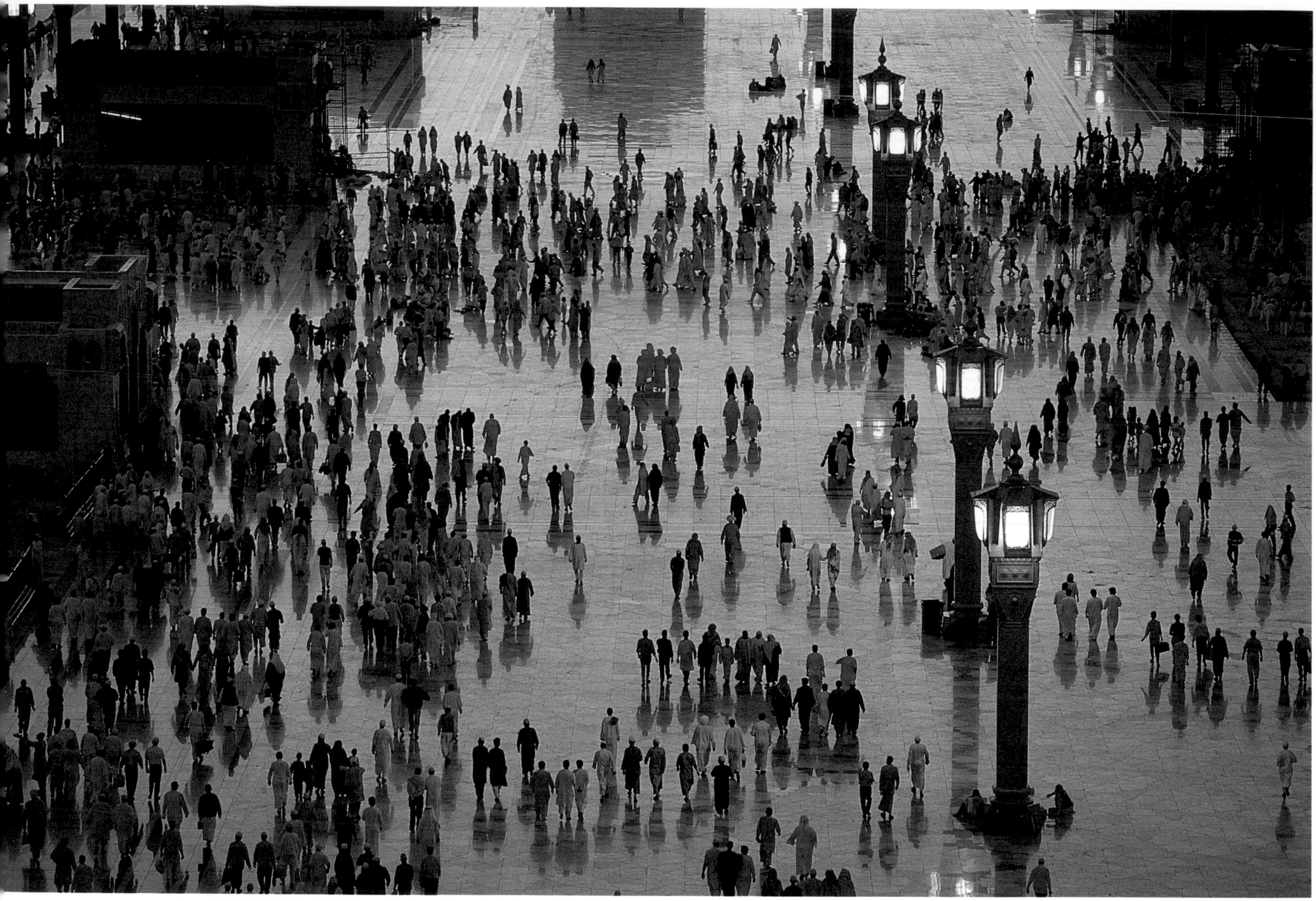

*(Above)*
Pilgrims heading for the evening (*maghrib*) prayers through the marble-floored complex of the Mosque of the Prophet. Usually the *maghrib* prayers are the most crowded.

*(Opposite)*
An enlargement of part of the inside of the Mosque of the Prophet belonging to the extension completed in 1995. The new parts of the Mosque have elaborate air-conditioning and a cooling water system to compensate for the extreme heat especially during the summer season.

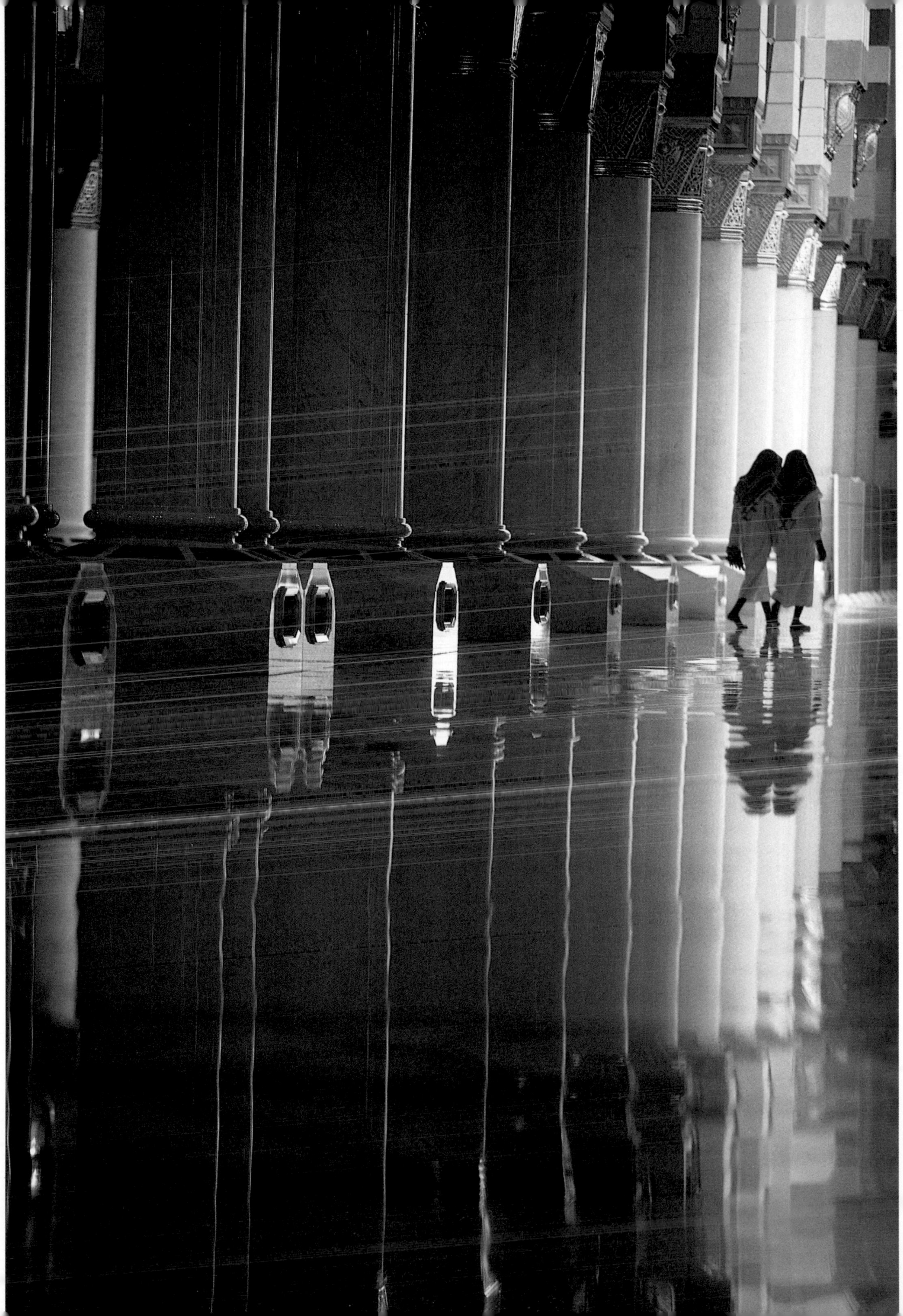

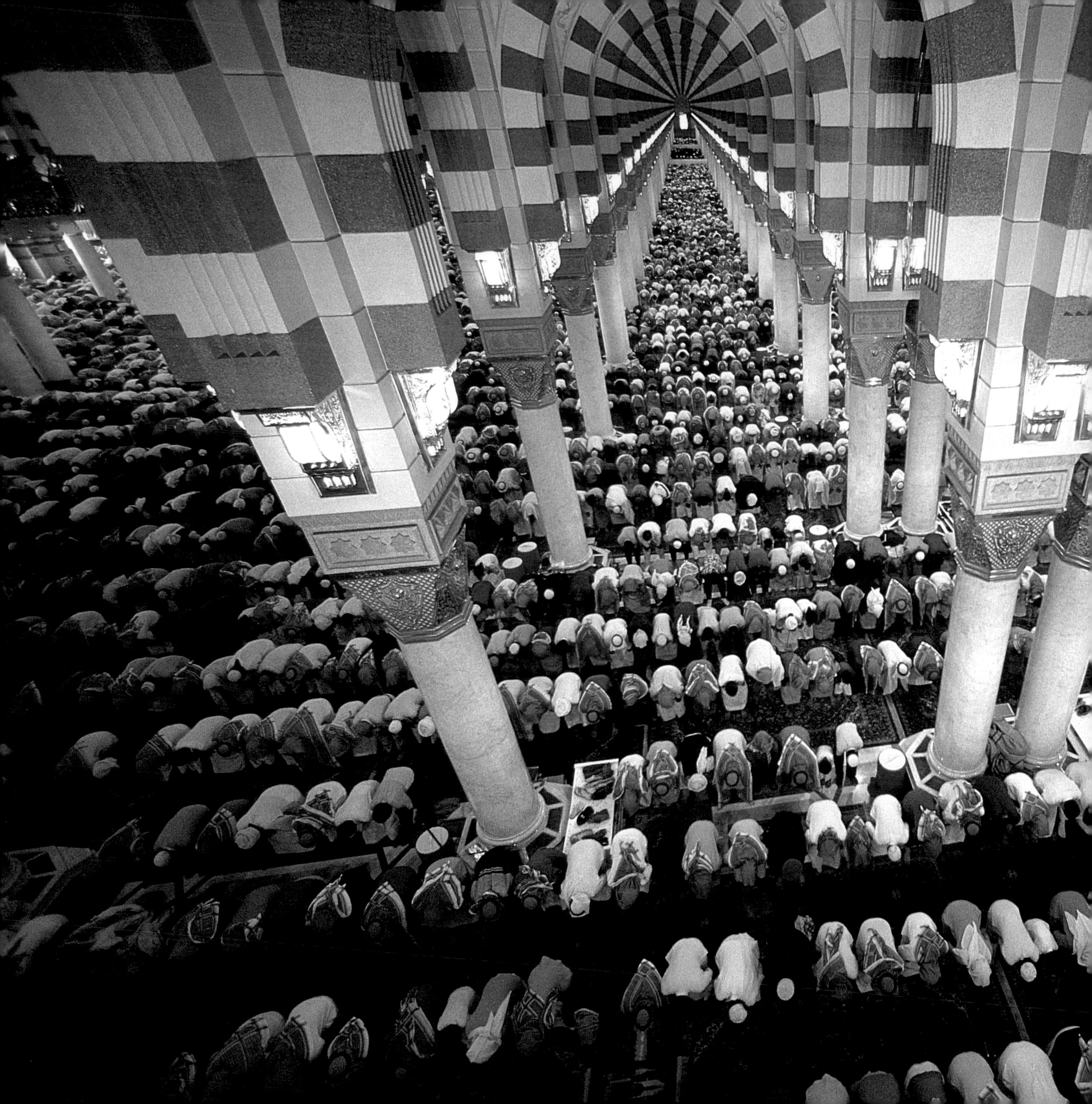

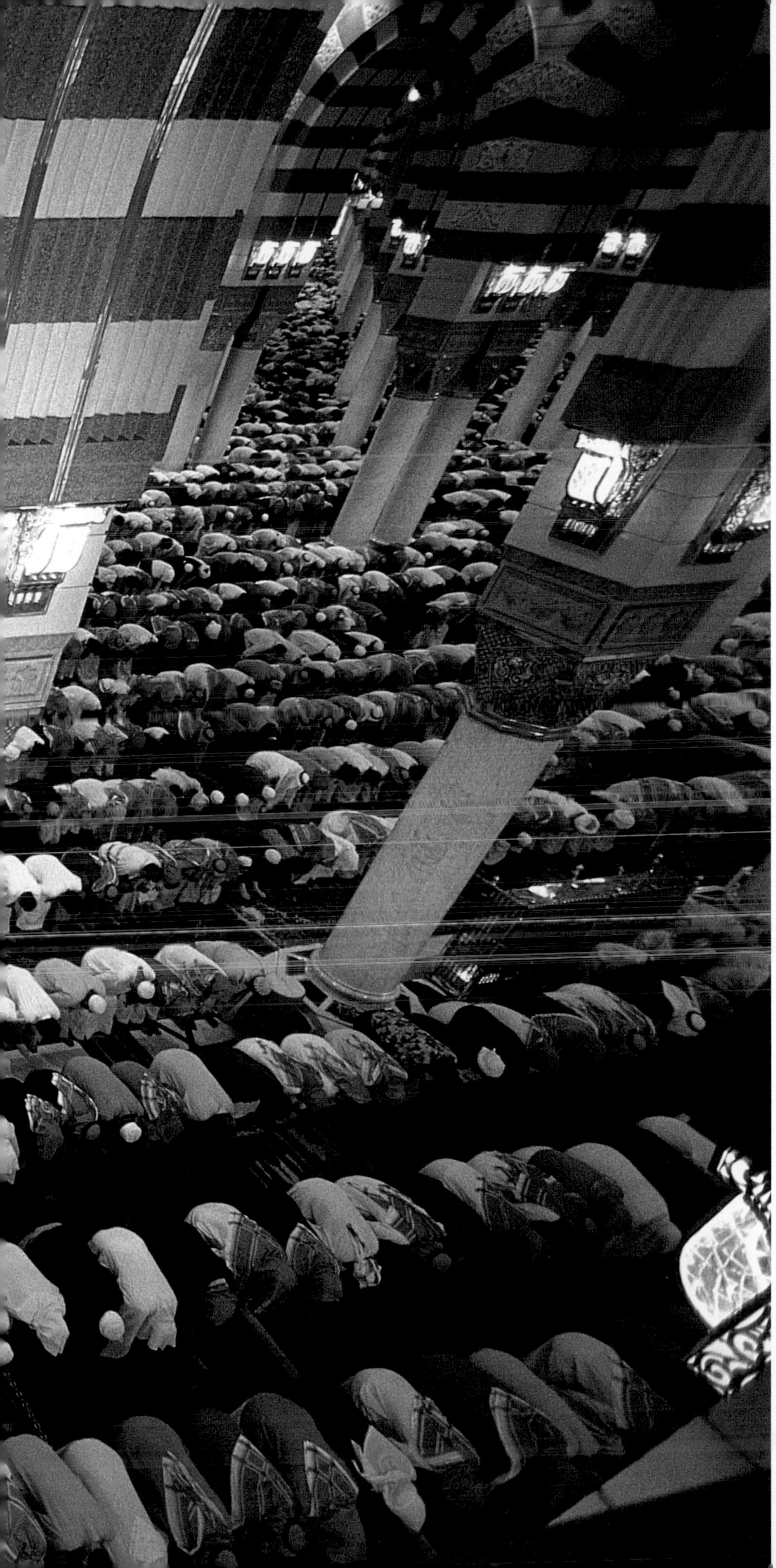

The Friday congregational prayer at the Mosque of the Prophet is always attended by the people of Medina as well as pilgrims. That is why the space holding 190,000 worshippers invariably becomes full and many listen to the sermon (*khuṭbah*), which forms part of the Friday prayers, outside under the heat of the sun.

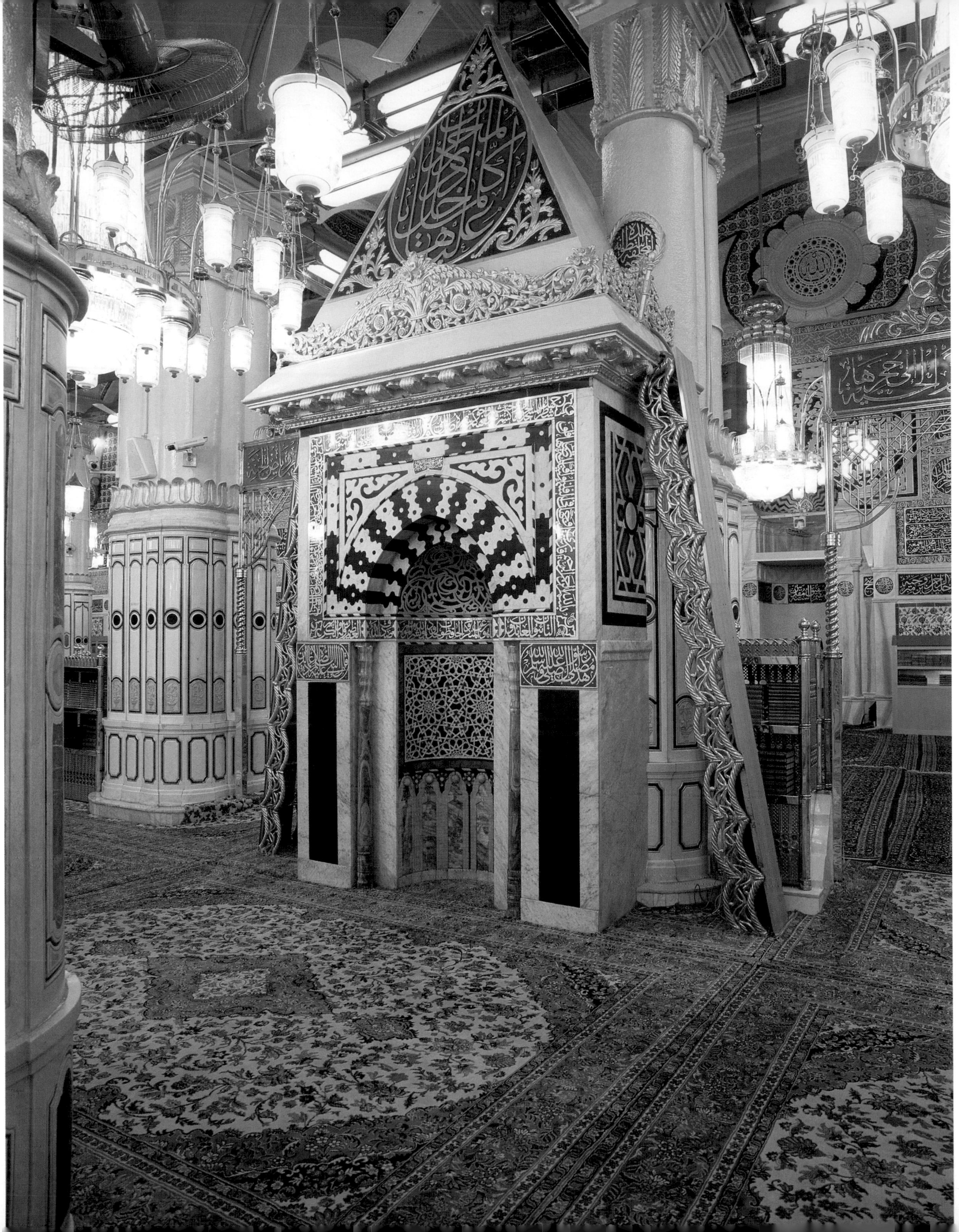

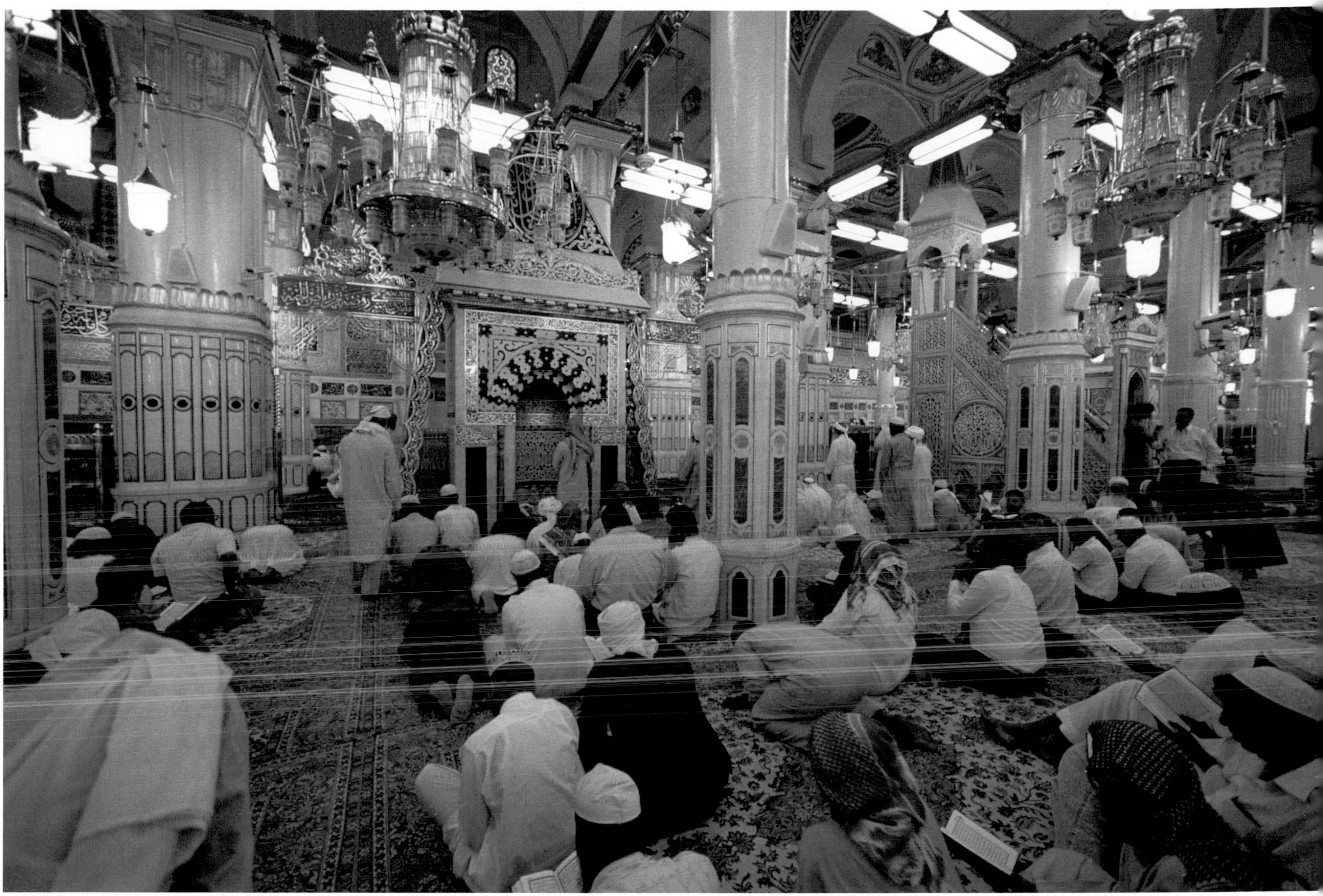

*(Opposite)*
The *miḥrāb* or prayer-niche built in the direction of Mecca before which the Blessed Prophet himself prayed, this mosque being the one built by the Prophet adjacent to his dwelling when he first migrated from Mecca to Medina.

*(Above)*
The Mosque of the Prophet adjacent to his tomb is, along with the *Kaᶜbah*, the most sacred place for Muslims.

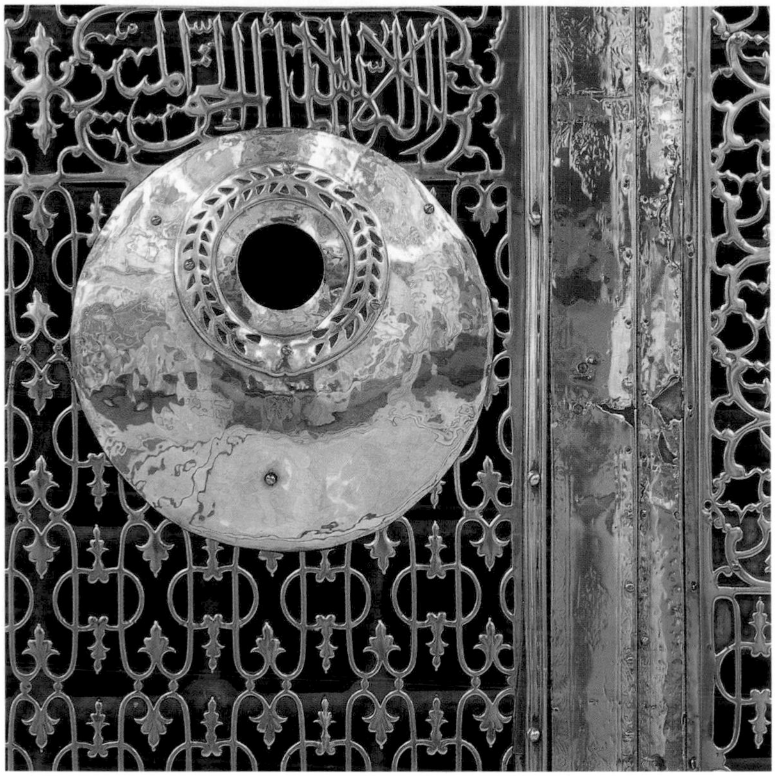

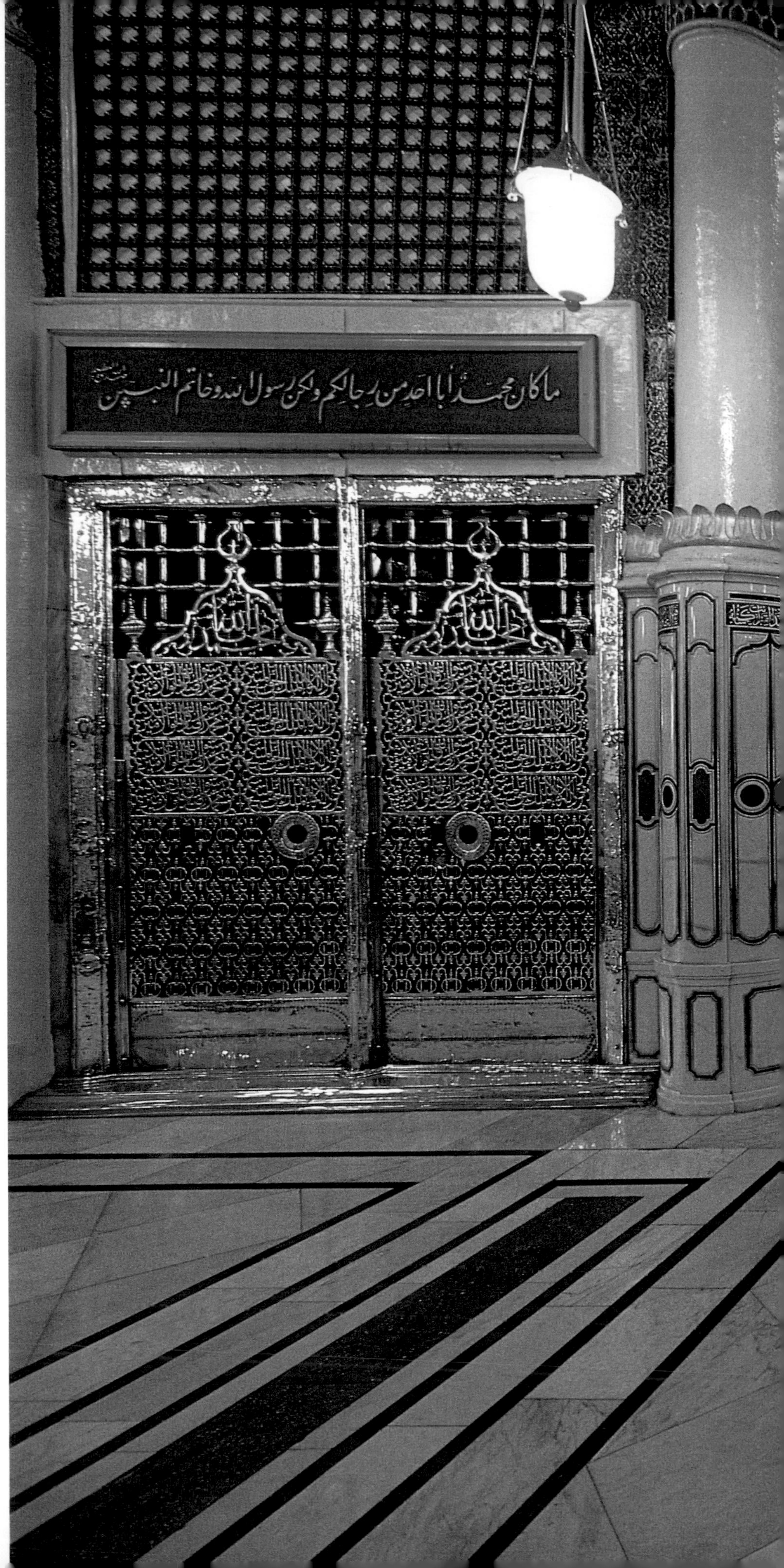


*(Above)*
This metal plaque indicates the direction of the head of the Blessed Prophet in his tomb that lies behind the wall.

*(Opposite)*
This photograph taken with special permission at midnight when the Mosque was closed shows the southern wall of the room (known as the "Blessed Room" by Muslims) in which the Prophet is buried with Abū Bakr and ʿUmar, the first two caliphs, beside him.

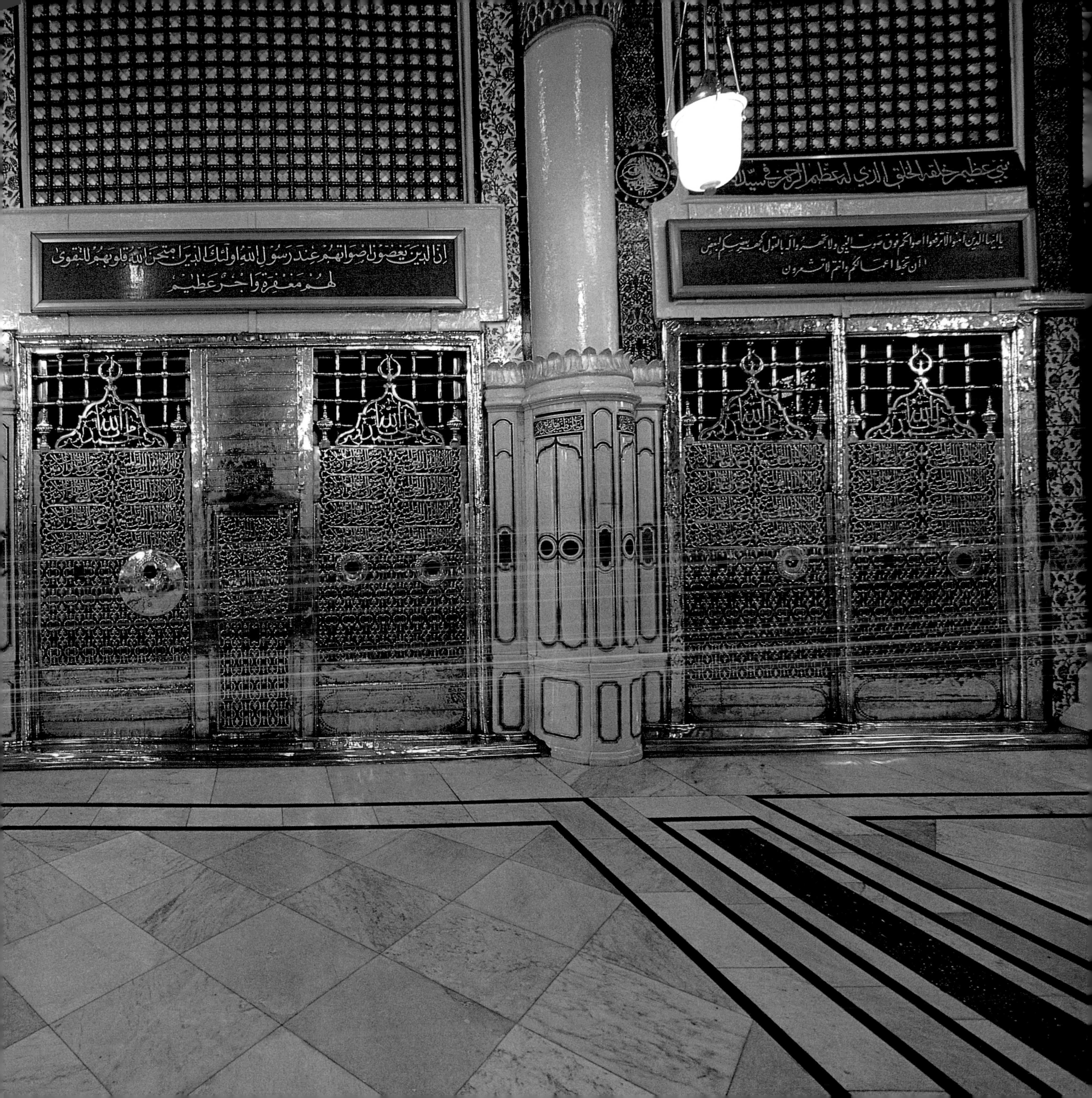
ان الذين يغضون اصواتهم عند رسول الله اولئك الذين امتحن الله قلوبهم للتقوى
لهم مغفرة واجر عظيم
يا ايها الذين امنوا لا ترفعوا اصواتكم فوق صوت النبي ولا تجهروا له بالقول كجهر بعضكم لبعض
ان تحبط اعمالكم وانتم لا تشعرون

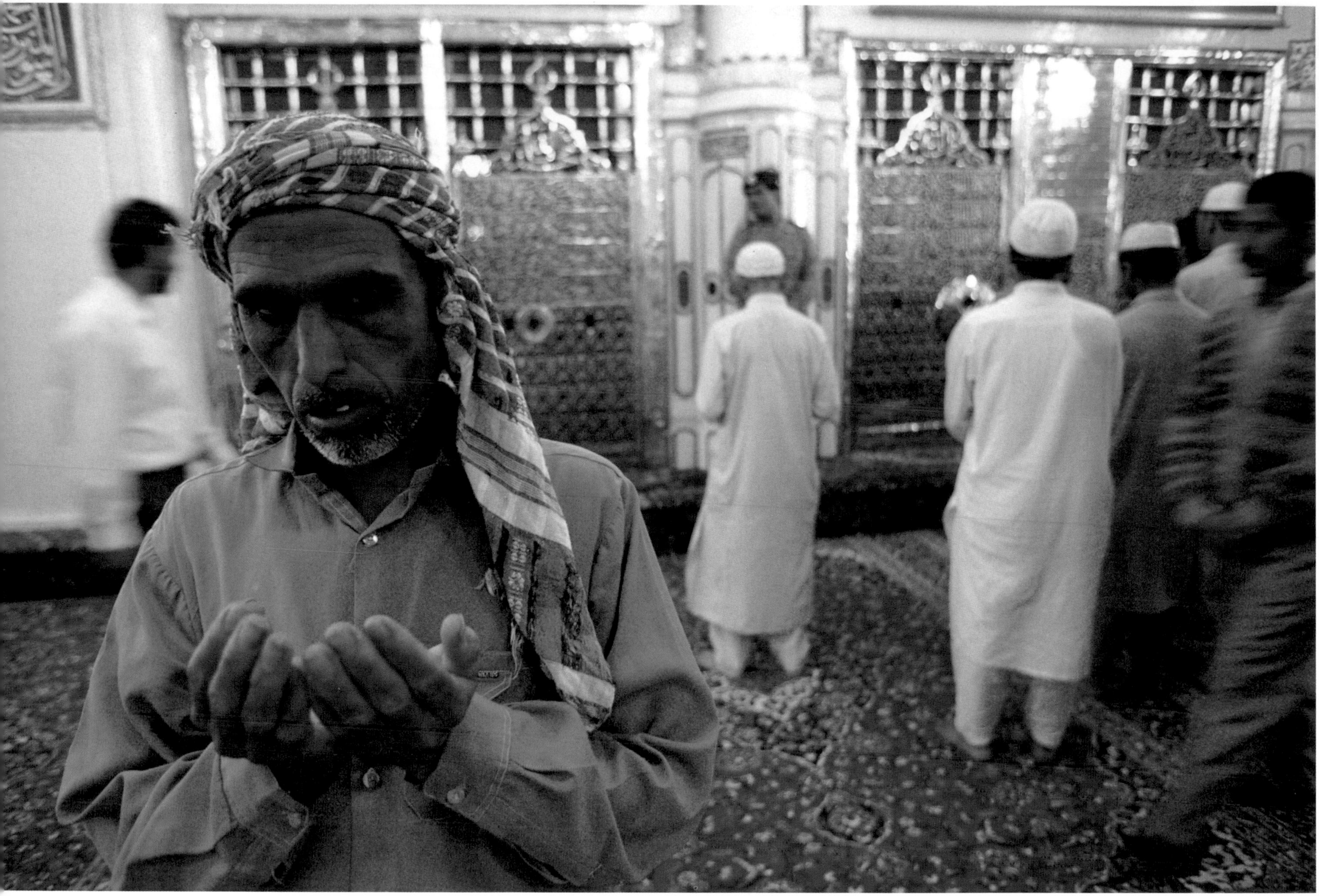

Pilgrims offering prayers (*du*ʿ*a*) next to the tomb known as the Blessed Prophet's meeting room. Pilgrims are forbidden to enter the chamber containing the Prophet's tomb and it is therefore here that they feel closest to him. It is here that their hearts are most uplifted, with most pilgrims praying intensely with tears in their eyes.

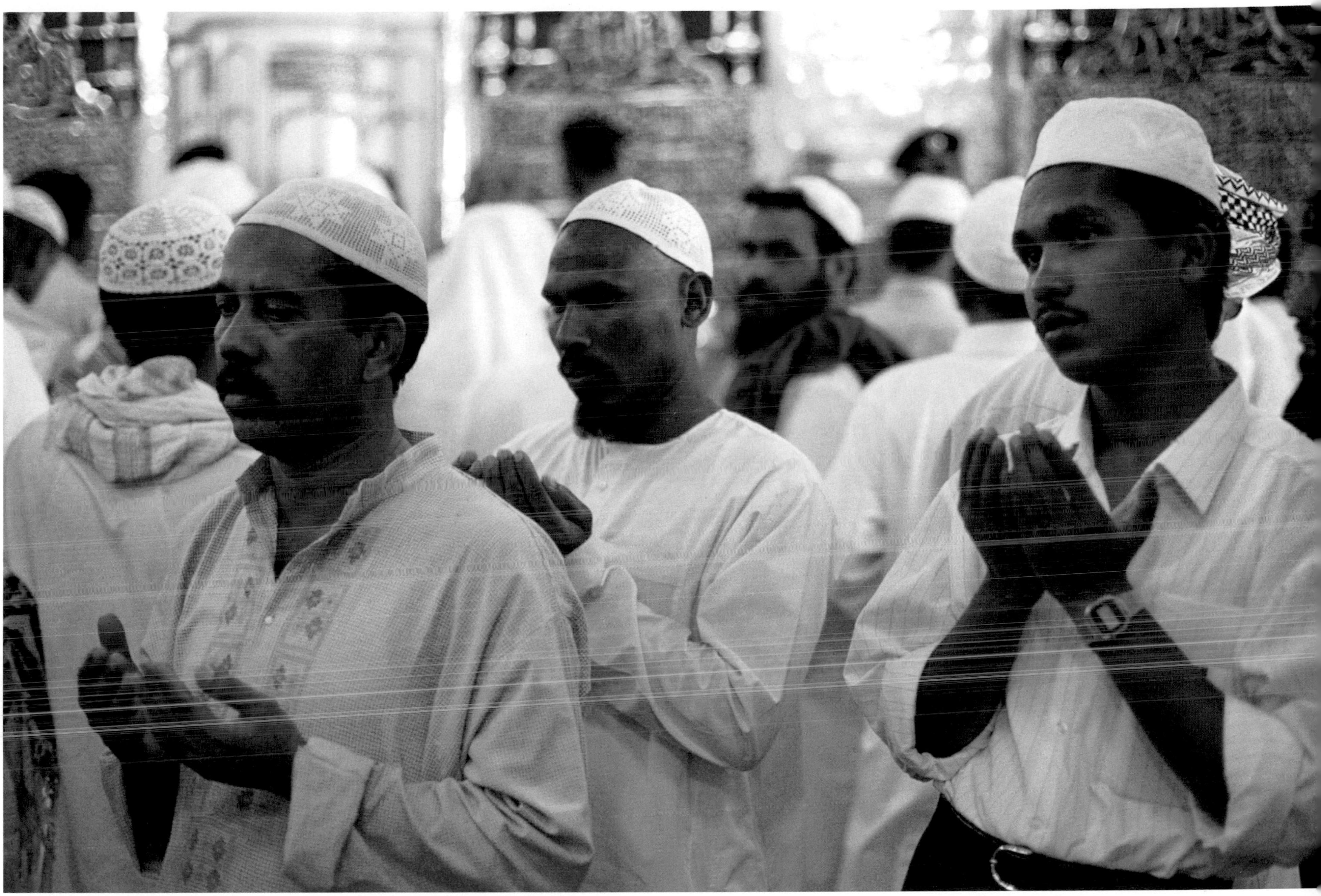

The Wahhābīs who dominate religious life in Saudi Arabia oppose visitation of the tombs of saints but offering prayers at the tomb of the Blessed Prophet is permitted. The love of the Blessed Prophet is central in Islam and it could not be otherwise.

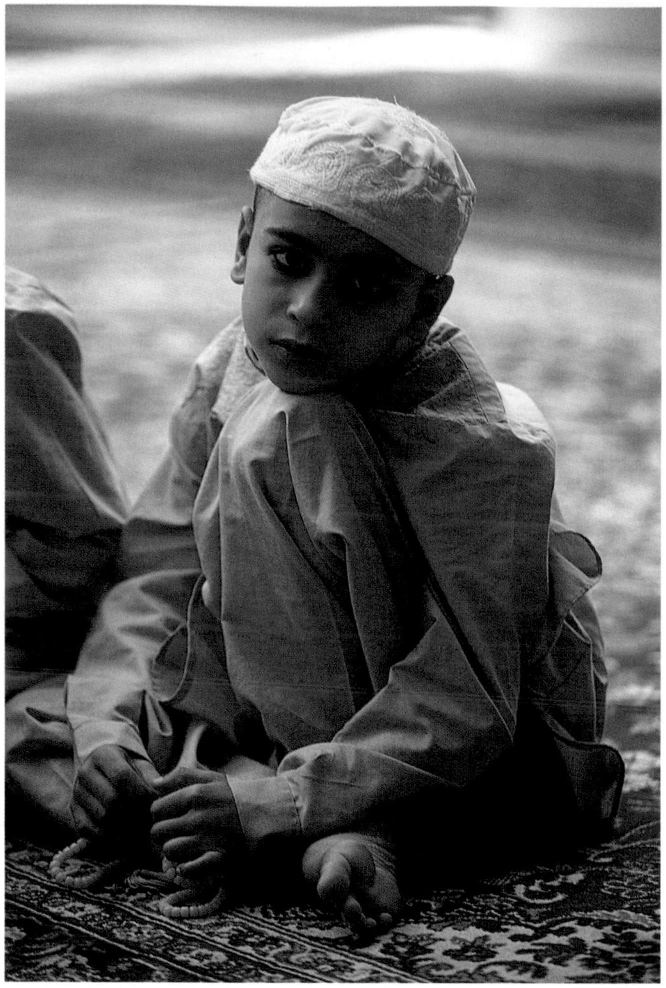

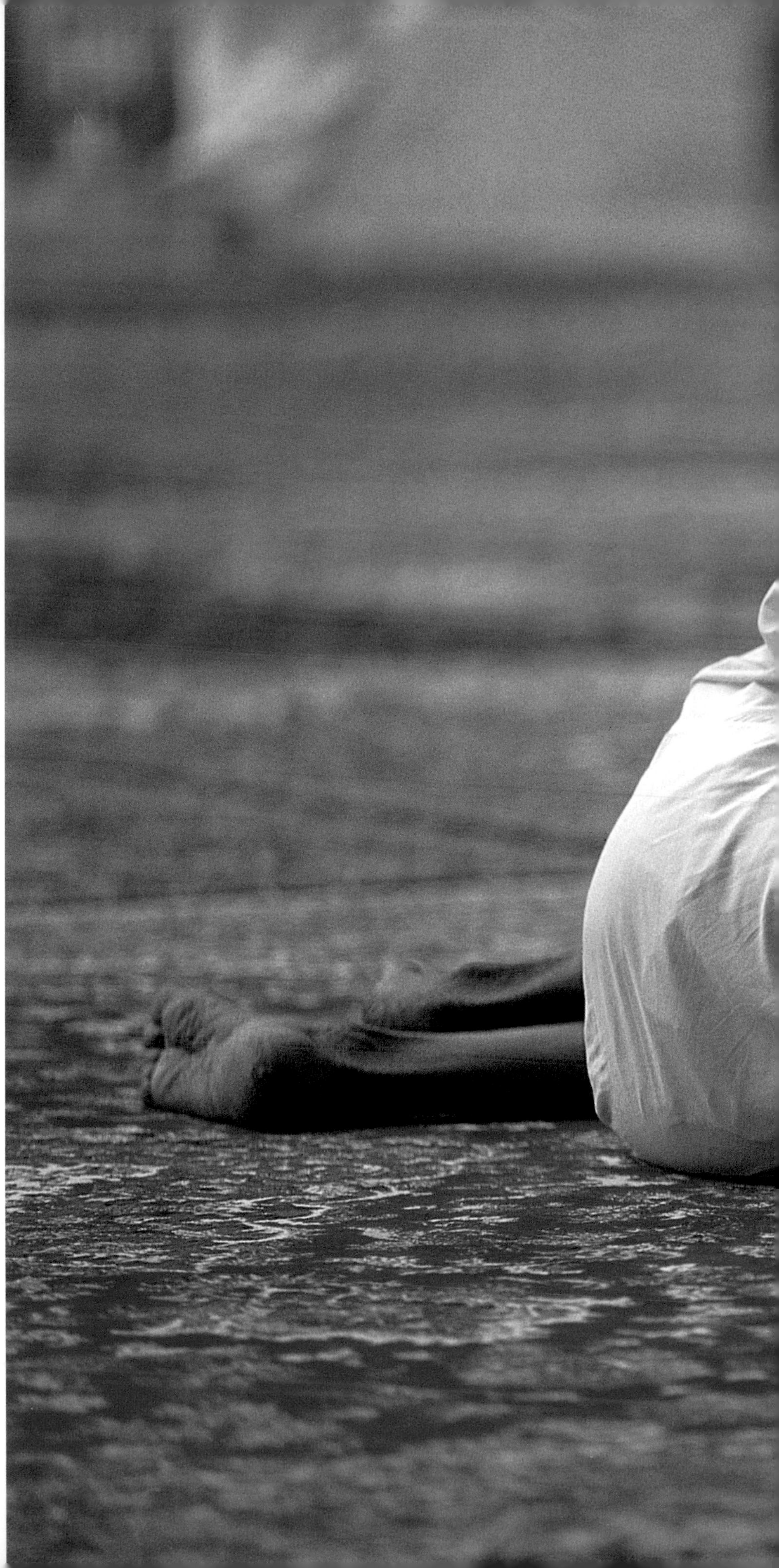

*(Above)*
A young Pakistani boy, son of a laborer in Medina, praying with the use of his rosary (*subḥah*) while awaiting the time of the canonical prayers (*ṣalāt*).

*(Opposite)*
A pilgrim from West Africa reciting the Qur'ān in the vast space of the Mosque of the Prophet outside the period of the *ḥajj*. The short pilgrimage (*al-ʿumrah*) can be and is performed by numerous people throughout the year so that the wave of pilgrims to Mecca and Medina never ceases.

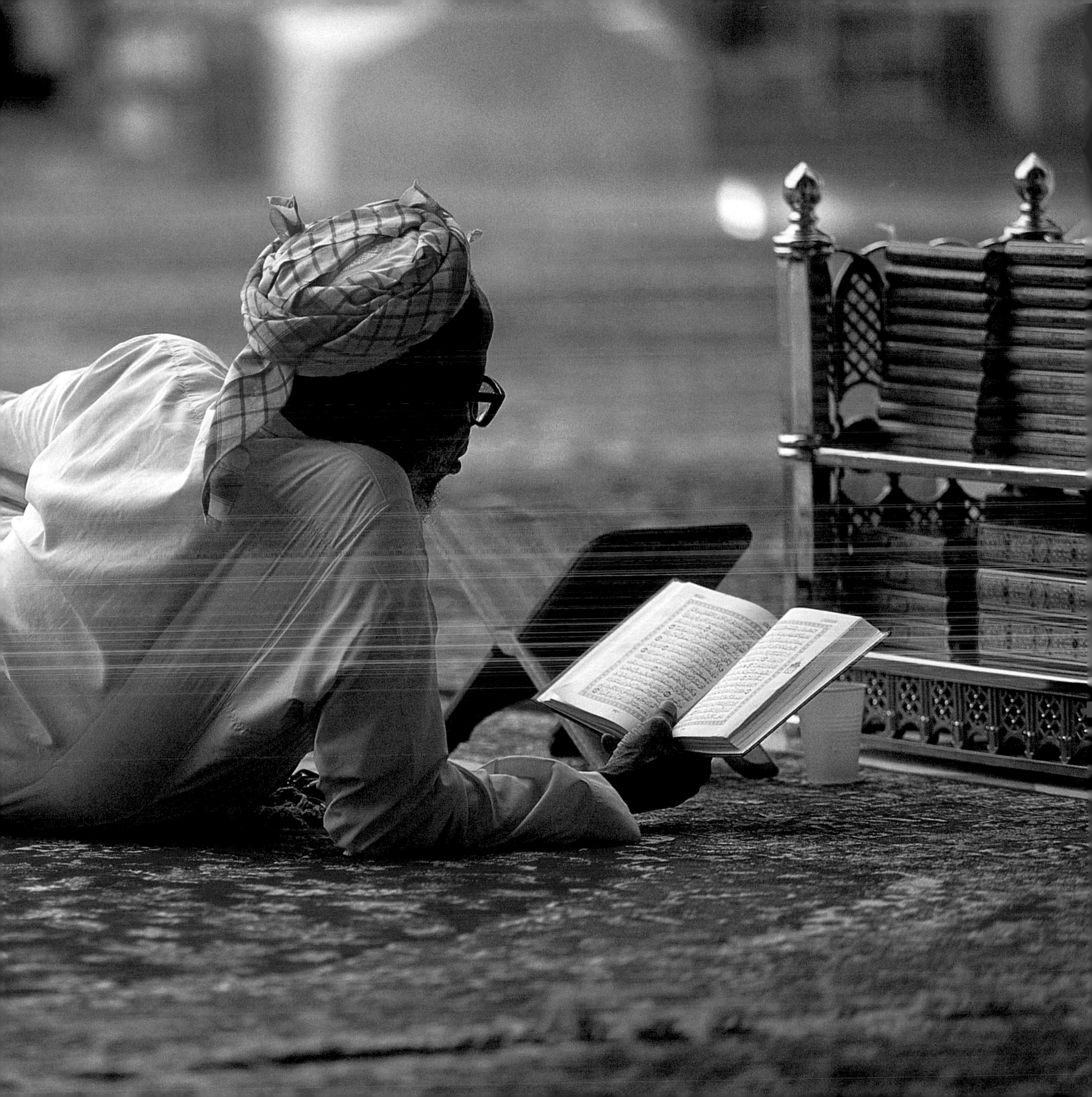

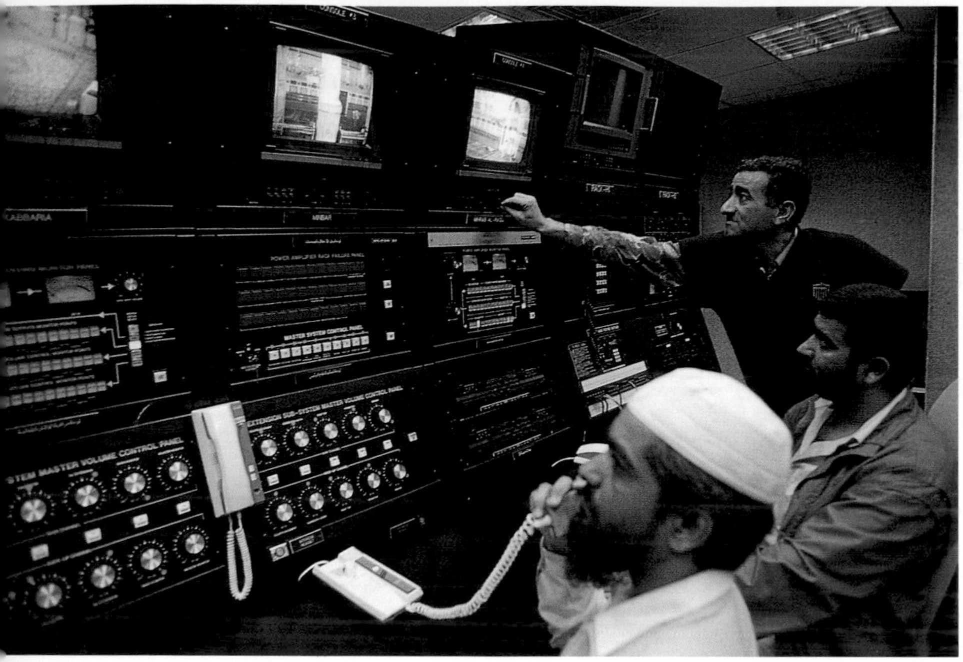

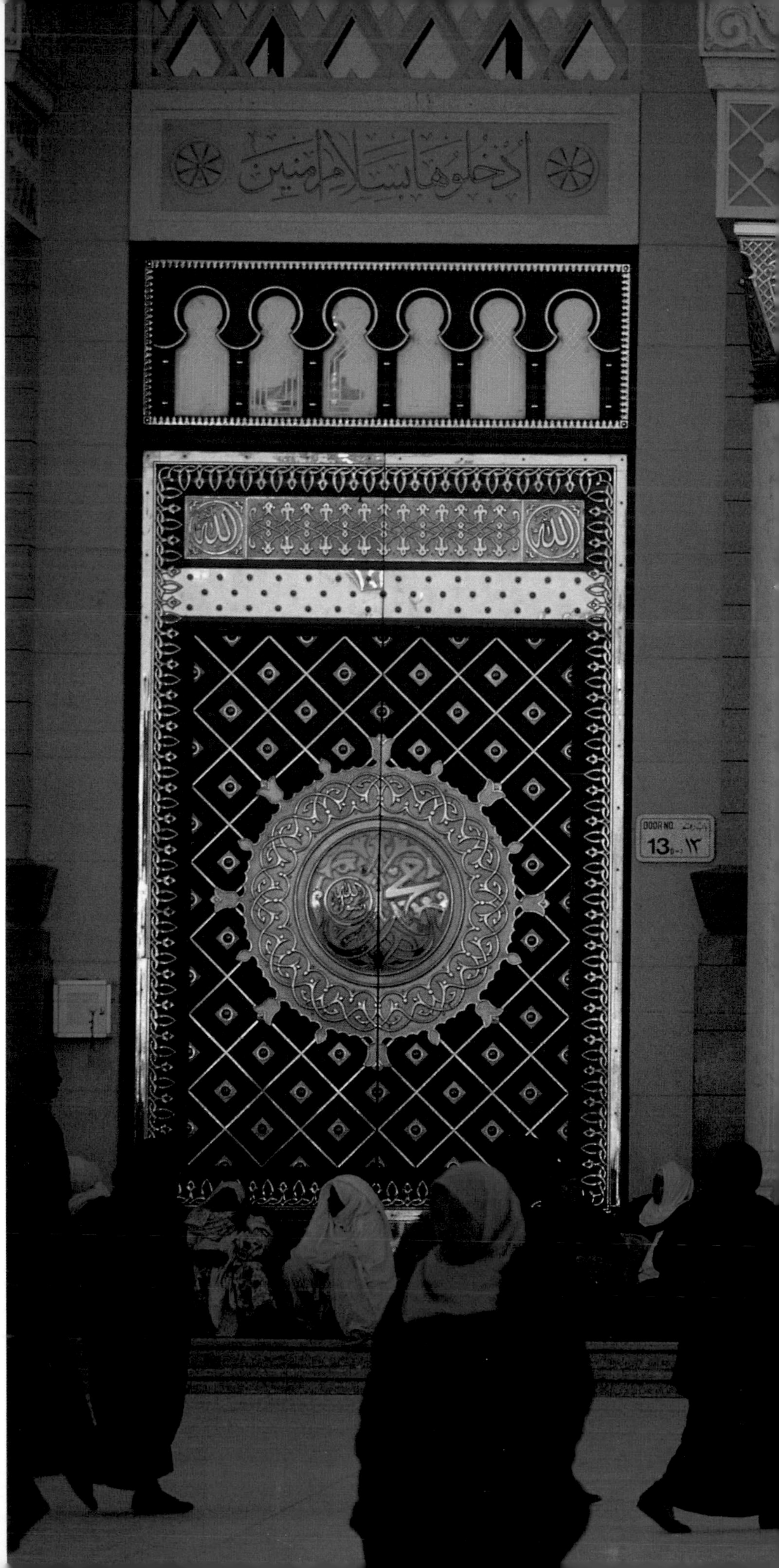


*(Above)*
A control room in the basement of the extension of the Mosque of the Prophet displaying the modern equipment including closed-circuit television used in the Mosque.

*(Opposite)*
The extension of the Mosque of the Prophet in Medina, which was completed in 1995, has provided a seating capacity of some 260,000 for prayers. With the outside space all covered with marble there is enough room for a million people to pray in the Mosque, making it the second largest mosque in the world after the Grand Mosque of Mecca.

ادخلوها بسلام آمنين
DOOR NO.
13 ١٣

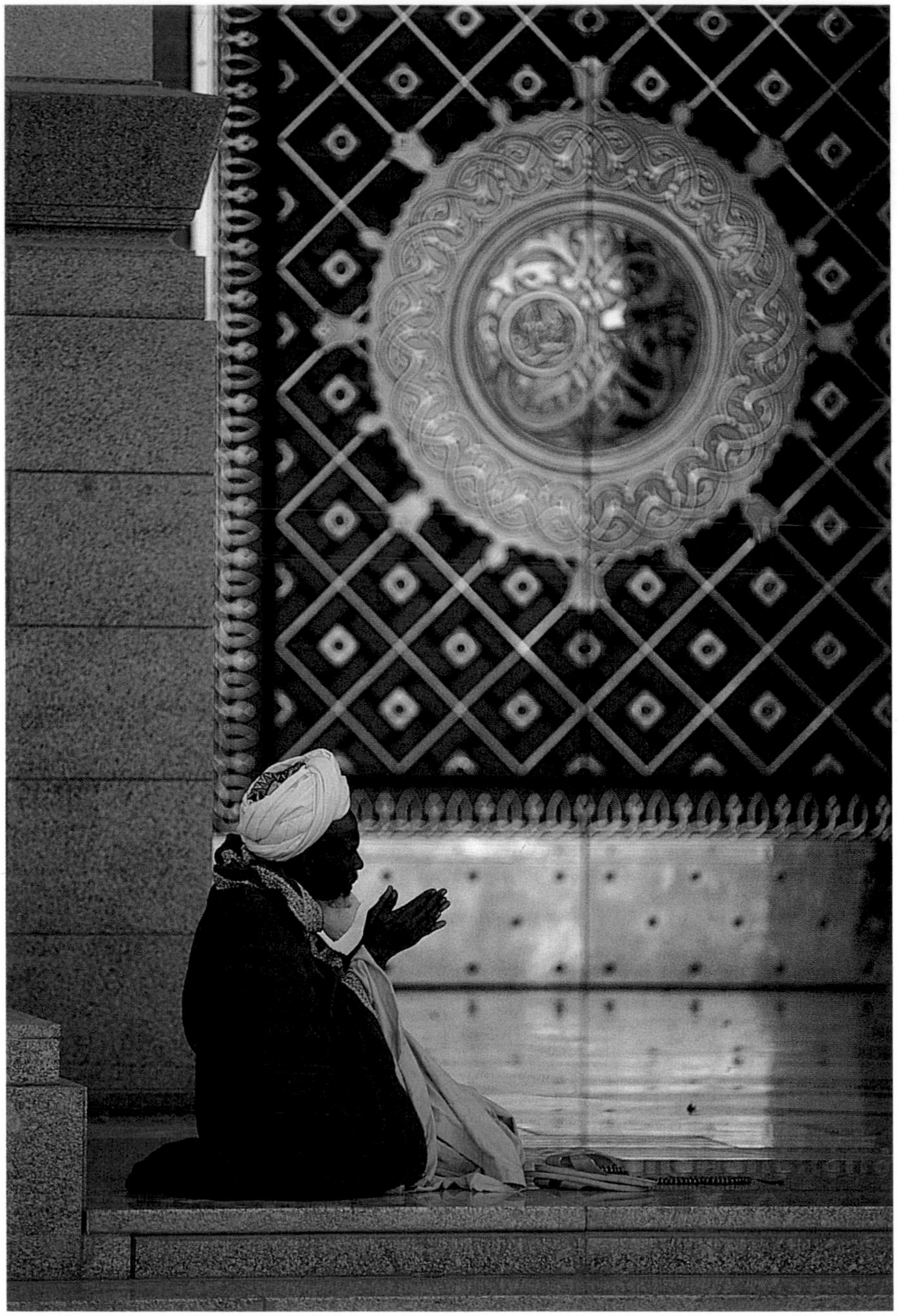

*(Above)*
A pilgrim from Nigeria praying by the door of the Mosque of the Prophet. Barring exceptional circumstances such as an epidemic, the Nigerians constitute the largest body of pilgrims from Black Africa.

*(Opposite)*
This group of women pilgrims from Kerala in southern India wear this distinct blue color to distinguish them from others so that the members of the group do not become lost amidst the vast crowds.

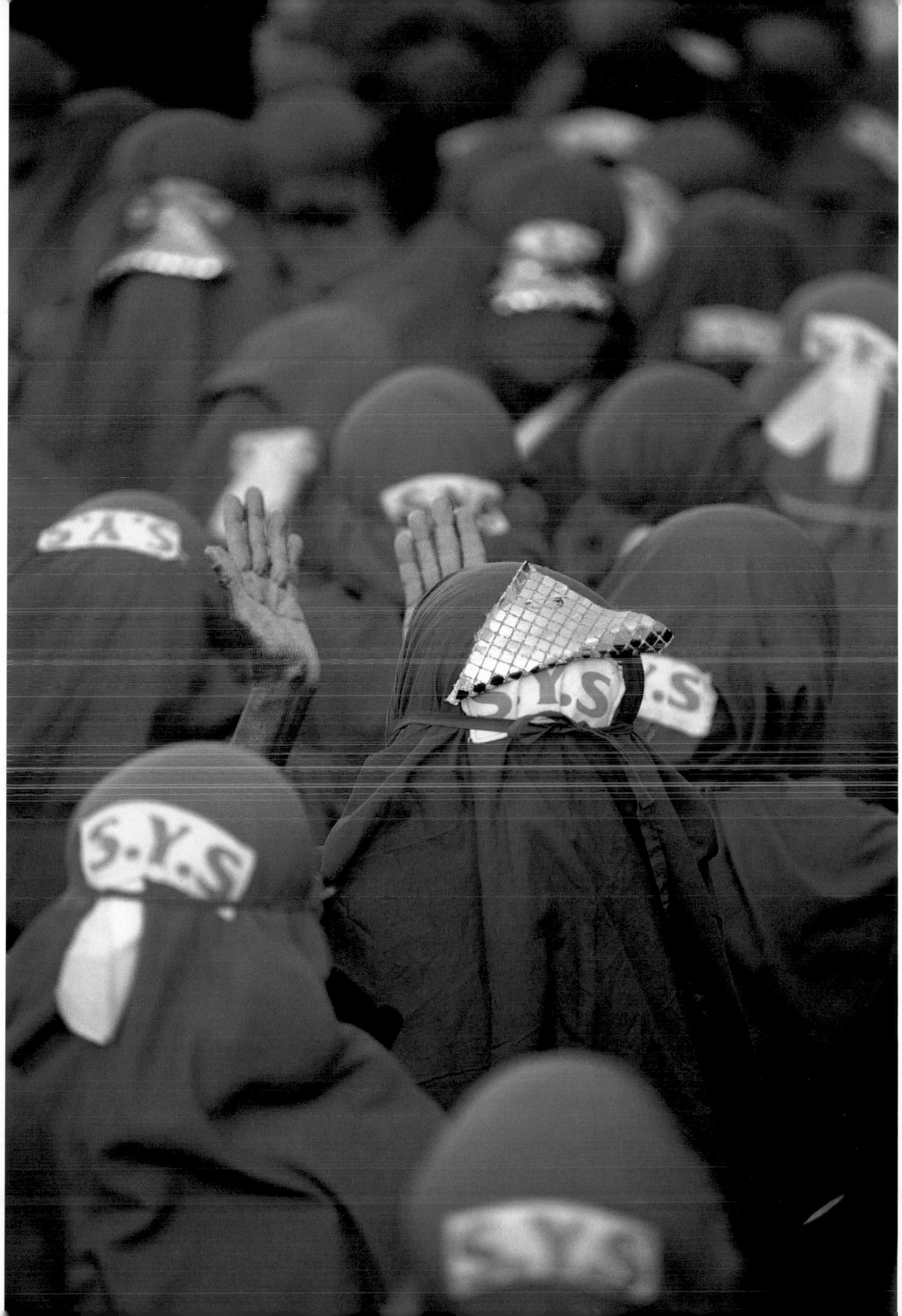
S.Y.S
S.Y.S
S.Y.S
S.Y.S

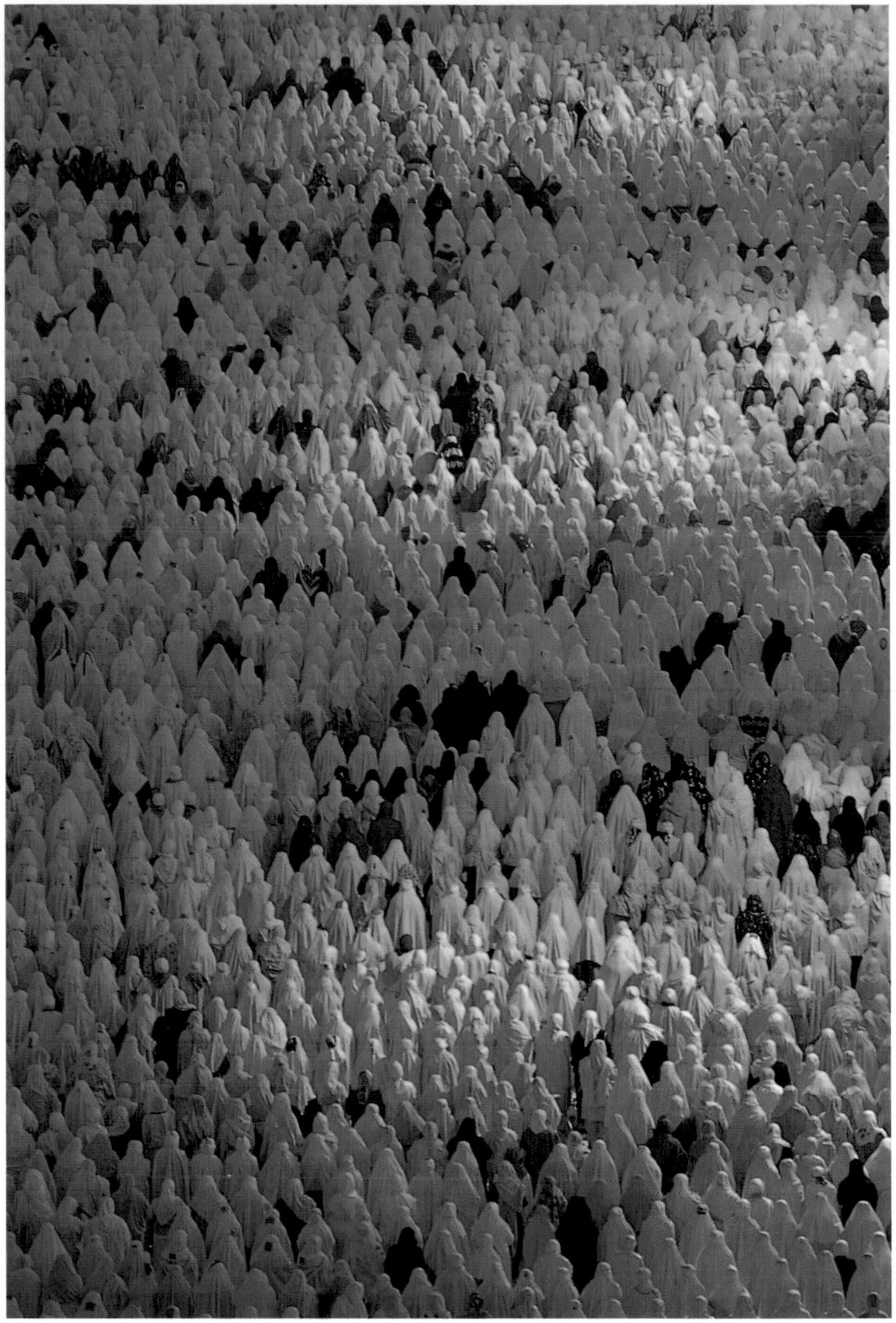

*(Above)*
Woman attending the evening prayers around the Mosque of the Prophet. Most of them stay there until the night prayer (*ʿishāʾ*) which is performed about an hour and a half later.

*(Opposite)*
The crowd leaving the Mosque of the Prophet at the end of the *ʿishāʾ* prayers after which the Mosque is closed and the inside cleaned. It is opened again at dawn for the morning (*fajr*) prayers.

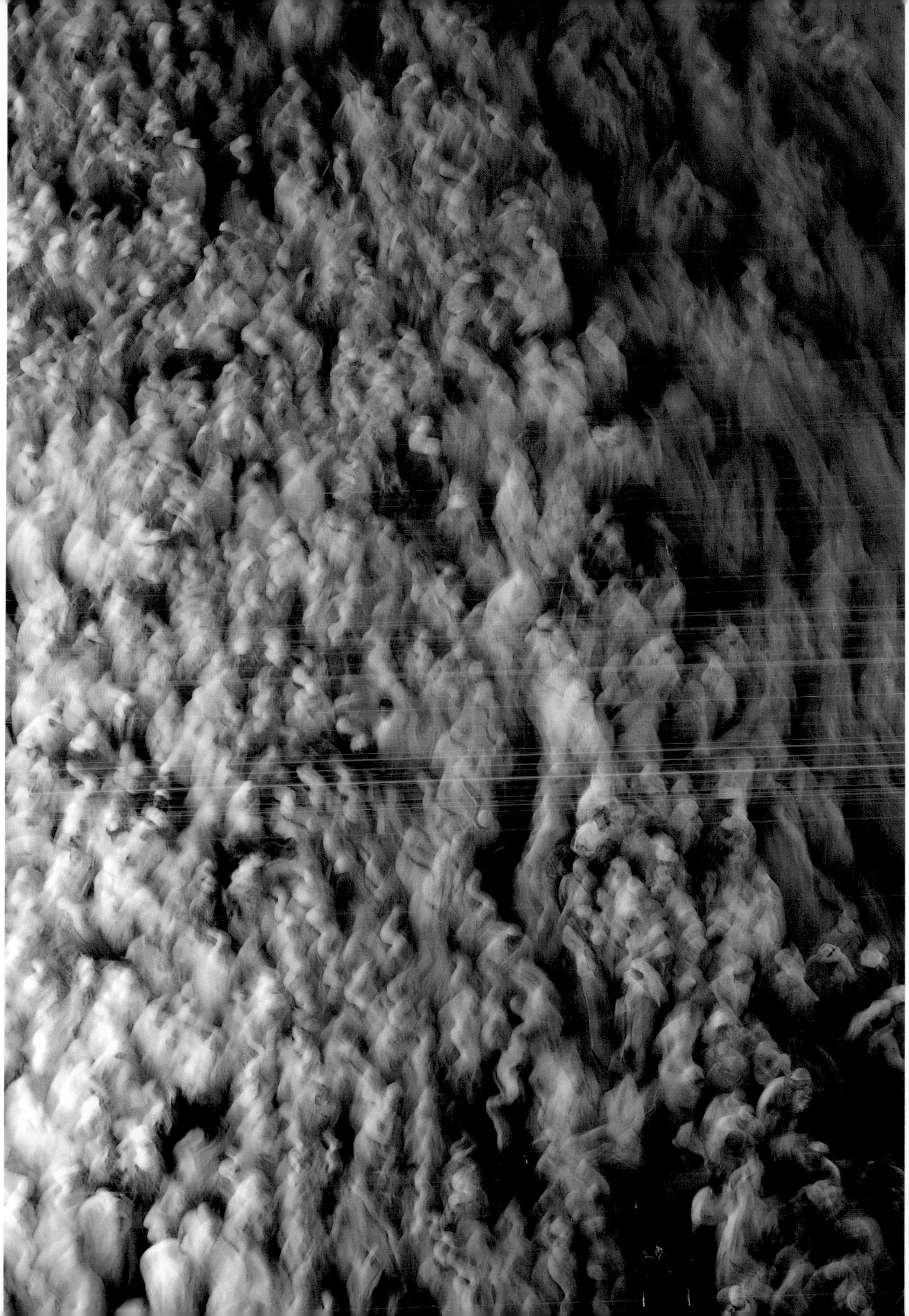

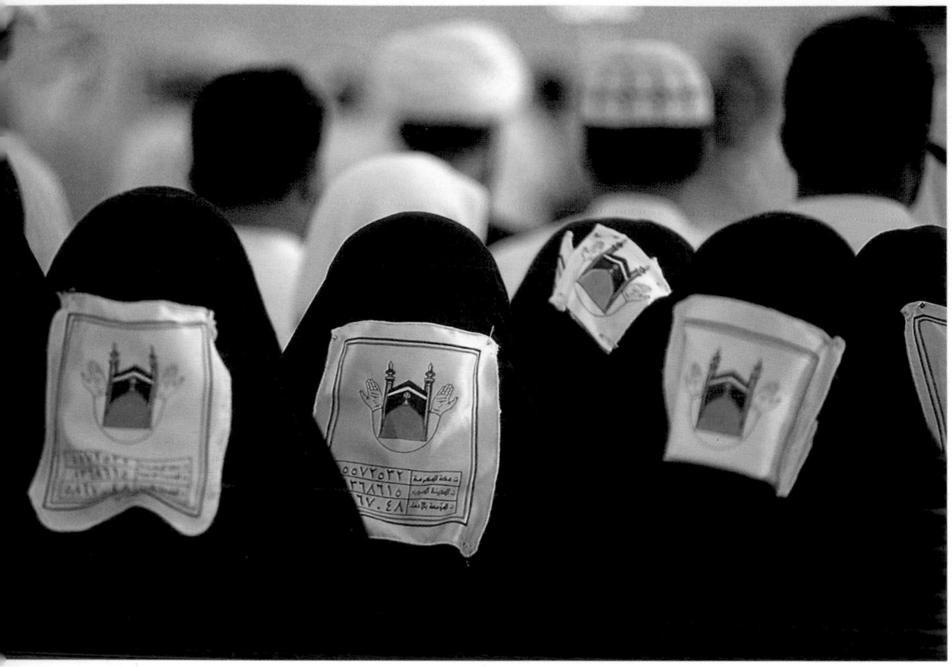

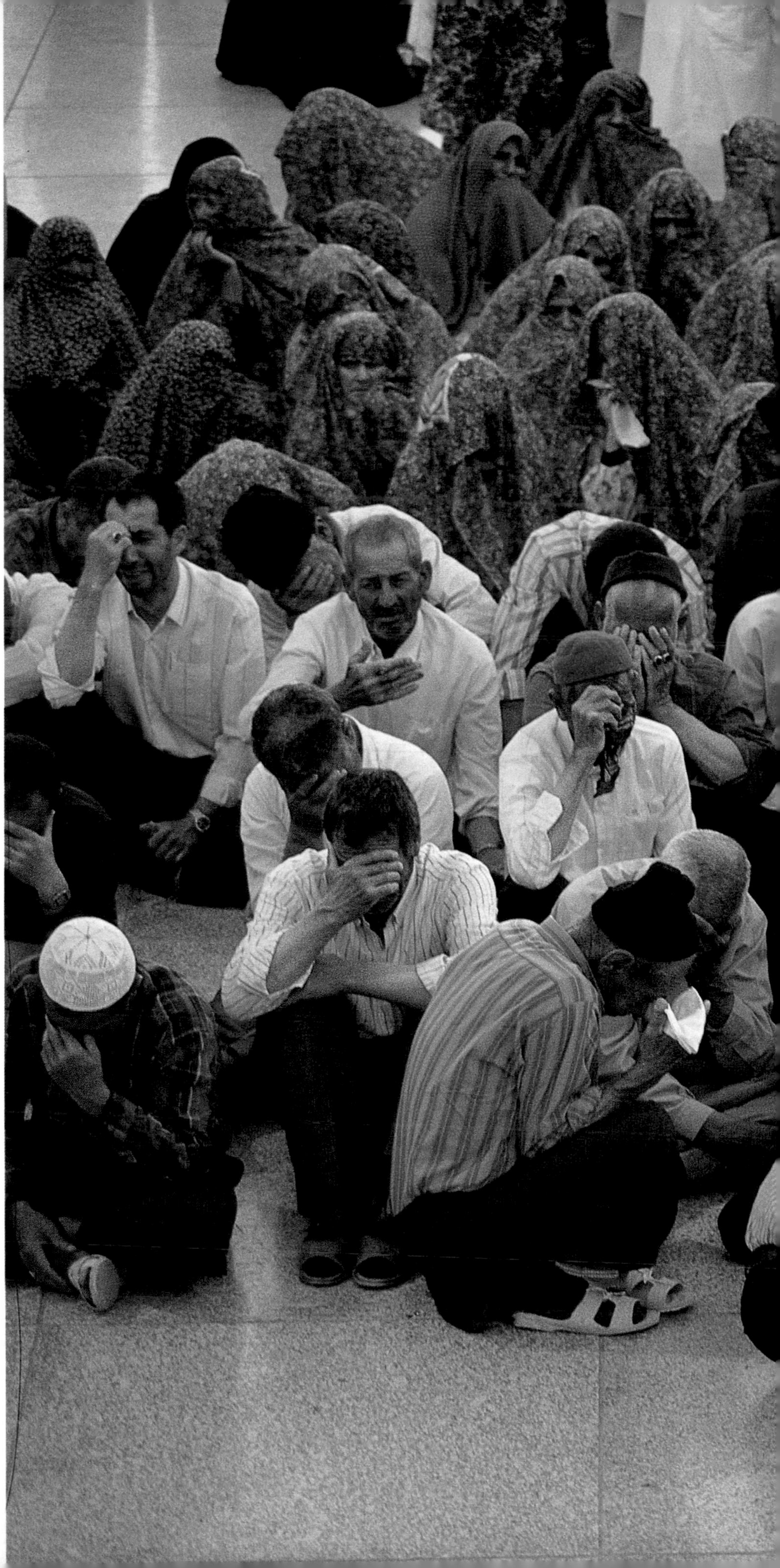

*(Above)*
A group of women pilgrims from Iran with a cloth attached to the back of their veils (*chador*) to distinguish them from other groups.

*(Opposite)*
Iranian pilgrims grieving as they move toward the cemetery of al-Baqīʿ near the Mosque of the Prophet where Fāṭimah, the daughter of the Prophet, his grandson Ḥasan, the second Shīʿite Imam, and many other members of the Household of the Prophet (*ahl al-bayt*) are buried. Being Shīʿite and therefore holding the members of the Household of the Prophet in great reverence, this group like most Iranians hold this cemetery in special esteem.

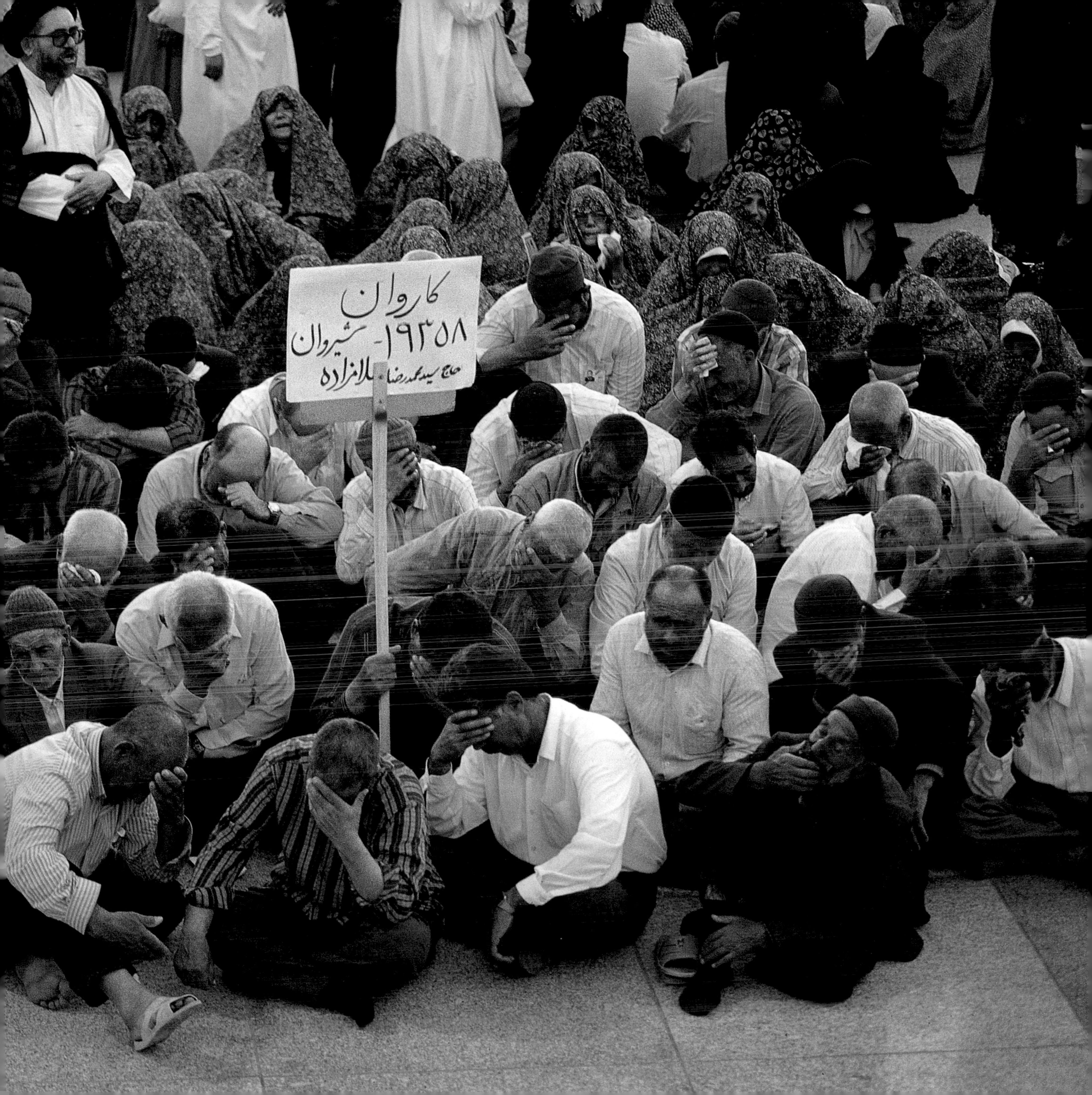
کاروان
۱۹۳۵۸ - شیروان
حاج سید محمدرضا لازاده

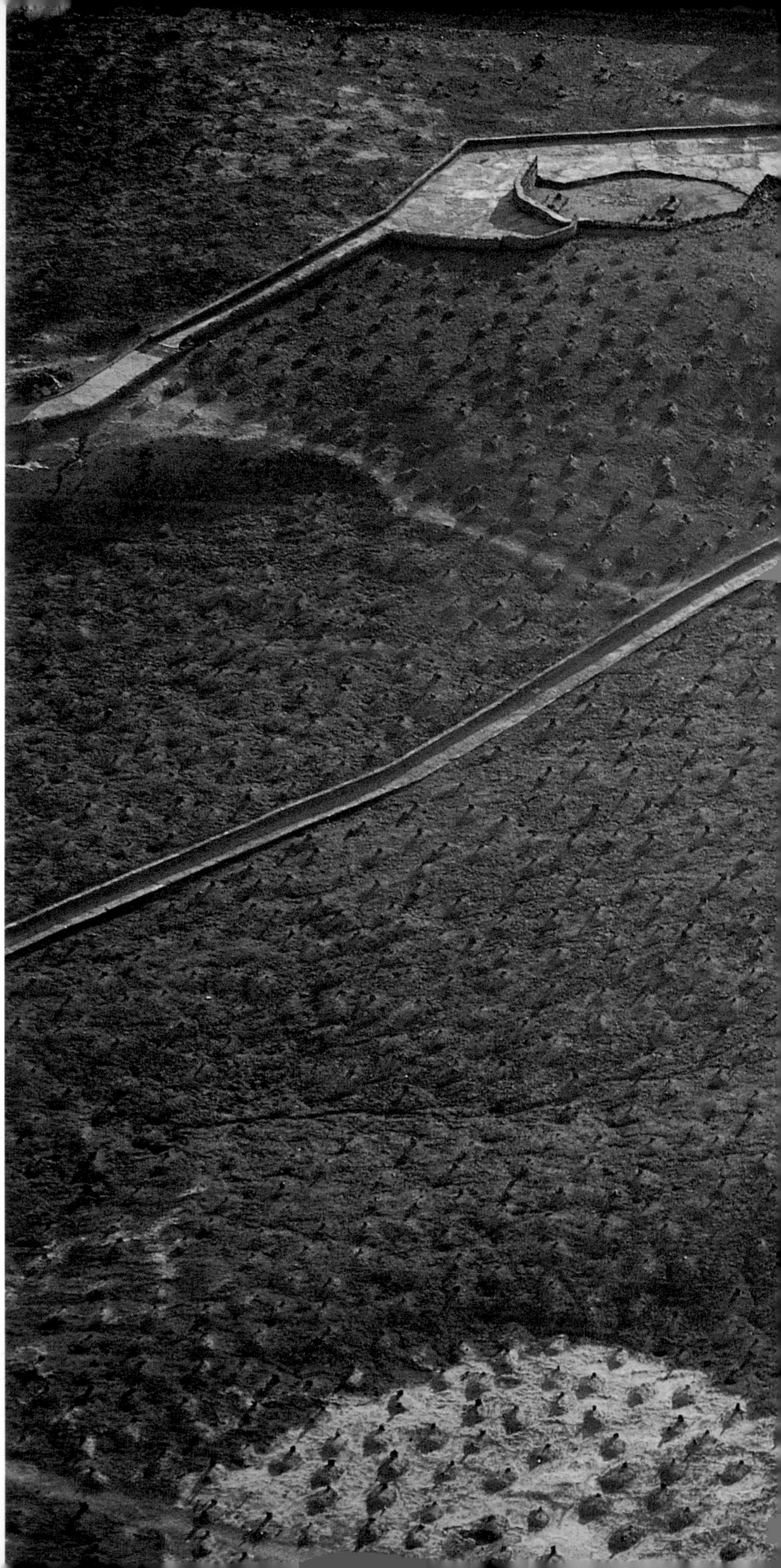

An aerial view of al-Baqī[c] cemetery, the oldest and historically the most significant cemetery in Medina.

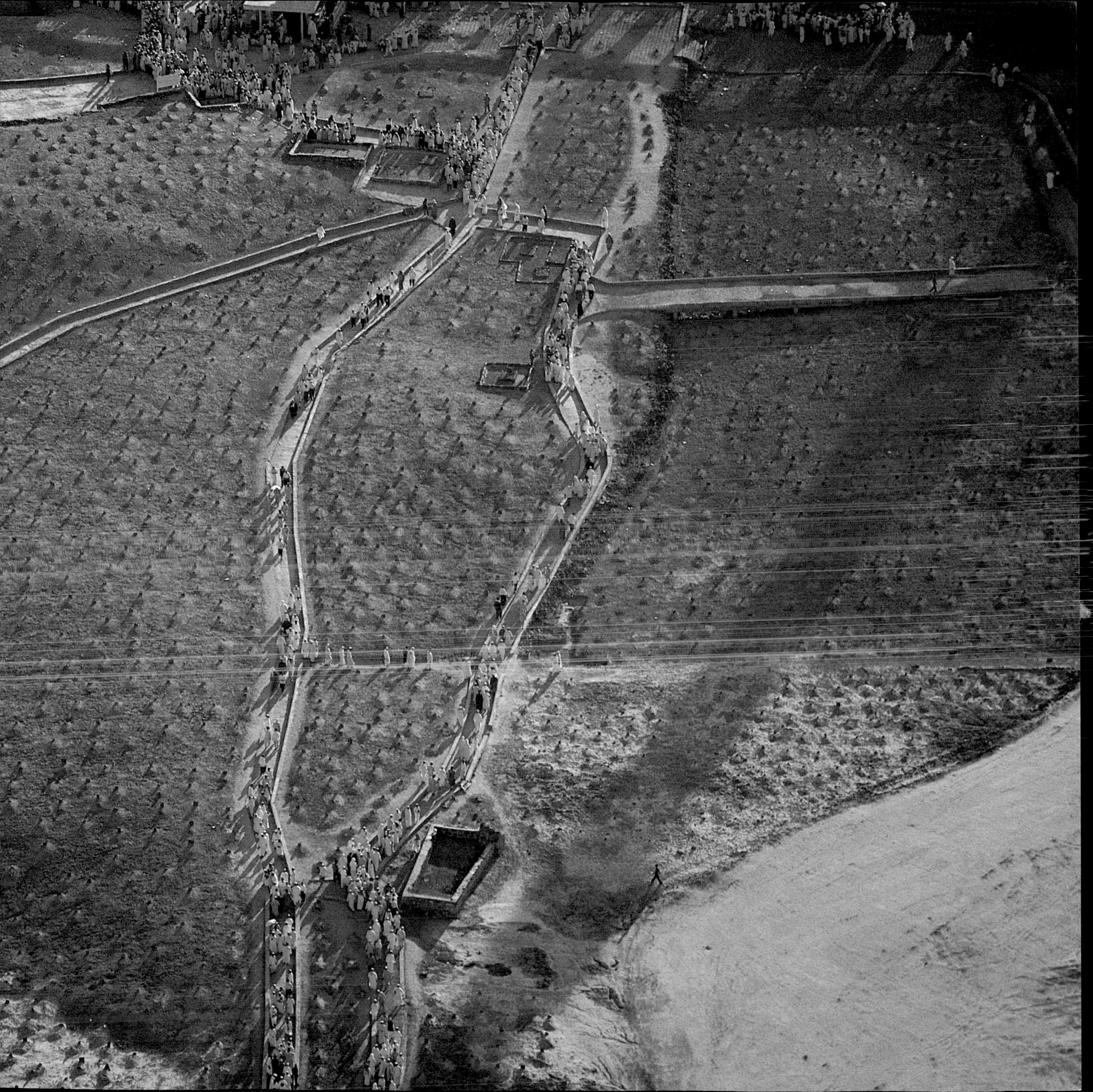

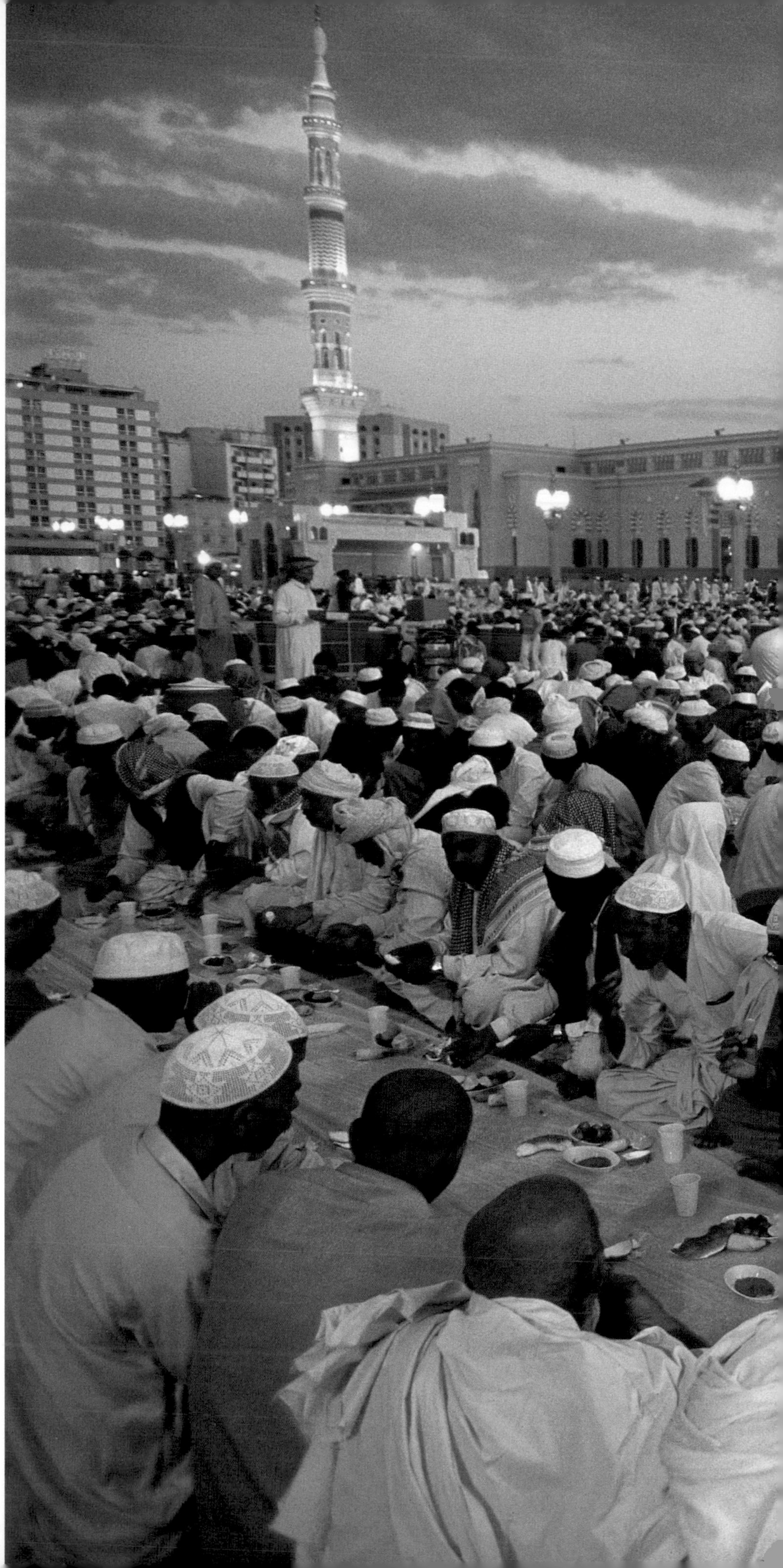

During the holy month of Ramaḍān, the most sacred month of the Islamic calendar, all adult Muslims who have the physical capability are obliged to fast from dawn to sunset. Here pilgrims are offered food to break their fast at the Mosque of the Prophet.

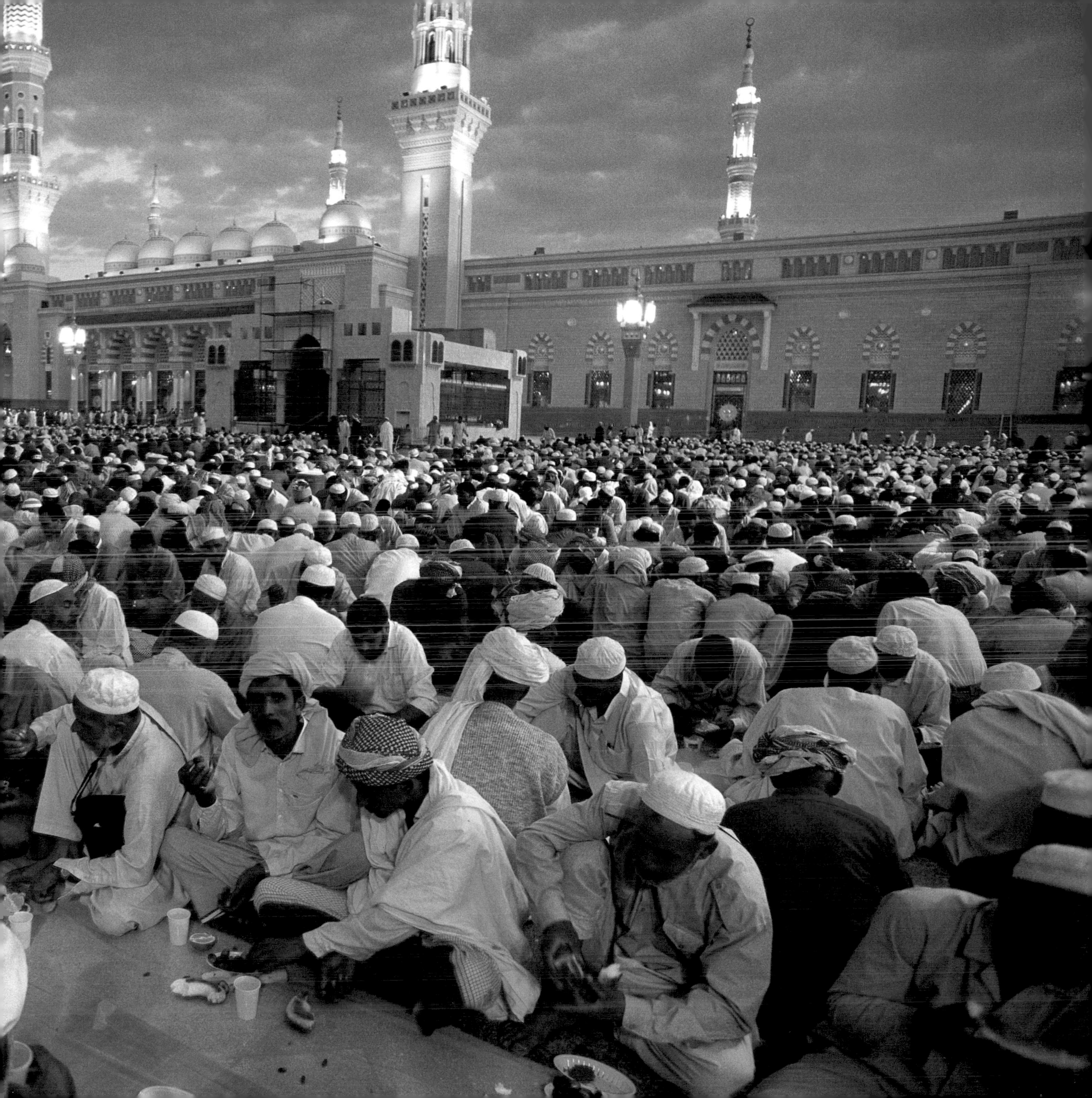

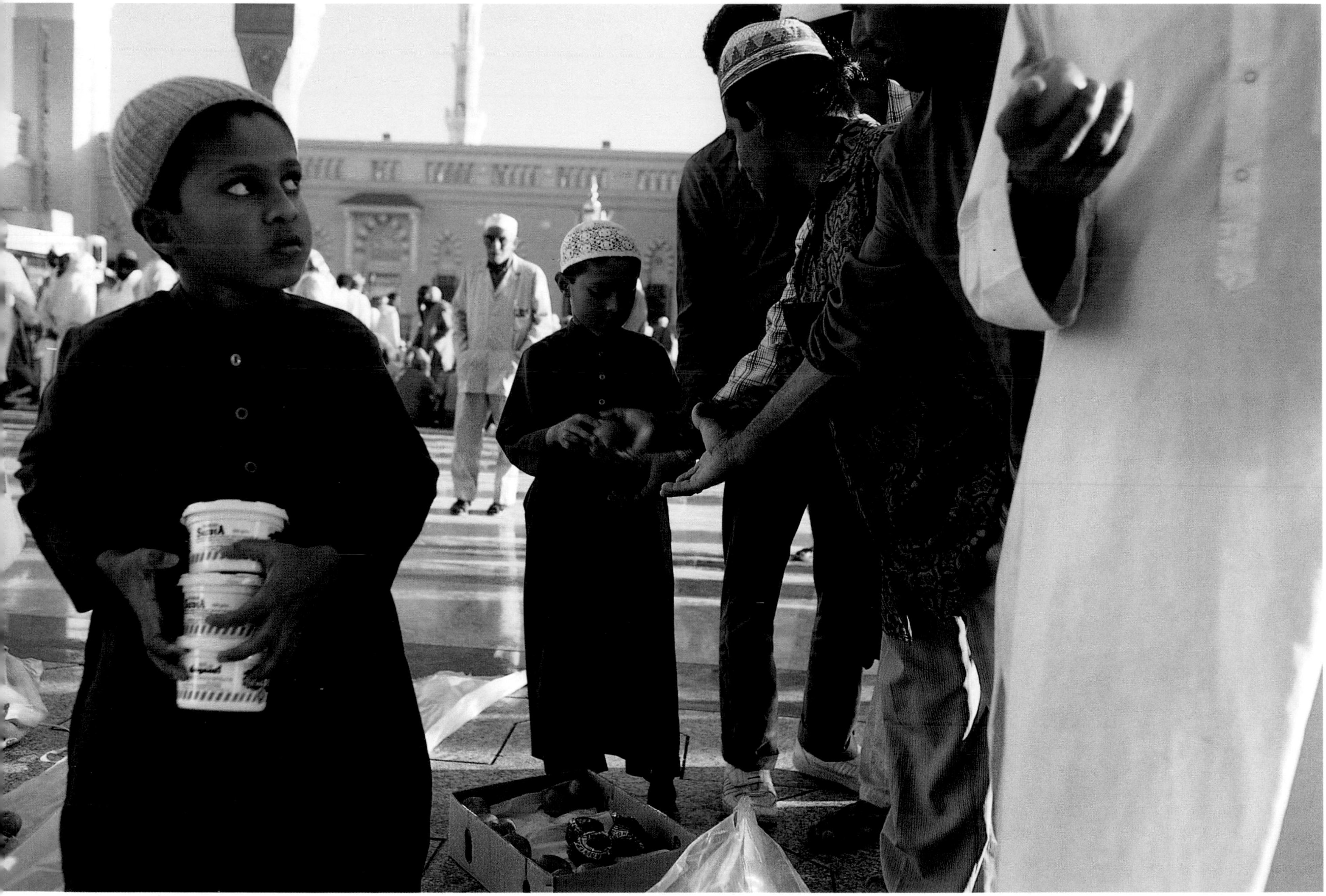

Saudi children help in the preparation of the meal to break the fast (*ifṭār*). Wealthier Muslims by tradition prepare food for the needy at this time. Here during every evening of Ramaḍān, wealthy Saudi families provide *ifṭār* for whoever requests it.

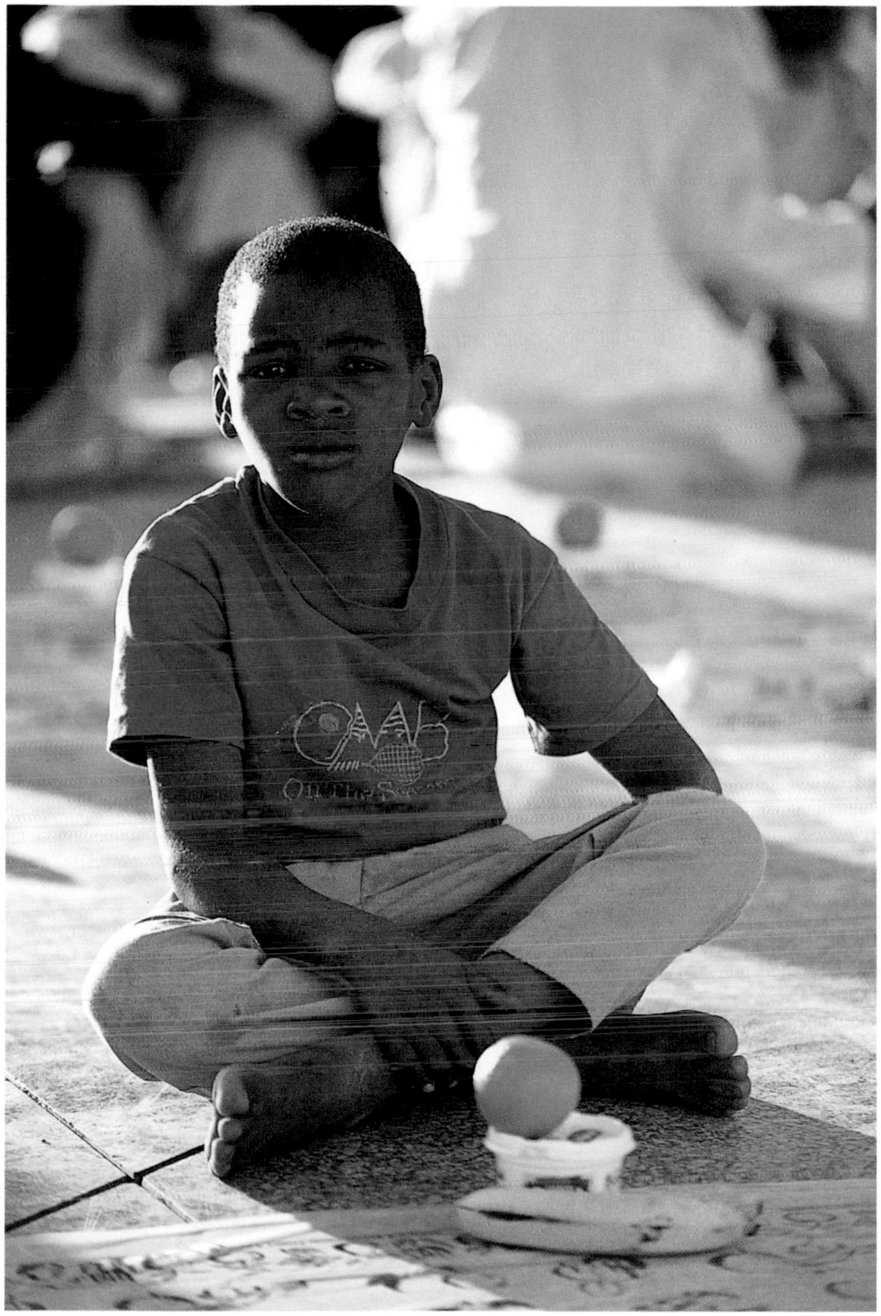

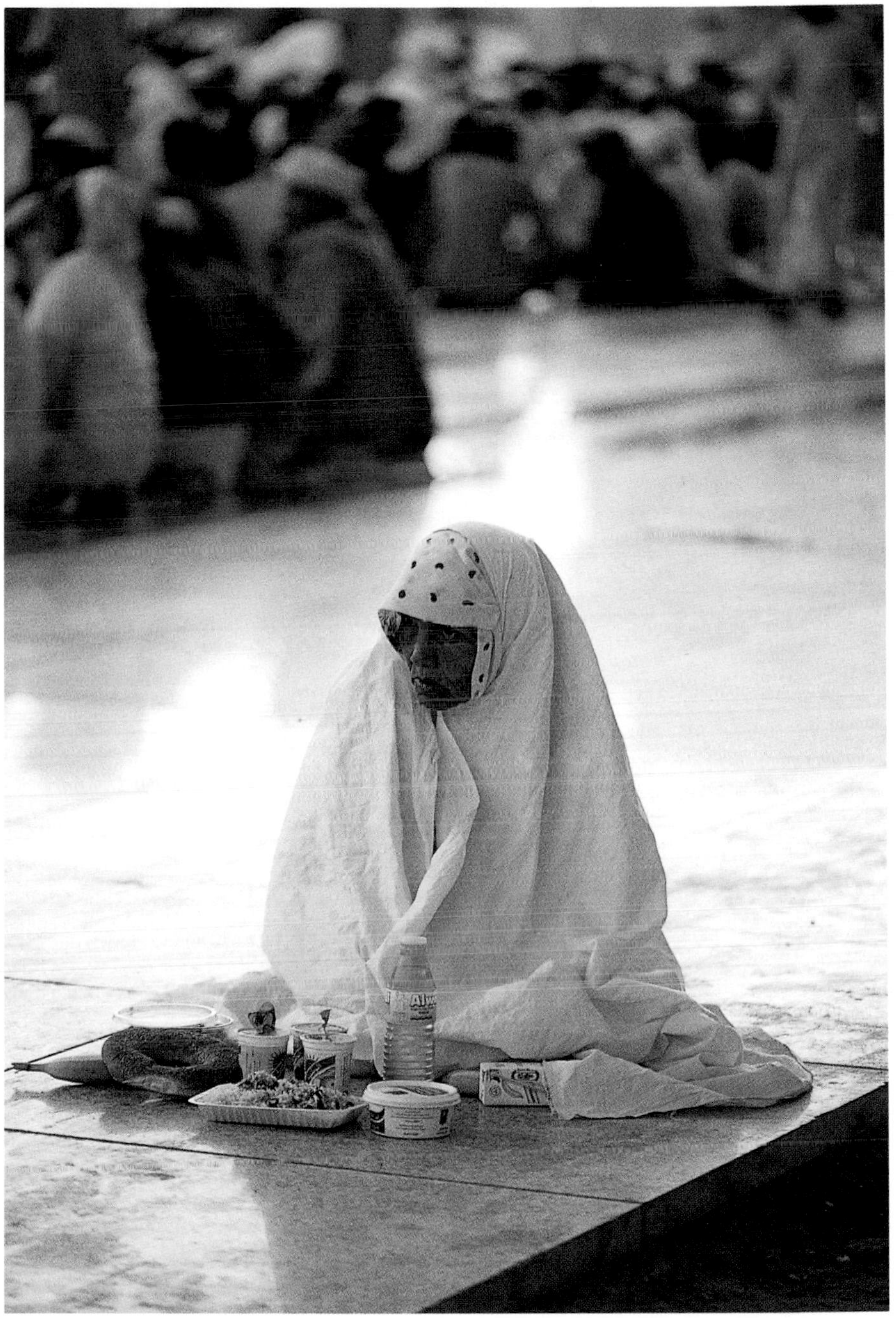

*(Left)*
People being offered *ifṭār* in Medina. Other than pilgrims, laborers often participate in these free meals. Feeding the poor is a religious obligation in Islam.

*(Right)*
A woman pilgrim from Indonesia has wandered into an area designated for men and is awaiting the time to break the fast. In the early days of Islam *ifṭār* consisted usually of dates, bread and water but now a variety of dishes are prepared for the occasion.

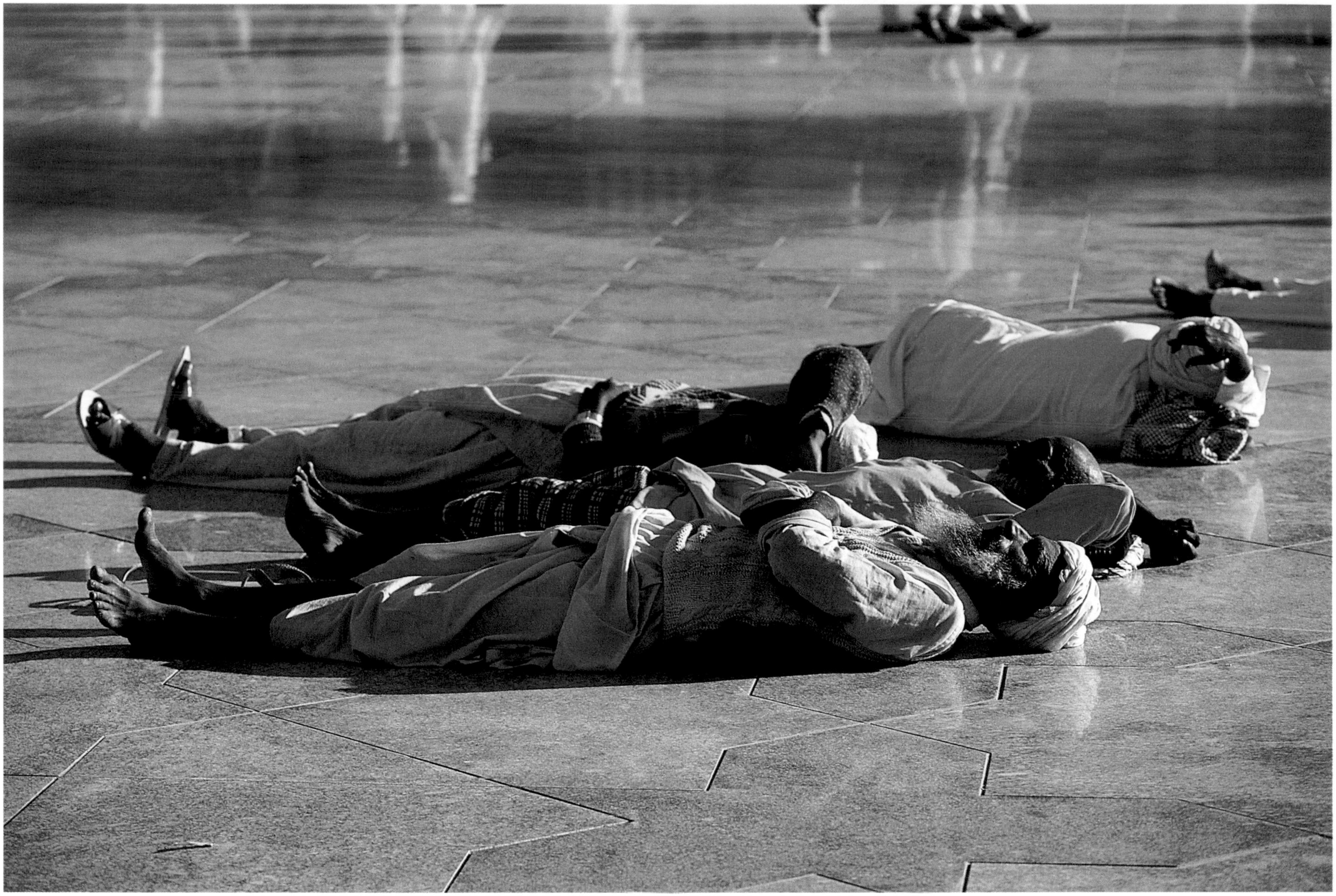

Pakistani pilgrims fatigued by the fast await the end of the fast. One of the purposes of the fast is to distribute food among those deprived of regular meals during the year.

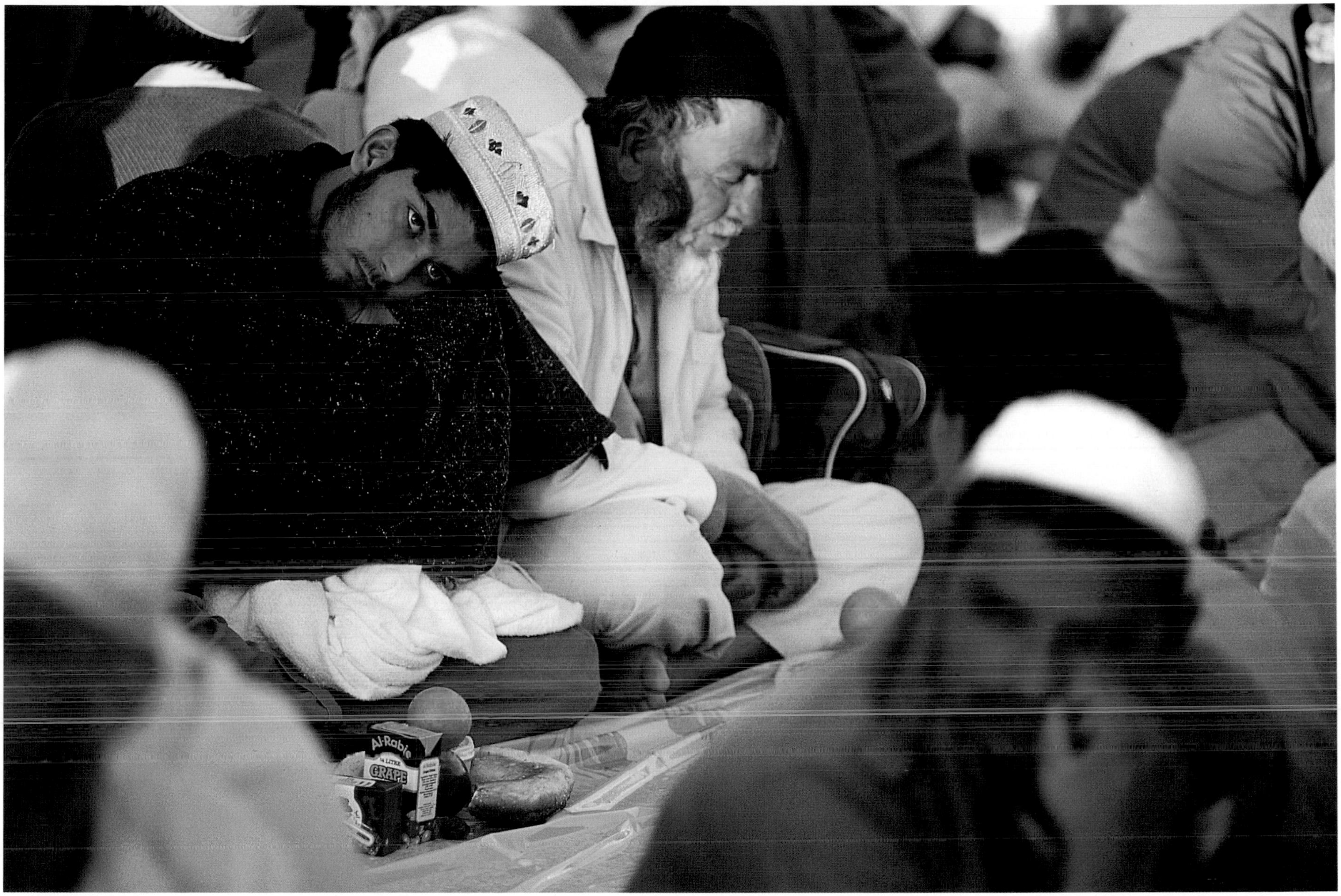


*(Above)*
A young Pakistani tired from fasting awaits the arrival of the end of the day which is announced by the call to prayer (*adhān*) for the *maghrib* prayers. In cities cannons are also usually fired at that time to make certain that everyone hears that the time for the breaking of the fast has arrived.

*(Following pages)*
Over one hundred thousand people are having *ifṭār* in the vast garden surrounding the Mosque of the Prophet. Before breaking their fast, people offer a prayer of thanksgiving to God for having been able to fast during the day.

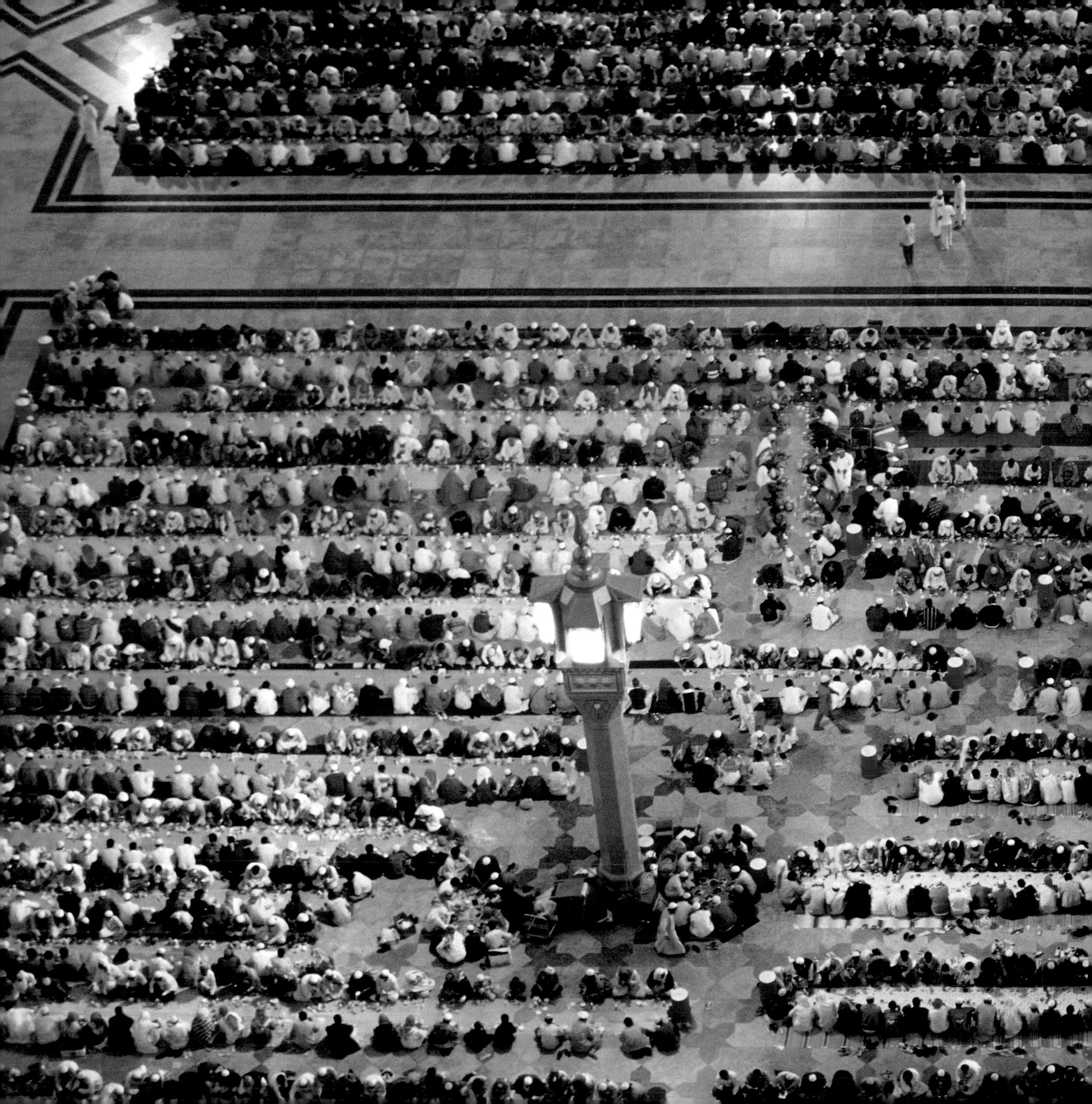

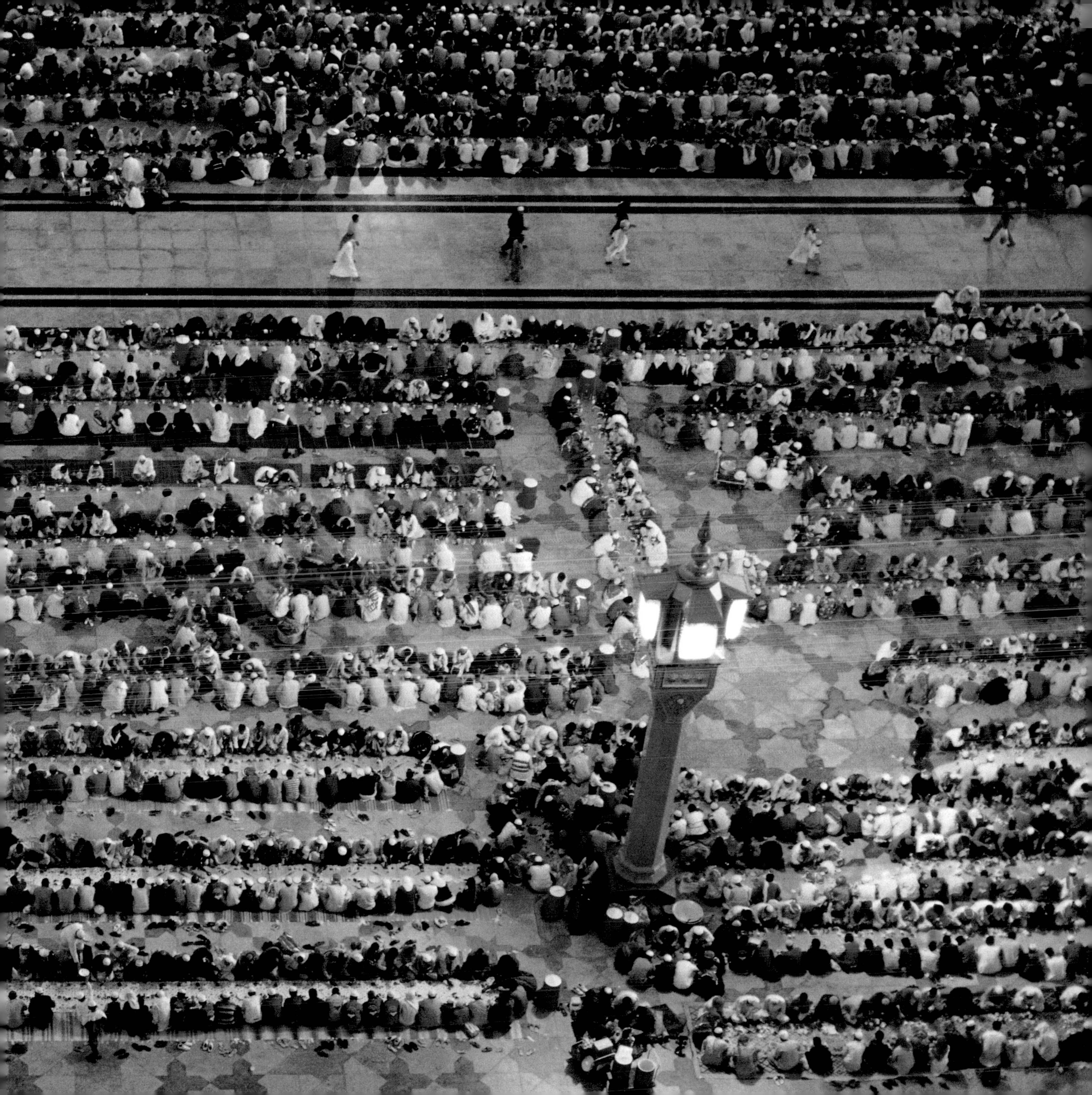

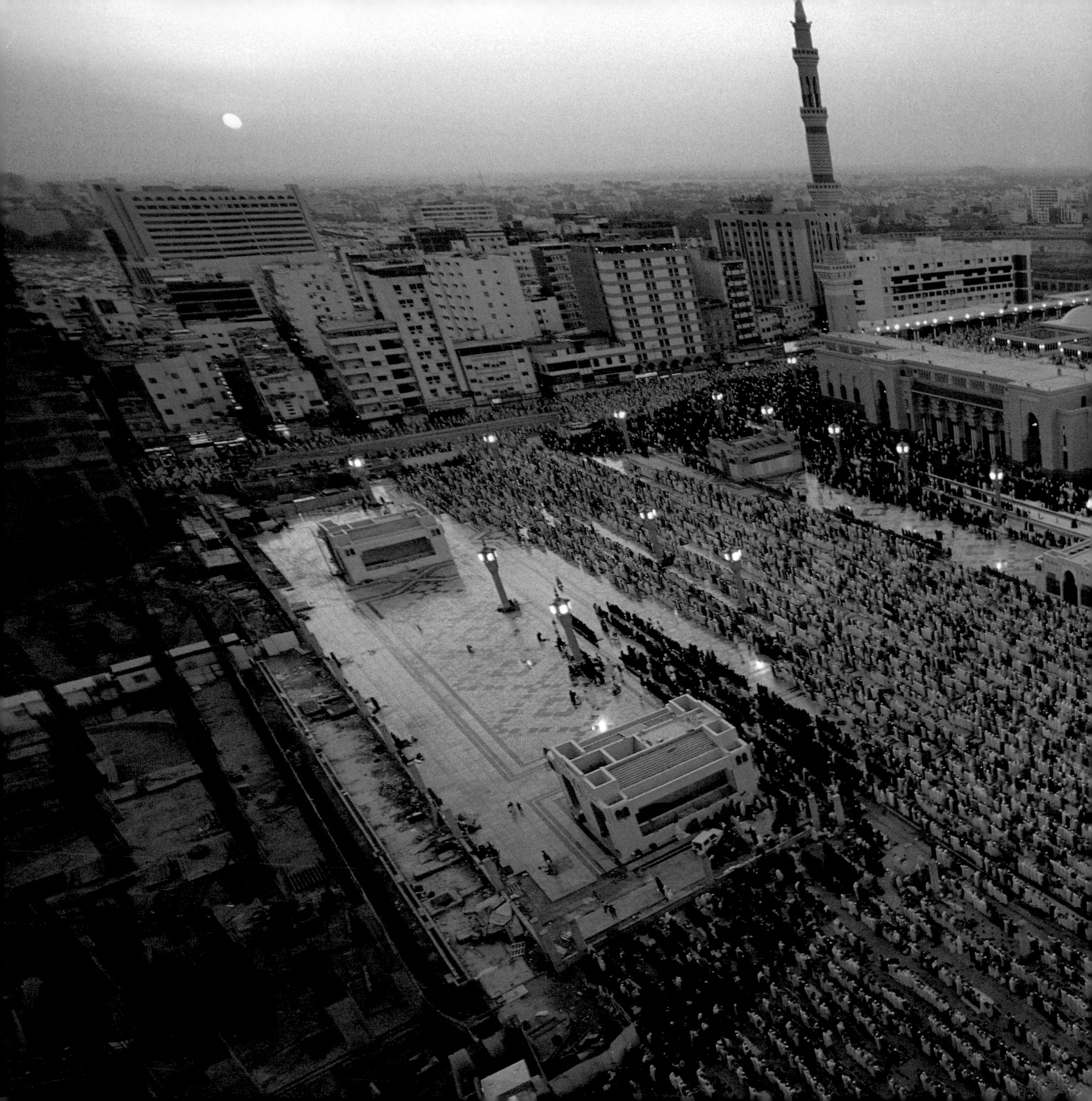

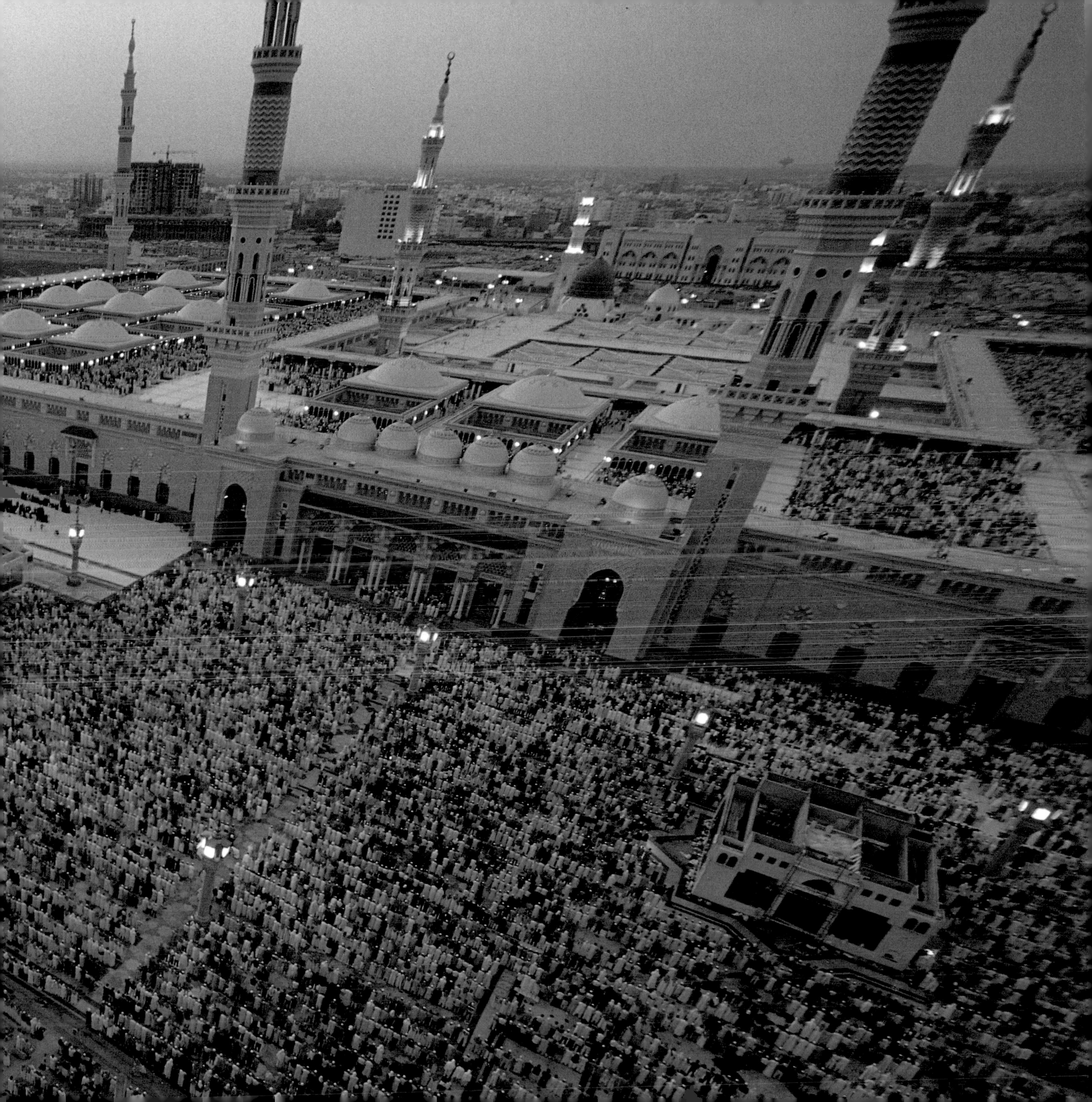

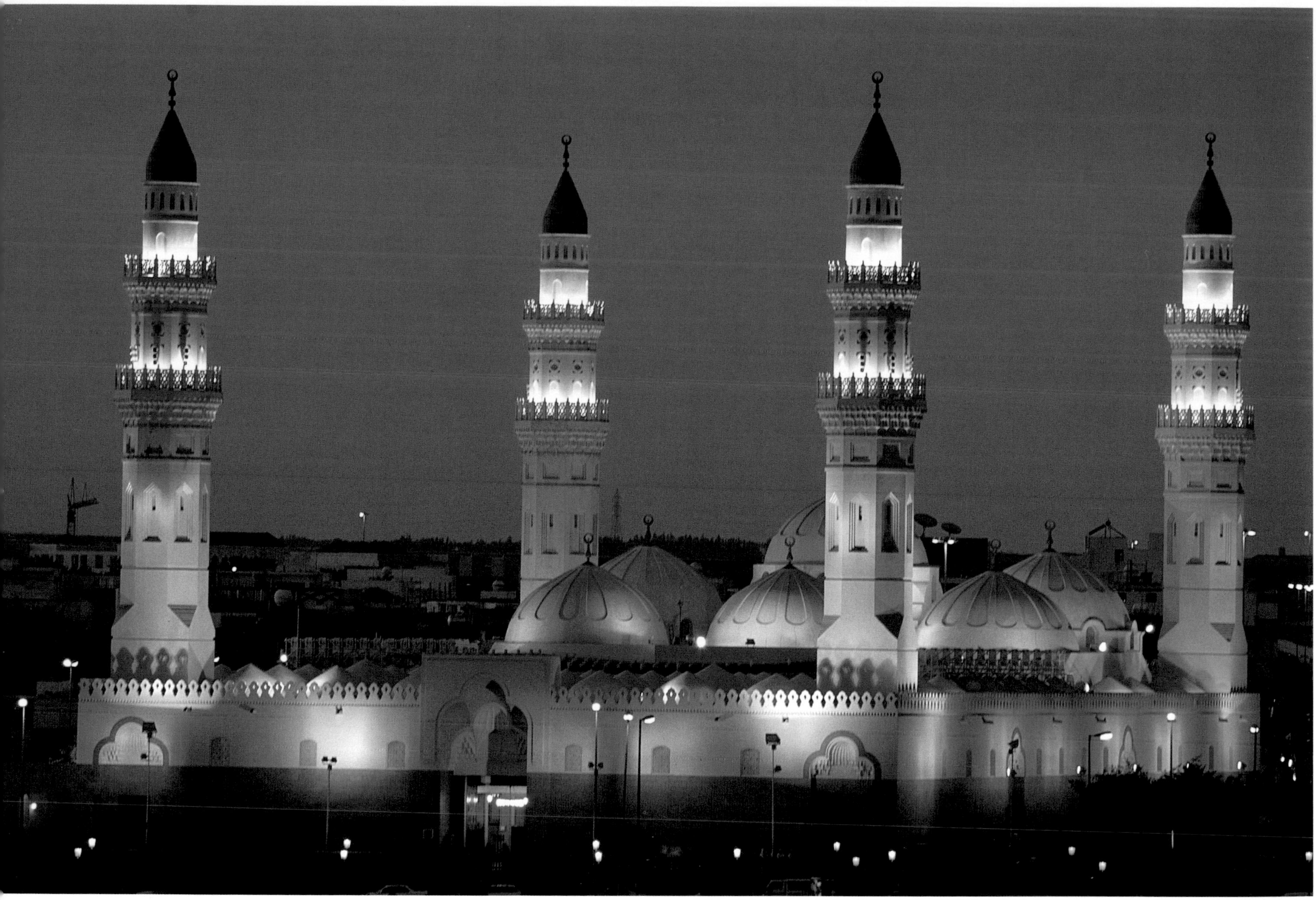

*(Previous pages)*
The early prayers on the morning after the end of Ramaḍān marking the ʿĪd al-fiṭr which is the great Muslim holiday. On this occasion over a million people consisting of pilgrims as well as the people of Medina come to the Mosque of the Prophet, the worshippers overflowing to the spaces around the Mosque.

*(Above)*
This is the Qubā' Mosque where the Blessed Prophet first prayed when he entered Medina. He gathered stones with his own hands and with the help of his followers built a simple edifice which is considered to be the first mosque in the world.

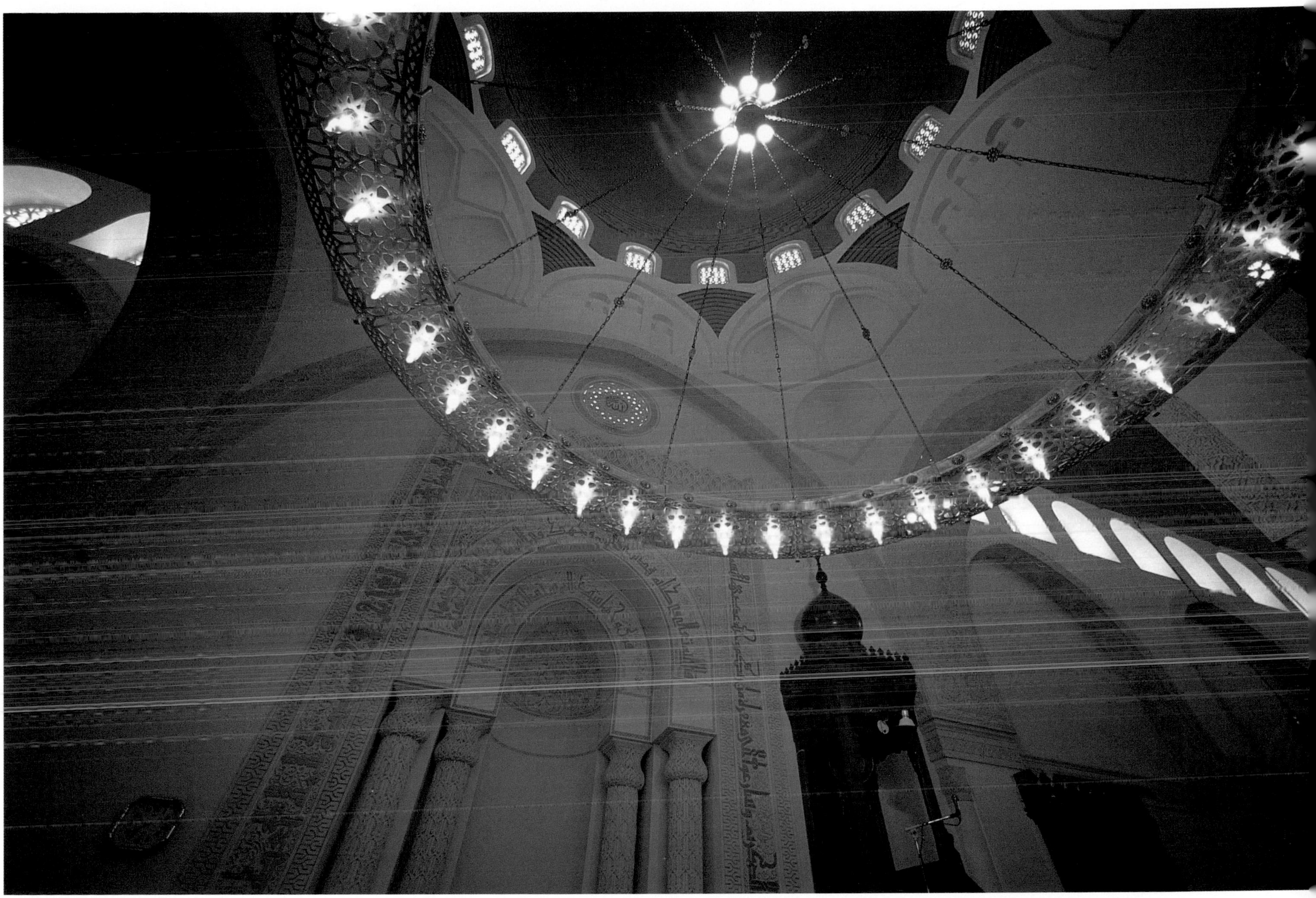

This is the *miḥrāb* of the Qiblatayn Mosque (literally meaning having two *qiblahs* or directions of prayer). During the first years of the advent of Islam the *qiblah* was in the direction of Jerusalem and then by Divine Command the direction was changed toward Mecca. The original version of this Mosque was used during that transitional period and therefore had two *qiblahs*. The current edifice was constructed recently at the site of the earlier mosque.

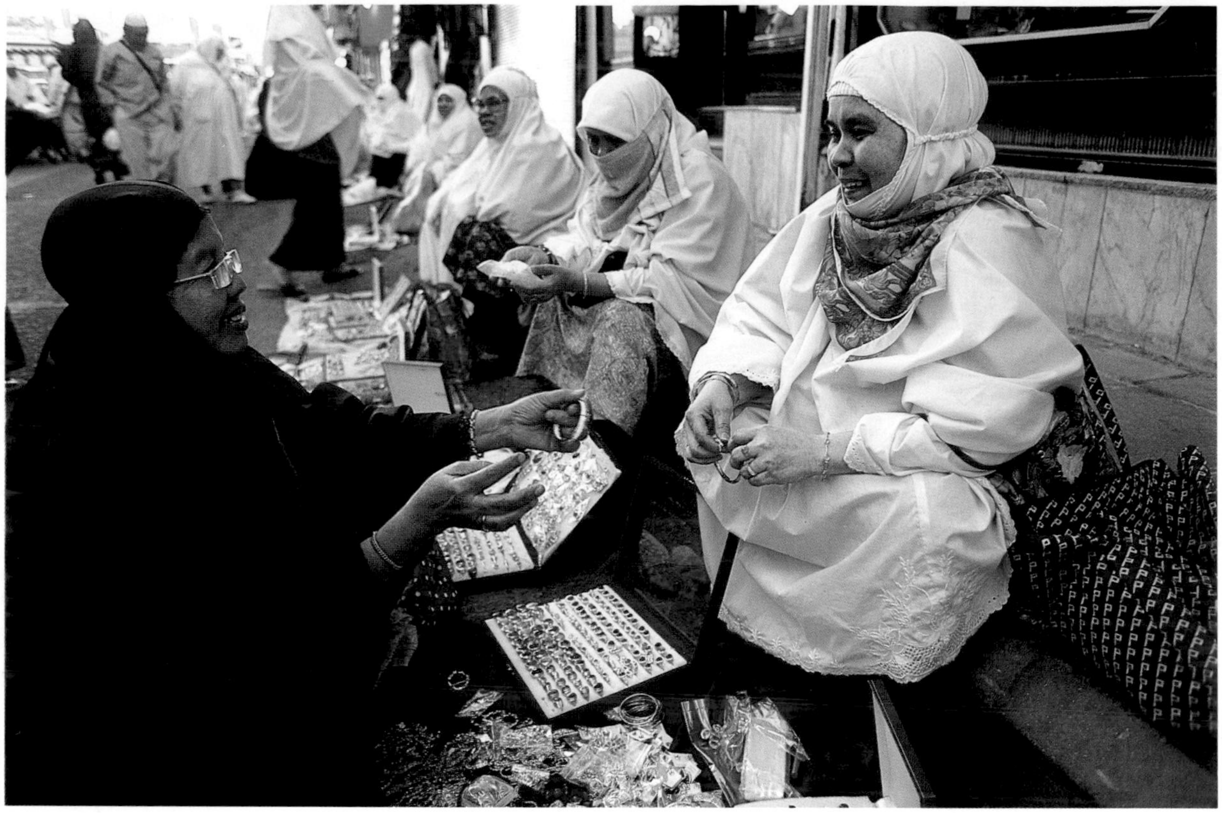

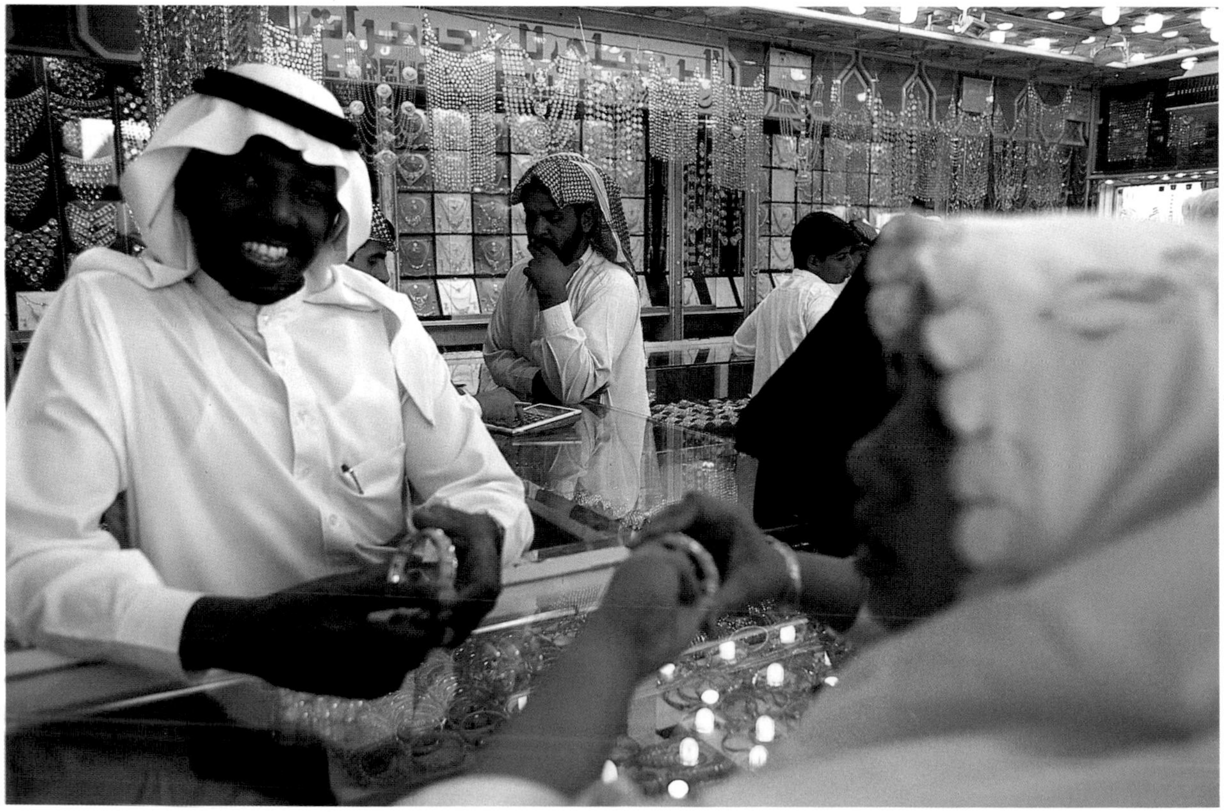

*(Top)*
Thai pilgrims selling merchandise from their homeland. During the pilgrimage people are allowed to buy and sell goods which often provides for the expenses of their journey. This tradition goes back to the earliest days of Islam.

*(Bottom)*
Jewelers in the bazaar around the Mosque of the Prophet. Many women purchase jewelry during the pilgrimage and jewelry shops have the largest number of customers during the months of *ḥajj* and Ramaḍān.

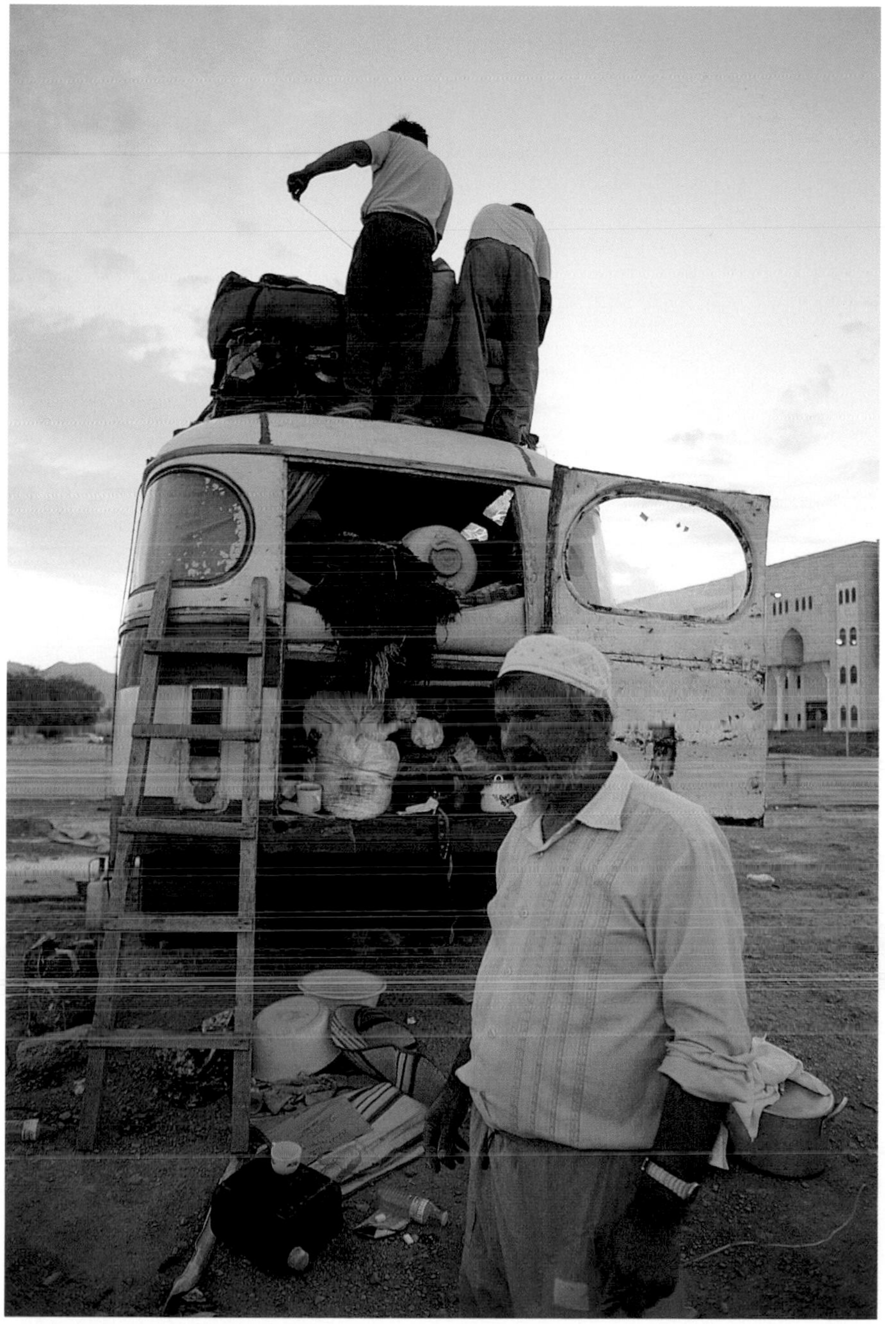

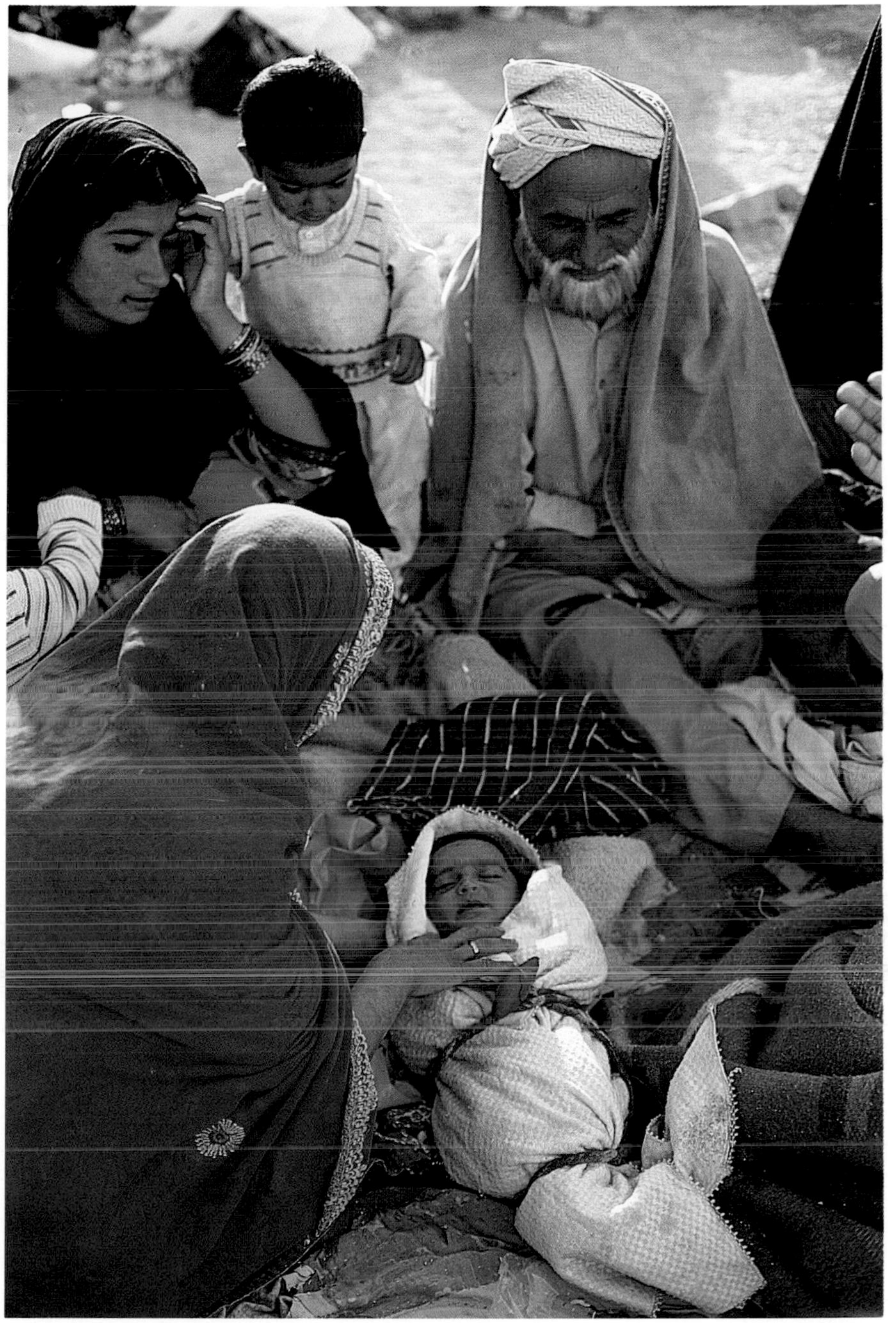

*(Left)*
Pilgrims from Daghestan, a Muslim land in present-day Russia. They had made the journey of 5,800 km in eight days through Iran, Iraq and Jordan.

*(Right)*
A poor family of pilgrims from Pakistan who were camping on vacant land adjacent to the Mosque of the Prophet for a whole week.

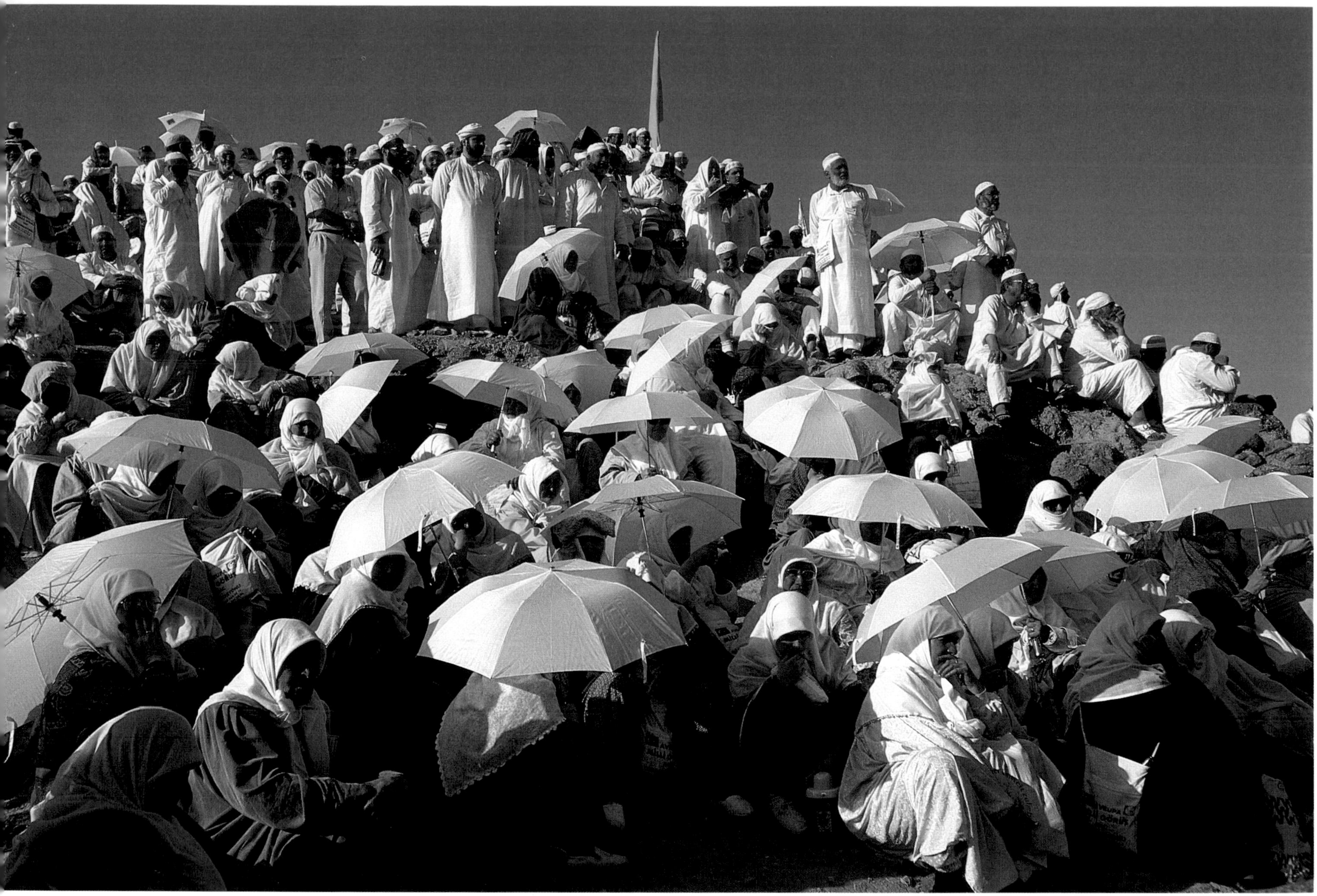

A group of Turkish pilgrims staying at the foot of Mount Uḥud the site in northern Medina of the famous and intense battle in Islamic history during which the idolatrous Quraysh tribe from Mecca defeated the Islamic army. During this battle the Blessed Prophet was injured but the Meccans did not pursue the Muslims and returned to their own city.

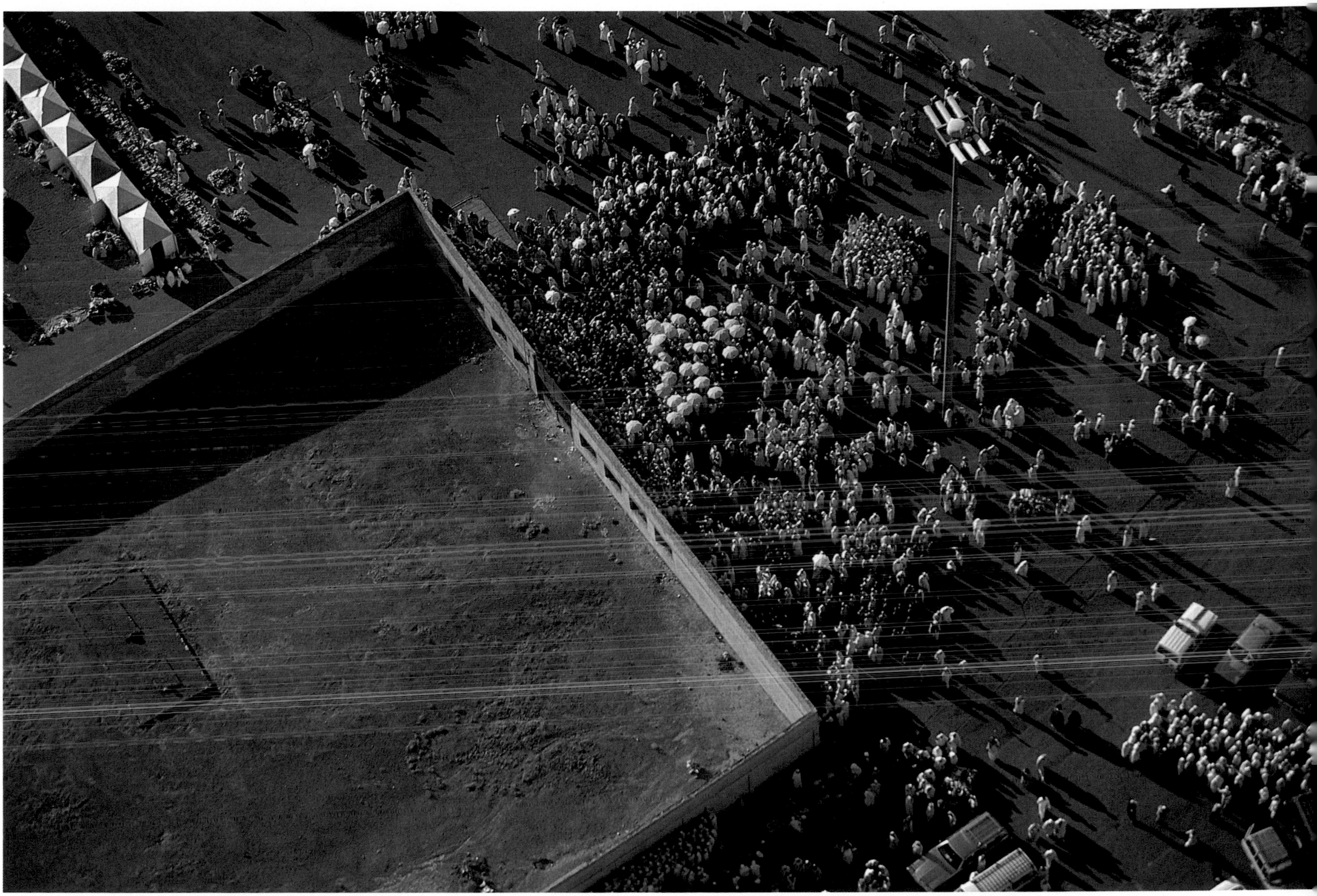

Pilgrims praying at the tomb of the Blessed Prophet's uncle, Ḥamzah, who died at the battle of Uḥud along with 70 other martyrs. In this battle which took place on the 23rd of March AD625, the Islamic army consisting of 1,000 men faced an army three times its size led by the Quraysh from Mecca.

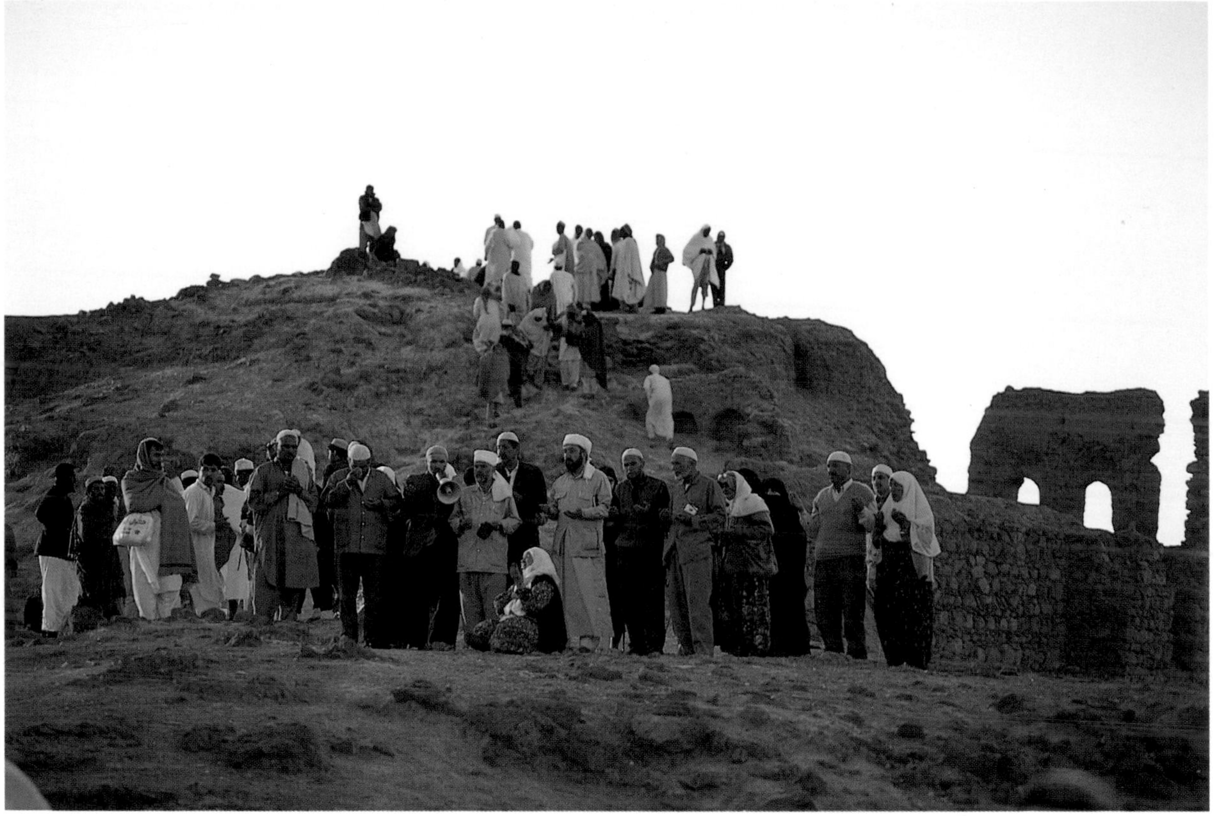

A group of Turkish pilgrims praying and mourning at the battlefield of Uḥud.

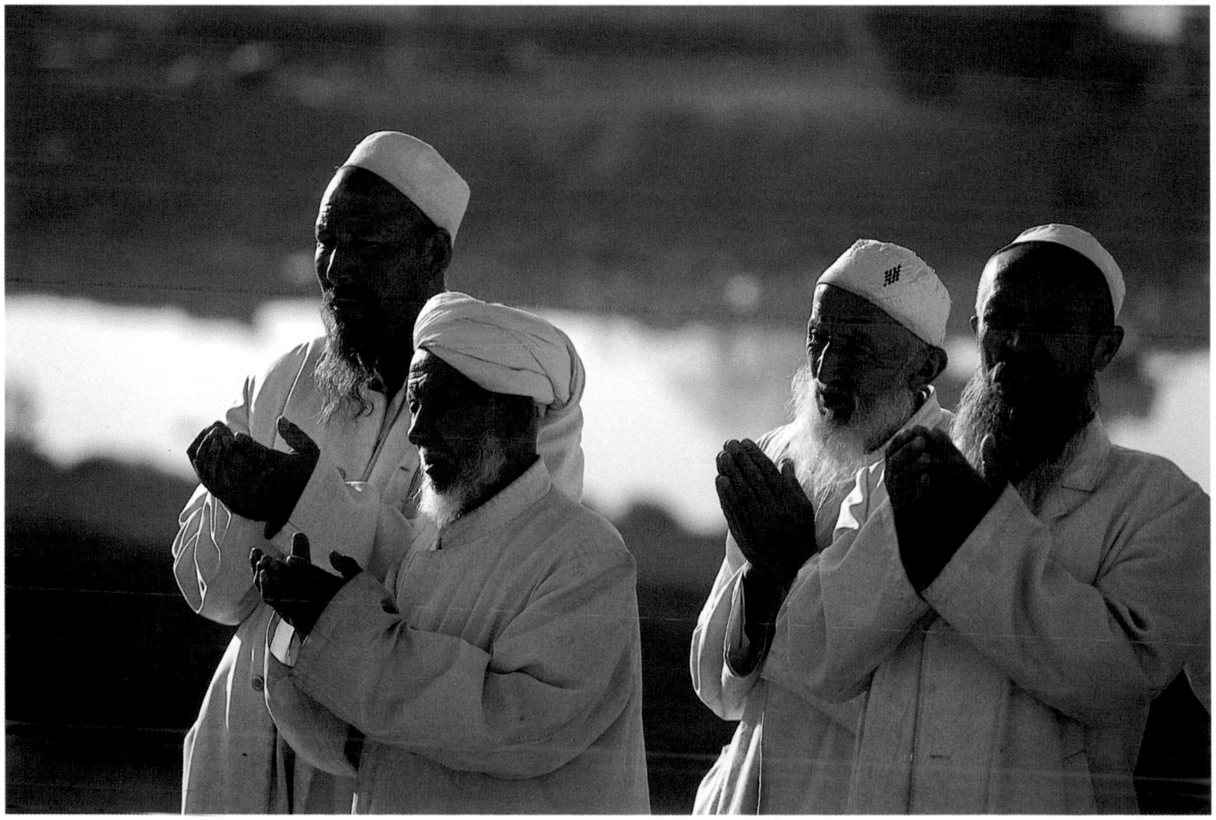

A group of Chinese Muslims from Kashghar/Kashi visiting, like almost all other pilgrims, the battlefield of Uḥud.

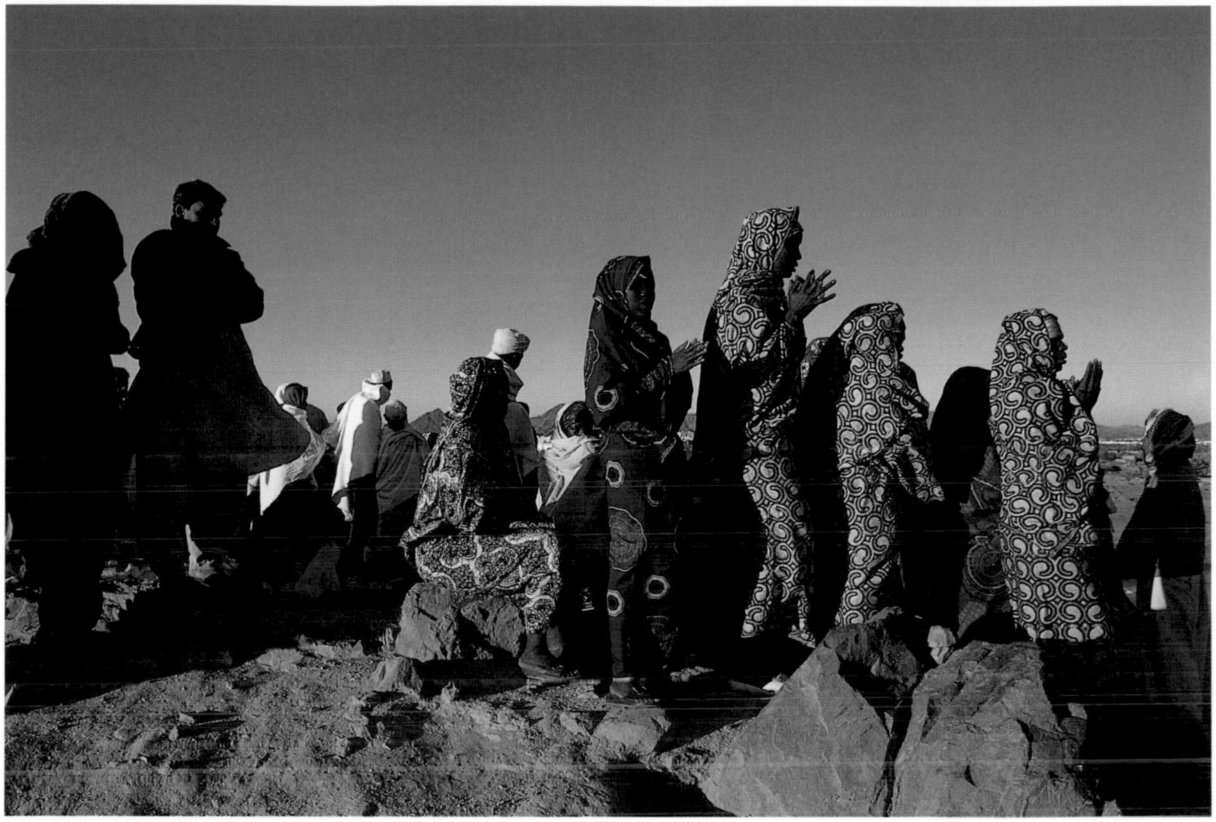

A group of Nigerian pilgrims at Uḥud.

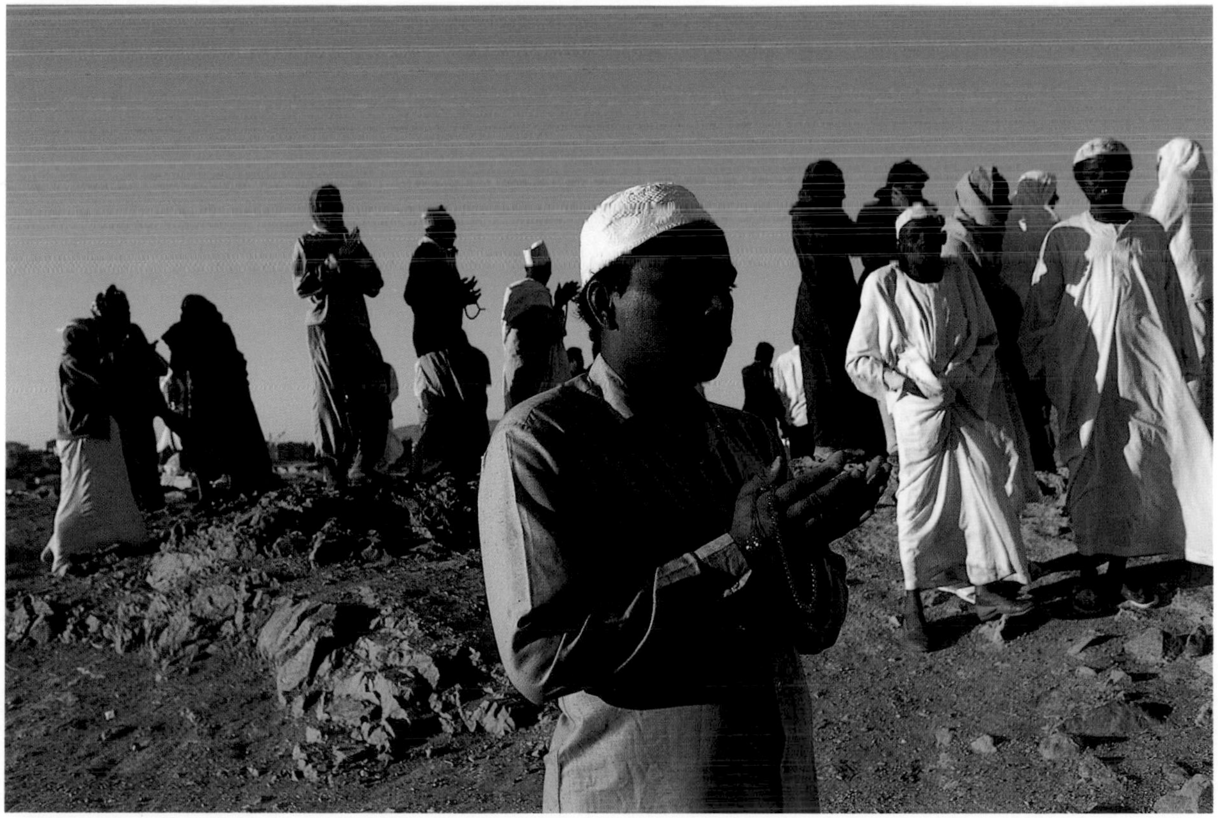

A group of Pakistani pilgrims praying on a hilltop in the early morning hours.

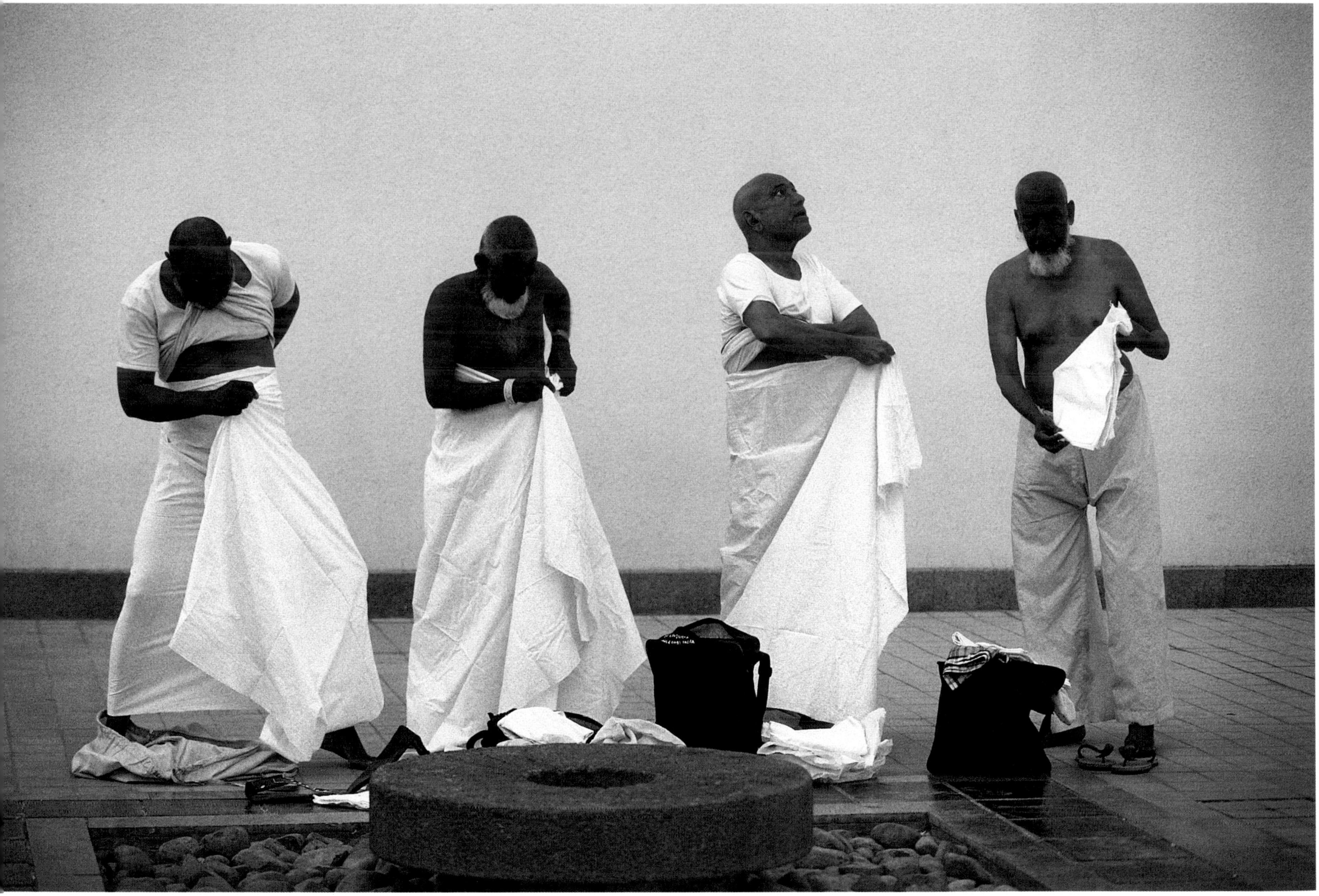

*(Above)*
Pilgrims donning the *iḥrām* at the Mīqāt Mosque to go to Mecca for pilgrimage. Before putting on the *iḥrām*, they perform the ritual washing of their bodies (*ghusl*).

*(Opposite)*
While wearing the *iḥrām*, the Muslim is forbidden from hunting, killing, arguing, violence, deceit and sexual activity.

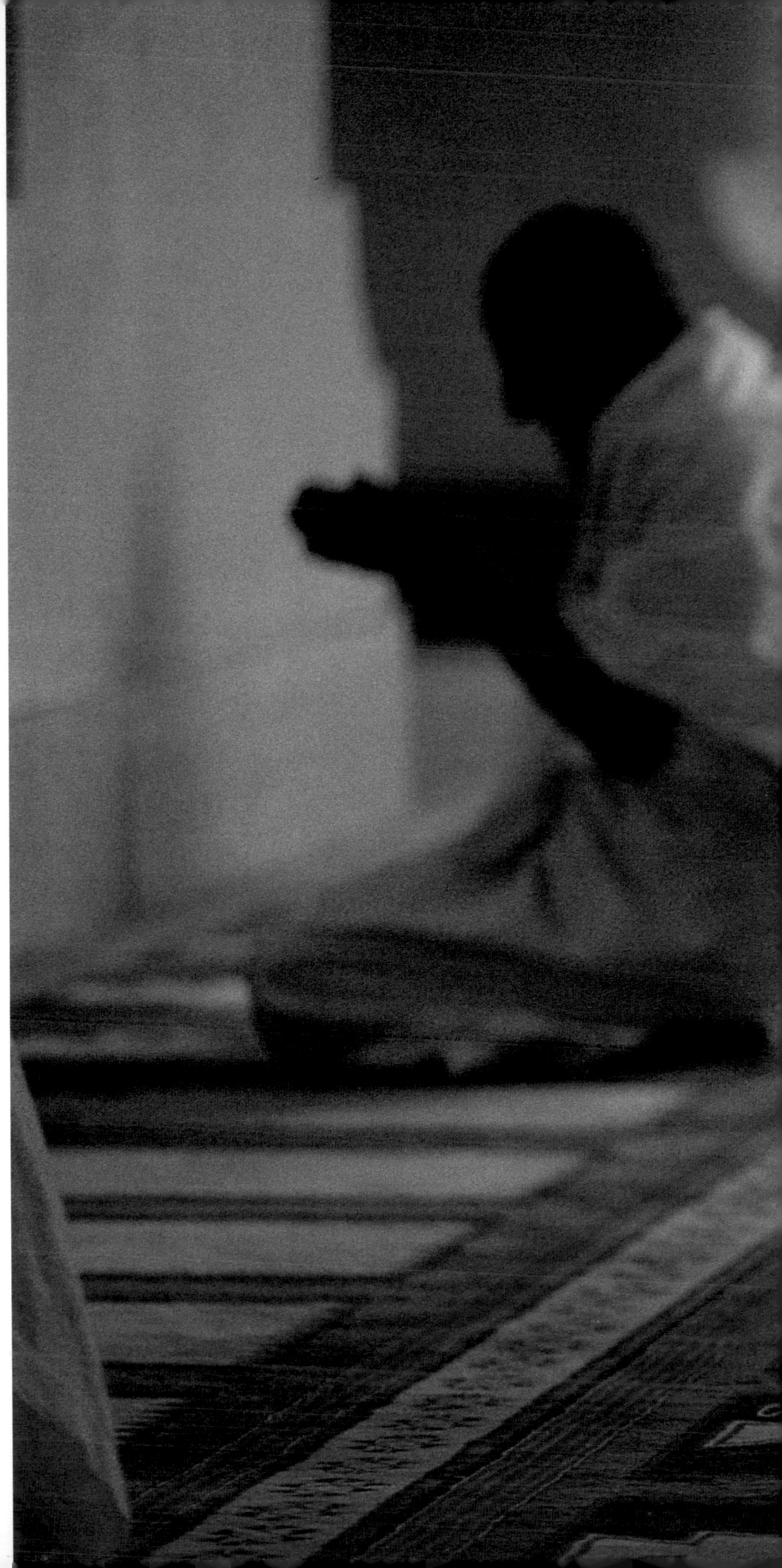

The *iḥrām*, consisting of two pieces of seamless white cloth, is worn on the naked body and symbolizes the state of man in his primordial condition.

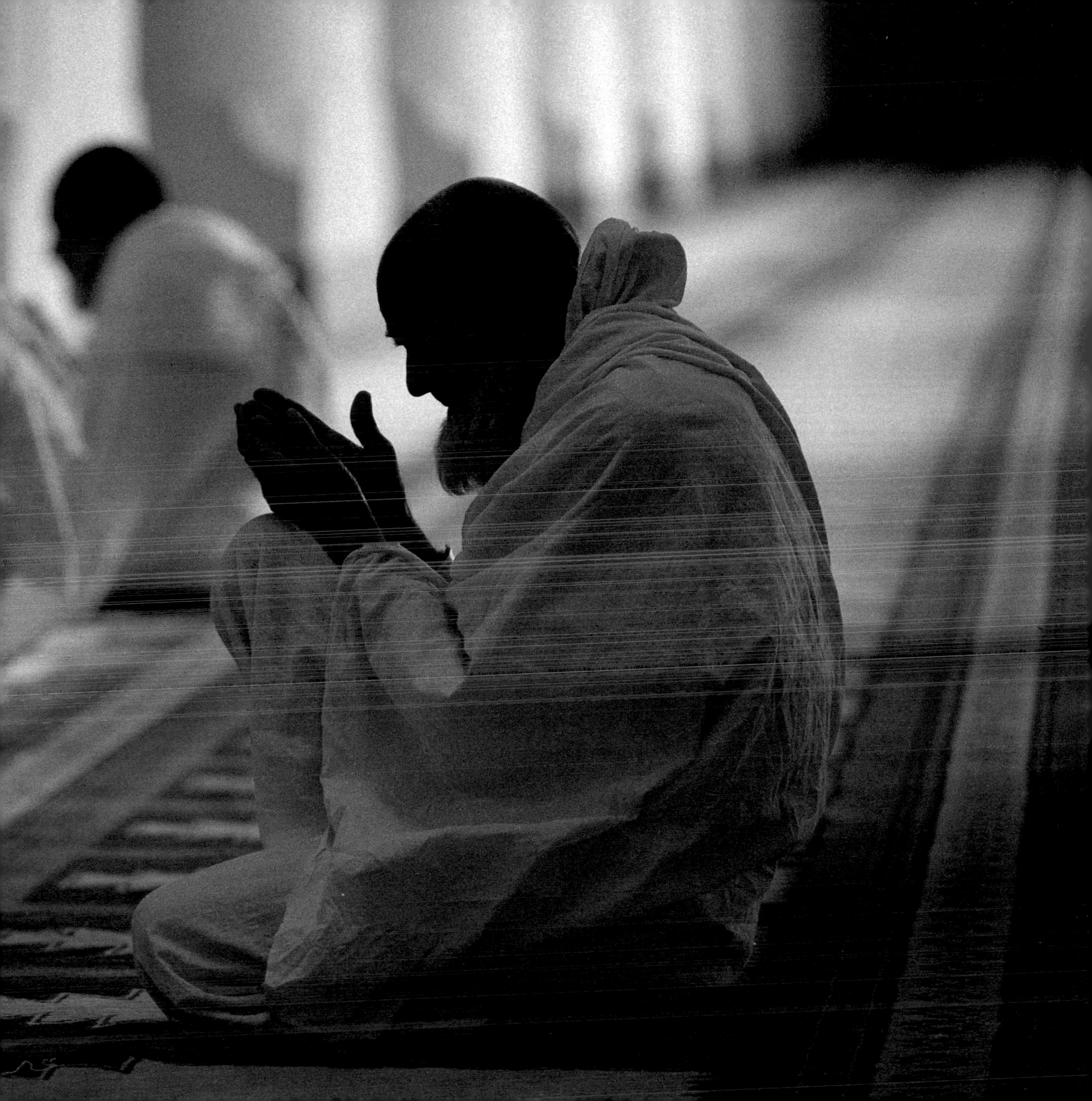

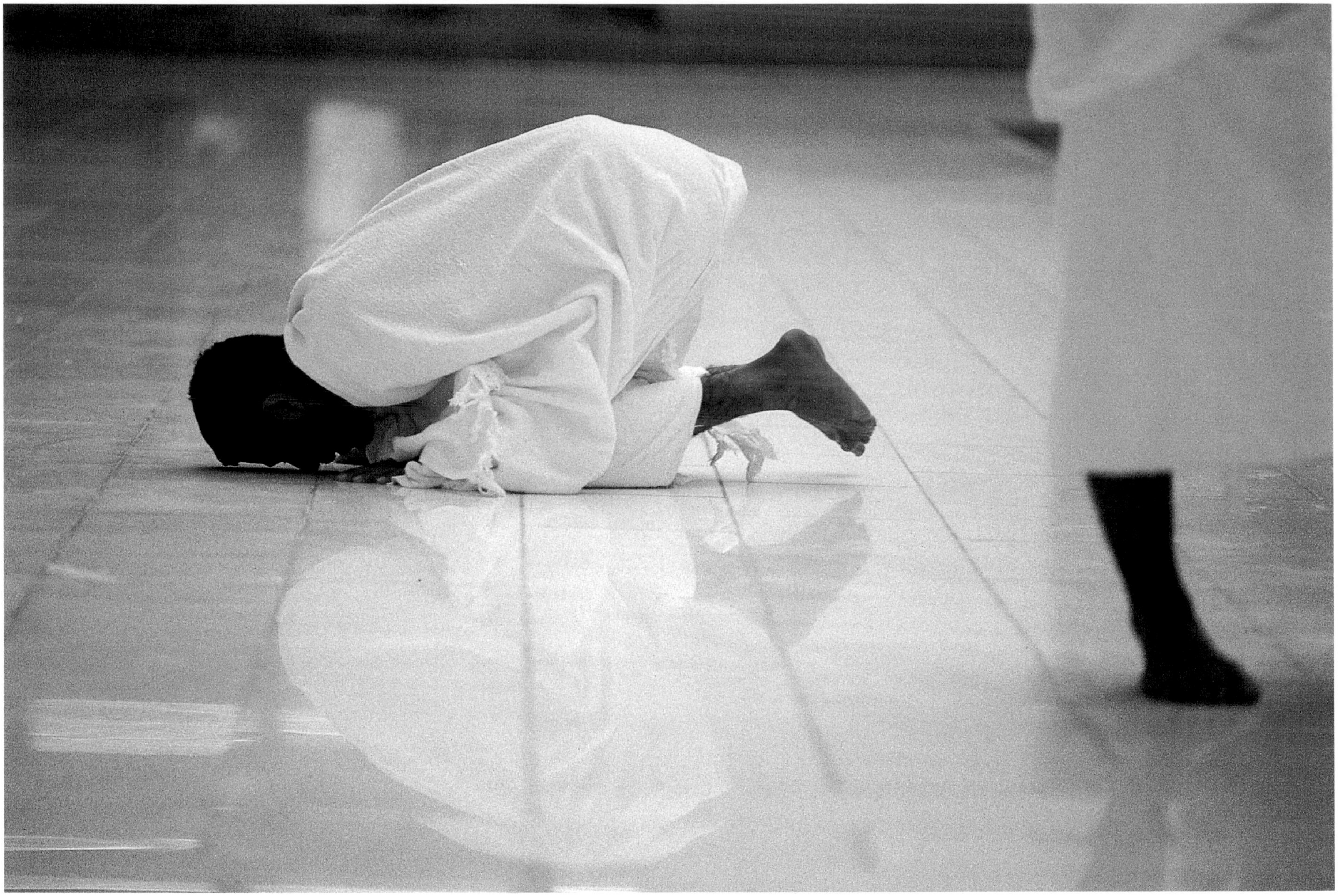

The *iḥrām*, especially of one's first pilgrimage, is washed in zamzam water and then put away to be used as one's shroud. To wear the *iḥrām* itself symbolizes having died to the profane world.

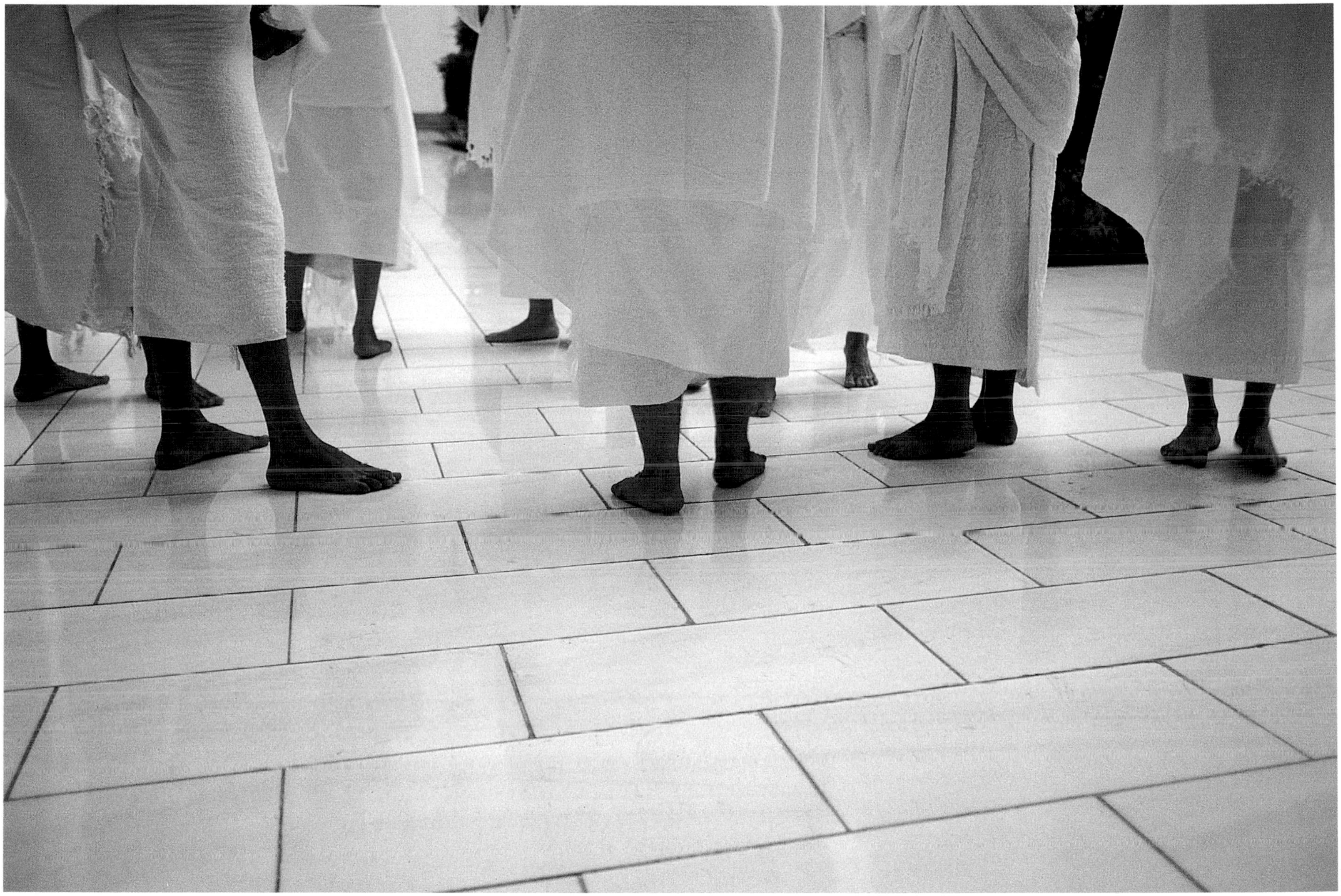

When wearing the *iḥrām*, one must remove all adornments. In fact all signs of position and status in society are removed and all men face God with their soul laid bare and independent of all worldly distinctions.

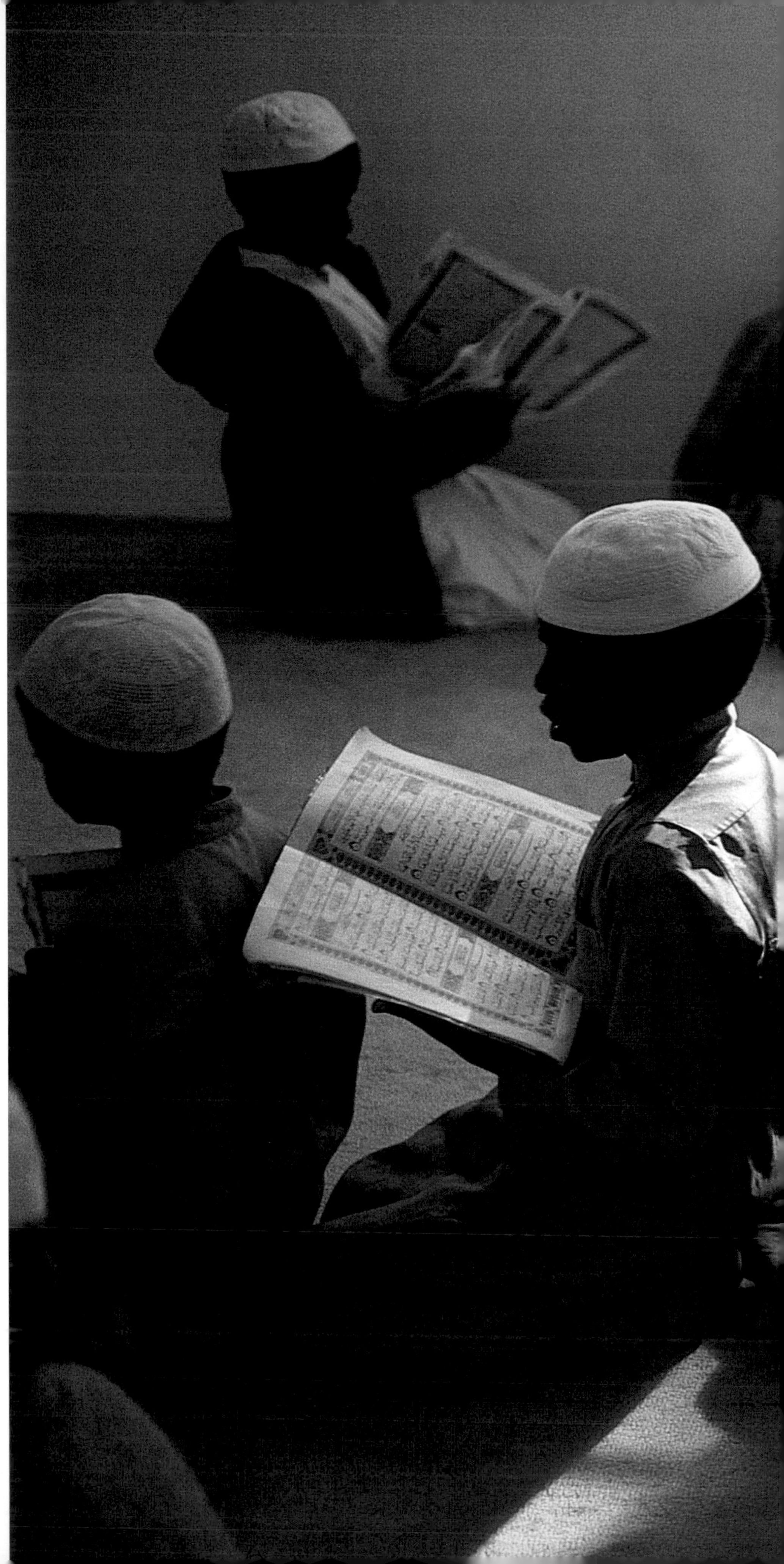

Children of foreign laborers and residents at one of the many Qur'ānic schools in Medina. The children are from many nationalities reflecting the different national backgrounds of the laborers and the many pilgrims who have come from all over the world to Medina and then have decided to remain there.

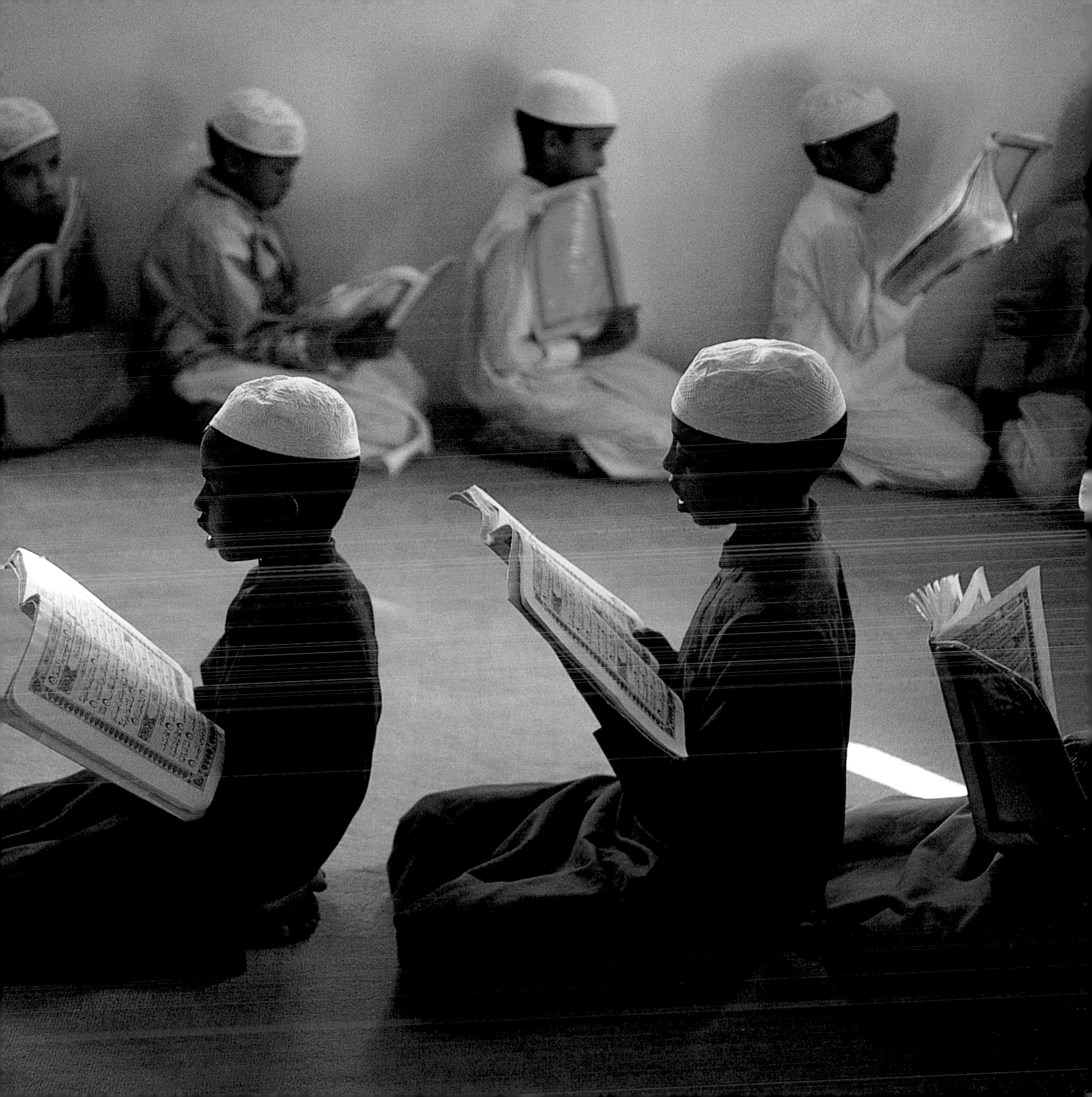

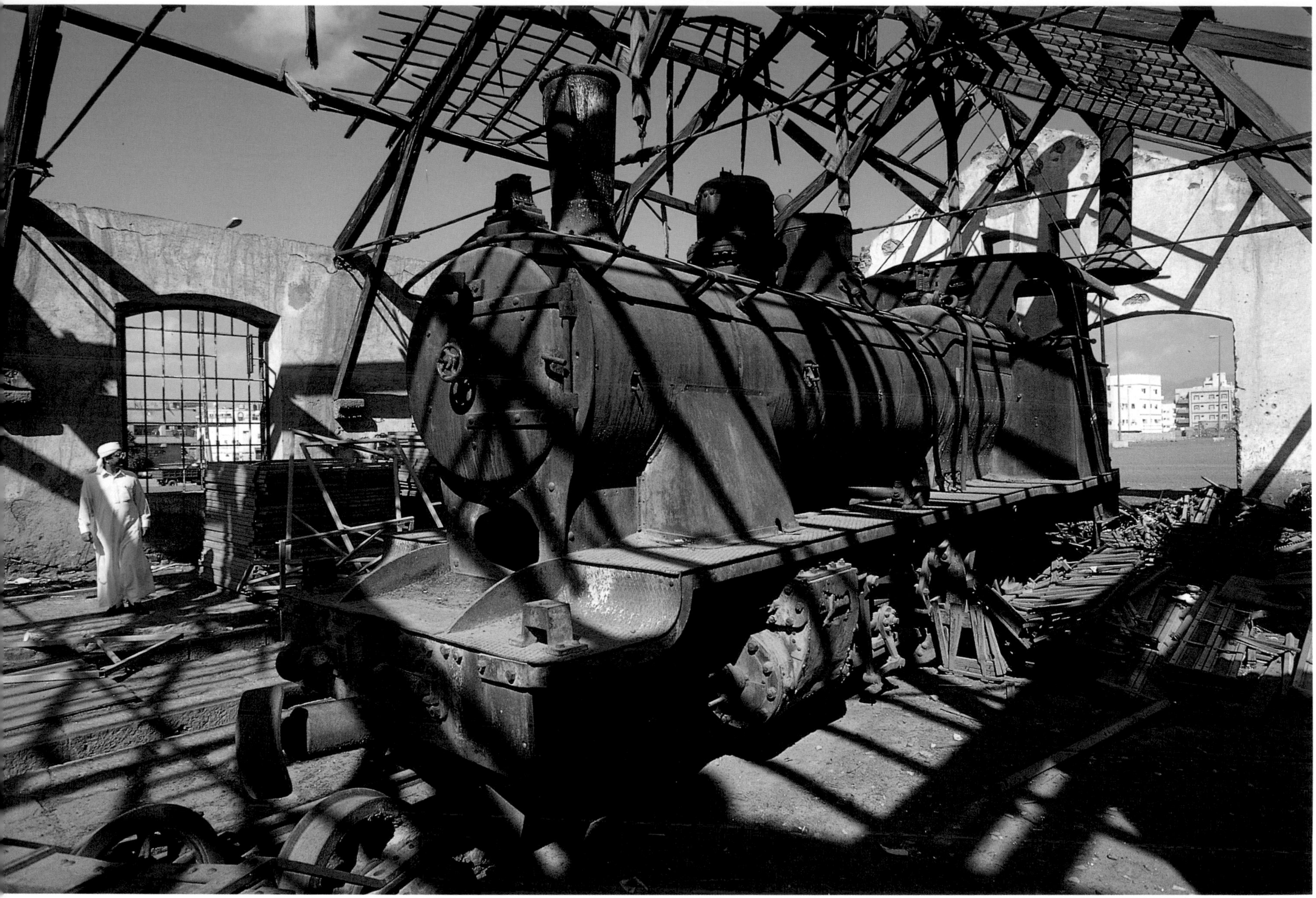

The Ottomans built a railway to link Damascus to Medina. The line was opened in 1908 and trains remained in service until 1924 when Medina fell to the forces of the Saudis. This steam engine remains in the station of the historic railway.

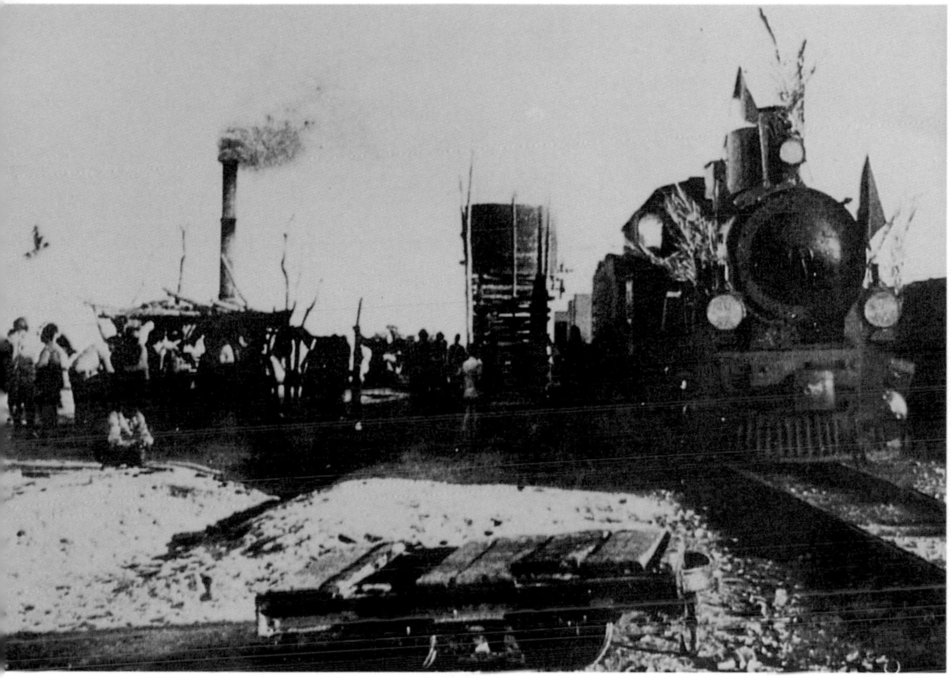

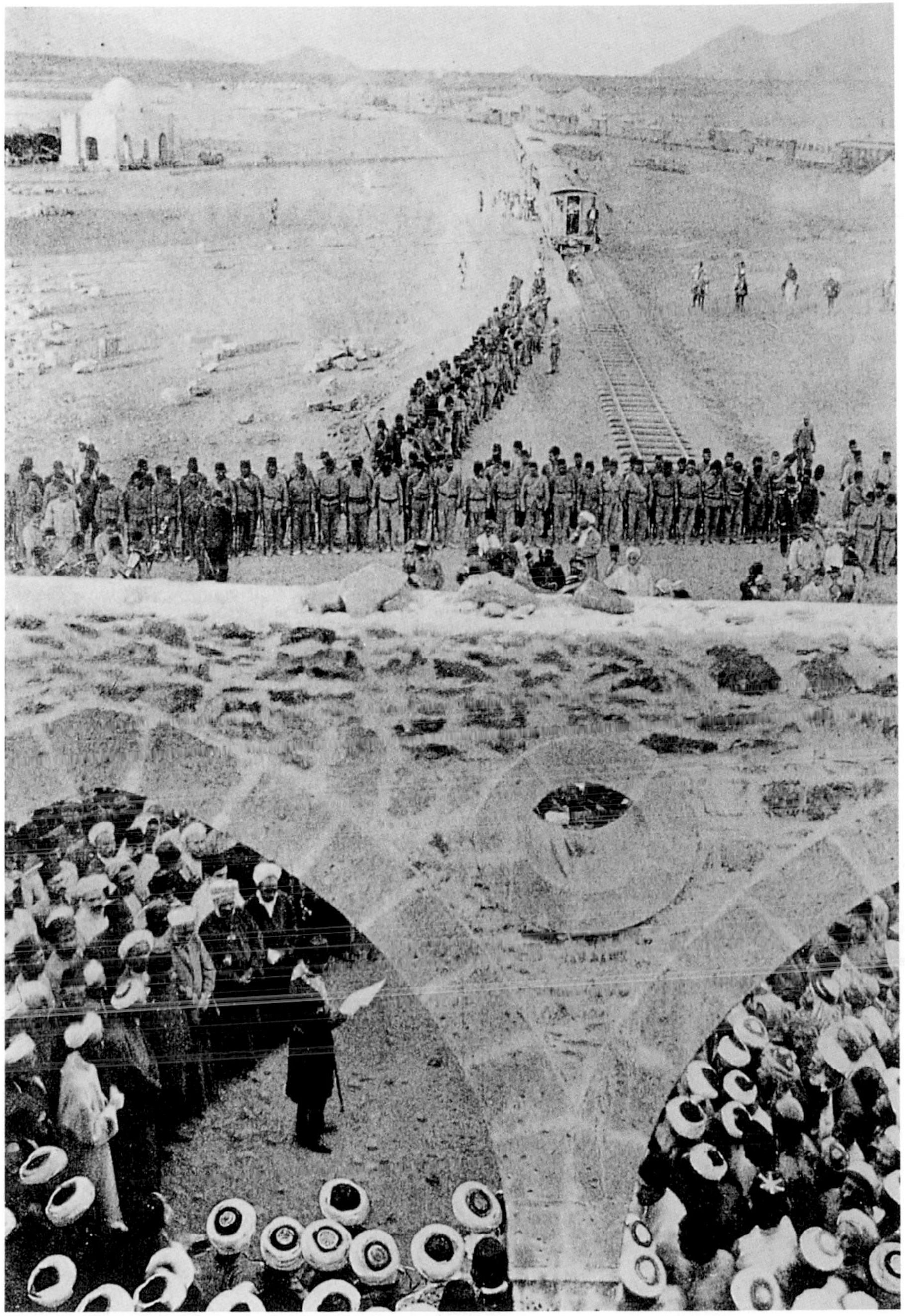

*(Above left)*
A historic picture of the train leaving Medina in 1908 when the railway was called the Hijaz Railway. Some of the track between Damascus and Medina is to be found to this day.

*(Above right)*
The opening ceremony of the Hijaz Railway in Medina in 1908. There were plans to extend the railway to Mecca, but they were never realized.

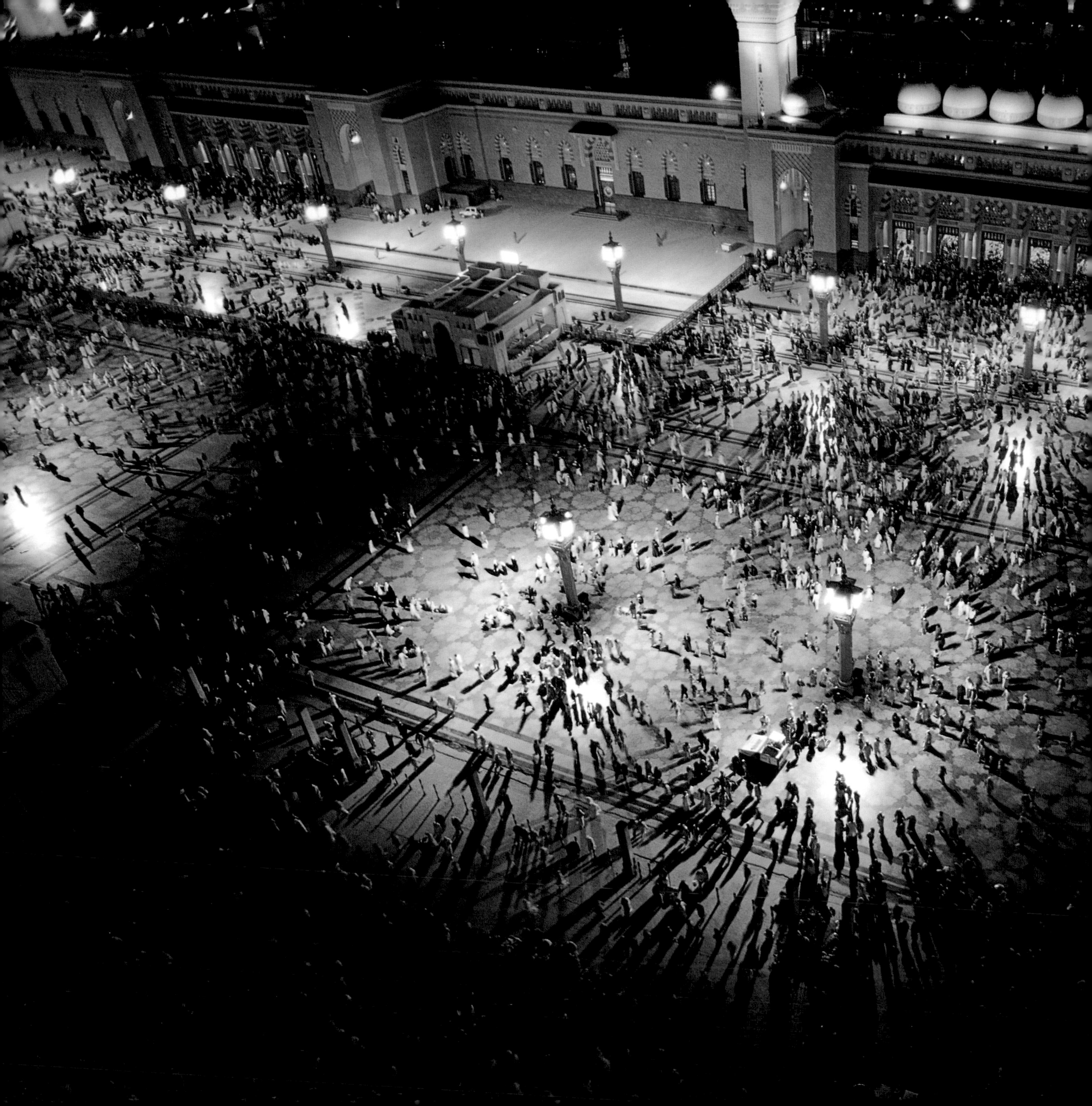

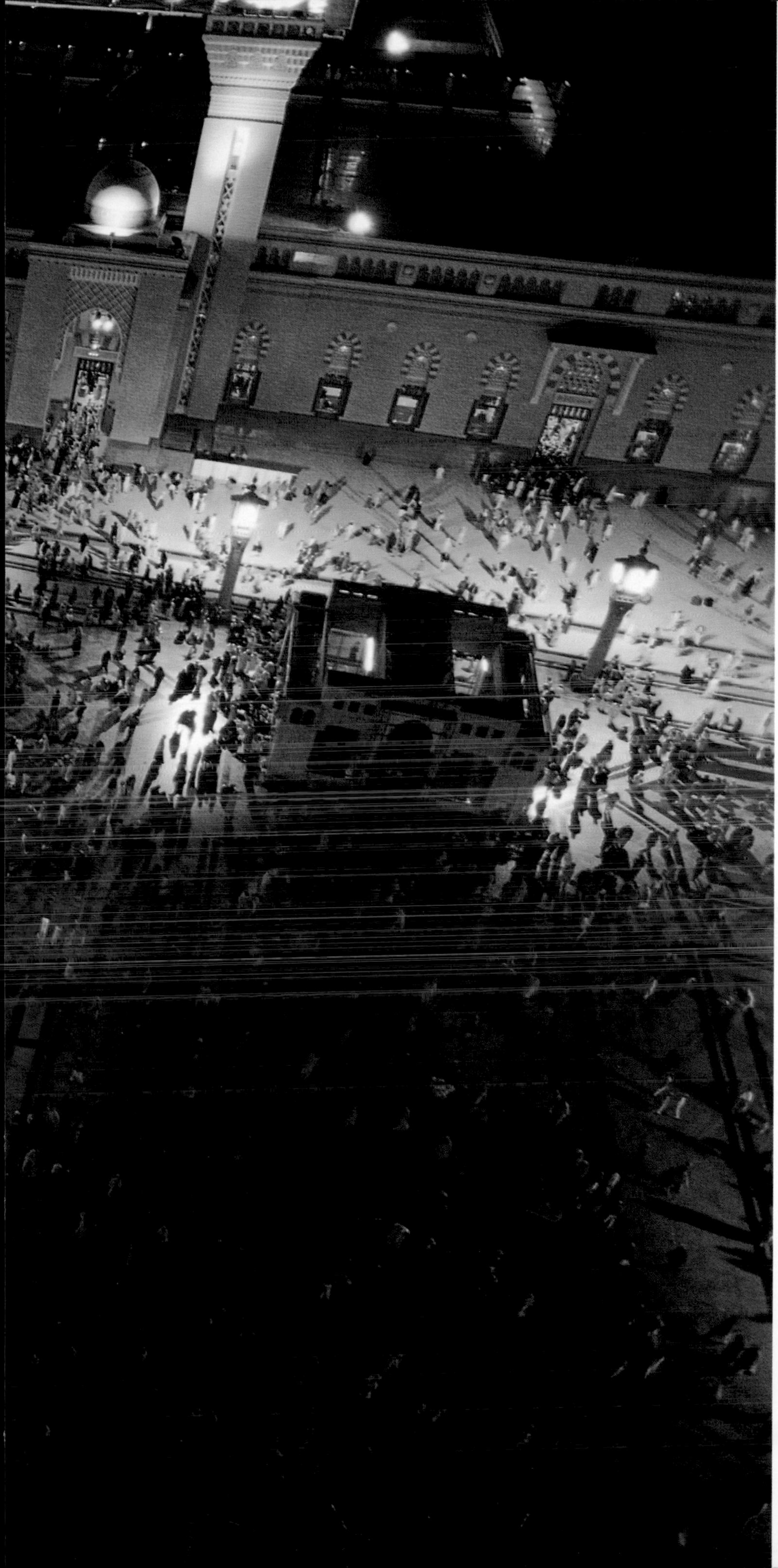

People coming out of the Mosque of the Prophet after the *maghrib* prayers when all the shops around the Mosque open their doors again and the area becomes very lively. As for restaurants, they begin to serve after the *ʿishā'* prayers.

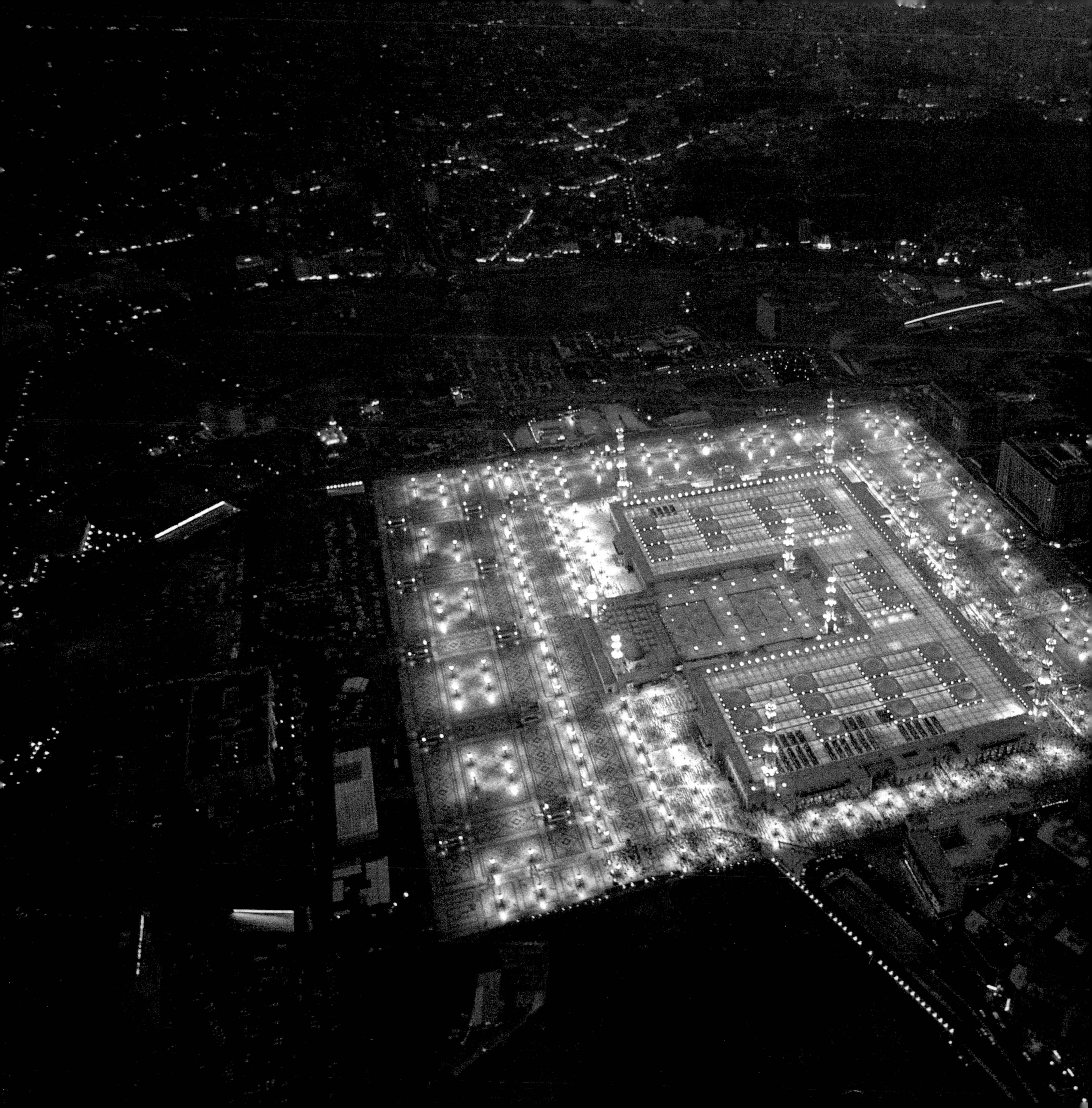

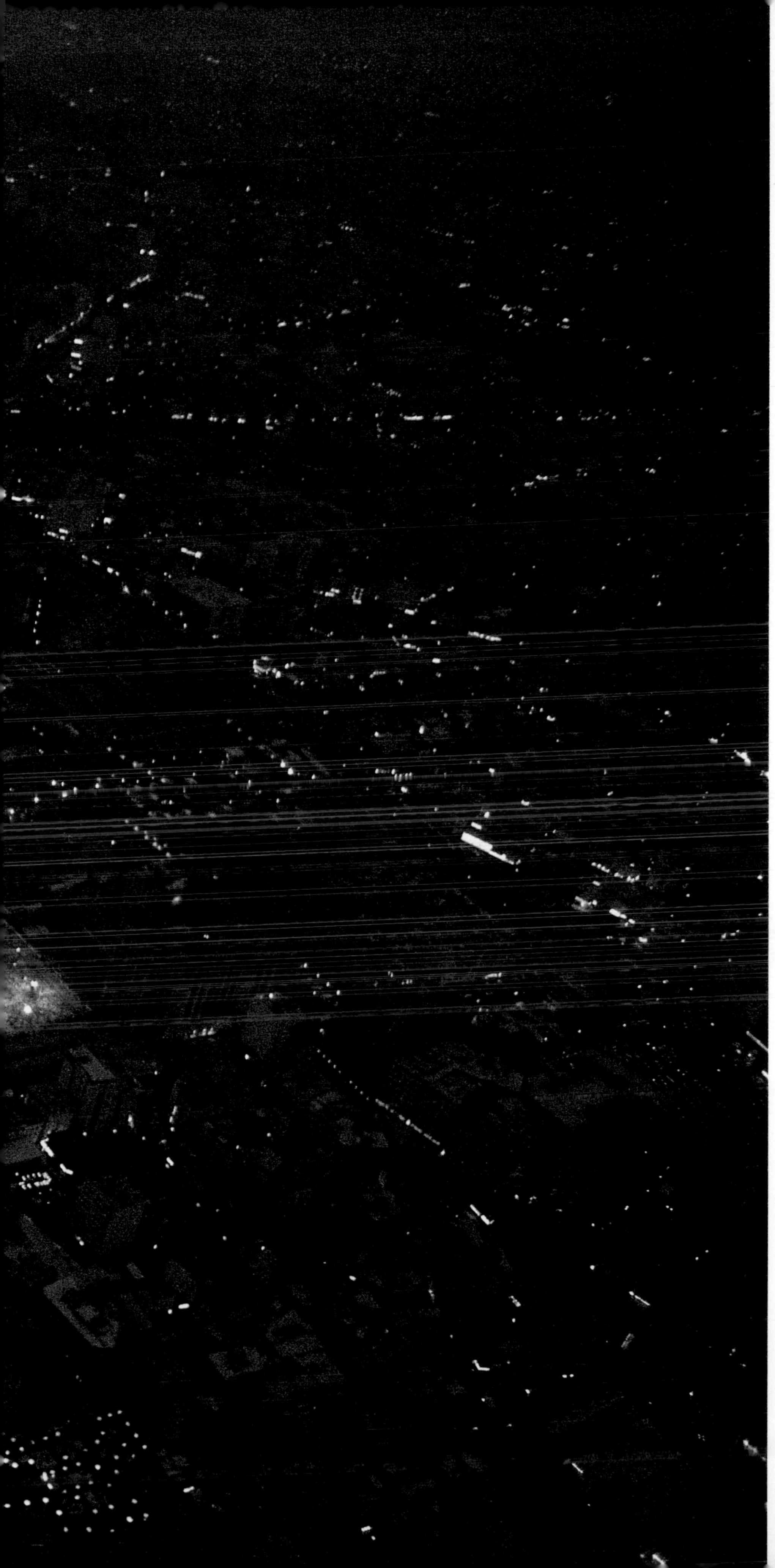

The Mosque of the Prophet at dusk. To counter the heat, the floor of the Mosque is covered by white marble, an important factor when the prayers are performed under the heat of the sun. The new extension of the Mosque has six minarets each reaching 104 meters and standing outside the four minarets of the old Mosque each of which has a height of 72 meters.

# *Arabia*

Bridge between three continents, neighbor to the African and Persian worlds as well as the eastern Mediterranean region, this stark land of great beauty and purity, was witness to many prophets and the scenes of many episodes of the sacred history of the Abrahamic world. But it remained outside of the arena of world history until it was visited by the Archangel Gabriel who, on the order of God, brought the Qur'ānic revelation and revealed the last total message of Heaven to one of the sons of Arabia, the Blessed Prophet of Islam. Henceforth the land of Arabia became inseparable from the life of the Prophet. In the same way that the aroma of the frankincense of this land reached the Roman Empire and medieval Europe, the spiritual fragrance of Arabia, holy to Islam, is sensed by Muslims near and far. Who among the Muslim faithful ever comes to Arabia without becoming deeply imbued with the sacred quality of the land chosen by God for His final revelation?

The very starkness of the landscape of Arabia opens the soul bare and naked before God and the intensity of the sun reminds man of the majesty of the One before whom all multiplicity dissolves in the same way that in the glow of the sun of the Arabian desert the "many" seem to disappear while the ubiquitous presence of light symbolizing the Presence of the One remains. And then there are the lush green oases growing as if out of nowhere in the middle of the arid desert, oases profuse with life reminding man of the Divine Mercy which according to a sacred saying *(ḥadīth qudsī)* precedes God's wrath. The central lands of Arabia and especially the Hijaz have been blessed by God with the seal of holiness, and this land with its vast deserts symbolizing infinity and majestic peaks reflecting the quality of absoluteness and transcendence, will remain to the end of time, and despite all that men may do to defile it, a land reverberating with the presence of the Sacred.

Seyyed Hossein Nasr

Although most Bedouins in Arabia have become settled in urban centers in recent decades, some still remain nomads as seen here where a Bedouin woman is holding her child in a traditional Bedouin tent.

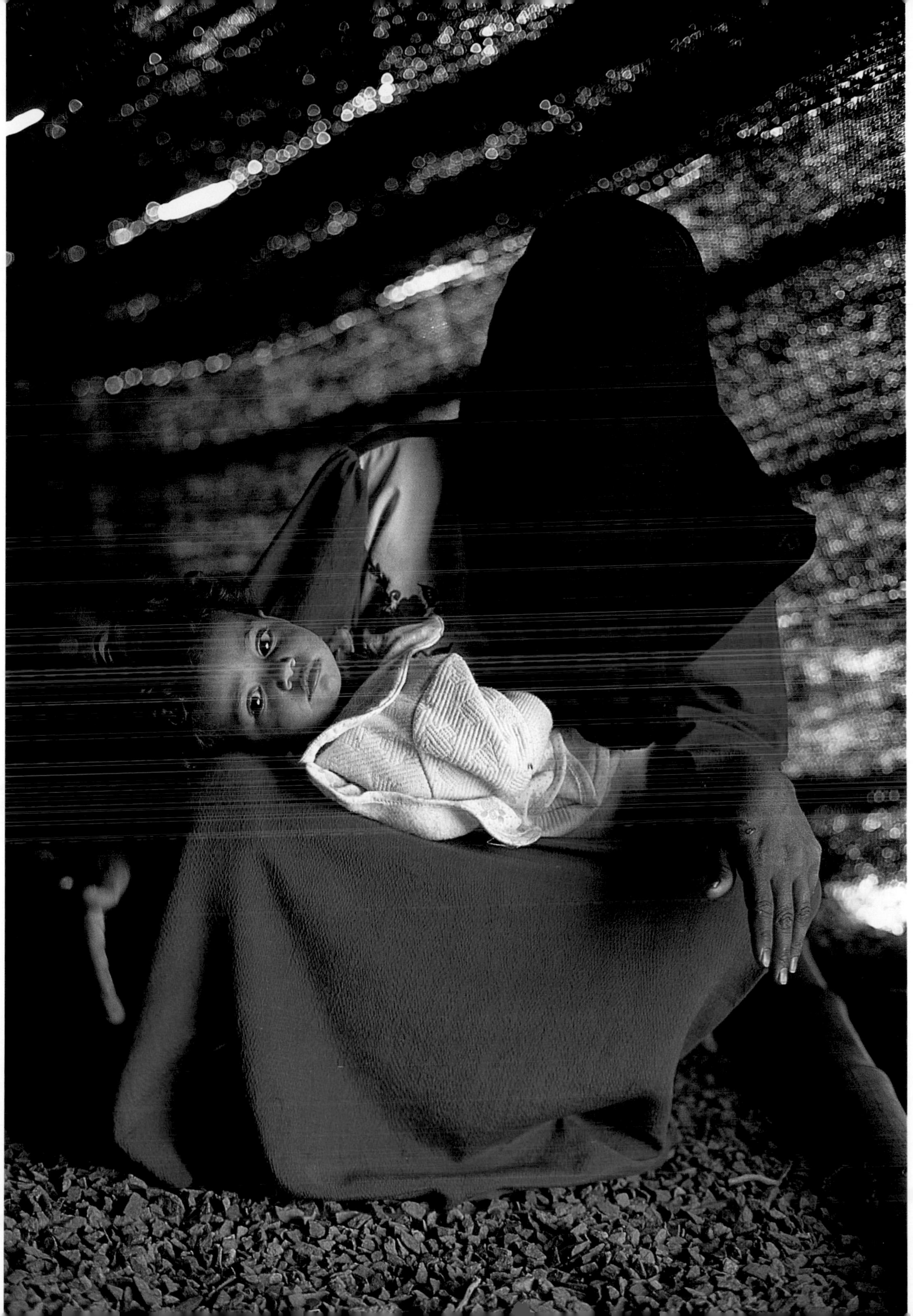

The ruins of Madā'in Ṣāliḥ which is part of a complex of ruins in the desert in the northwestern region of the Arabian peninsula, most of them being tombs of Nabataeans who formed a civilization in that region in the early centuries of the Christian era. The center of their civilization was in and around Petra in present-day Jordan.



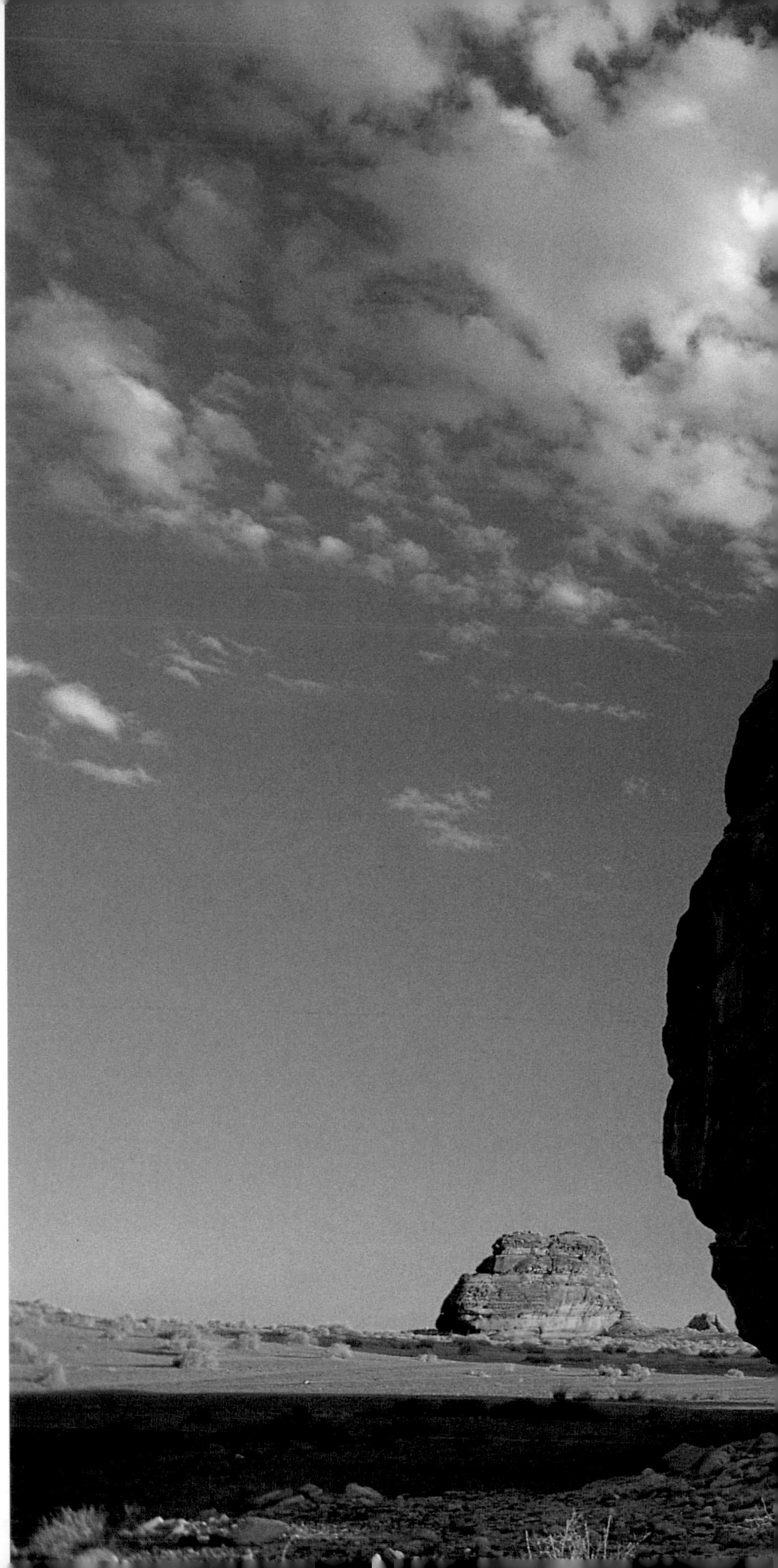

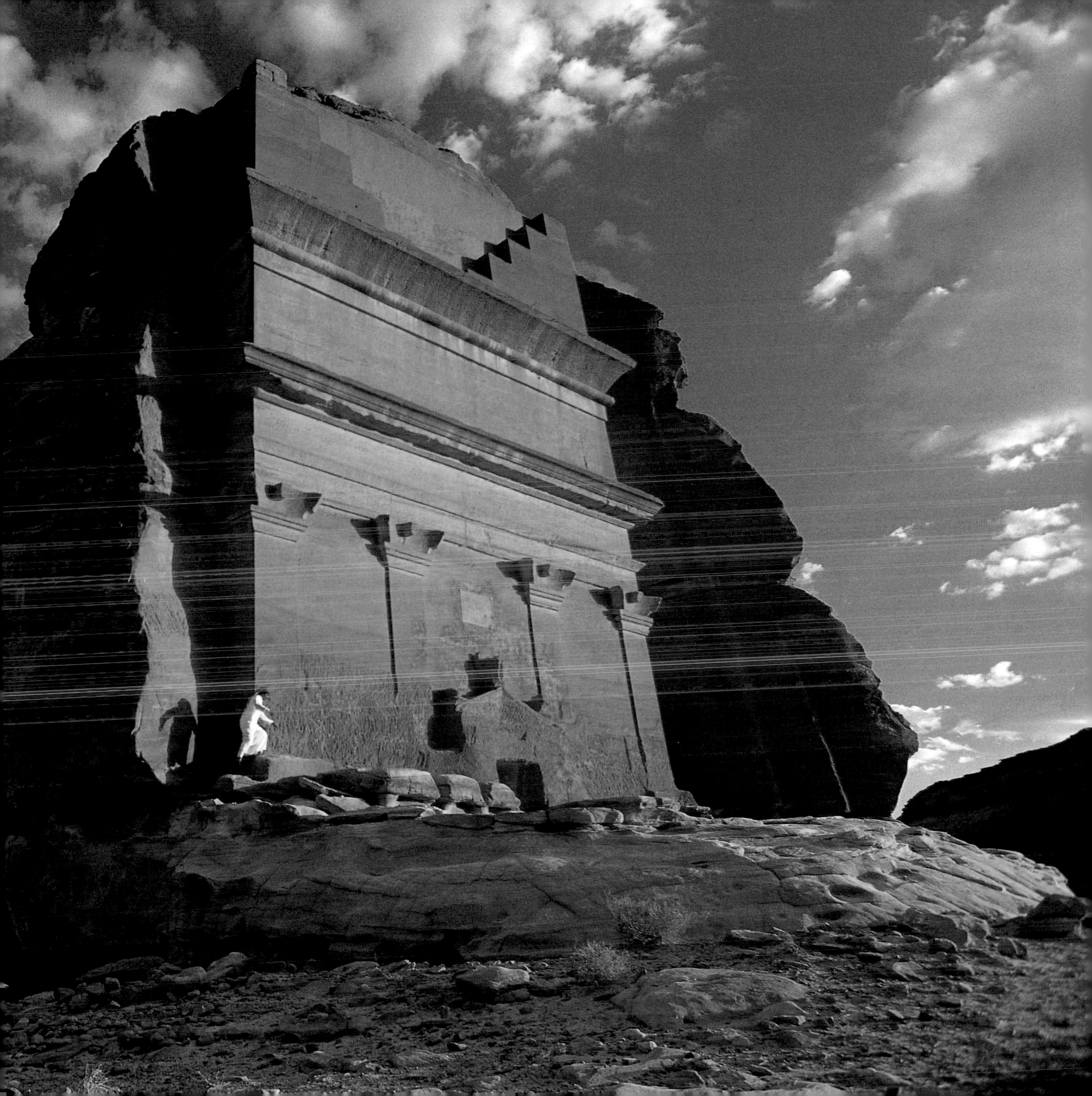

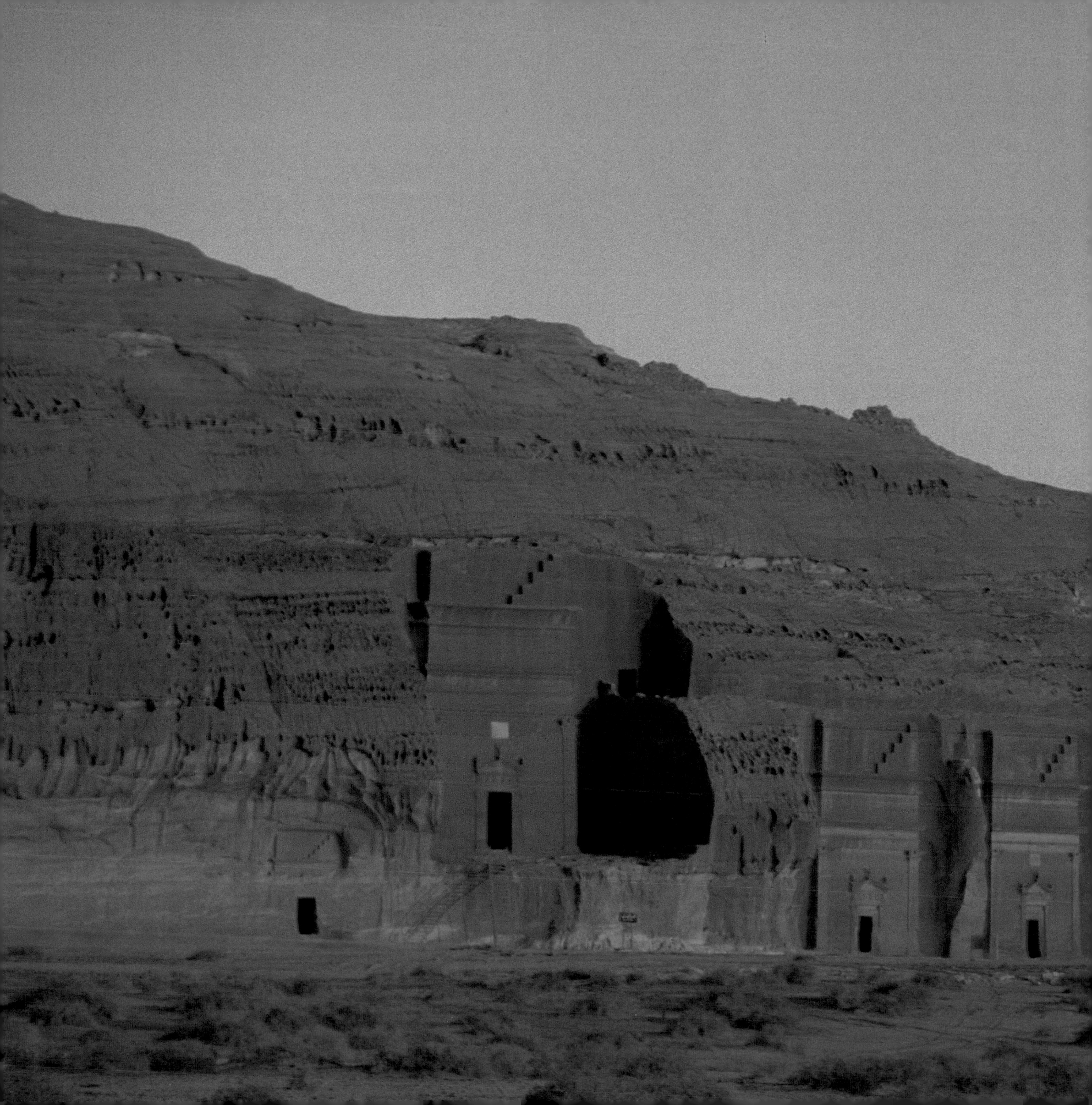

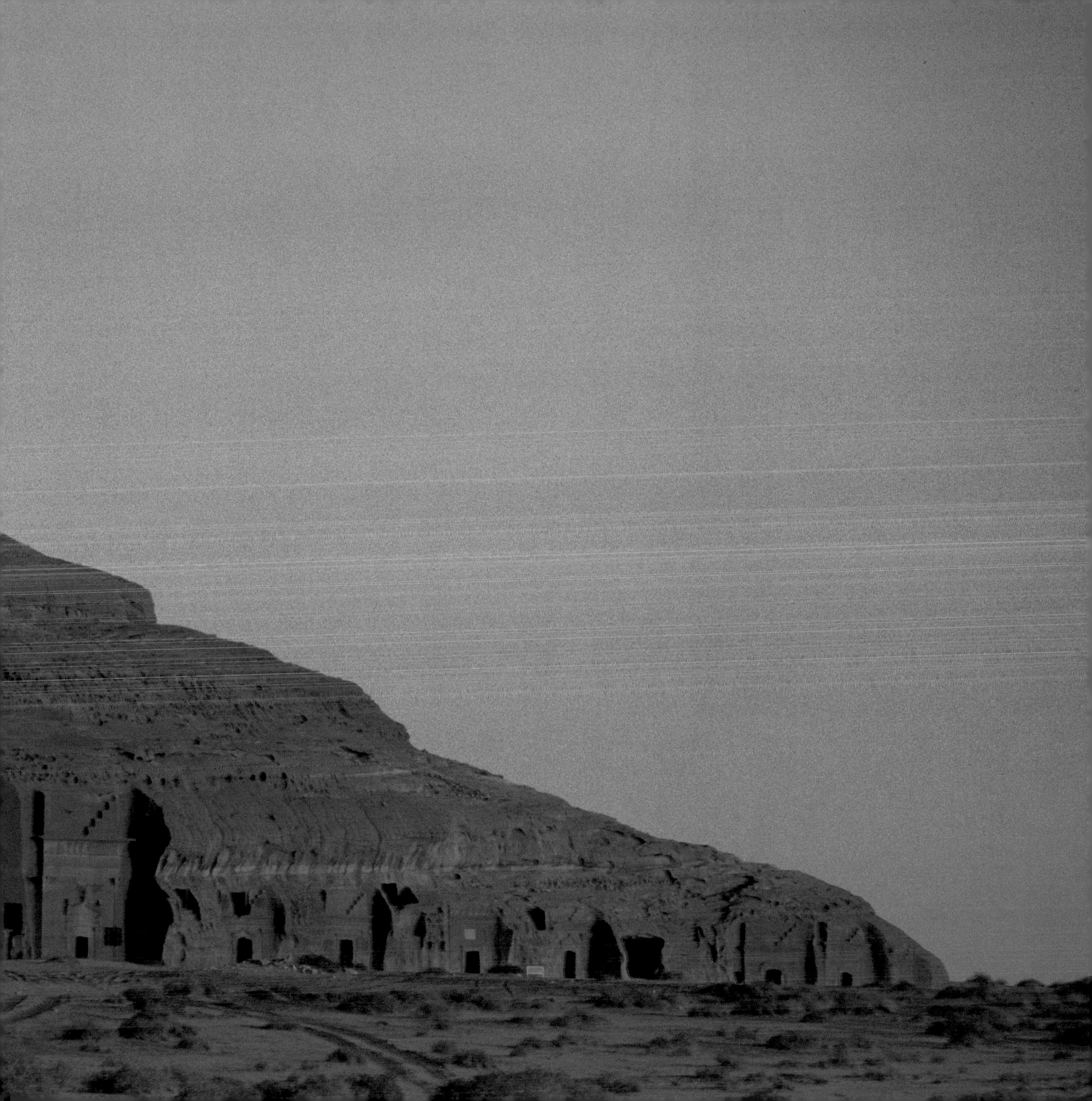

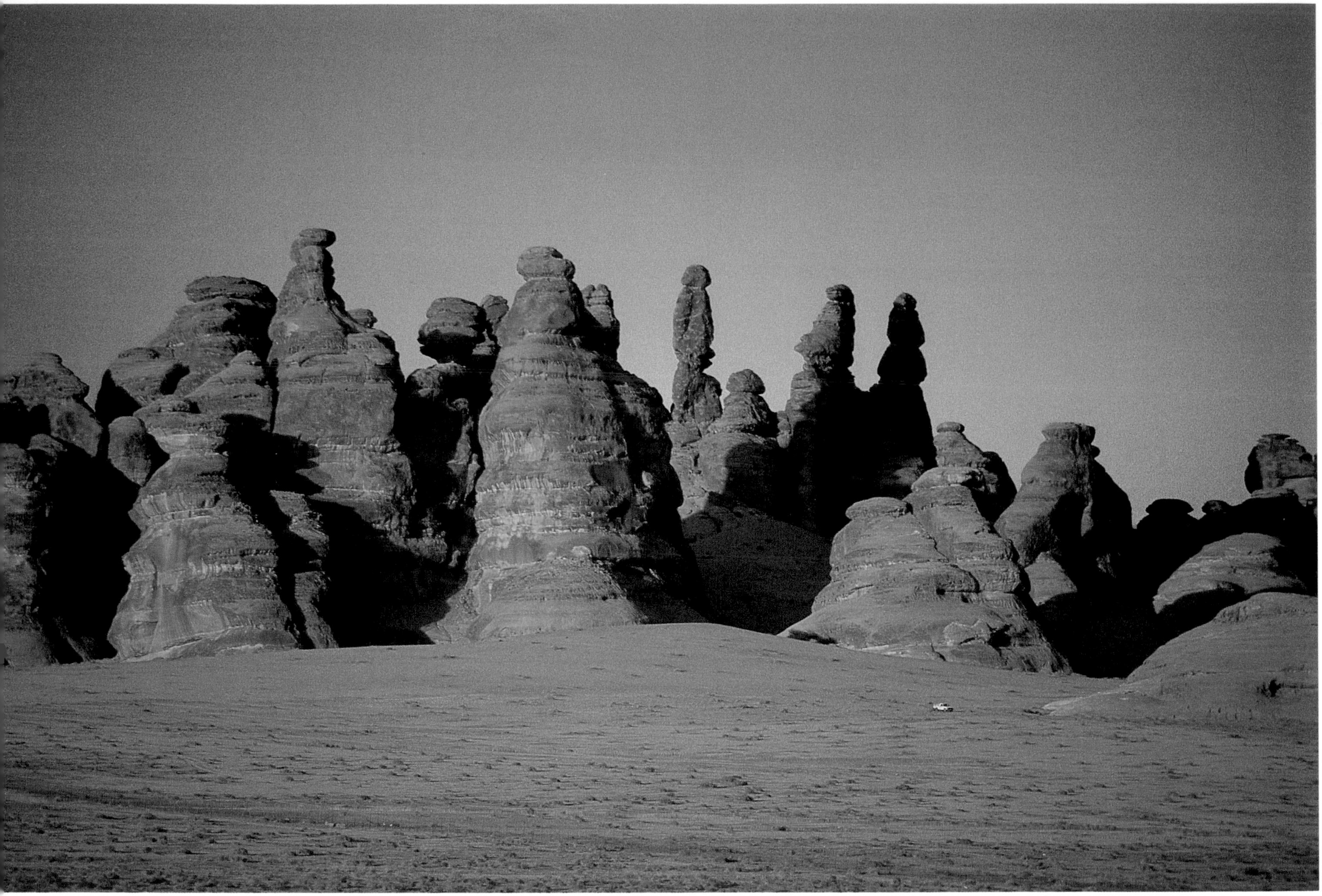

*(Previous pages)*
These graves have stylized decorations on flat surfaces cut from a giant sandstone wall. The graves belonged not to an individual, but to a whole family and funeral rites were performed there each time a family member died.

*(Above)*
This rock formation from a sandstone plate is the result of the metamorphosis of a sedimentary bed which lay under the sea some 400 to 600 million years ago, according to geologic time, then rose as a result of the movement of the earth's crust and became weathered. These strangely shaped rocks characterize the area of al-Ūlā where the ruins of Madā'in Ṣāliḥ are to be found.

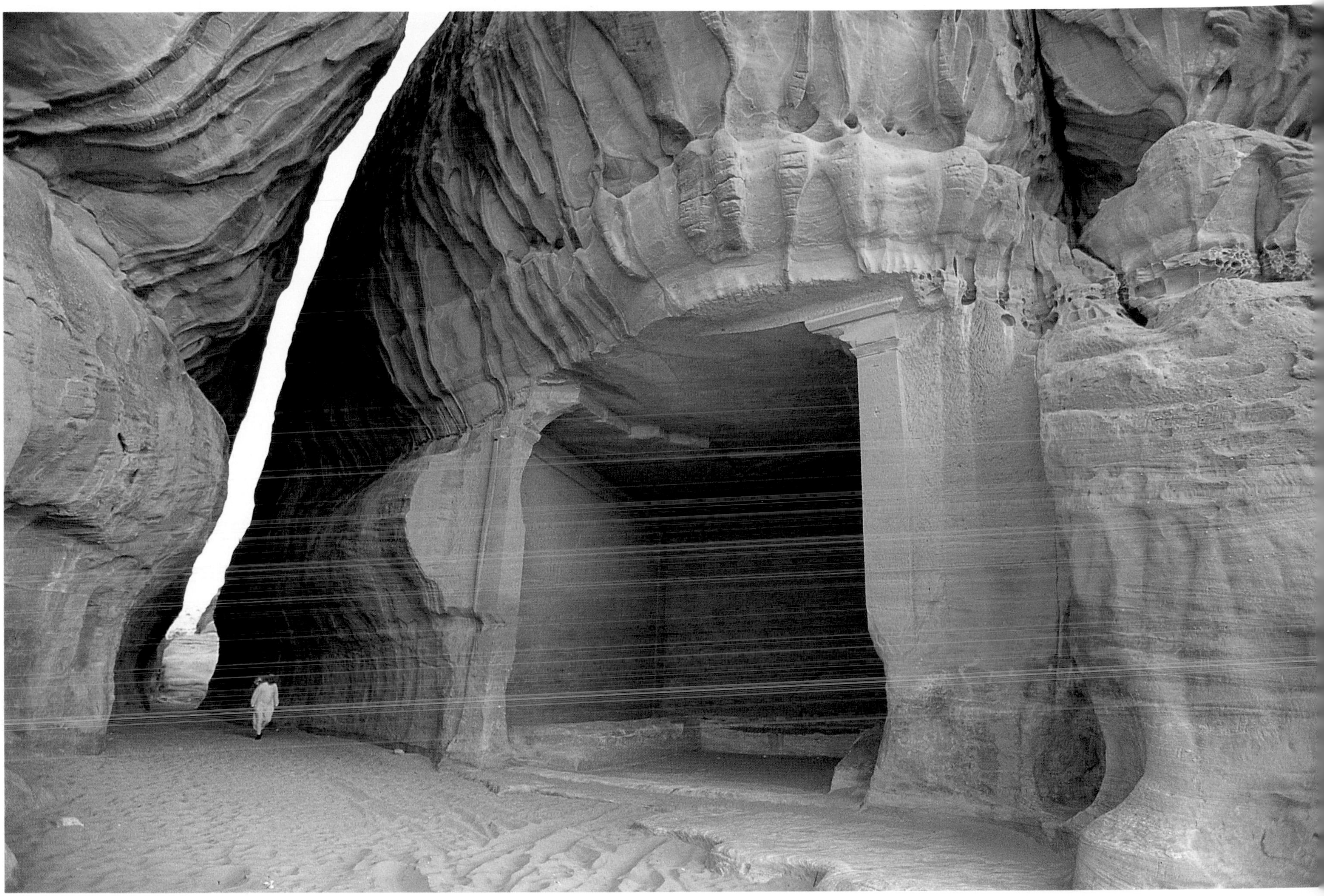

Ruins of a temple surrounded by corridors formed by rain erosion. Nabataeans ruled this land for several centuries until they were defeated by the Romans in AD 106.

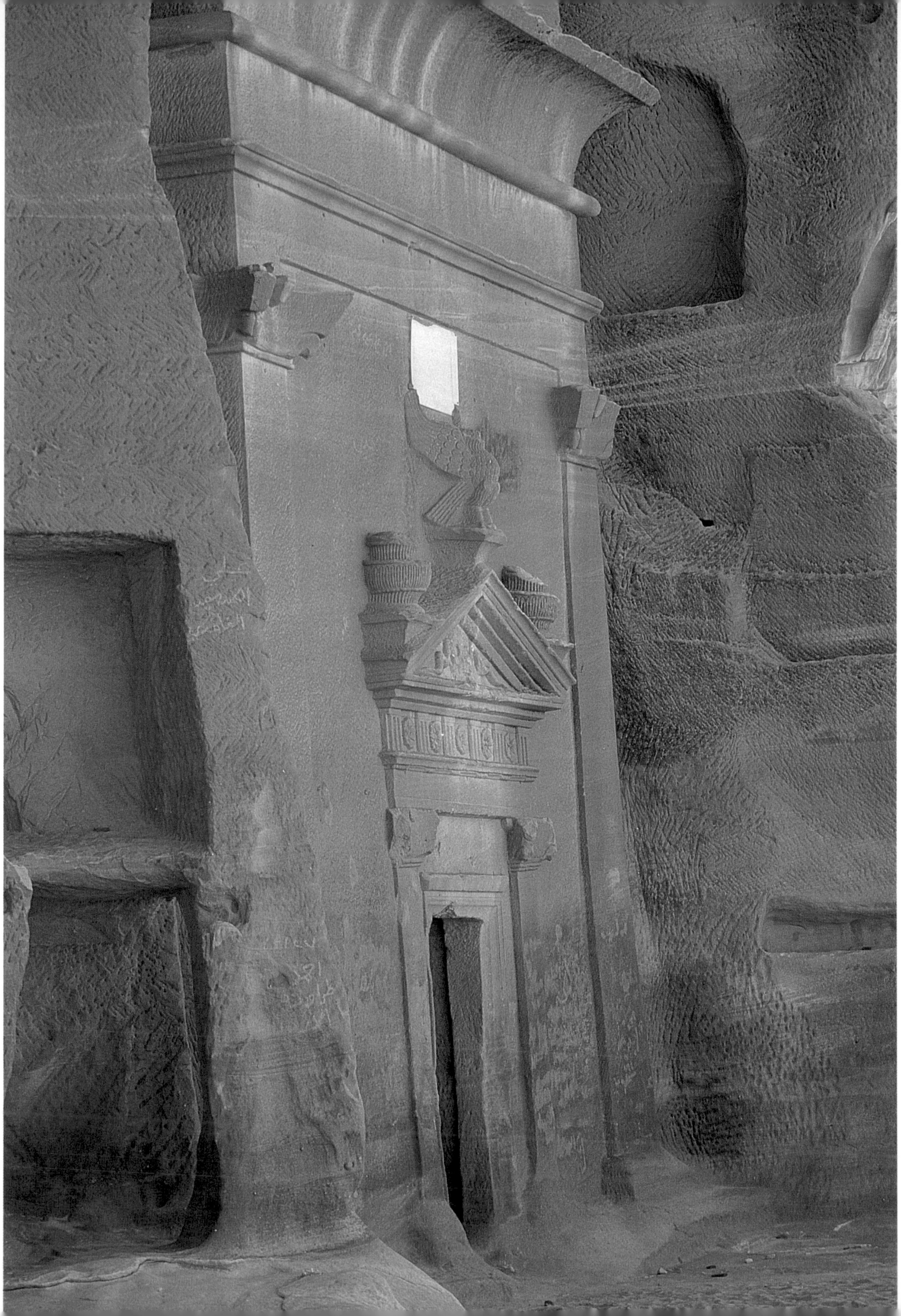

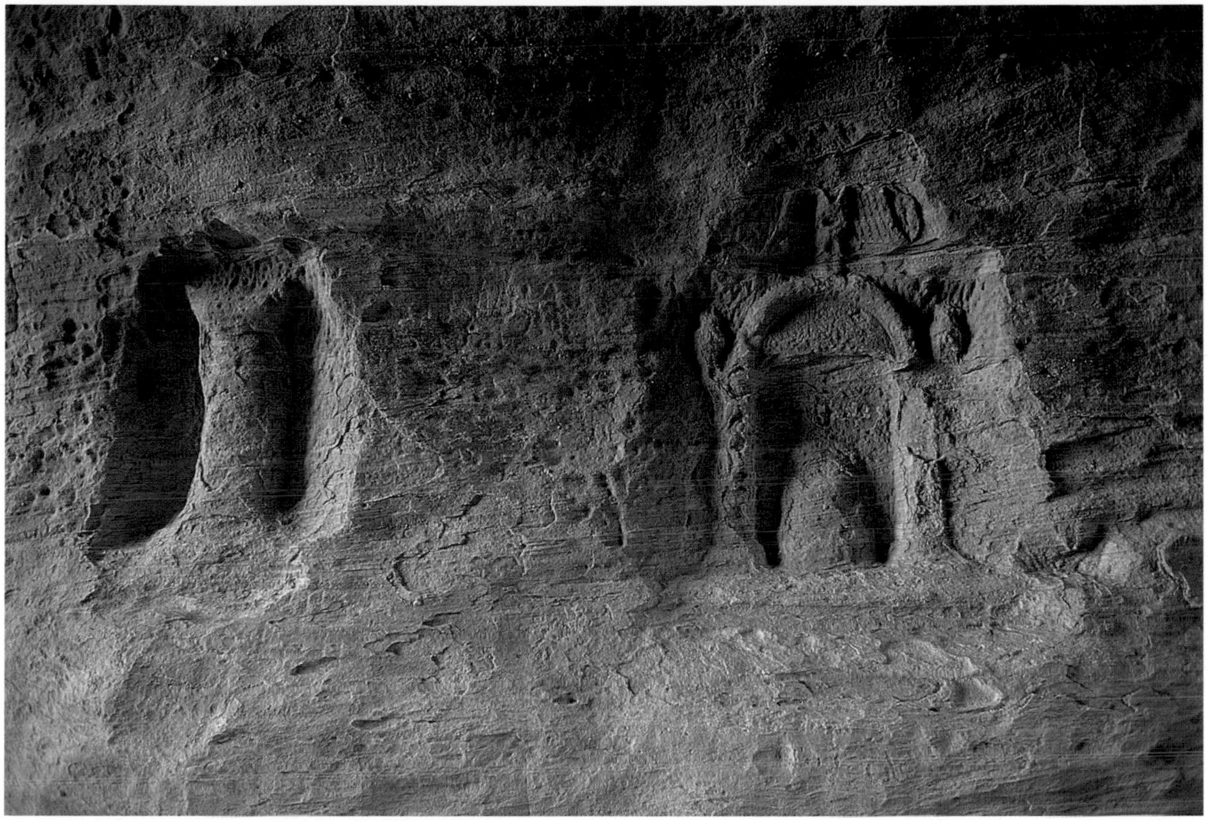

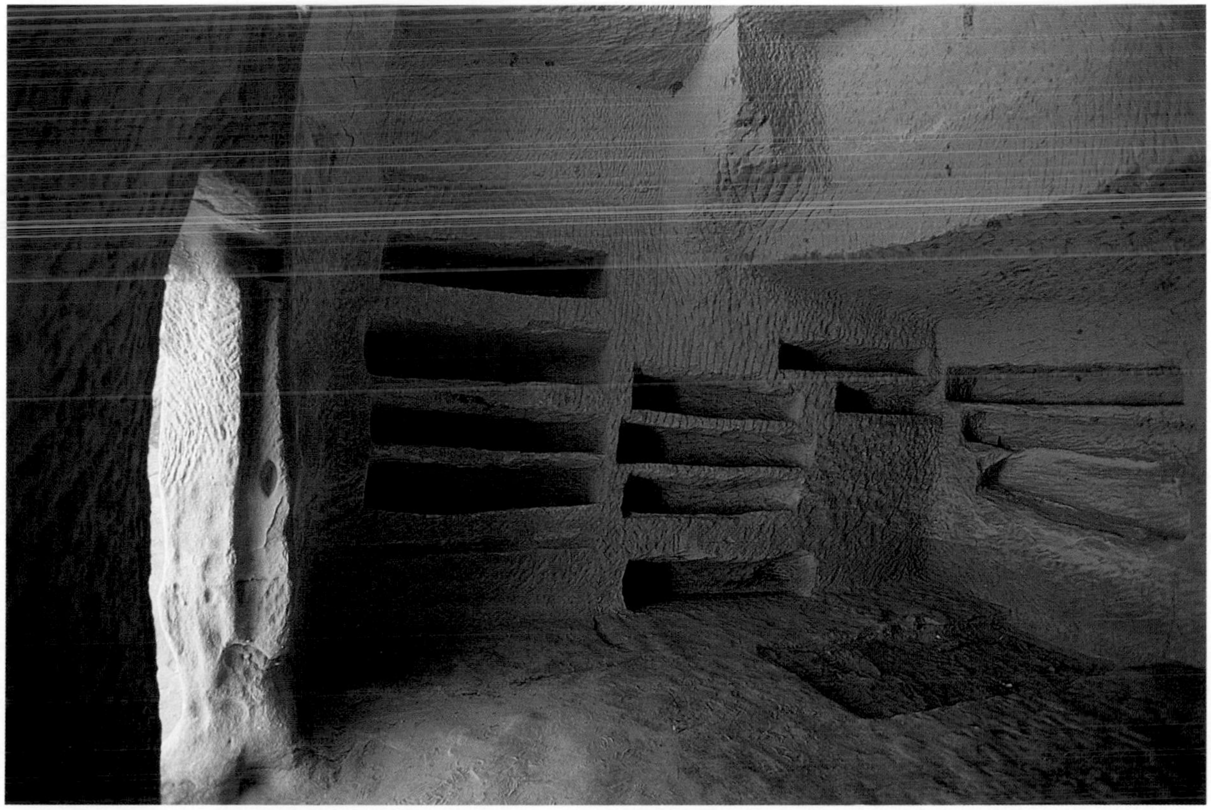

*(Opposite)*
An epitaph on a grave inscribed in the Nabataean language on the white section above the statue at the center of this photograph. A plastic board shining bright has been placed there to prevent erosion of the inscription. The Nabataean alphabet is considered as the forerunner of the Arabic alphabet.

*(Top)*
Statues in the prayer room of the temple point to the polytheism prevalent in Arabia before the advent of Islam.

*(Bottom)*
There are many small alcoves such as these in the inside wall. In ancient times when it was customary to rebury the dead, cinerary urns of various families were consigned to such shelves.

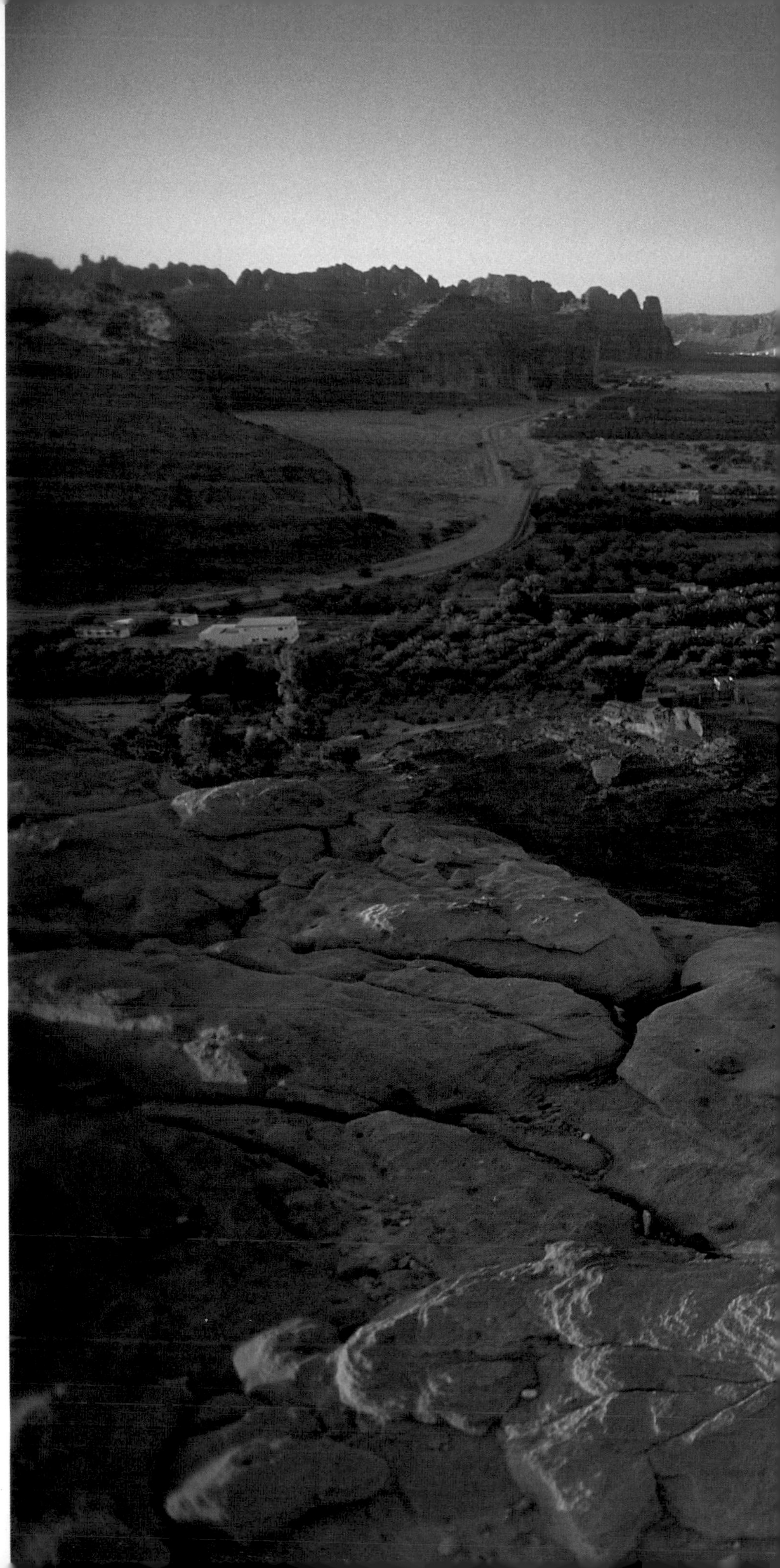

An oasis in al-Ūlā near Madā'in Ṣāliḥ where one finds water veins which have made possible the date-palm grove. This area was a transit point of the old caravan route stretching from the Yemen to Palestine.

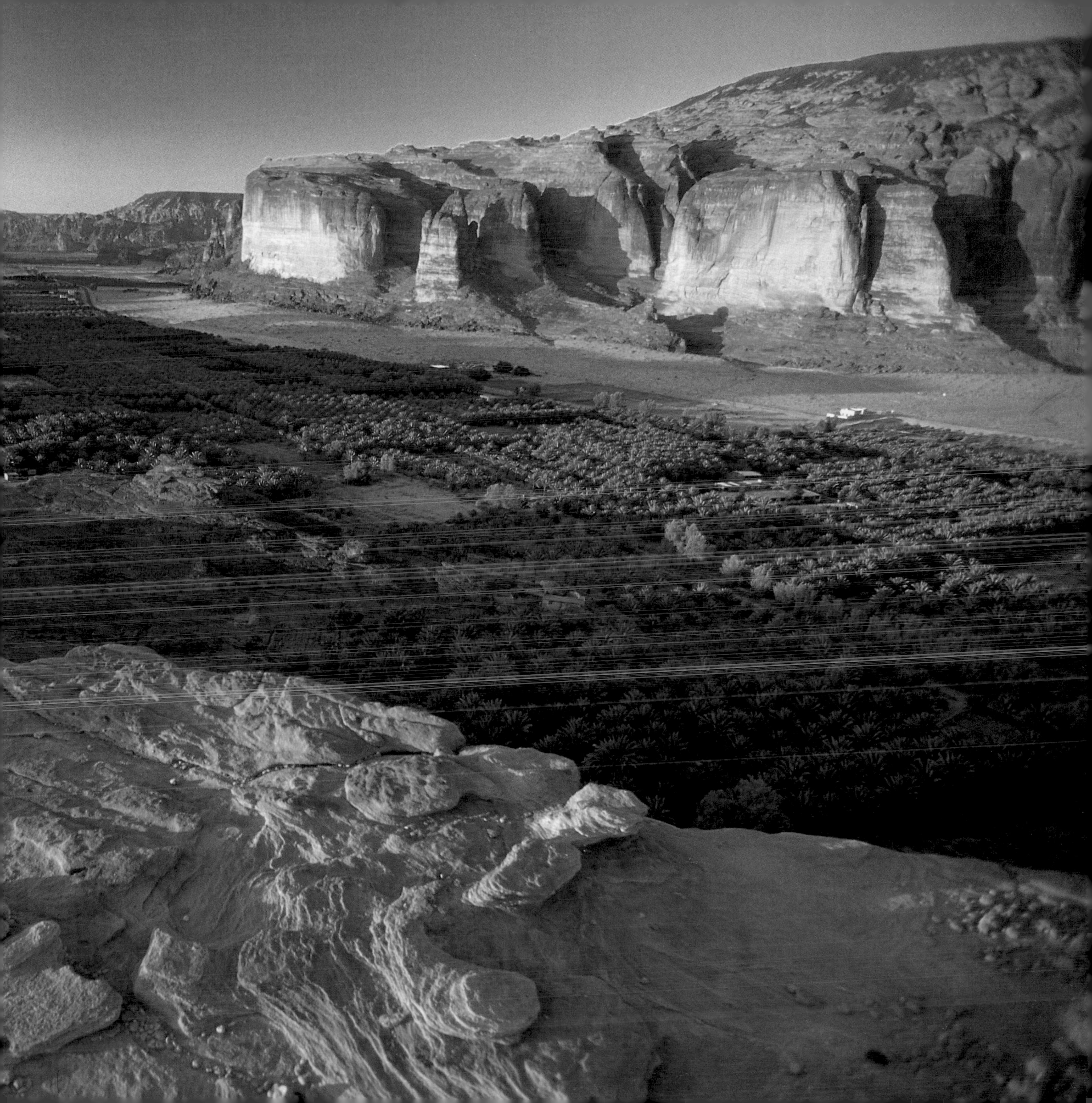

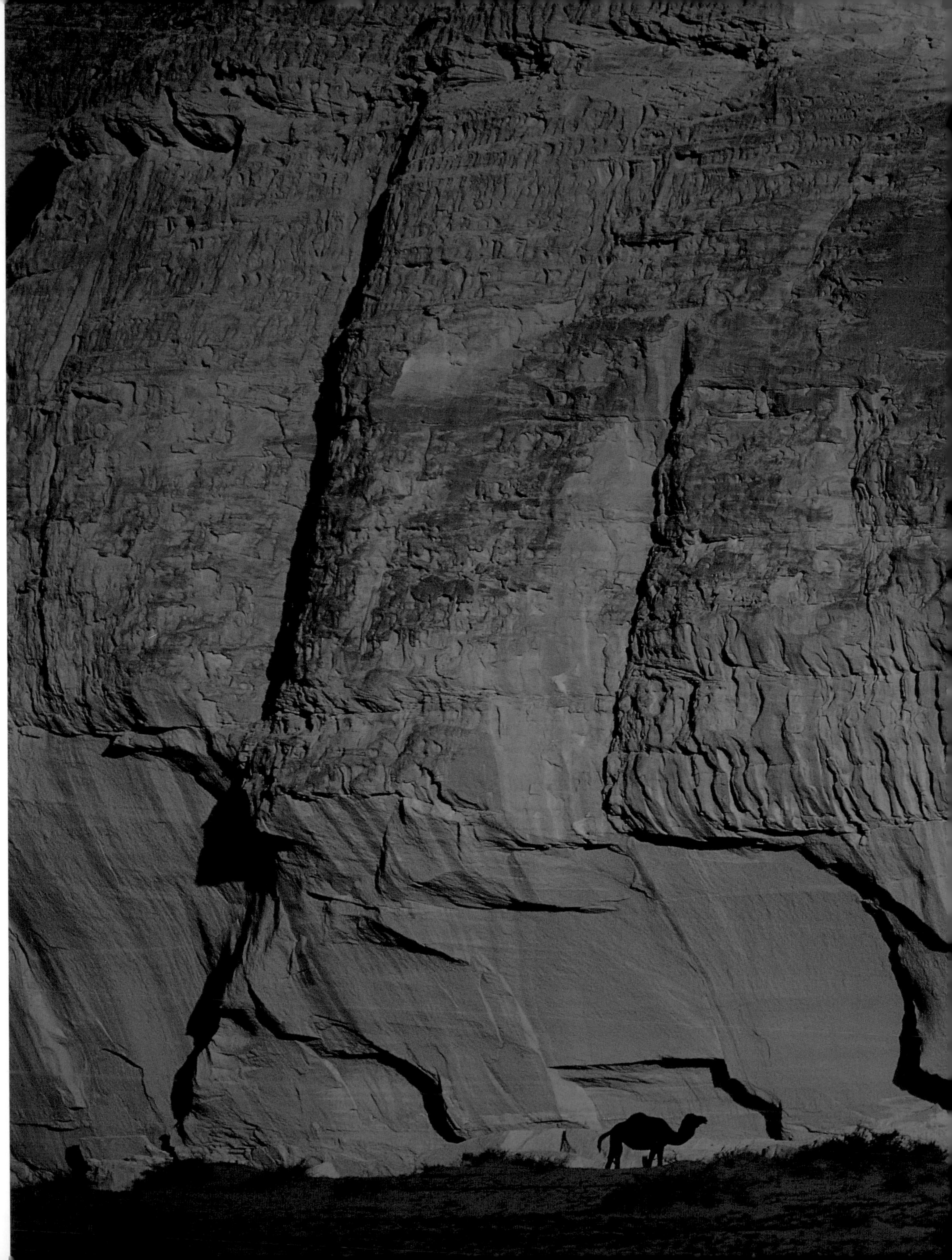

Camels grazing before a sandstone wall at Madā'in Ṣāliḥ bathing in the sun. This area is blessed with water and pasture is relatively abundant. That is why one finds Bedouins here to this day living their traditional life with their camels.

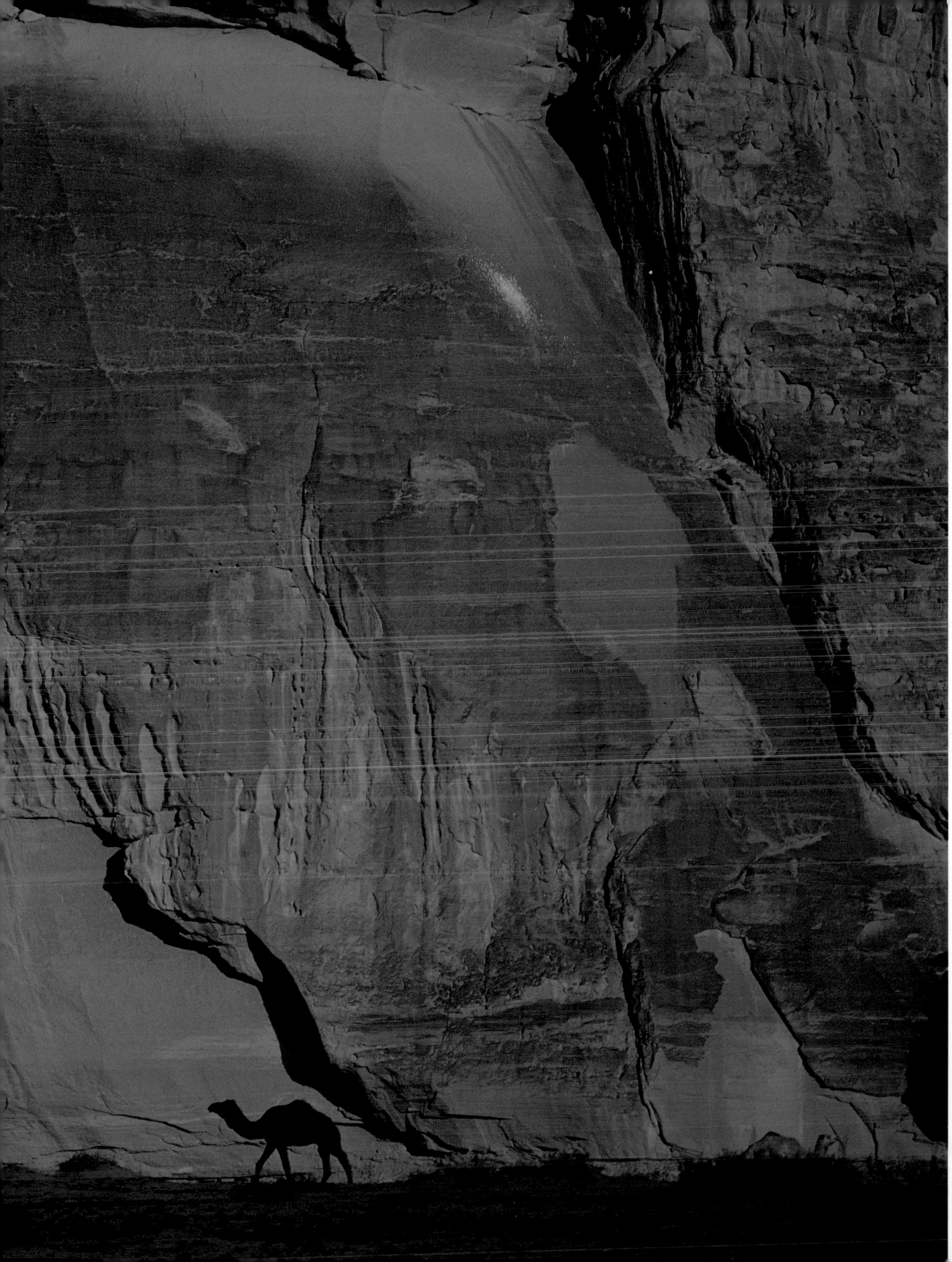

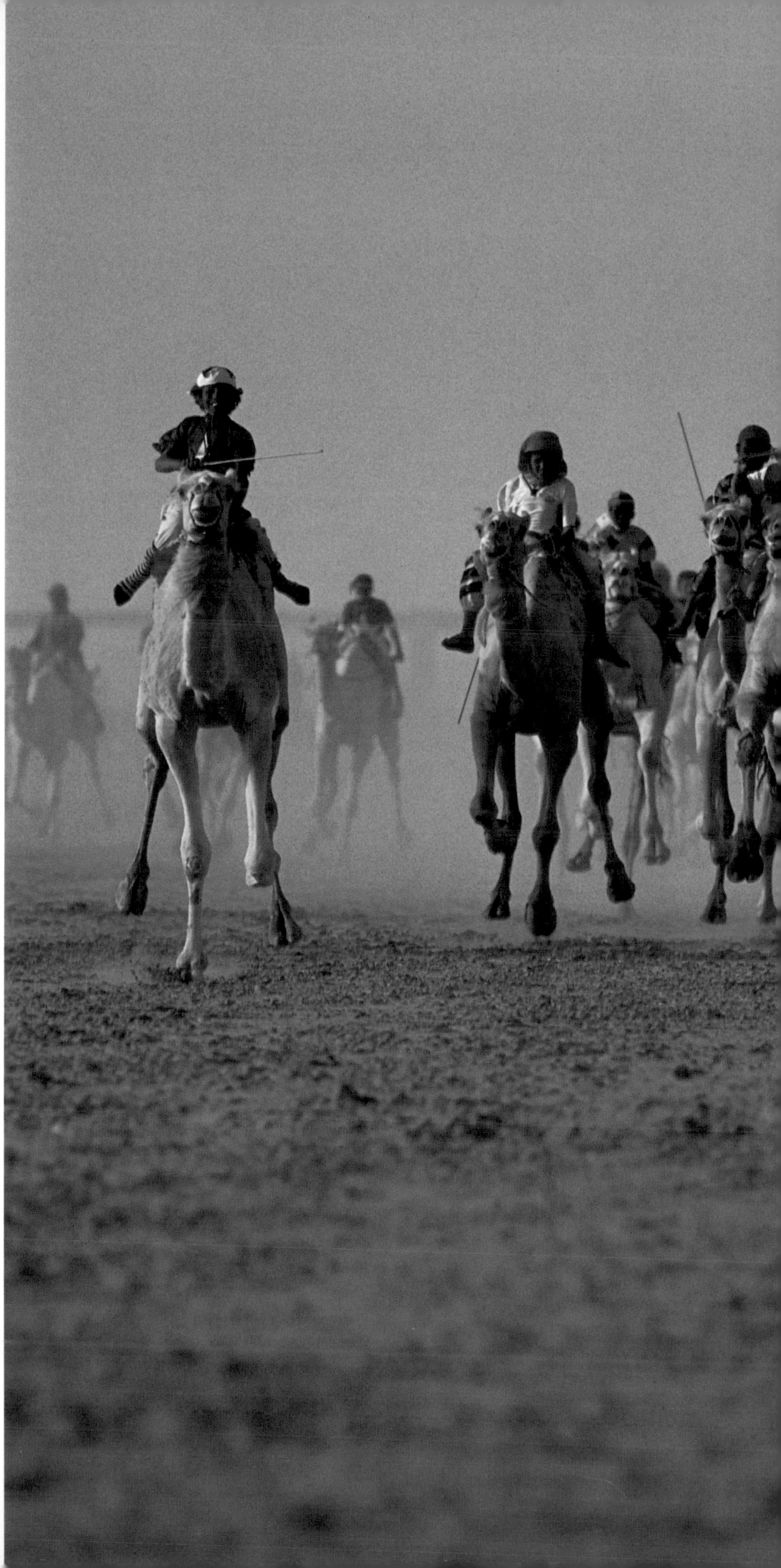

The traditional Arab sport of camel racing continues to this day. Here one can see the famous race for the King's Cup held outside the capital of Saudi Arabia, Riyadh. Some four hundred camels usually participate and the race takes about half an hour. In the 1970s and 80s around three thousand camels would partic ipate and dazzling sums were awarded to the winners.

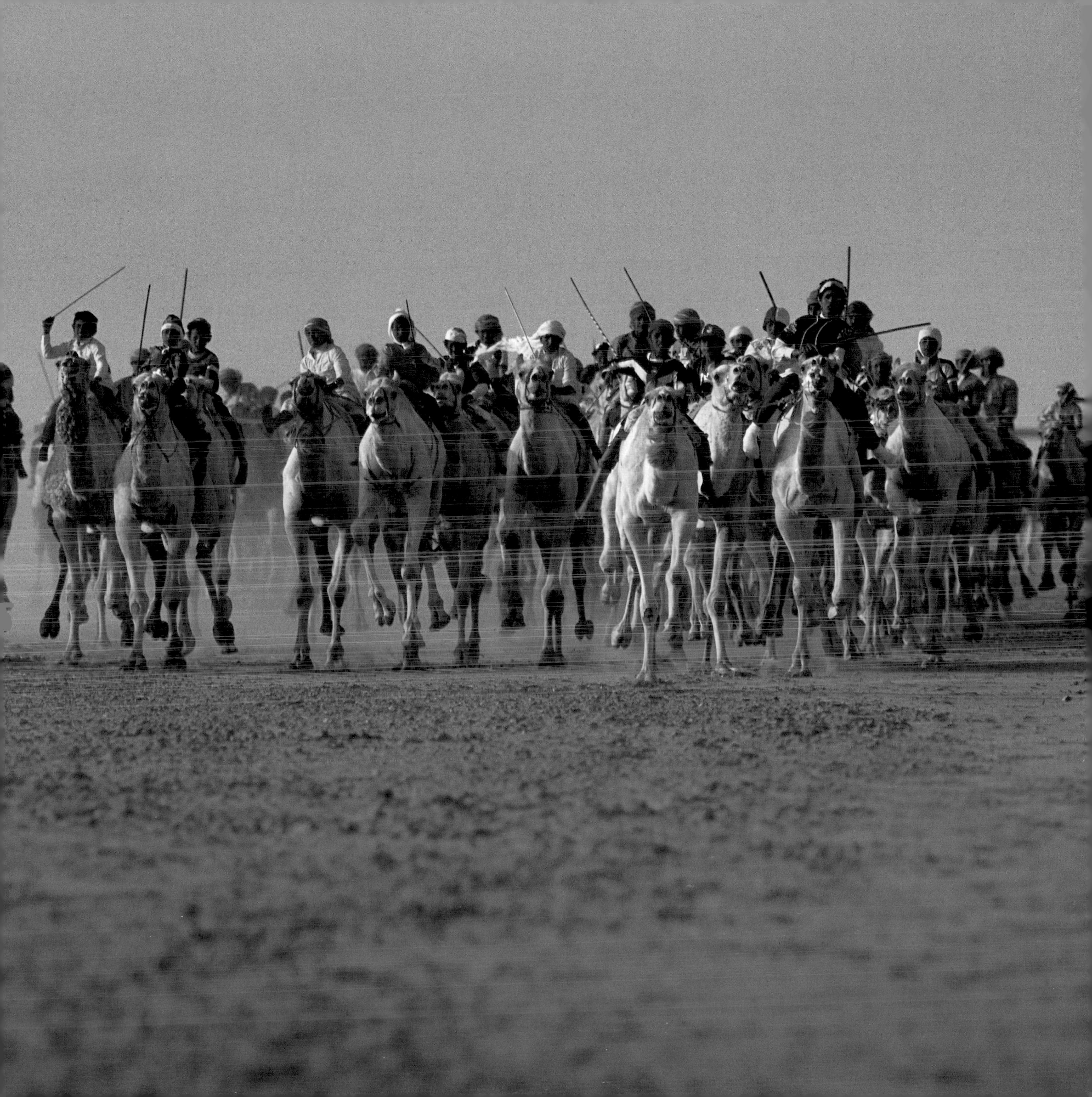

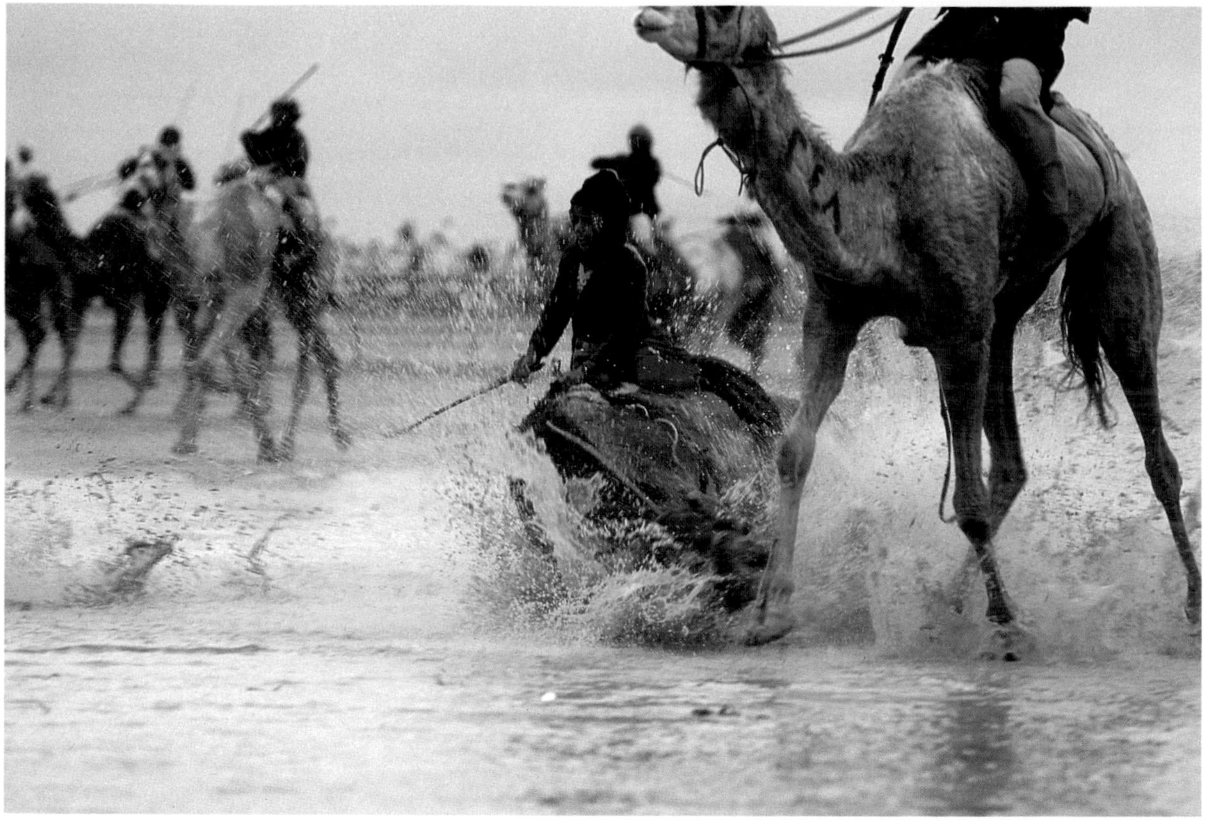

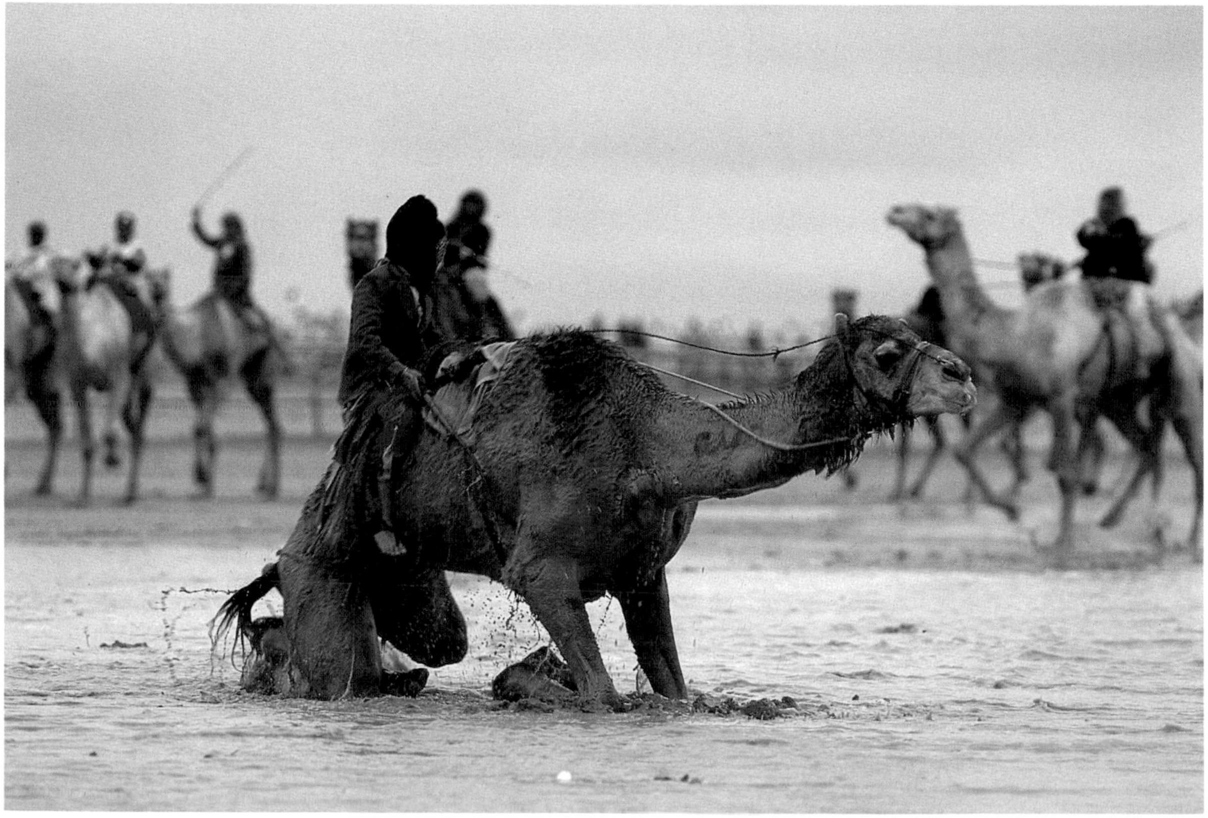

In 1995 the race began after a heavy rain so that many camels slipped and fell.

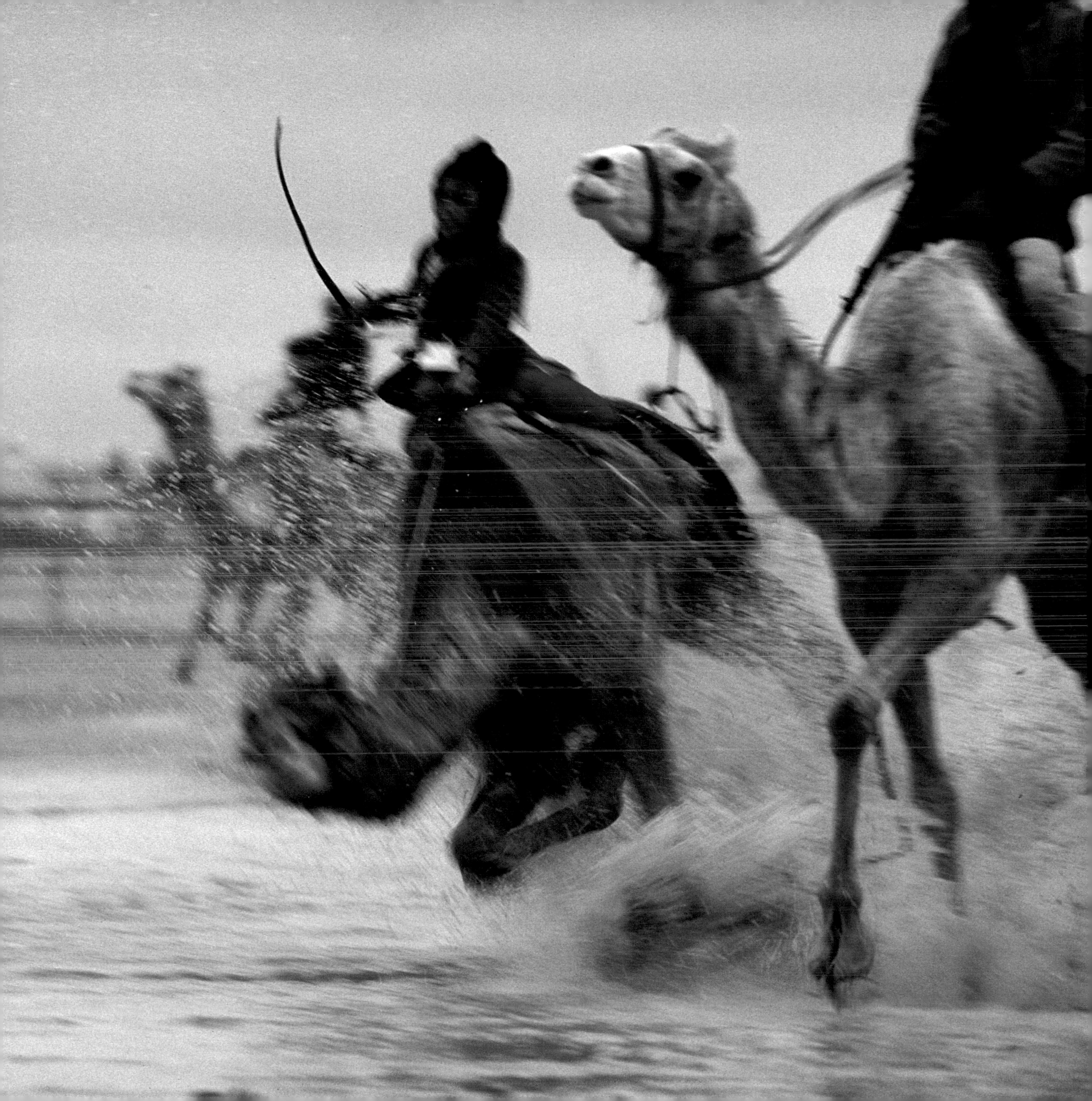

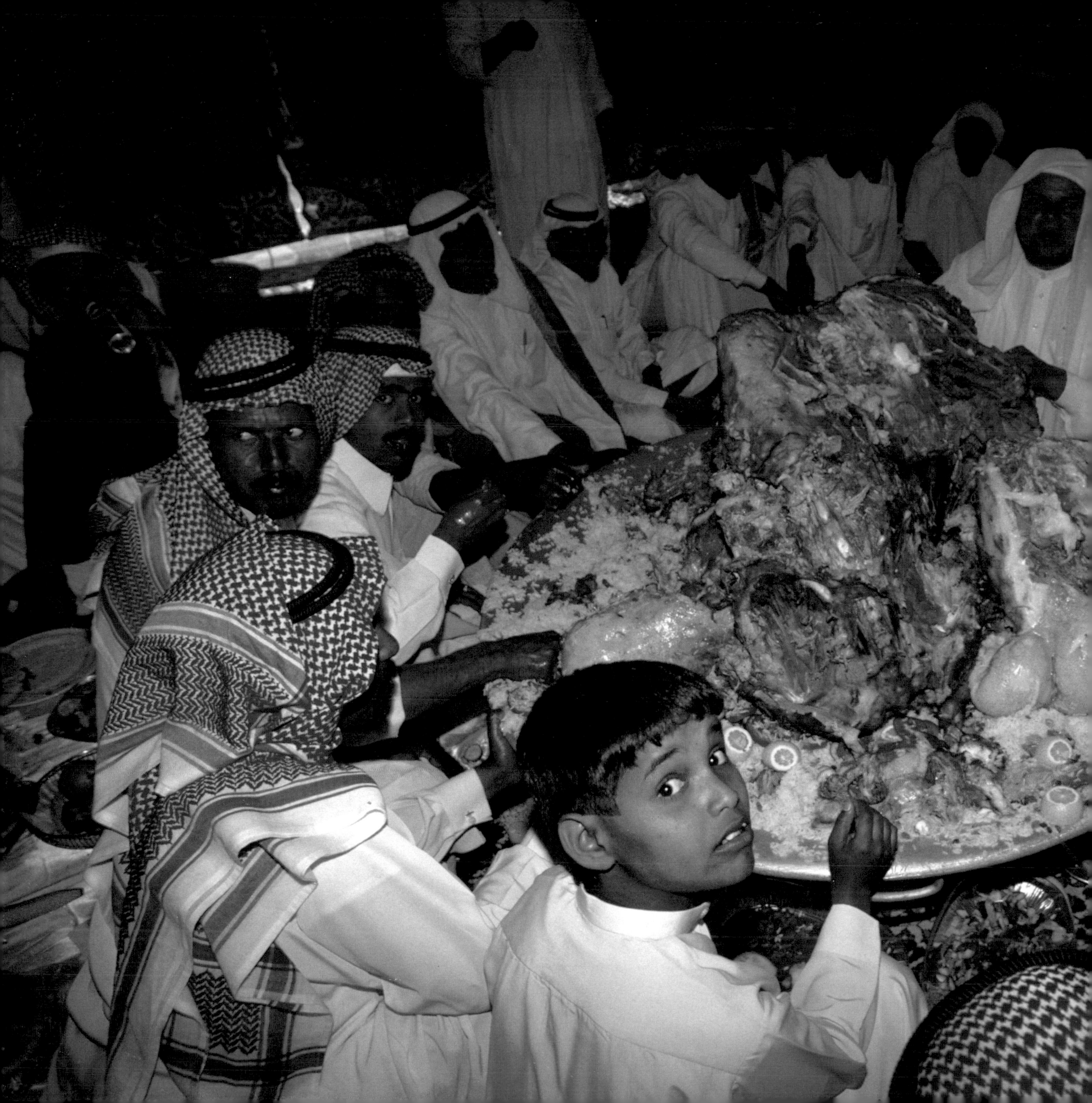

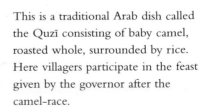

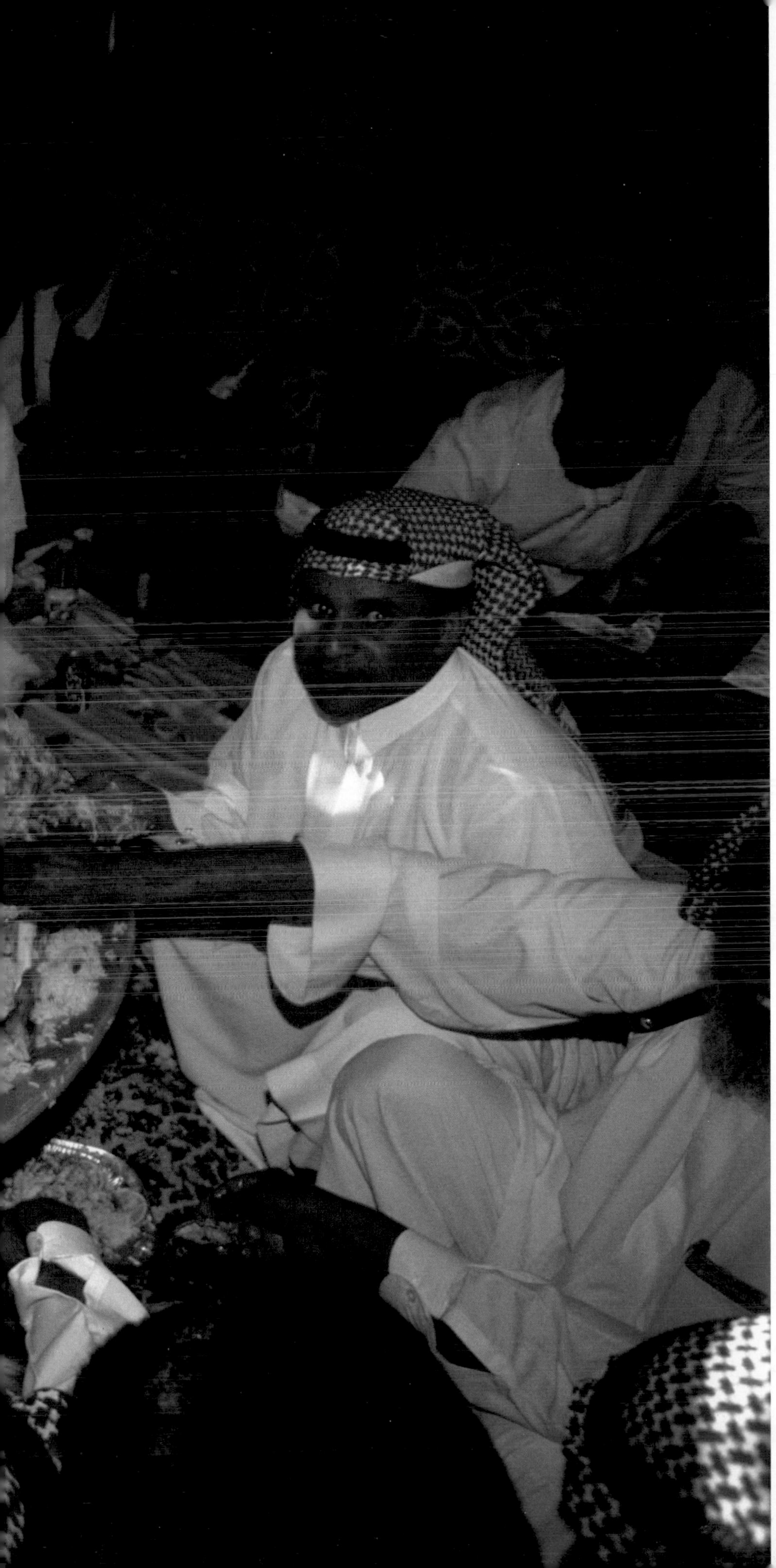

This is a traditional Arab dish called the Quzī consisting of baby camel, roasted whole, surrounded by rice. Here villagers participate in the feast given by the governor after the camel-race.

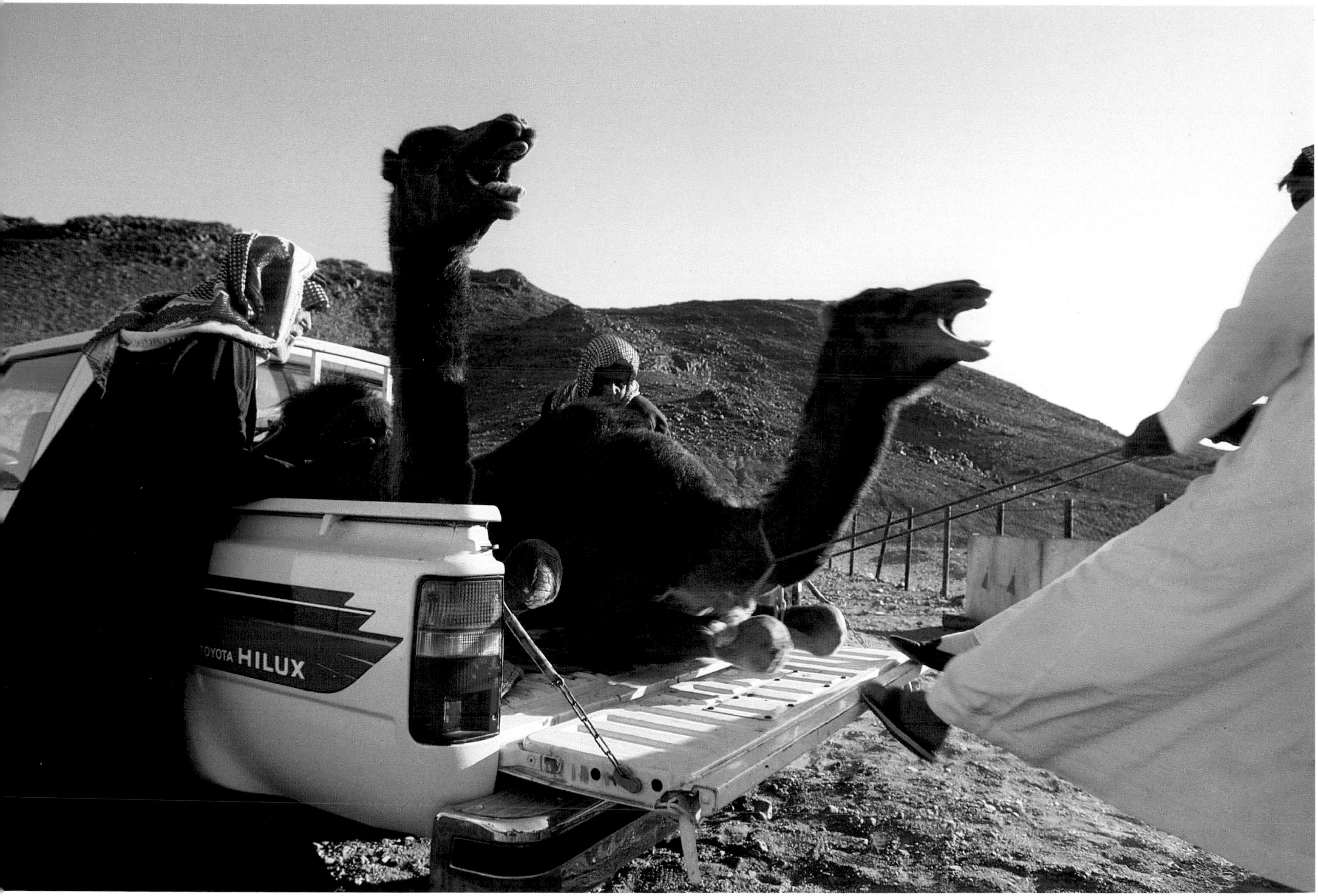


*(Above)*
Baby camel being transported to the meat market. The modernization of the past few decades in Saudi Arabia has decreased greatly the demand for camels as a means of transportation.

*(Opposite)*
A cattle-market run by Bedouins most of whom have now become settled. The rapid rise in population of Saudi Arabia in recent years has forced the country to acquire most of its cattle from its neighbors and abroad.

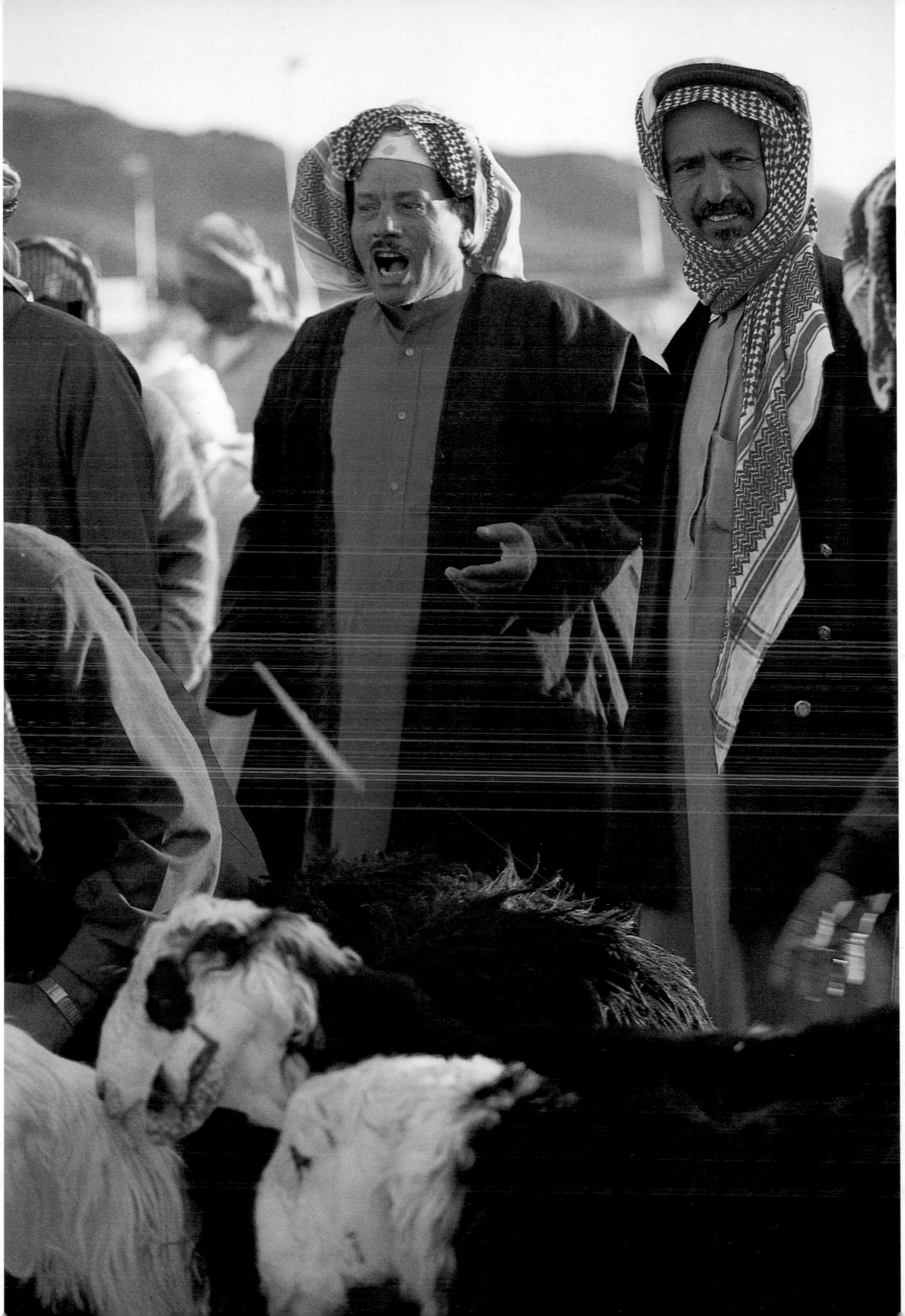

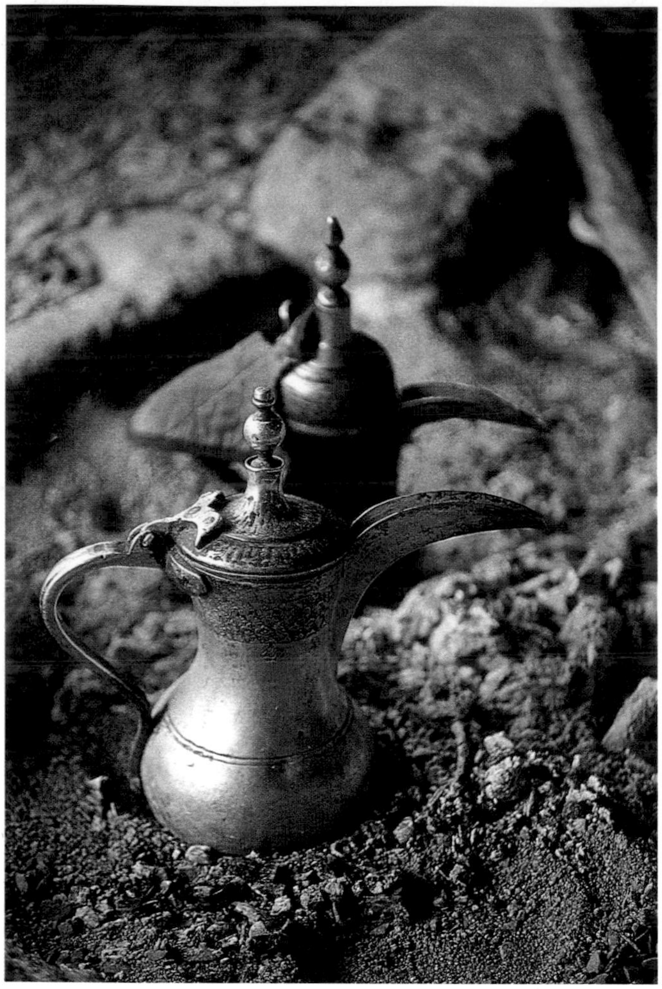

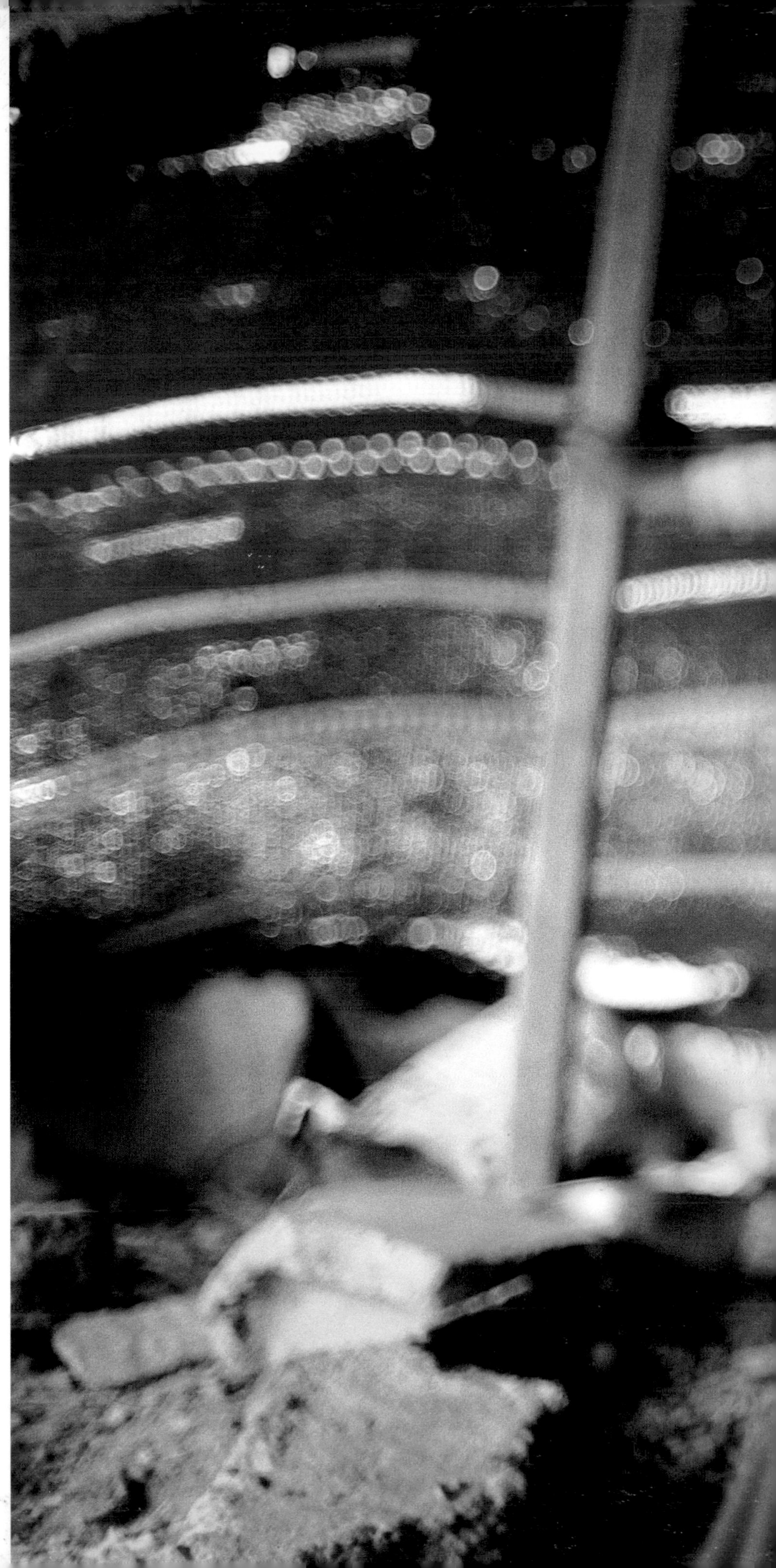

A Bedouin family living in a traditional woolen tent. Like many other Bedouins, this family has lived here for many years and even has some modern facilities in the tent such as a washing-machine run by a generator.

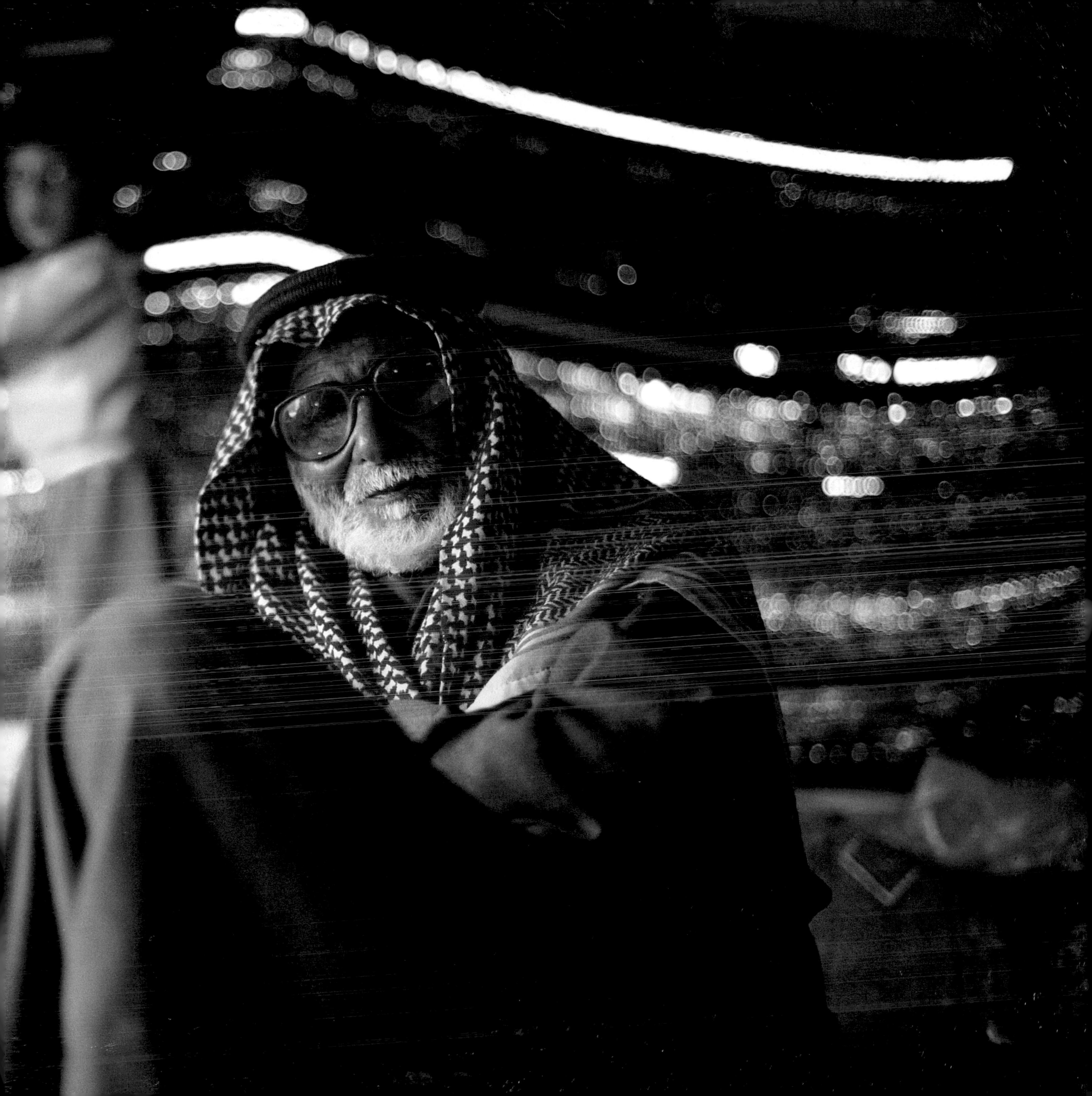

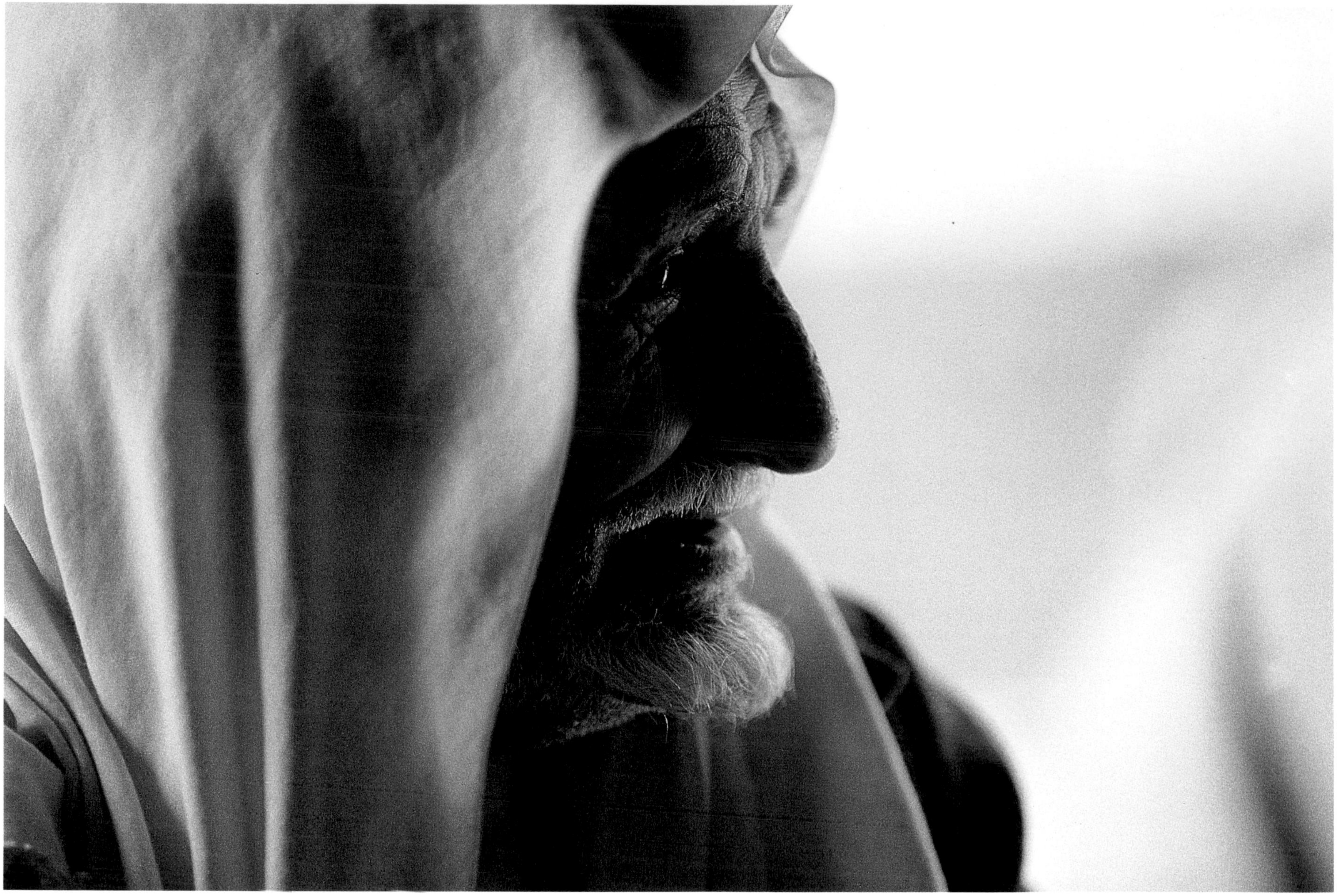

A village elder relaxing in his tent. Although many Bedouins have now taken up agriculture, love of the freedom of the desert still runs strongly in their veins.

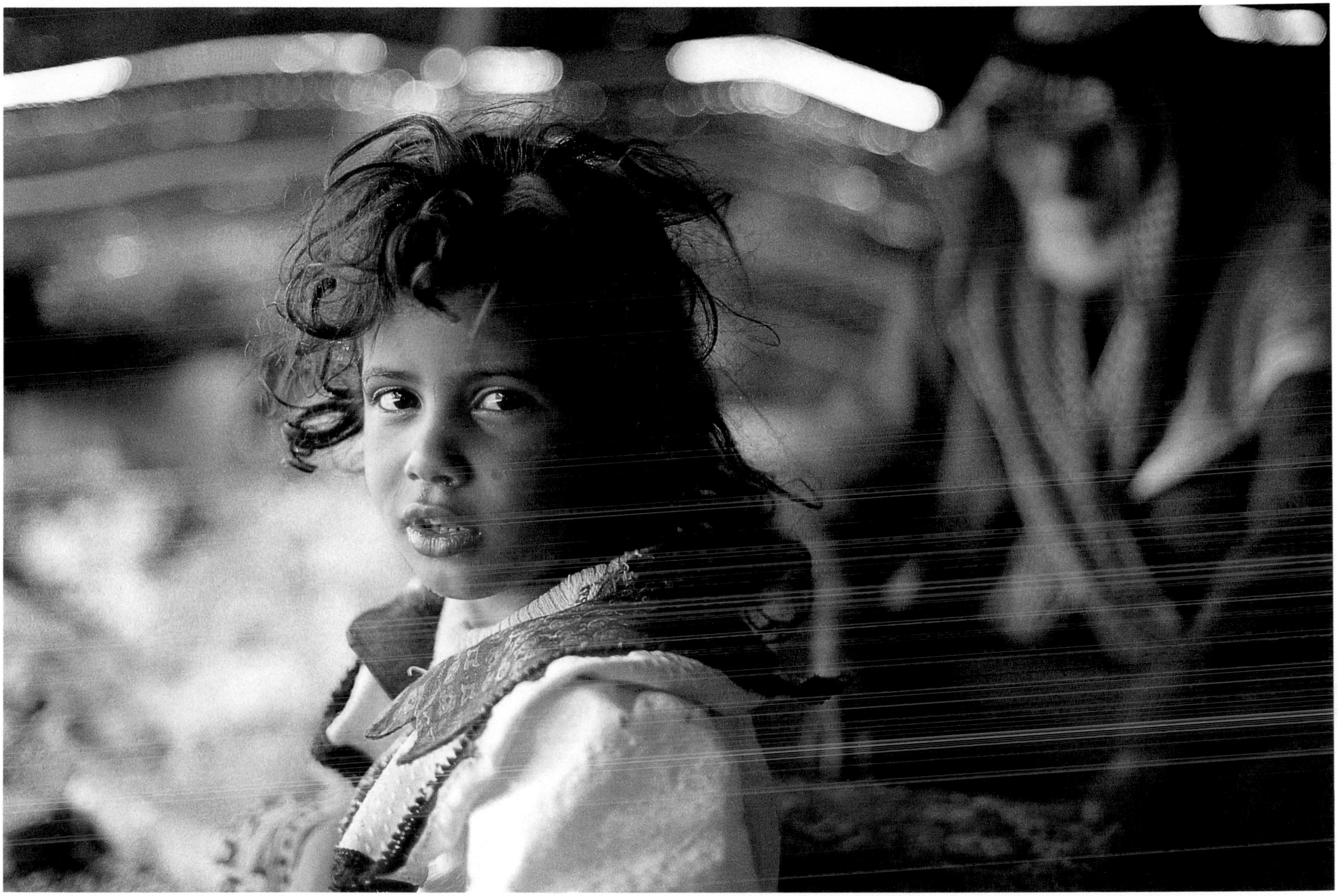

Although the living-space of these girls inside their Bedouin tents has not changed for millennia, they are watching television, bringing a completely alien world to their ambience in that traditional space.

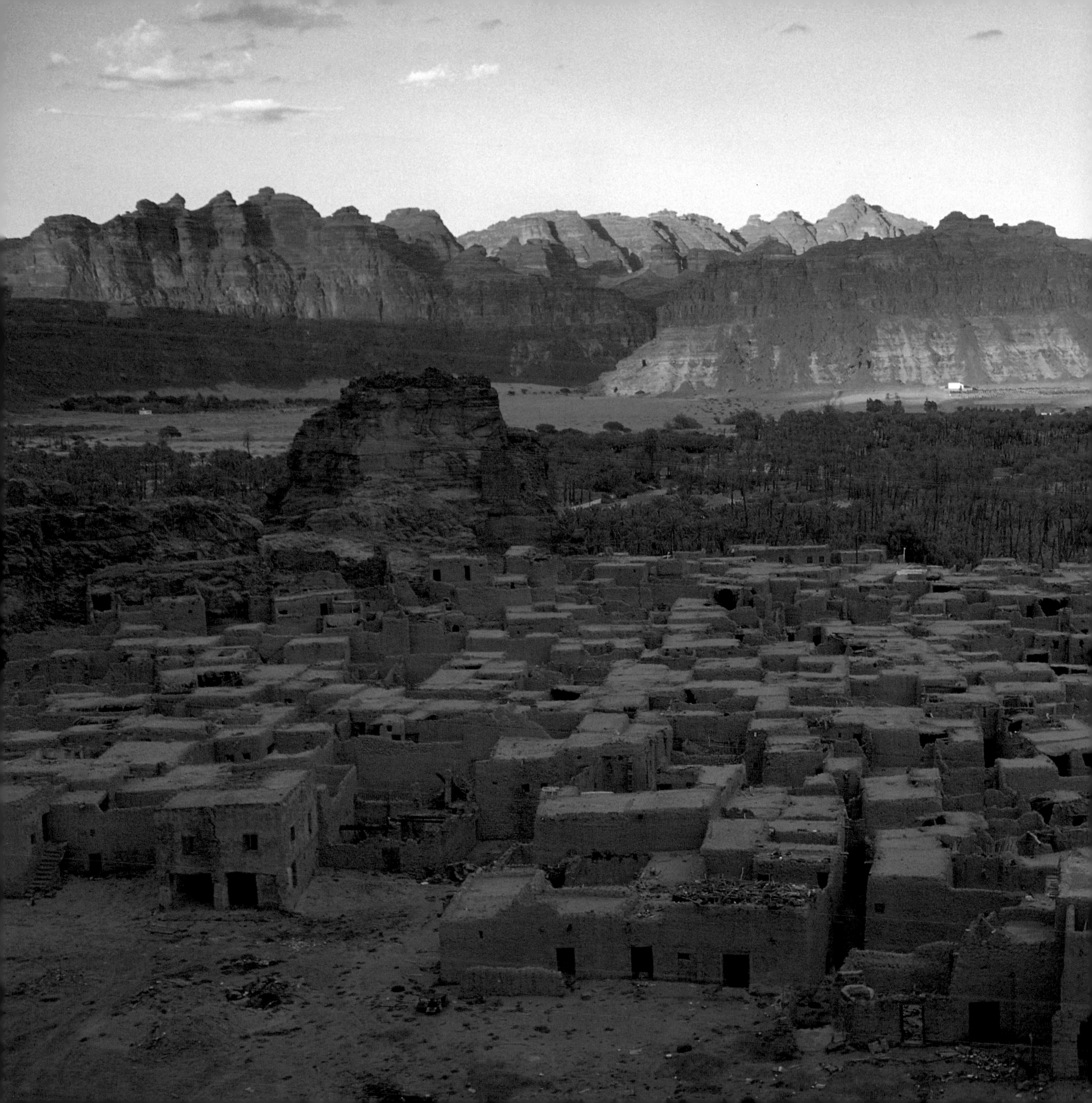

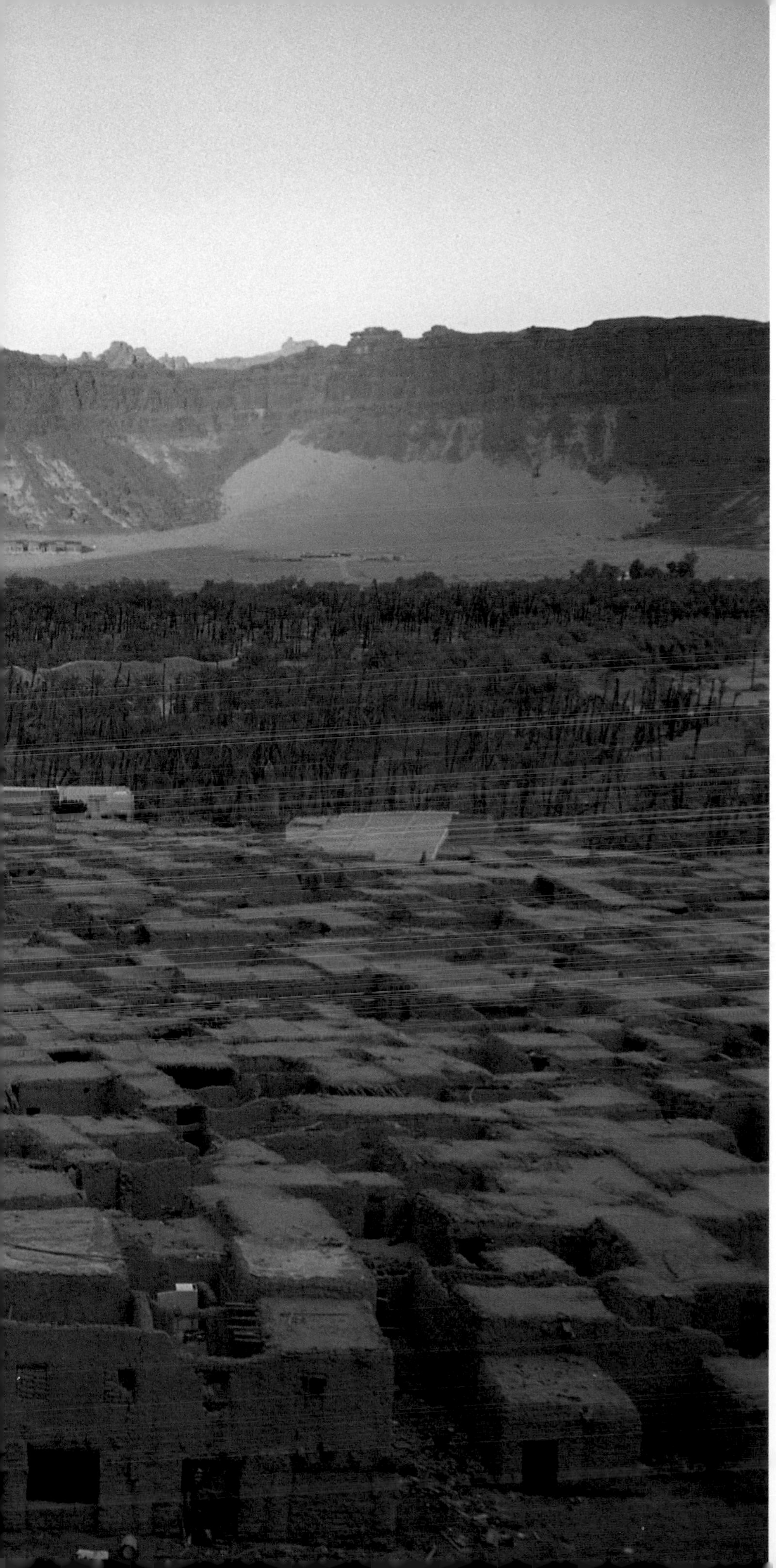

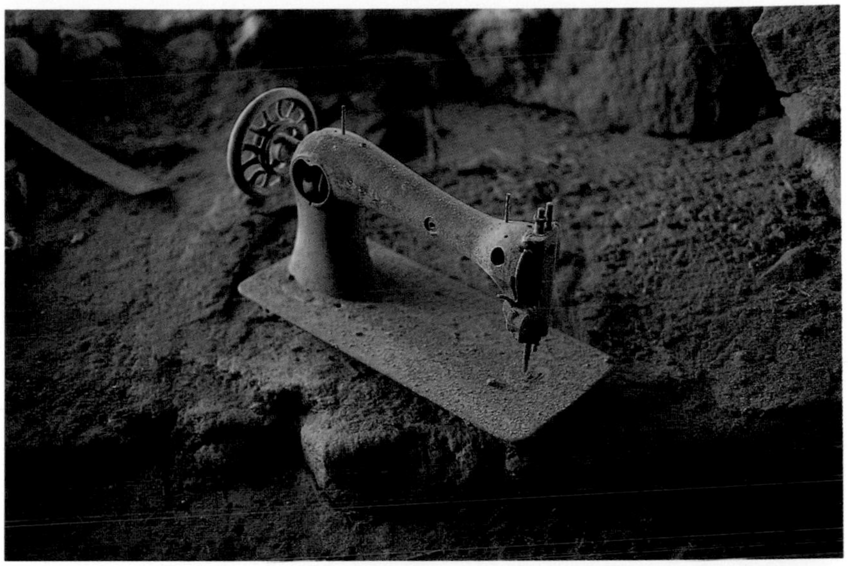

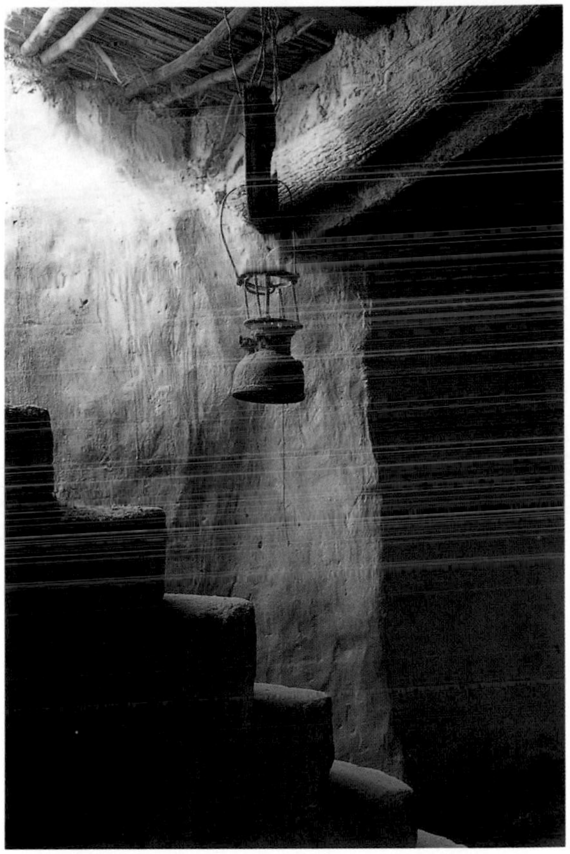

A deserted old village in al-Ūlā, its former residents having built new houses with money received from the Saudi governments in the 1970s during the oil boom.

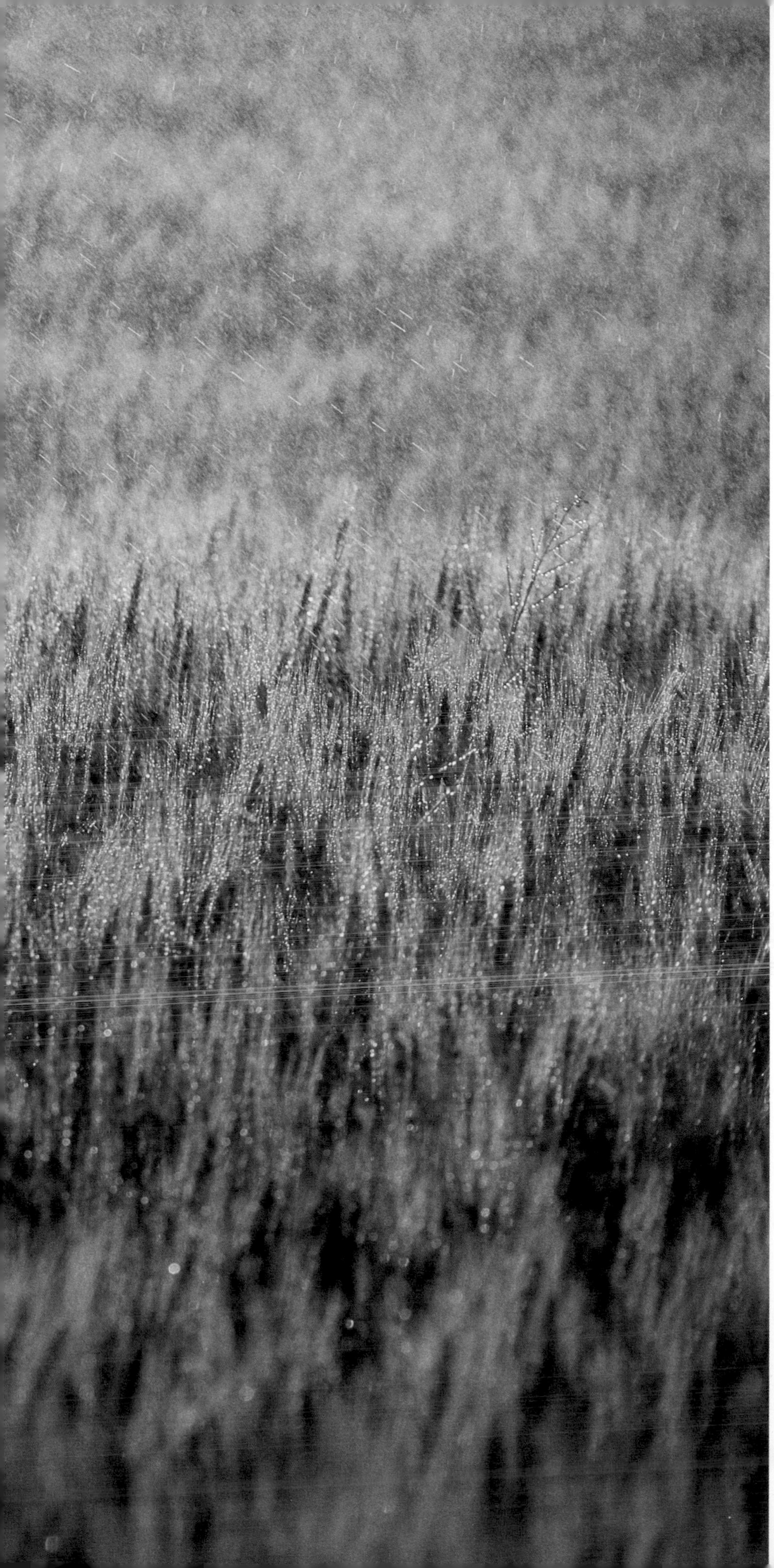

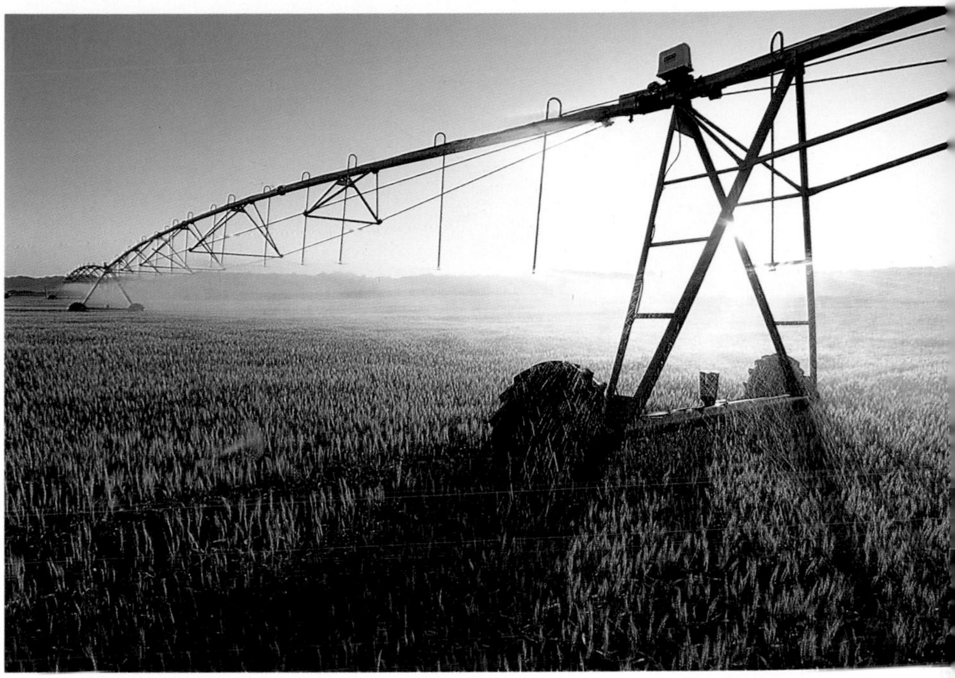

Although mostly a desert, Saudi Arabia has vast natural underground water that has been used in recent years for agriculture. Today Saudi Arabia produces four times its need in wheat and has become a major exporter

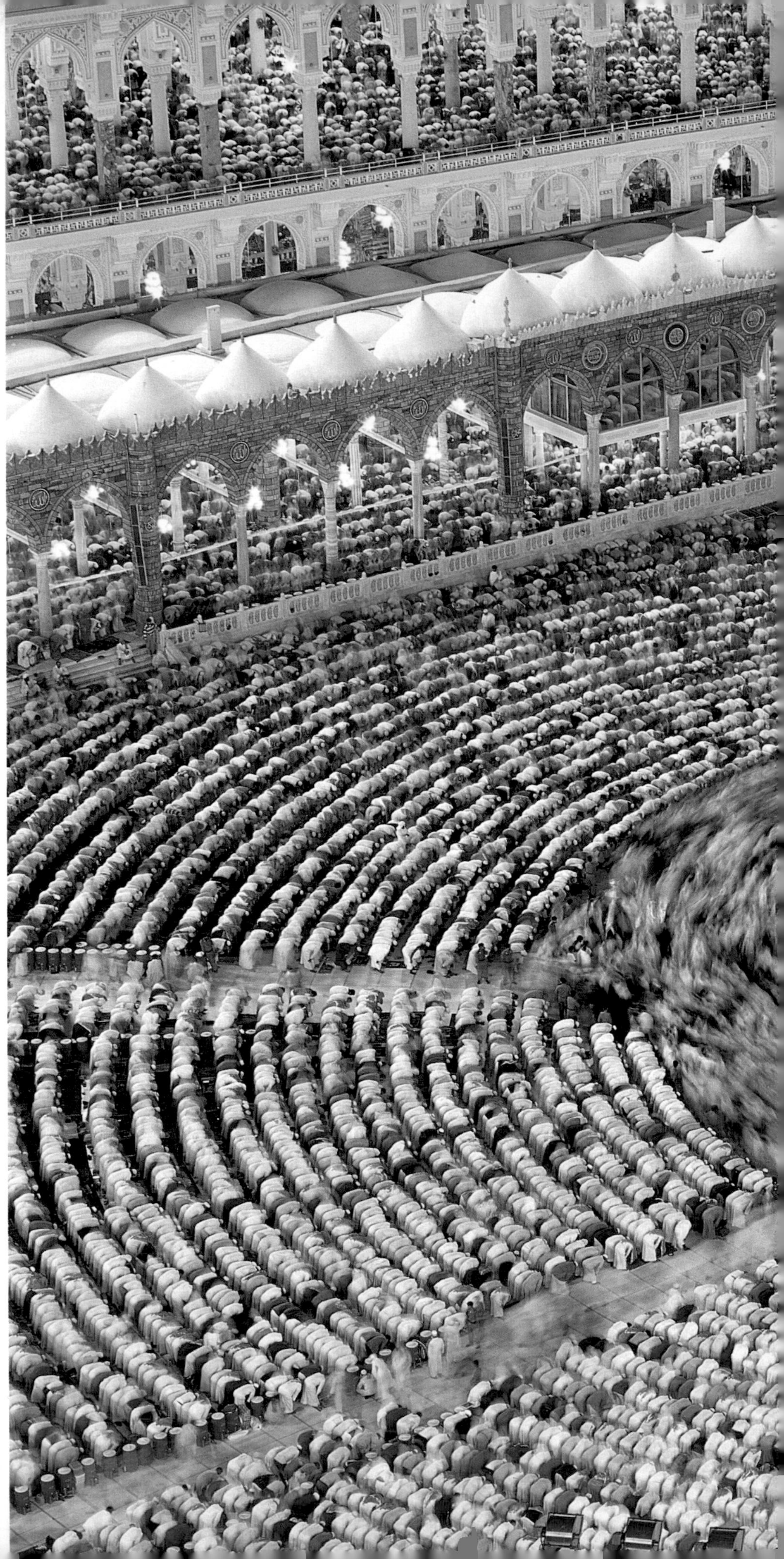

Prayers in the evening of *Laylat al-Qadr*, normally celebrated on the 27th of Ramaḍān.

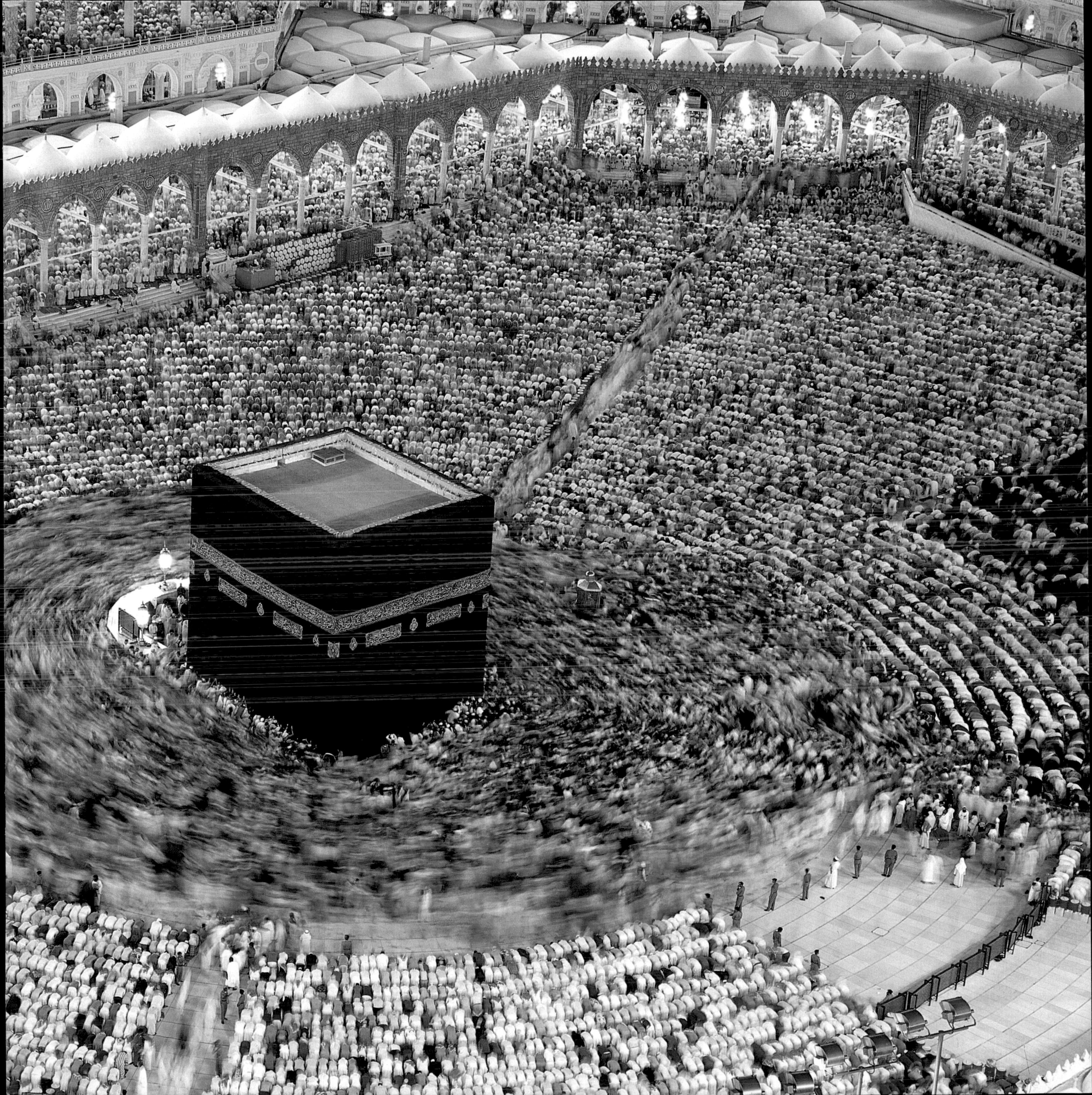

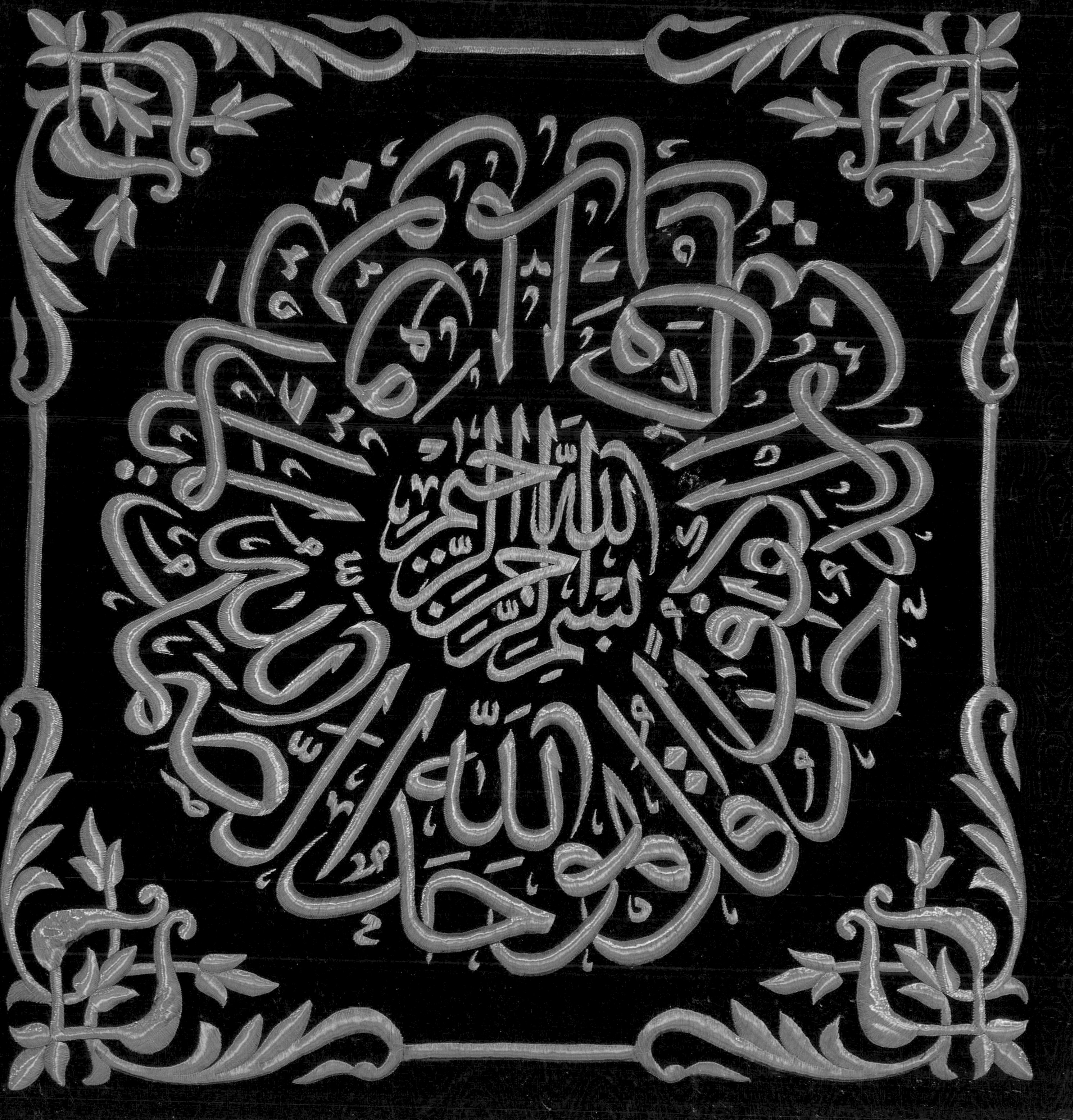
بسم الله الرحمن الرحيم